The 11th Wisconsin
in the Civil War

The 11th Wisconsin in the Civil War

A Regimental History

CHRISTOPHER C. WEHNER

McFarland & Company, Inc., Publishers
Jefferson, North Carolina

The present work is a reprint of the illustrated case bound edition of The 11th Wisconsin in the Civil War: A Regimental History, *first published in 2008 by McFarland.*

LIBRARY OF CONGRESS CATALOGUING-IN-PUBLICATION DATA

Wehner, Christopher C., 1969–
The 11th Wisconsin in the Civil War : a regimental history / Christopher C. Wehner.
 p. cm.
Includes bibliographical references and index.

ISBN 978-1-4766-8520-5
softcover : acid free paper ∞

1. United States. Army. Wisconsin Infantry Regiment, 11th (1861–1865)
2. Wisconsin — History — Civil War, 1861–1865 — Regimental histories.
3. United States — History — Civil War, 1861–1865 — Regimental histories.
4. Soldiers — Wisconsin — Biography. 5. Wisconsin — History — Civil War, 1861–1865 — Biography. 6. United States — History — Civil War, 1861–1865 — Biography.
7. United States — History — Civil War, 1861–1865 — Campaigns. I. Title.
 II. Title: Eleventh Wisconsin in the Civil War.
 E537.511th.W44 2020   973.7'475 — dc22   2007049756

BRITISH LIBRARY CATALOGUING DATA ARE AVAILABLE

© 2008 Christopher C. Wehner. All rights reserved

No part of this book may be reproduced or transmitted in any form or by any means, electronic or mechanical, including photocopying or recording, or by any information storage and retrieval system, without permission in writing from the publisher.

Printed in the United States of America

*McFarland & Company, Inc., Publishers
Box 611, Jefferson, North Carolina 28640
www.mcfarlandpub.com*

Dedicated to all those who fight for freedom

Table of Contents

Preface and Acknowledgments	1
Maps	3
CHAPTER ONE: 1861—The "Glorious Opportunity"	7
CHAPTER TWO: From Farmers to Soldiers	13
CHAPTER THREE: A Godforsaken Place	22
CHAPTER FOUR: 1862—In This Land of Rebeldom	41
CHAPTER FIVE: Contraband and Cotton	57
CHAPTER SIX: 1863—A Midnight Battle	67
CHAPTER SEVEN: Champion Hill	87
CHAPTER EIGHT: Vicksburg—Through the Mouth of Hell	95
CHAPTER NINE: 1864—Bivouacked in the Sand	118
CHAPTER TEN: Damn the Torpedoes!	126
CHAPTER ELEVEN: 1865—Down on the Bayou	136
CHAPTER TWELVE: What an Awful Destruction of Human Life	143
CHAPTER THIRTEEN: Back Home and to the Frontier	161
Appendix A: Roster of the 11th Wisconsin	169
Appendix B: Civilian Occupations of 11th Wisconsin Soldiers	207
Appendix C: Muster Sites for the 11th Wisconsin Regiment	209
Appendix D: Victory Sermon by 11th Wisconsin Volunteer George Wells	210
Appendix E: Army of the Tennessee Officers	214
Chapter Notes	217
Bibliography	231
Index	237

1906 Reunion of Eleventh Wisconsin Volunteer Regiment (Wisconsin Veterans Museum).

"Heu! quanto minus est cum reliquis versari quam tui memmenisse!"
(Oh — to live with them is far less sweet than to remember thee!)

Preface and Acknowledgments

On April 9, 1865, just hours after Robert E. Lee surrendered to Ulysses S. Grant and for all practical purposes ended the Civil War, the Eleventh Wisconsin Volunteer Infantry Regiment charged across a hellish field of abatis, snarled debris, and ravines loaded with landmines. Their target was Fort Blakely, Alabama. A needless assault that took only minutes to complete cost the Eleventh Wisconsin 61 casualties, and was ordered by a general trying to save face for numerous failings.

When the Eleventh Wisconsin was formed in the fall of 1861 outside of Madison at Camp Randall, it would have been hard for any of those Boys of '61 to imagine that three and a half years later they would take part in the last significant land battle of the war.

Leading up to the assault on Fort Blakely, the Eleventh Wisconsin had traveled some 9,000 miles all along the Trans-Mississippi region, to as far away as Texas and the Gulf of Mexico. It was an odyssey of epic proportions for the farm boys of Wisconsin who dominated the regiment's ranks; many had never left their county, let alone their state.

The Eleventh Wisconsin was made up primarily of wheat farmers (around 72 percent) from south central Wisconsin, with a strong showing from Dane County and Madison, where their beloved colonel, Charles L. Harris, resided. Their journey had been a hard one in more ways than simply distance: it included long and exhausting marches across an often desolate, hot, humid and unforgiving landscape. Many died of exposure, exhaustion, and, of course, disease. They also saw hard combat, especially during Grant's Vicksburg Campaign, where the regiment suffered high casualty rates during the siege of Vicksburg.

* * *

This is not the first history of this regiment to be written. James J. McMyler in 1864, while the regiment was stationed outside New Orleans, wrote a short history of the regiment from its organization to its situation in Louisiana in 1864. This history was published in 1865 by a New Orleans publisher and was of some use for this work, but unfortunately it was a short publication, not even reaching one hundred pages.

I first became aware of the regiment as a young boy when my grandfather, a World War II veteran, showed me the diary of our ancestor William Henry Oettiker, a member of the Eleventh Wisconsin. It was years later, as a college student, that I returned to the diary and began to seriously read and study it.

My goal when I first started writing, years ago, was simply to document the events surrounding William Henry Oettiker and his regiment during the Civil War. As I continued my research the book began to take on a life of its own. History has always interested me and today as a high school history teacher it is what I use to try to impart some knowledge and understanding of the world to my students. The details of everyday life during the Civil War fascinated me, right along with the tactics and maneuvers of battle. To me it was about finding the epic nature of the daily lives of these men being played out in an epic age. As we know, it was not just the generals and leaders who created history.

My research centered primarily on unpublished letters and diaries and I was quickly astounded by the number of documents left behind by the men and boys of the Eleventh Wisconsin. Nearly 400 letters were exchanged between two soldiers alone, Samuel C. Kirkpatrick and Henry P. Strong. Though I have lost count, there were easily over 1,000 letters I read and consulted during the writing of this book. Whenever possible I did not alter the spelling or punctuation unless absolutely required for reading purposes. I tried to remain as true to their writing as possible.

Another goal was to tell a story within the historical narrative of the documents. The narrative flair of such Civil War historians as Shelby Foote and Bruce Catton inspired me. A history book should give a truthful account of an event. It is the job of the historian not only to research an accurate book, but to find the thrust of the account and provide the reader with something more than facts and exposition. I wanted to write a book about a tragic event in our history that anyone, without any knowledge of the Civil War, could pick up and read.

I am indebted to the Wisconsin Historical Society, in particular, archivist Harry Miller. Anyone interested in doing any type of research regarding Wisconsin I strongly urge to visit their Website (wisconsinhistory.org), which is easily one of the best I have encountered. I would also like to thank Abbie Norderhaug and the Wisconsin Department of Veterans Affairs for her invaluable aid in hunting down documents and photos. Mary-Jo Miller and the Nebraska State Historical Society, the Department of the Army staff, and researcher Bob Doepke of the Sauk County Historical Society were all very important contacts for specific elements of my research. Randy L. Bixby, manuscripts curator/archivist, Southern Illinois University at Carbondale, the Illinois State Historical Society, and the Arkansas Historical Society were helpful, too. There are also dozens of online databases and collections that were used. I list the most important ones in the bibliography. I would also like to thank Rhylin Bailie for her watchful eye, and Ted Savas for quickly producing several maps for me, most notably the Battle of Bayou Cache.

I also want to thank Melvin Kirkpatrick, who in the early 1980s rescued Samuel C. Kirkpatrick's letters from oblivion. One day while visiting a relative in Wisconsin, he came across a pile of old letters in a box that had been forgotten while stored in an old chicken coop. The letters were badly damaged by weather, but Melvin spent months faithfully transcribing the documents. Without his intervention, the story of Samuel, and perhaps the Eleventh Wisconsin, would not have been told. It was Samuel's letters that inspired me to tell this story.

Years ago it was Marsha K. Taylor who provided me with some very important information regarding my ancestor William Henry Oettiker, and sparked my interested in the Eleventh Wisconsin regiment, for which I am grateful.

Finally, my thanks to the men and young boys of the Eleventh Wisconsin, and all those who left for posterity a treasure trove of insights and ramblings. I got to know these men during my research and the writing of this book. I found that I could not easily pull myself away from my desk once raptured by their words. I hope you enjoy reading about their journey as much as I did discovering it.

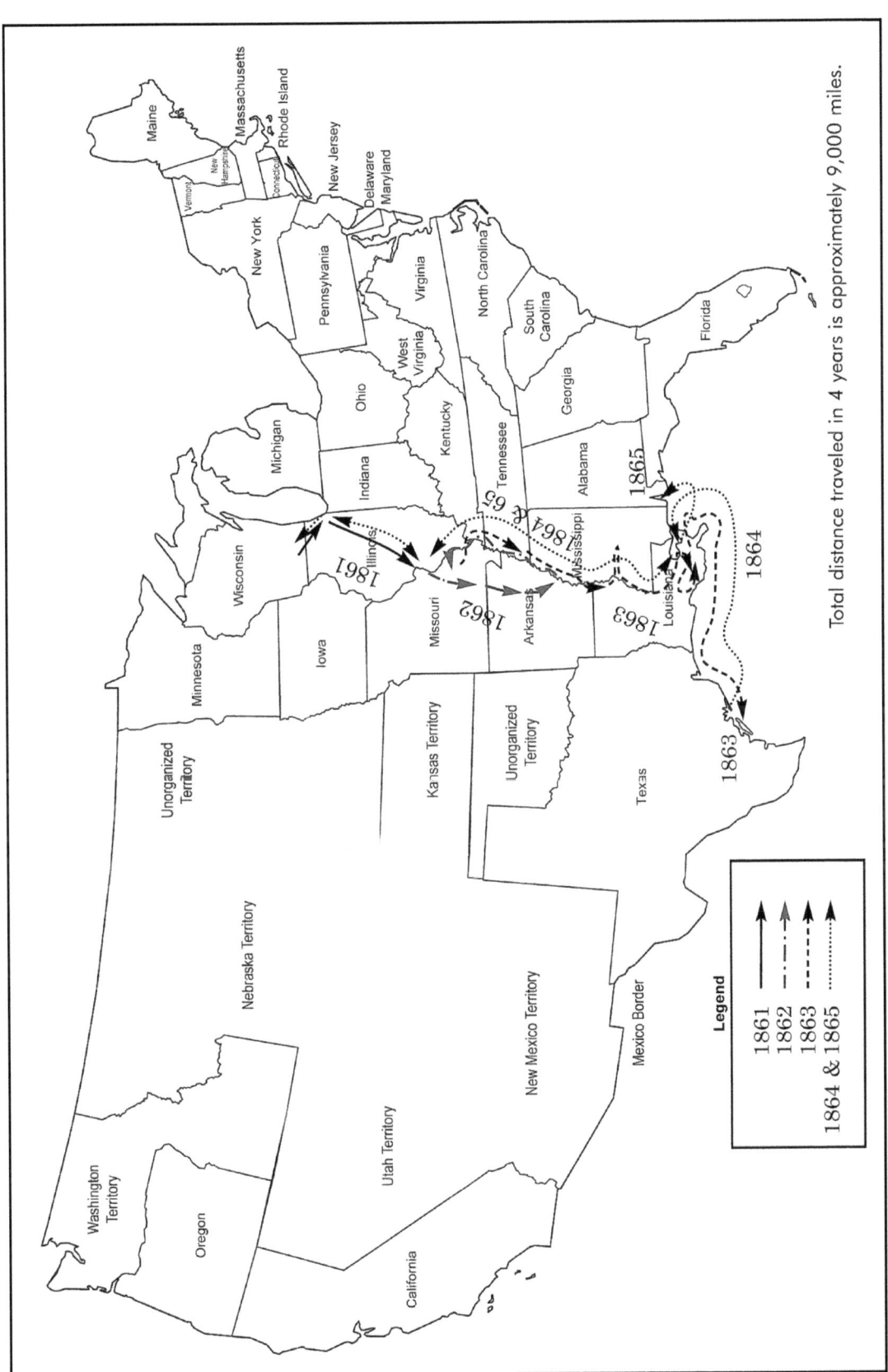

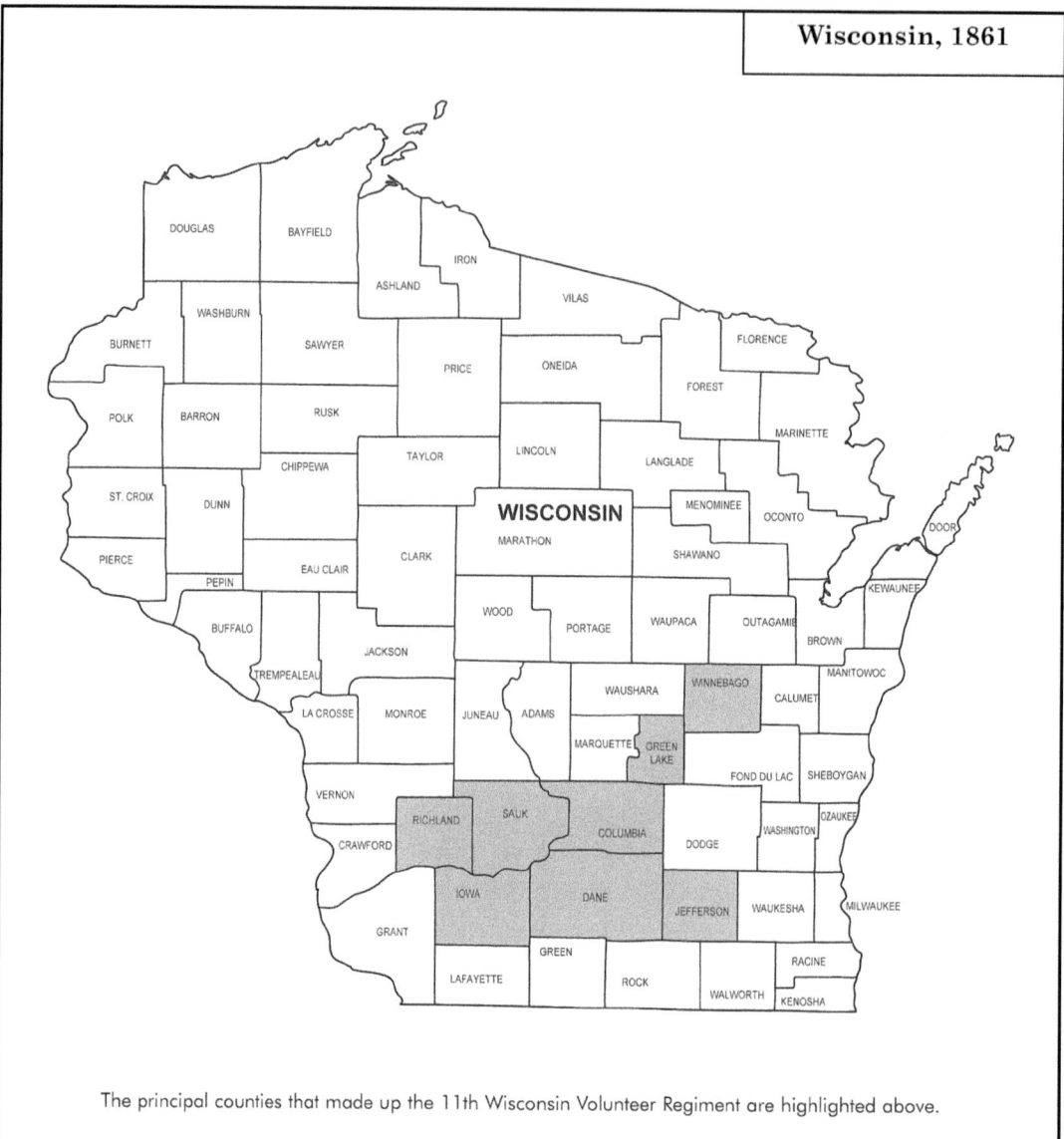

The principal counties that made up the 11th Wisconsin Volunteer Regiment are highlighted above.

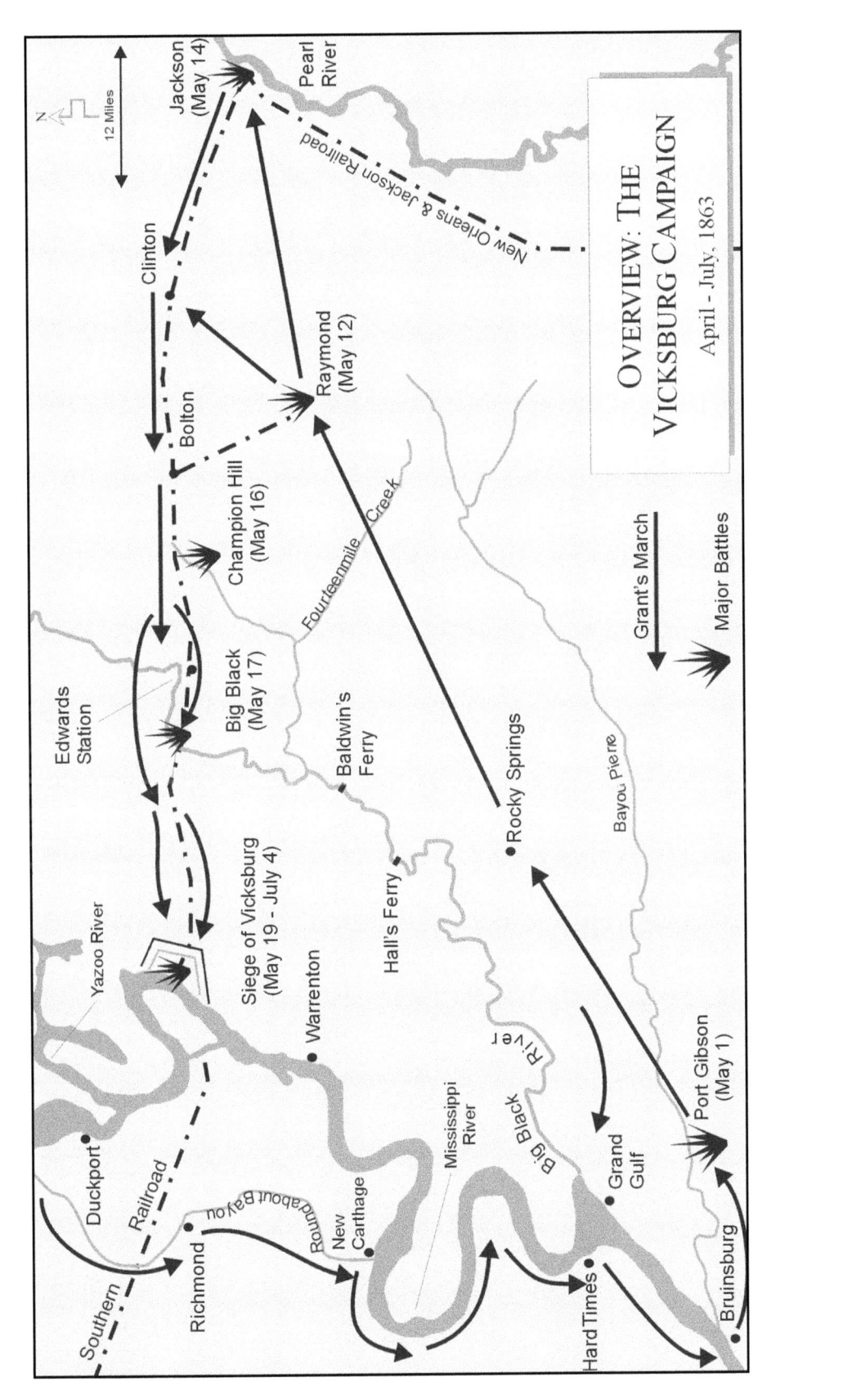

CHAPTER ONE

1861— The "Glorious Opportunity"

On the afternoon of March 4, 1861, a cool breeze swirled above the streets of the Wisconsin state capital of Madison. The flag in the town square fluttered gracefully, lending an aura of regality to a town already filled with excitement and anticipation. Today President Lincoln would be inaugurated. At 2 o'clock folks lining the streets were greeted by the boom of a cannon near Capital Square. A marching band struck up patriotic tunes as onlookers' hearts swelled with pride. Capital Square was filled with nervous chatter as an impromptu meeting convened in the assembly chamber. Politicians took turns filling the air with "patriotic and stirring remarks as resolutions were passed adapted to the occasion. Everybody seemed to feel well."[1]

Few could have anticipated the days to come. Just a little over a month later, Fort Sumter would be fired on, followed by the surrender of its garrison on April 13. On April 15 Lincoln would issue his proclamation calling for 75,000 militiamen for 90 days to put down the rebellion. The possibility of a wicked civil war lasting four years at the cost of 620,000 lives seemed unfathomable to virtually everyone. From New York to Chicago, the North was almost delusional in its estimation of how long the war would last. The *New York Commercial Advertiser* considered the South to be controlled by only a small minority. The *New York Times* boldly predicted the rebellion would be put to rest "effectually in thirty days." The *Chicago Tribune* saw no need to think the war would go beyond two or three months.[2]

Lincoln carried Wisconsin by a vote of 86,000 to Democratic nominee Stephen A. Douglas' 65,000. Though decidedly in Lincoln's favor, the state was far from unanimous on issues of secession and slavery. Some Wisconsin Democrats were still calling for continued appeasement, even after southern states seceded. The *Milwaukee Sentinel* went so far as to suggest the North try to "win the South back by kindness," a suggestion so controversial that Wisconsin governor Alexander W. Randall had to make a special trip to Washington to meet with Lincoln. After the fall of Fort Sumter, the large majority of Wisconsin newspapers declared the "Rebels must be put down."[3]

There was little doubt about the opinions of people in rural south central and southwest Wisconsin, home to the majority of young volunteers in the Eleventh Wisconsin regiment. The small farming community of Kingston, in Sauk County, quickly passed a law changing the town's name to Sumpter in honor of Fort Sumter. The name was misspelled, but it was never corrected.[4]

Just days after the fall of Fort Sumter, the *Beloit Free Press* described a "glorious demonstration" that took place with a "grand" and "patriotic" spirit. It was the largest meeting ever held in the city at the time. In response to Lincoln's call for more troops, men and women crowded into Hanchett's Hall, ready to defend their "flag and freedom." Though it was a cool spring night outside, the temperature rose steadily inside as the meeting wore on. The patriotic spirit reached a fever pitch when a call went out to all those "willing to PERIL THEIR LIVES for their country, to SPILL THEIR BLOOD in her defence." Dozens of young men signed up on the spot.[5]

After the fall of Fort Sumter, the Madison Guard and Governor's Guard marched the streets of the state capital, which soon led to a large gathering of people. The parade stopped at the park, where Captain J.P. Atwood gave a speech after presenting his men. Governor Randall was on hand and gave his own speech. Wisconsin historian E.B. Quiner noted, "[The] dangers which surrounded the Nation awakened the liveliest sentiments of patriotism and devotion. For the time, party fealty was forgotten in the general desire to save the Nation."[6]

Still, the fury with which the public and press responded to the national crisis was not entirely supportive. Some antiwar Democrats were outspoken, including the mayor of Madison, George E. Smith. After the firing on Fort Sumter, Smith told those who showed up for a rally that "I would forgive the South in many things—even for firing on the American flag when we sent a steamer into Charleston."[7]

In courthouses, halls, and on street corners, locals gathered to discuss the latest news, spread gossip and rumor, and debate. Most expressed their growing hatred of the South. From Manitowoc to Platteville, Madison to Janesville, there were ruminations on the enemy. Jefferson Davis and his Southern brethren were "cut-throats," "blood thirsty traitors," "murderers," and "outlaws" who sought to destroy the Union and undo what the founding fathers had worked so hard to accomplish. Most would have agreed that the traitors should be "put to the sword." Governor Randall implemented a plan to supply President Lincoln with nine regiments. He called Charles S. Hamilton out of military retirement to organize and establish a training camp to prepare these volunteers for war. Hamilton decided on a location outside of Madison, to be known as Camp Randall.[8]

By the end of April, the *rage militaire* had crescendoed across the state as town hall meetings became an almost daily event. One such impromptu Union meeting held on April 25 practically shut down the town. At 3 o'clock, men packed into the town hall for the purpose of forming a home guard. Dozens signed up and were then led by a small band on a parade down Main Street. By half past seven that evening the mayor was on hand and locals gathered to sing songs and say a prayer. The upcoming confrontation was seen as a "glorious opportunity" for young men to "distinguish themselves" and prove their manliness and patriotism.[9]

At one enthusiastic meeting in Beloit, a senator, a reverend, and a college professor addressed upwards of 100 men who had just volunteered. It was reported that the "most active and best young men of the city" were quick to join up. Among them were students, clerks, and businessmen. But it wasn't just the men who were enthusiastic. Some women urged friends and family to do their part. Mrs. Mary Hyde of Lancaster had several sons, and if any failed to "answer his country's call to arms" she would "disown" them on the spot, she announced. Not surprisingly, her sons were among the first to sign up.[10]

Once the town meetings got going, noticed one witness:

> It needed only the first man to step forward, put down his name, be patted on the back, placed upon the platform, and cheered to the echo as the hero of the hour, when a second, a third, a fourth would follow, and at last a perfect stampede set in to sign the enlistment roll, and a frenzy of enthusiasm would take possession of the meeting. The complete intoxication of such excitement, like intoxication from liquor, left some of its victims on the following day, especially if the fathers of families, with the sober second thought to wrestle with; but Pride, that tyrannical master, rarely let them turn back.[11]

At various times in 1861, Wisconsin, like other states, had more volunteers than she could handle. States, both North and South, simply were not yet organized to accommodate and arm their amateur soldiers made up of militia units and social clubs. Fortunately, Governor Randall urged the state legislature to approve appropriations to organize more companies, and to sanction a $200,000 war loan. Randall then telegraphed the U.S. secretary of war, Simon Cameron, informing him that the "First Regiment of Wisconsin" was ready. Though only one regiment was requested by the government, Wisconsin had an extra twenty companies, or enough for two more regiments.[12]

Wisconsin had been a state for only 12 years when the war broke out. Her largest city, Milwaukee, was the thirteenth largest in the country, with just over 45,000 inhabitants. An 1860 census put the state's population at 775,881, an increase of 48.6 percent over the census in 1855. During the first 12 months of the war, 20,000 volunteered throughout the state. Of those, 33 percent were foreign born. By war's end the Badger State would send 91,000 men into the fray, organized into 53 infantry regiments, 4 cavalry units, 13 light artillery batteries, and one regiment of heavy artillery serving in both the eastern and western theaters. Wisconsin lagged behind other Midwestern states, however, with fewer troops furnished in proportion to the number of eligible males.[13]

In 1861 the U.S. government had only a small organized army, most of it scattered west of the Mississippi and stationed in forts and garrisons. In all, about 16,000 men occupied its ranks. By summer, nearly a third of its officers joined the Confederacy, along with a number of its soldiers. The entire country was mobilizing rapidly in an effort to bring the largest possible army to some future battlefield. By 1862 there would be 575,917 men organized into over 500 regiments for the Union. As would be the case for the next 80 years, the U.S. militarized for war only after getting into one, and this was never more evident than in 1861. Without the proper mechanisms in place, states awkwardly tried to deal with thousands of young men seeking enlistment in regiments not yet formed. Fortunately, by the end of the year the U.S. War Department had taken over the cumbersome responsibility of feeding, clothing, and arming the soldiers.[14]

On the Wednesday before July 4, nearly the entire town of Johnston gathered round a 188-foot pole residents had erected. It was marvelously painted in three colors, "the lower third painted red, the middle white and the top blue." When they hoisted the pole into the air, the town's new flag spanned 30 by 20 feet across the clear blue Wisconsin sky. As it fluttered in the air, three cheers rang out from the crowd. Those gathered then saluted local veterans of the War of 1812, and gave another cheer for the young men of their community who were about to do their duty for their country. After a short "entertaining and patriotic" speech by the town sheriff, a final salute went out, along with "three cheers for President Lincoln and his cabinet."[15]

In 1861, July 4 celebrations across the country held more meaning than ever before. In Wisconsin emotions were split between a heightened sense of patriotism and a relative "coolness" that filtered through the festivities. There were no fireworks in Janesville. Instead, a large portion of the town gathered and took turns reading the Constitution, followed by a few speeches. Others stayed at home and had a quiet time with family and friends. The mood was a little too somber for some, who hoped that "another fourth of July will not [pass] without a good, old fashioned, rousing celebration, in this city. The non-observance of the day, in a becoming manner, is not creditable to the public spirit of our city." Earlier in the day, downtown Janesville witnessed a poignant scene. Young boys playing in the street pretended to be a company of soldiers, parading about town as shopkeepers and passersby stopped and watched. The boys must have made an impression, for folks cheered them on and it was reported, "they mean to do business ... when they get a little older." These images of innocence at play would come back to haunt many a small Midwestern town in the years to come, though, as these boys became young men and went off to fight, many never to return.[16]

Just a few weeks later, patriotism gave way to a sense of urgency as the news of the Union's defeat at Bull Run reached Wisconsin communities. "We have no heart to comment upon the news today," wrote one newspaper. "Our army has suffered defeat, and Washington is in danger." The press had prematurely announced victory the previous day, so the defeat came as a shock. Federal troops indeed appeared to have victory close at hand early in the battle, until Confederate general Thomas J. Jackson stood like a "stone wall," and the arrival of Confederate general Joseph E. Johnston and part of his army. The resulting rout at the end of the day sent Union soldiers fleeing from the battlefield. The report continued: "It is unaccountable, and will bring sorrow and shame upon the whole north. Out of it, however, will grow a fiercer determination on the part of the friends of the Union to strike once more for the honor of the country."[17]

As news spread that the war's first major battle was decisively lost, the North gained clarity and renewed vigor for the conflict. The people realized "we are really at war," and that only steadfast resolution would "save the country from the despotism which the slaveholders are endeavoring to fasten upon us. Good will come out of this reverse, terrible as it is; let us all profit by the lesson."[18]

In ensuing days, descriptions of the battle began to trickle back to the newspapers. One came from Captain Ely of the Second Wisconsin regiment (it combined with the Sixth and Seventh Wisconsin regiments and the Nineteenth Indiana and Twenty-fourth Michigan regiments to become the famous "Iron Brigade"), who fought in the battle. His description was poignant and wrenching. "We went down 3 miles at a tremendous pace," he wrote, "cheering all the way and in high glee till we got just in front." There all hell broke loose as cannonballs began "singing" over their heads. Ely continued with his narration in detail:

> We remained under this fire three quarters of an hour.... Most of the balls passed over our heads. We had but four casualties and those all in company B, the La Crosse company, and I think all from one rifled cannon. One man had his leg shot off near the thigh. He died this morning. One had his ankle broken, and one was blinded by the stones the ball threw up as it entered the ground. I have not learned what the fourth injury was. But through it all every man was quiet and cool, and did not budge an inch.[19]

The sorrow and shame that swept over the North in the days after defeat was soon replaced by a vigorous spirit of determination: "The excitement ... throughout this region of country, was very great yesterday and to-day, upon the receipt of the news of the defeat of our army at Bull Run." But some thought it was just wishful thinking. During the fall of 1861 wheat and corn prices plummeted. Corn sold for ten cents a bushel, forcing some farmers to burn their crop for fuel. Economic fallout hit Wisconsin farmers the hardest and caused many to question whether a war was prudent. But it also meant there were a significant number of farmers and laborers with nothing to do except join the army.[20]

At Maxon's Mill in Bradford it was a packed house as the enthusiastic gathering brought forth speeches by a reverend and two captains of the newly formed regiment. The meeting was a success, as seven new volunteers were obtained. The meeting adjourned with the hope that "more names will be obtained and that portions of the county will do their share in the final fight between freedom and despotism."[21]

The amount of disinformation, political blather, and brazen patriotism that local papers released upon the young minds of Wisconsin was not unlike any other state. Civil War soldiers were the most literate combatants of their time, and the writings of the Eleventh Wisconsin regiment bear witness to that. A European observer, French army officer Gustave Paul Cluseret, noted that because of the literacy of the soldiers and their willingness to read newspapers, they possessed an unusual "knowledge of the cause." Even while on the march, about to face battle, Civil War soldiers hungered for war news. "Daily papers command any price," wrote one soldier in the Eleventh Wisconsin. "I will pay one dollar ... for a paper not more than 5 days old." War was described as heroic, and men felt the need to "do their duty." The young men who volunteered in September 1861 did so with patriotic pride, a sense of duty and honor, and a desire to punish the South. These were important values in Victorian America, something less understood and appreciated today. Historian James M. McPherson has noted that, though the tone of this era may strike us as "mawkish posturing" or "hollow platitudes" today, we cannot forget that this was an age of "romanticism in literature, music, art and philosophy." It would take a world war to destroy that romanticization of war. One could argue that the Civil War killed the American idea of war being glorious first. But what should be understood is that "what seems like bathos or platitudes to us were real pathos and convictions to them." The men who signed up in 1861 would not have to be driven to battle like their European counterparts, only led. As historian John Keegan noted, "The Blue and the Gray [were] the first truly ideological armies in history." They fought for a cause and they fought for each other.[22]

But not everything was so serious. As the summer wore on, the Wisconsin press found its sense of humor with some amusing headlines:

History of Secession in six easy Lessons—Defalcation, Depredation, Repudiation, Assassinations, Trepidation, Extermination.
The Southern Insignia "C.S.A."—Can't Stand Artillery.[23]

By the fall of 1861, newspapers featured almost daily reports of regiments formed, marching off to Camp Randall, or sent to the "seat of war." Often named after towns, communities, or the people who organized them, units and companies were placed into regiments (10 companies) and given a regimental flag to be carried into battle by color-bearers—a position of honor. Individuals who organized a company or a regiment were usually elected as captains and sometimes colonels. Units such as the Lodi Guards, Marquette Sharpshooters, Berdan Sharp Shooters, Manitowoc Guards, Waukesha Union Guards, Beaver Dam Rifles, North Star Hides, German Turners, Janesville Light Guard, Berlin Light Guard, Richland Volunteers, Farmers Guards, and Milwaukee Zouaves formed into companies and regiments.

BERDAN'S SHARP SHOOTERS. We are glad to see that Col. Berdan's success in raising his regiment of sharp shooters has been so great, that he is now likely to organize three regiments instead of one. Ten companies are now ready, with a hundred men in each; and every man has been put to the test, and has made the required "string," which is ten consecutive shots at six hundred feet distance, averaging not more than five inches from the center of the target.[24]

Frontline letters from Wisconsin regiment correspondents continued to circulate back home and were published in local papers during the summer and fall of 1861, and indeed throughout the war. "The First Wisconsin Regiment in Battle," read one headline. The battle was really a skirmish, though not the way the article told it. The fighting was always fierce, and what a glorious thing it was to be fighting in the great War of Rebellion.[25]

One anonymous soldier (he signed his letters with the pseudonym "Badger") contributed several stories to his local newspaper. He apparently had time to spare, and was having "such good times" since his last letter. Letters and reports were usually filled with the heroic deeds of Wisconsin soldiers. But there were also stories of sacrifice, followed by listings of the dead and wounded. Since newspapers could report casualties within a week, families and relatives often read about the fate of their loved ones in these reports. The importance of these daily reports grew with the war.[26]

On August 20, 1861, Governor Randall issued an order for 14 new regiments in response to Secretary of War Simon Cameron's telegram to organize as many regiments as possible. The timing of the announcement could not have been better for Wisconsin. Though the state was the country's second largest wheat producer, with over two million acres of production, by the end of September the harvest had pretty much ended and thousands of young laborers and farmers suddenly had time on their hands. Many of these farmers volunteered, thinking they would go down South, take care of the rebellion, and be back home in time to plant the next crop. Indeed, the vast majority of volunteers (72 percent) for the Eleventh Wisconsin were farmers. Fathers, brothers, and sons would all go — some without their family's blessings — leaving home for the first time, to travel thousands of miles, face battle and death, and not return for three years, or until the war was over.[27]

Announcements of the formation of new regiments were greeted with both excitement and trepidation: "The Governor has commissioned Chas A. Hamilton, of Milwaukee, as the major of the 7th Regiment.... George Robbins, of Dane County, is appointed Lieut. Colonel of the 8th Regiment." Was time running out? Was it now or never to sign up and fulfill one's duty? These had to be questions the young men who would make up the Eleventh regiment were asking as they saw regiment after regiment organized in the fall of 1861.[28]

Colonel Charles L. Harris (Wisconsin Veterans Museum).

On September 4, 1861, Charles L. Harris was commissioned as colonel of the Eleventh Wisconsin Volunteer Regiment along with Charles A. Wood (lieutenant colonel) and Arthur Platt (major). Harris was a veteran, having served briefly as a lieutenant in the First Wisconsin regiment. By September 21, nine companies had been formed and ordered to report to Colonel Harris at Camp Randall: the Watson Guards (Mazonmaine), Waterloo Rifles, Richland County Plowboys, Baraboo Rangers, Farmers Guards (Mineral Point), Randall Zouaves (Madison), Mendota Guards, Dane Co. Zouaves, and the Mendota Fire were among them.[29]

It would not be long before the regiment was complete. Where they would ultimately be headed was unclear. Would it be the Army of the Potomac in the East, or somewhere else? For now, all the volunteers knew for sure was they would soon be going to war.

Chapter Two

From Farmers to Soldiers

South central Wisconsin before the war boasted beautiful lakes and virgin prairie, with forests of oak, fresh rivers, and rolling hills. There were massive open spaces with trees dispersed as in a vast orchard. The land was "extensive and beautiful" and the prairies and timber were easily cleared, making much of the land appealing to the early pioneers. From Columbia County in the east toward Sun Prairie in the west, the drumlins gave way to sealike tall grass, spreading as far as the eye could see. The Kegonsa, Waubesa, and Monona lakes were first visible from the Yahara River. Nestled near the third lake was the state's capital, Madison, located on a thin neck of land between Monona and a fourth lake, the Mendota. Southward, towards the Rock River, was a "mostly wild, uncultivated land" with rugged inhabitants, hardy people of Norwegian descent living in mud houses and rude log cabins. Further south, along the rivers, was Stoughton, then Janesville, and on the Illinois border was Beloit.[1]

West of Madison along the old military road, a vast prairie joined with Military Ridge just north of the Blue Mounds. At first the hills were rounded and easily crossed. But the land gradually transformed from forests, prairies, and drumlins to an uneven terrain. Valleys give way in all directions to steeper edges with numerous rock outcroppings. Lakes and rivers that were once visible were engulfed by hills. The southwest corner of the state was mining country, from whence the establishment of Wisconsin really began. Lead was discovered in the 1820s, and prospectors flocked to the region, though by the 1860s production was in a downward spiral and people were more interested in California's gold. Nearby Mineral Point (50 miles west of Madison) was described as a beautiful town with "stone houses on Shake Rag Street" constructed by expert Cornish stonemasons. Another 20 miles west was Platteville, settled about the same time by Cornish lead miners. At one point, in the early 1850s, native Cornish folk made up one-sixth of the population in parts of the region the Eleventh Wisconsin was recruited from. Soon there arrived German and Irish immigrants, followed by a wave of Italians. The Winnebago Indians were eventually forced out by the swarming miners. After the Black Hawk War (1831–1832), farmers began to settle into the area and, along with the transformation of lead miners into farmers, the fertile land ideal for wheat and corn helped to make south central Wisconsin known for its large farming community, furthered by the outbreak of the Civil War.[2]

Prairie country was abundant throughout south central Wisconsin, in Rock Prairie east of Janesville and Liberty Prairie north of the Rock River. Further north in Sauk County, at the base of the Baraboo Range near the Wisconsin River, oak forests mixed with lush prairies. The people from these areas were hardy, stout, and tough. The pioneers of Wisconsin were constantly clearing the land and erecting log houses:

> Many of the young men, when not necessarily at work on the small farms, went into the "pineries" for employment in the winter; and in spring "ran the river" with the drive. Those who had only small fields to grain at home went down at harvest time to work on the prairies.[3]

Except for men from a few urban areas such as Madison, the regiment's ranks were filled mostly from agricultural communities where wheat farming was the center of the social and economic system: "The harvest was the harvest; on it depended the prosperity not alone of the farmer but of the merchant, the doctor, and everybody who had a stake in the community."[4]

* * *

Standing six feet tall with brown hair, Jesse Mather was 17 years old when he followed his brother Oliver, 20, from their family farm in Sauk County to nearby Kingston to enlist in the United States Army. They were both eventually assigned to Company F in the Eleventh Wisconsin Volunteer Regiment. Jesse and Oliver often reminisced about home in their letters, of which several dozen have survived. Jesse lied about his age to join, and both brothers seemed to have enlisted without their parents' blessing. Volunteers under 18 were required to have parental consent. At first the boys' letters were addressed to their sister Sarah, presumably because their parents would not accept them.[5]

William Henry Oettiker of Company E, born in Allegheny, Pennsylvania, in 1841, was a farmer near Belmont in Lafayette County. He stood just a shade under 5'9" and had blue eyes and a medium build. Two of Henry's diaries have survived. Filled mainly with simple entries such as the weather, they do offer occasional tidbits and subtle insights into soldiering and other aspects of army life in the 1860s.

The Civil War has often been called a brothers' war, and for more than one reason. Henry Twining and two of his brothers served with the Eleventh Wisconsin. Four Emilys (Abram, Anthony, William, and Webster) served in Company A, and miraculously all survived. The Emilys were from Berry, a small rural farming community surrounded by steep, wooded hillsides and verdant lowlands in Dane County. In 1861, the Women's Club of Berry planted 17 fir trees (they would eventually plant 38), one for each man who joined the Union Army and went off to fight in the Civil War. It was a memorial that was probably "not duplicated anywhere in the state," as each soldier had a specific tree dedicated to him and a metal tag attached with his name engraved. The initial seventeen men who enlisted in 1861 were all assigned to Company A. Three of those trees still stand today at the junction of Highway 19 and Old Settlers Road. Nine men perished and their bodies were brought back and buried on Sunning Hill overlooking the valley, along with Civil War nurse Annie Roberts Taylor, who died in 1870.[6]

Henry Twining, standing nearly 6 feet tall, was nineteen years old when he enlisted as a corporal on September 14, 1861, three weeks after his brother John joined up. It would take almost eight weeks for the final Twining brother, Aaron, to follow rank and enlist. All three were placed in the Eleventh Wisconsin in Company C. About a dozen of Henry's letters have survived, dated from September 29, 1861, to August 27, 1862, and addressed to a Miss Harriet "Hattie" Perkins. Henry and Hattie were likely just friends, as they never married and the letters did not reflect any intimacy.[7]

Thaddeus Rice was born on May 30, 1841, and lived in Cross Plains. He and Baylis Rice were mustered into service on September 9, seven days after Obadiah Rice. All three brothers served in Company A. There are dozens of instances of brothers and cousins signing up together, some fighting and dying side by side. Thaddeus left behind several letters.

Samuel Kirkpatrick was born in Grant County, Wisconsin, in 1841 and was also a farmer before enlisting at Washburn (now Arthur) on September 11, 1861. He was assigned to Company E. Standing six foot four and weighing 185 pounds, Kirkpatrick towered over the average solider and had a physical presence that demanded respect. He was mustered into the service as a corporal. A confident and handsome young man, with "fair hair" and light eyes, he would eventually earn the rank of sergeant first class. Samuel was a prolific writer, with over 100 letters to his credit.[8]

A half dozen letters from Charles A. Stevens of Richland County survived. Charles had a family history rich in military tradition; two of his great-grandfathers fought at the battle of Bunker Hill during the Revolutionary War. Born in Franklin County, Maine, on November 6, 1843, Charles was the third of ten children of Alonzo and Mary Stevens. When Charles was very young, he and his family moved to Rockbridge in Richland County, Wisconsin. Charles and two of his brothers (Joshua and Adelbert) volunteered in the fall of 1861.

Calvin P. Alling was born in Braceville, Ohio, on April 2, 1840. He stood 5'8" with dark hair and dark complexion. When he was three his family moved to Grant County, Wisconsin, where his father purchased some land outside Platteville. Calvin enlisted early in April 1861, but it wasn't until July that he joined the Richland County Plowboys and marched off to Camp Randall to join the Eleventh regiment, where he was assigned to Company D. Calvin wrote a short memoir of his experiences during the Civil War, and also left behind part of his diary.[9]

Sergeant Samuel C. Kirkpatrick (Author's Collection).

When Oliver S. Robinson was a boy he moved from Ohio to Port Andrew, Richland County, with his family. He grew up to be a farmer, and joined Company H of the Eleventh Regiment on October 21, 1861, at the age of twenty. Several of Oliver's letters to his parents have survived.

Robert R. Sherrill, born in Galena, Illinois, and raised in Bethel Grove, Lafayette County, signed up on September 16, 1861, and was assigned to Company E (Farmers Guards), along with his brother Edward. Robert was twenty years old when he joined the regiment. He wrote frequently (16 letters have been recovered) to his aunt and uncle, John and Caroline Dunlap, in Calamine. Caroline's brother, James Dain, was also a member of the company.[10]

The first head surgeon for the regiment, twenty-eight-year-old Henry P. Strong of Beloit, was perhaps the most prolific writer in the group, having penned over 300 letters and reports. He also wrote to several papers, including the *Beloit Journal*, authoring a dozen or more correspondences using the pseudonyms "Major" and "Monterry" and perhaps others. Henry was born at Brownington, Orleans County, Vermont, February 8, 1832. He graduated from Castleton Medical College, Vermont, with honors in 1853. That same year he followed his parents to Beloit, where he began the practice of medicine. He joined the Eleventh Wisconsin when the war broke out and by April 1863 he was made surgeon-in-chief of the Fourteenth Division of the Thirteenth Army Corps.[11]

Charles L. Harris, born August 24, 1834, in Bridgeton, New Jersey, was a prominent Madison resident when the war broke out. He immediately enlisted and became a lieutenant in the First Wisconsin regiment. Three months later he welcomed the rank of colonel in the Eleventh Wisconsin, at the age of 27. A confident man of medium height (5'8"), Harris was well educated, having graduated from West Point, and had considered a career in the military but chose to study law. He was also ambitious and had an early interest in politics. When war broke out, the opportunity to defend his country and advance his political career must have made Harris' enlistment an easy decision.[12]

While on the march, infantry regiments would sometimes be unable to send out letters. The Union army had post offices near most forts and camps and a mail service that followed them whenever possible. After one march, which took the Eleventh Wisconsin away from these lines of communication for 21 days, it was reported that as many as "1500 letters" were sent off immediately upon their return. "Newsboys," as they were called, carried mail from camp to the post office for "2½ cents" per letter. They also sold newspapers and writing materials, and it was reported that on one occasion a "thousand papers" were purchased at the hefty price of "20 cents" each." Typically, once in camp, soldiers purchased ink, paper and covers from the sutlers. It's reasonable to suggest that the Eleventh Wisconsin sent home as many as 20,000 letters during their first year of service. Even taking into account the reduction of its ranks as the war continued, the regiment easily authored 50,000 or more letters during their four years of service. That does not take into account the number of letters sent from home to the soldiers. Unfortunately, as time went by, most soldiers were forced to burn or destroy letters received because they simply could not carry them (perhaps as much as several pounds worth at a time) during many of their long marches. This accounts for there being virtually no letters to be found from loved ones to the soldiers.[13]

* * *

In April of 1861, Governor Randall had an abundance of volunteers. Believing they would soon be needed, he decided not to disband them, and sent them instead to the State Agricultural Society's fairgrounds outside of Madison. This makeshift camp grew steadily into Camp Randall. By war's end, over 70,000 of the state's soldiers would be sent to the camp. By the end of September, men assigned to the Eleventh Wisconsin started to arrive.[14]

They traveled by foot, wagon, boat, and train. As each local militia unit or company guard prepared to head out, towns and farming communities gathered to see them off with "bands playing, banners flying, and people shouting." For most of these young men, this was their first significant trip away from home. "It was a new experience to me," said one soldier from La Crosse. "I was wide awake the whole way." The first train ride was a revelation to many. "I was afraid we were off the track every time we crossed a switch or came to a river," recalled one soldier. As each company traveled to Madison, at almost every stop "girls swarmed ... ask[ing] the boys for their pictures and to kiss the best looking ones."[15]

A procession of wagons carried the men from Waterloo to just outside Madison. There they unloaded and marched through the capital as well-wishers cheered them on. "When we got there we met the Dane County Zouaves," wrote Henry Twining. "They opened ranks and the Corporal marched us through them and when we got in the city we met our Colonel [Harris] and he gave us three cheers." From there they marched a couple of miles west of capital square to Camp Randall. It started to rain when the Eleventh Wisconsin arrived, and the rain continued for several days. They had a "good dinner" that first night, but had to sleep in the barn. Though out of the rain, the men itched from the flea-ridden straw in the bunks. Within a few days they had tents, and some pretty nice ones, Henry thought: "They are 18 ft on the ground, 15 feet high, round ... and hold 20 men." Though camp life was likely not what some of them had imagined, spirits soared, along with a complete lack of understanding for the gravity of the situation facing both them and the nation. "It will be a pretty good time," wrote Henry.[16]

Samuel Kirkpatrick and his company from Mineral Point, known as the Farmers Guards, came in a few days after Henry. Not long after his arrival, Samuel picked up his pen, as he would often do, and wrote home to his beloved mother and father, brothers and sisters:

Dear father and mother

I take up my pen in hand to let you know that I am well and I hope that these few lines will find you in the same health. We all left Mineral Point Wednesday the 25th and went to Arena in wagons and it rained all the way on us and then we took the cars for Madison. We got in the barracks about three o'clock and then we got dinner. The boys are in good spirits. John Dean is fierce as a mink. We go in the eleventh regiment. There is four companys in the eleventh. It is Sunday and the boys are all writing. Yesterday we all marched up town and got free dinner and we had a good time. It is very nice every evening to see them [his fellow soldiers] on dress parade. The officers look splendid. It was a great sight for me. I wish you all could see us here.... You must excuse the bad writing. No more at present. Write soon.[17]

Samuel C. Kirkpatrick

By October 18, formation of the Eleventh Wisconsin Volunteer Regiment was complete. It was organized into ten companies with about 100 men per company, for a grand total of 1,029 men. By war's end, because of replacements due to death, injury, disease, desertion, and discharge, a total of 1,965 men served in the regiment.[18]

Camp Randall consisted of ten acres surrounded by a wooden fence eight feet high. Two guarded gates opened every afternoon so locals could enter and watch the soldiers drill. "The evening [dress] parade was witnessed by a large concourse of visitors," said a newspaperman visiting the camp before the Eleventh Wisconsin arrived. After dress parade the men were given passes so they could go to town, get a decent meal, and visit the ladies. After a while some townsfolk felt the soldiers were visiting too frequently, and sometimes too late at night. After drill and dress parade, while inside the camp, the men often played cards and chess, gambled, and drank. Sutlers were allowed inside the camp to sell snacks, beer, liquor, tobacco, and other necessities. As the monotonous nature of camp life wore on, the men were prone to drunkenness and fights, which resulted in guardhouse confinement.[19]

On October 17 Jesse Mather and his brother Oliver arrived with one of the last companies to join the regiment. Jesse wrote home to his sister Sarah after his arrival:

Dear Sister

I thought I would write you a few lines to let you know that we had got here. We got here in time for supper last night. We had bread and butter and hot coffee. We were swore into the United States service this morning and then went to the clothing office and got two shirts and two pairs of drawers and two pair of stockings a pair of shoes and a cap and a cloth blanket. Our big woolen blanket we got last night fine and course comb and towel to wipe on we have to get up at six o'clock in the morning sit up till after nine to go to bed for the roll is called at nine o'clock. We have not got a gun yet but expect one soon the officers are drilling this after noon the privates have to begin at three o'clock and is almost time. They have a cannon that is fired twice a day it makes every thing jingle and the cars come along and wake us up two or three times a night. good by I must fill in the ranks.[20]

Jesse Mather

Once settled in, the men received uniforms, knapsacks, canteens, and hats, and eventually their rifles. "Our uniforms will be blue and long coats. We have got our caps and they are blue," wrote Samuel Kirkpatrick. After the excitement wore off and the daily routine of rationed food, drilling, and dress parade kicked in, soldier life lost a little of its luster. "I tell you, Hat, that if anyone wants to live a dogs life let him enlist in the U.S. Service," wrote Henry Twining to his dear friend Harriet "Hattie" Perkins, back in Waterloo. "When we first came here they had a pretty good living but we live now on rations and we don't get but very little to eat. French soup and bread is about all we have with one pt. of coffee." The men often used their passes into town to get a decent meal — on their own dime, of course.[21]

In July, an Appleton correspondent at Camp Randall sent a series of reports back home. The correspondent noted a change among the men as they shed their individual identities and took on the look of a soldier. Though as citizens and amateur soldiers they would never truly lose their individuality, the correspondent noticed "quite a change" among the men of the Fifth and Sixth Wisconsin regiments. It was more than just the appearance of the men in their uniforms, he thought, but that, together with "their increased proficiency in drill, gives them quite a soldierly appearance, and if they were called into active service immediately, they would do honor to the State."[22]

The men were eager and "anxious," he wrote, though they had only trained for a few weeks: "To-day, we assume the position of United States Soldiers." That evening was the soldier's dinner, which consisted of a feast unlike anything they had seen. They gathered around large tables with the men and women from Madison. "The bands played the sweetest music," he added. The estimation later was that six to ten thousand people arrived that evening after dinner to honor the soldiers. They held dress parade and were presented with two handmade state flags for the regiment. "They are made of blue silk, with yellow fringe around the edges, with a large spread eagle in the center, underneath which is a scroll with the number of the regiment." This flag would be carried into battle. After receiving their regimental flag, the colonel of the Sixth Regiment was so moved he turned to his men and asked if they would "stand by him in its defence," which was answered with a thunderous, "Yes, we will!"[23]

In October, while the Eleventh regiment was still training at Camp Randall, an article appeared in a local paper outlining the "Rudiments of Military Drill." Camp life and military training was a mystery to many in south central Wisconsin, and those left at home were fascinated to hear what their friends and family were experiencing. Each man received two elements of training while at camp, described as individual and collective drill. This training was supposed to prepare the soldier for battlefield survival and maneuver. Soldiers learned simple things, such as how to salute an officer, fall in, and stand at attention. They learned facings, which is the command given for when and where to face (for example, "about face.")[24]

Though their training was by no means extensive, the ability to maneuver — the precision required in battle — was important for Civil War soldiers. With lessons such as "Lesson IV — The Mechanism and Rhythm of Marching in Common Time," soldiers were taught how to side-step, flank step, balance step, and change formations. They had to be able to change direction on the field while taking fire. In "Oblique Marching," and instead of going straight forward the regiment would march at an angle; being able to change direction, move in angles, and go right or left as a group without losing "squareness of position" was crucial. They drilled and drilled for hours, and then they drilled some more, nearly six hours a day. They learned what quick and double quick time were. Precision in the number and speed of steps for certain maneuvers was very important. And when they finished drilling, soldiers did gymnastic movements, which were thought to be "of great use in giving steadiness and suppleness to the recruit." The gymnastic movements focused on the arms and shoulders to build muscle and flexibility; as the men became stronger and more focused, they grew more confident in their abilities as soldiers.[25]

About mid October, the Eighth Wisconsin* regiment left Camp Randall for the war and were sent off with the customary celebration. A band and a large crowd from town gathered to wish them well. "The boys of the 11 were drawn up in a line as the [8th] regiment march out of the gate and bade their comrades farewell with rousing cheers," noted Samuel Kirkpatrick. "The band played by the track till all were aboard." It must have been a sight. Hundreds of people waving goodbye, with tears no doubt shed, and the sounds of patriotic tunes filling the air. Then the whistle blew, and the train chugged away. The music continued until the train was out of sight, and the crowd quietly broke up. The Eleventh regiment stood at attention in honor of their comrades (many of whom they knew and considered friends); no doubt the men were lost in thought wondering what was in store for them and when it would be their turn to leave.[26]

Unknown soldier in full uniform: knapsack, rifle, and bayonet (Library of Congress).

The Eleventh included one of the better regimental brass bands. "We have a splendid brass band in the eleventh," wrote Samuel Kirkpatrick. "We got out muskets and we had a

---

*The Eighth Wisconsin regiment carried a bald eagle (named "Old Abe") with them and became famous throughout the country after the war.

big time cleaning them." The rain fell throughout most of October, and they continued to drill in the sloppy mud. Though they were getting the hang of it, Samuel knew they needed a lot more training before they would see action: "I expect that we will be here a good while."[27]

During their stay at Camp Randall, the regiment had a steady flow of visitors, as family and friends sometimes traveled long distances to come and see the men one last time. When family couldn't visit, they wrote. It was lonely for a soldier who had few or no visitors or, even worse, no letters from home (which was a rarity). But few of the men commented on such things. Early topics of conversation centered on the girls in town and a longing for home. "Frank has had a letter from a girl but I have not," wrote Samuel. "We all like to see the girls when they come down from town. I would like to see you all. I haint got homesick yet. I don't have any horses to rub down or feed."[28]

Pay became an issue for the men after only a few weeks, for they still hadn't received any by mid November. According to one newspaper article, the entire regiment was due $14,000 from the time of enlistment, which was no small sum of money in 1861. As the average soldier made only about $13 per month, the regiment was owed at least a month's pay.[29]

By the end of October it was rumored the regiment would soon be heading to Missouri. The army of the Trans-Mississippi was in great need of men. Missouri, though a slave state, was neutral and still up for grabs. Both Federal and Confederate armies were hastily formed and began fighting it out. Fortunately, St. Louis and its large armory were held by the Union, while the southwest fell to the Confederates.

On the last Sunday of October, the entire Eleventh Wisconsin regiment, minus those who were sick or injured, marched from Camp Randall into Madison for church services. The band came along, playing inspirational melodies. Correspondent C.D. Waldo was on hand to document the occasion for the *West Bend Editorial*: "On Saturday last, by invitation of its Chaplain, the 11th marched up town and attended a divine service at the Episcopal Church. It went with officers mounted, and band playing, and without arms.... the marching was splendid, and was a site worthy to behold." Spirits soared. These former farmers were about to head to the "seat of war." Waiting in Madison were family and friends, smiling and waving at the marching soldiers, wiping away tears, and winking at familiar faces in the crowd.[30]

A week later some of the ladies of Madison treated the regiment to a nice meal along with a selection of cakes and pies. C.D. Waldo noted, "The fair ladies of the city have been treating them [Eleventh Regiment] to an abundance of fine things, the inmates of each tent receiving two or three baskets full of such goodies as none but the ladies know how to provide, and from the cheers and shouts that continually rant the air, to the soldiers, I should judge that their kindness was duly appreciated, and long to be remembered by them."[31]

By now they were certain it was only a matter of days until they too would ship out. "I think we shall leave here the 8th [of November]," wrote Samuel Kirkpatrick to his father. "The boys is in good spirits and are glad that we are a going to leave." After the Soldier's dinner, Governor Randall came down to the camp and presented the Eleventh regiment with their regiment flag. Samuel wrote, "... as the good old stars and stripes were unfurled to the breeze every heart leaped anew at the sight." It was a sure sign they were only days from leaving.[32]

William H. Cope of Aurora, originally from Canada, stood five feet five inches and was described as handsome, with dark eyes and sandy blond hair. Like virtually everyone else he was a farmer. He wrote home often to his father, Thomas, who was a carpenter (from England) by training, but like so many immigrants had moved his family to the frontier and became a farmer, starting first in Canada then migrating south to Wisconsin. William's mother had passed away a few years before. Thomas was left to tend to the farm without William, who was his only son. William wrote his first letter (that has survived) to his father on November 1, describing the sight of sixteen hundred men drilling and marching. It was the grandest sight he had ever seen. His enthusiastic descriptions of the state capital and surrounding buildings gives a clear indication that it was all new to him. This was most likely the farthest he had ever been from the farm.[33]

Soldering so far, for virtually everyone in the regiment, was "first rate" as they prepared to start their journey: two miles down, about 8,998 to go.

Receiving only four weeks of training before moving out was not unusual for Civil War regiments. Some only received a week or two. For some in the Eleventh, like Jesse and Oliver Mather who arrived in mid October, two weeks of training would have to be enough.[34]

CHAPTER THREE

A Godforsaken Place

On November 19, 1861, the Eleventh Wisconsin Volunteer Regiment was ordered to St. Louis, Missouri. They were now part of the Department of the Missouri; the Union liked to name its departments and armies after rivers. In charge was Major General Henry W. Halleck, a West Point graduate and an intellectual who was fascinated with military strategy and even wrote on the subject. He was known as "Old Brains" before the Civil War. Under him were a series of generals, two of whom would become famous: Ulysses S. Grant, positioned in Cairo, and William T. Sherman in St. Louis.[1]

Before Halleck took over, Missouri was commanded by Major General John Charles Frémont,* known as the "California Pathfinder" after he, with the aid of guides such as Kit Carson, mapped the trail that carried settlers through the Rocky Mountain passes. When war broke out, President Lincoln assigned him to Missouri. He didn't last there long. His fate was sealed after he made a proclamation that disloyal Missourians would lose all possessions, not only those who owned slaves. Frémont essentially emancipated all Negroes not already free in Missouri, causing a tidal wave of backlash. The Union was still fragile, and Lincoln was between a rock and a hard place. He had no choice but to remove Frémont from command.[2]

Before his removal, Frémont made an urgent plea for more troops after the military debacle at Wilson's Creek. He called on the governors of Ohio, Illinois, Indiana, and Wisconsin to send more troops. Missouri was a battlefield unlike any other. Bushwhackers, guerillas, and spies battled in some of the most vicious fighting of the war. Without warning, guerillas would show up and decimate families, pillage, and burn homes. Martial law was declared and Frémont issued his proclamation.[3]

The Eleventh Wisconsin was assigned to guard the Iron Mountain Railroad near Sulphur Springs. One of only four slave states (Kentucky, Maryland and Delaware being the others) not to secede, Missouri was divided and still up for grabs in 1861 and early 1862. It was one of the wealthiest states along the Trans-Mississippi, with a population of 1.2 million. St. Louis was one of the largest and most important cities in the Union. Most importantly, its large arsenal contained some 60,000 muskets, 90,000 pounds of powder, and 1.5 million ball cartridges.[4]

Federal soldiers felt the locals could not be trusted, sometimes with good reason. It was almost impossible to tell who was a "secesh" (Confederate sympathizer) and who wasn't. Federal soldiers often sent money home through the local post office — money that never reached its destination, disappearing somewhere between the post office and St. Louis. Local spies reported Union troop movements to the enemy. Lawless bushwhackers roamed the countryside, disturbing communication lines and destroying railroads. Guerillas attacked Union

---

*Maj. Gen. David Hunter replaced Frémont for a short time before Halleck was appointed.

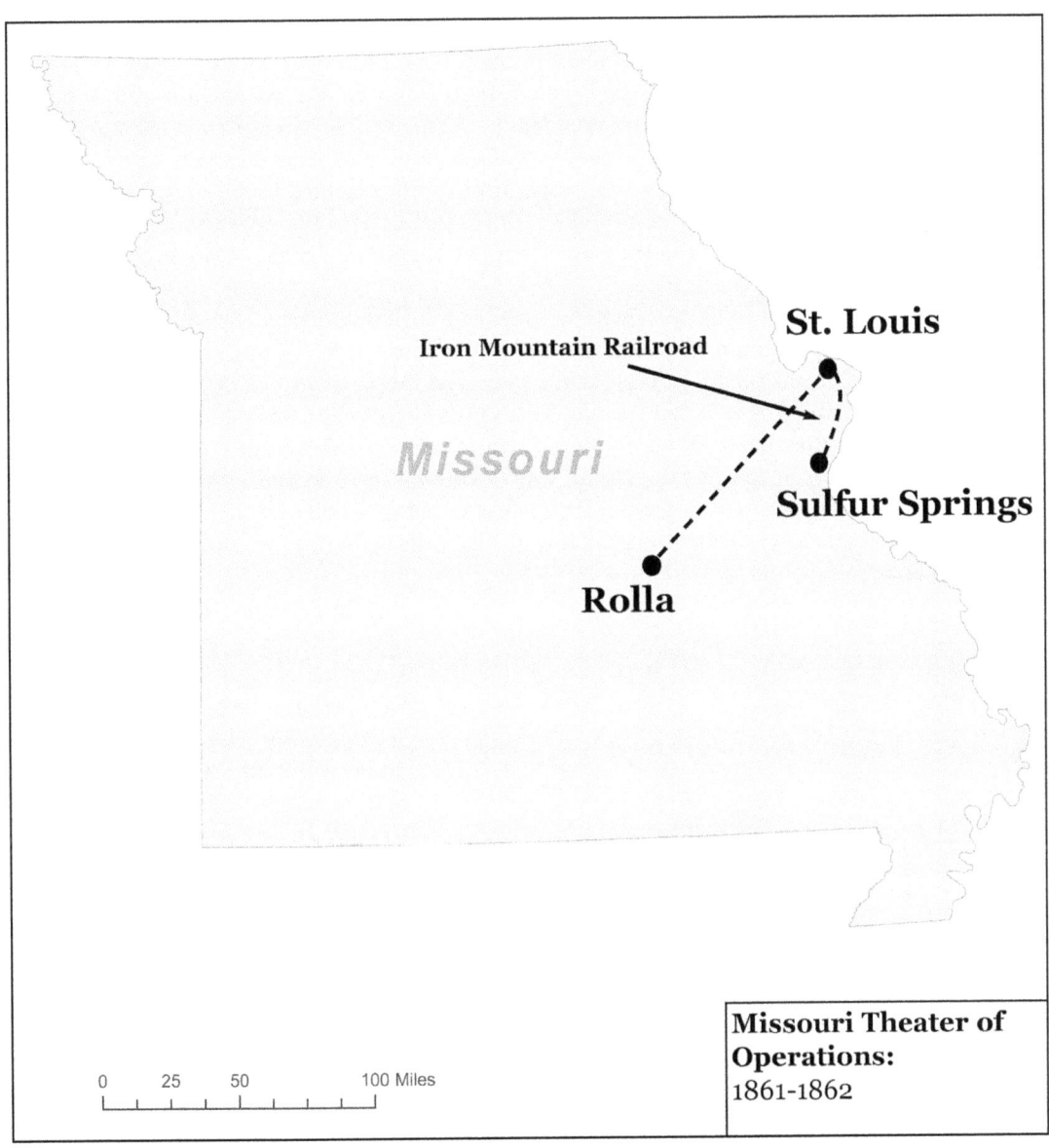

Missouri Theater of Operations: 1861-1862

stragglers. Halleck was so concerned he issued stern orders that all secessionists who were thought to be spies were to be arrested, jailed, or even shot.[5]

Halleck's most pressing issue in Missouri was the strength of Confederate major general Sterling Price's army, located somewhere near Springfield. Price's army was estimated at 12,000 to 40,000, a huge discrepancy that caused Halleck much unease. Halleck was also informed of a possible force of 18,000 Arkansas, Texas, and Native American troops marching to rendezvous with the Confederates in his region. After the Union army defeat at Wilson's Creek in August, Halleck's hold on Missouri felt tenuous at best.[6]

In January, General Grant, along with naval flag officer Andrew H. Foote, proposed an attack on Fort Henry on the Tennessee River. Halleck hesitated at first, but Grant persisted and eventually got his way. About the same time, Brigadier General Samuel R. Curtis and his army launched a winter campaign in an attempt to push Price from southwest Missouri.

There were essentially three lines of attack in the west along the Mississippi, Tennessee, and Cumberland rivers. Lincoln himself realized the value of attacking on these lines. In January, he sent memorandums instructing Halleck to move on the Mississippi line, and General Don Carlos Buell in Louisville to move along the Tennessee. Access to water transportation allowed them to move their troops almost without hindrance from weather, an advantage over the Federal armies in the east. Yet, a major problem remained in the west. Halleck and Buell disliked and mistrusted each other; each wanted to gain the upper hand in hopes of becoming overall commander in the west. Lincoln was continually mediating to get the generals to do anything in concert.[7]

The key to the war in the west was the rivers and the lines of attack they offered; the Mississippi River was the main prize. To take and hold the states that squeezed its shores would secure the region, cutting the South off from Texas and its supply of cattle and other goods. But control of anything as lengthy as the Mississippi begins with control of its head. Without securing Missouri and Arkansas, Union armies could not move much farther south. By controlling the rivers from St. Louis all the way to the Gulf and into Tennessee, Federal armies could cleave a large section of the South. Then it could take offensive action into the heart of the South to smash it. Unfortunately, it was some time before Union commanders formulated a plan.[8]

Major General Henry W. Halleck (Library of Congress).

In February, Grant was finally allowed to move on forts Henry and Donelson along the Tennessee and Cumberland rivers, scoring impressive victories. These lines of attack allowed the North to drive at the South's center. The Tennessee River was particularly important, enabling the Union to "thrust between Memphis and Nashville," outflanking the other armies. The river also crisscrossed a crucial Confederate line of communication between east and west. But although Grant was thrusting his "harpoon" deep into the "bowels" of the enemy, this action was away from the field of danger for Halleck. Missouri and Arkansas had to be dealt with.[9]

* * *

The Eleventh Wisconsin arrived in Chicago at six o'clock on the 20th of November. They unloaded from the train and marched to another depot, then packed into another set of train cars headed for Alton. They arrived in Alton the next day and marched down to the Mississippi River. The march to the river must have been a welcomed event — after spending the better part of two days in train cars — with the smell of the water, the cool breeze, boats and fishermen bringing in the day's catch.

Upon the regiment's arrival in Chicago, city officials delivered the following address to the officers of the Eleventh Wisconsin as the enlisted men loaded into the trains:

> Welcome ... to this great metropolis of the northwest, and to bid you God speed on your journey from the northern lakes to the banks of the Missouri. You have taken leave of the beautiful oak lands, the silver lakelets, and broad and rich prairies of Wisconsin, where peace and joy and contentment reign, to endure amidst the sleet and storm and snows of a northwestern winter the grim and dreadful realities and sufferings of war, on the plains, along the rivers, and amidst the now desolated and ruined and blackened and deserted homes of the once prosperous and beautiful Missouri. The change to most of you is a great and trying one; for us mere holiday soldiers, as carpet knights who have not yet realized the horrors of war, you know little of the onerous duties, the fearful responsibilities and the dreadful sacrifices that lie along your pathway, and no one but that of God can see or tell how far or how many shall ever return to those dear homes and precious wives and bright-eyed children you have left behind. Your presence, Colonel, and yours, officers of the Wisconsin Eleventh, reflect the highest honor on yourselves, and add another and yet another leaf to the chapter of immortal glory that Wisconsin, one of the fairest, youngest and most joyous daughters of this Union, has woven for herself during this dreadful crisis of our republic.[10]

It was dark when they boarded steamers and headed down the Mississippi for St. Louis. As men sprawled out on the large decks and caught up on sleep, others, like Samuel Kirkpatrick, enjoyed their first trip down the Mississippi. It was a clear night and the water was calm. "It was a great sight to me to see the boats passing one another that night all lit up with lights," he said. "We had a pleasant trip."[11]

It was only a three-hour voyage from Alton to St. Louis, where they docked around midnight. The next day they marched to the train station, where they loaded up and headed south 30 miles to Sulphur Springs on the Mississippi, arriving around five o'clock that evening. They pitched tents and cooked their dinner. Sulphur Springs, a small place of no more than a dozen buildings, was home to Camp Curtis, where parts of the Eleventh Wisconsin would spend the winter guarding the Iron Mountain Railroad and capturing "butternut secesh" and bushwhackers.

The weather for the most part was mild, and food was plentiful. Their diet consisted of sweet potatoes, grapes, peaches, corn, apples, nuts, wheat, and dried salt meat. The eating was so good that Samuel was worried about gaining weight. "I am fat and rugged. I weigh a hundred and 87 pounds," he informed his parents. Henry Twining was also very impressed with the food: "They raise the largest corn here that I ever saw."* The farmers of Wisconsin constantly wrote home comparing the land and crops to their own. For the most part, they were thoroughly impressed with the South.[12]

The men came to know their commanders a little better as they settled in. Captain Jesse S. Miller was second only to Colonel Harris in popularity. He was described as "clever" and "plucky" after he "was attacked by four Rebels" but somehow managed to escape injury or

---

*Henry Twining offers an excellent description of what was available: "I went in the woods last Sunday and got a lot of Hickernutts and Peacans which were the best nutts I ever ate. We can get a lot of Butternuts, Black walnuts, apples 40 cents a bushel, Sweet Potatoes 75 cents, Potatoes 25 cents, Dried Peaches $2.50, Corn 20 cents" (Henry Twining to Hattie, December 3, 1861). Soldiers tended to put weight on during their first few months of training until their first long march and food rationing. One newspaper noted that, as was the case with "all others, the Twelfth Wisconsin Regiment gained weight during its first month. Each regiment is weighed on enlistment and then about a month later it is weighed again." The correspondence also documented that "One company was weighed [and] found that all had gained - no one less than 5 pounds!" (Richland County Observer, December 27, 1861).

capture. "He fired six times at them," wrote Charles A. Stevens, "[and] he brought one of their hats with him, he says that one of them fell over and he got his hat. That is al we can get out of the captain, but we herd from another that our captain had been attacked by four Rebels and that he had kill three of them. The longer we stay with our captain the more we are set by him. I dont believe ther is a man in the company that would hear a word against Captain Miller."[13]

Jesse Miller was 23 years old, about six feet tall, strong and handsome — a born leader who knew how to take care of his men. "He let us work out and get a little spending money," Charles continued. When some found part-time jobs to make extra money, he let them work on their own time: "We hav chance here to take jobs choping cord wood and grabing out stumps and loading cars with wood for which we can make a dolar a day prety easy."[14]

At this time the greatest threat to the Eleventh Wisconsin came not from the enemy, but from themselves. During one incident in early December, a corporal in Company E shot off the "1 and 2 fingers ... of his right hand," apparently during target shooting. He was immediately discharged from the army. At night, guards would inadvertently fire at each other, sometimes wounding one another. On one occasion, two guards patrolling some distance apart both opened fire, not knowing what they were shooting at. Then one charged and struck the other guard "twice with his Bayonett and almost killed him," said Henry Twining. A few days later another incident occurred. "I was corporal of the guard last night," wrote Samuel Kirkpatrick. "At ten o'clock the pickets guard was fired upon. One of them came into camp and gave the alarm." Robert Sherrill told his aunt and uncle that "a party of eight rebels" were the culprits and were flushed out by the cavalry. The entire regiment was ordered to fall in with cartridge belts and muskets and most "thought [they] were going to have a battle rite off." As the alarm sounded, men sprang from their tents half dressed, rubbing sleep from their eyes, and hastily formed ranks as Captain Miller lined them up and ordered them to load their rifles. "The boys fell in very quick but some of them was skeered so bad that they took the buck ague," said Samuel. Luckily it was a false alarm. According to Samuel, the cavalry was returning from patrol and decided to fire a couple shots at the guards "for fun." It was most likely another case of the jitters.[15]

What flustered the soldiers of the Eleventh the most was the continual discovery and arresting of spies and bushwhackers. "We thought there was no rebels in this part of the country when we came here," wrote Robert Sherrill. "Our pickets fired at three men last night.... I find there is a great many." It became a regular event for patrols to bring back two or three men a week. These men were part of Jeff Thompson's Missouri State Guards and sworn enemies of the Union. Better known as the "Missouri Swamp Fox," Thompson, along with his band of guerrillas, terrorized Northern sympathizers and harassed Union supply lines and patrols. Some conflicts involved hundreds of men. Things were tense for the regiment during January of 1862, with almost nightly alerts and alarms. "We are drawed up in the line of battle every night or so but it has not amounted to much," wrote Samuel. "Yet the pickets get skeered the other night."[16]

A few nights later it would be Samuel's turn to feel some anxiety and fear. He and five others had traveled several miles from camp on patrol when they began to hear things: "About 2 o'clock in the night we heard something coming through the bushes and we cried out, 'who comes there.'" They received no answer. The men took aim towards the sound. Their pulses quickened. Then suddenly through the brush burst a magnificent horse. They fired and in a flash it vanished. The sounds of it grunting and hissing as it stormed off echoed around them. Giving chase, they found it a short distance away, dead in the woods without its passenger. "It was a very fine horse with a bridle on," said Samuel, clearly saddened to have killed the animal. But he took the bridle as indication that its rider must have been a spy. Local Confederate sympathizers would sometimes take pot shots at patrols, probe their lines at night, and even attempt broad daylight attacks when soldiers relaxed in town. The men were always on edge.[17]

After looking around for a possible spy, Samuel and the others headed back to camp. It was about 3 o'clock in the morning as they approached camp when a shot rang out. An off-duty guard was returning to another part of the camp when a picket (guard) mistook him for a spy and opened fire. "I heard a shot it was a picket fired at one of our own men," Robert Sherrill reported home. The distance was not far and the shot proved fatal as it struck "one of his arms and passed through the left lung." According to Robert, the guard ordered the soldier to halt three times but for some reason he did not. Henry P. Strong, regimental head surgeon, was soon on the scene. Before falling unconscious the soldier told him "he thought the picket knew him," and that is

Private Robert Sherrill (Wisconsin Veterans Museum).

why he did not respond. Strong noted that the wounds were fatal: "the ball ... entered the chest on the left side & passed out of the back on the right side" with enough velocity left to strike a hill some distance away. The soldier made it through the night but "died the next morning," wrote Samuel sadly. "It was a hard sight to see him cut off so quickly." The soldier, Robert A. Tollard of Cottage Grove, was the regiment's first casualty of the war, killed by his own men. Though Samuel didn't know Tollard, this was his first experience with violent death up close and in person. Strong summed up the event: "The picket did his duty & the men will now understand that they cannot fool in the enemy's country." The first violent death of the regiment cast a gloom over everyone, noted a correspondent. Two days after Tollard's death the entire regiment attended his funeral.[18]

Death cast a dark cloud over the entire regiment as men continued to die from disease, sickness, and accidents. As each company lost men, correspondence back home to local newspapers in early 1862 noted with melancholy the first death in their company. Company H lost Amos Colburn of Sauk County on February first. The correspondent wrote, "His death cast a gloom over the whole company. It was the first, and one least expected." Colburn collapsed and died within minutes; an official cause was never declared. By the end of January 1862, the regimental surgeon would report "seven accidental gun-shot wounds," five of which resulted in "amputation of either the thumb or the first two fingers." But the emergence of disease—"measles and typhoid fever are fast filling up our hospital"—brought with it the realization that "more men in the army die of disease than of bullets." This was something that rural farmers of the Eleventh regiment simply did not expect. By the time February arrived, some 200 in the regiment would be stricken with measles, mumps, typhoid fever or

*In line of battle the men stand side by side, 2 ranks deep, in order to be able to quickly reload and fire their rifles.

pneumonia. And of the bullets that had killed or wounded, their own men had fired them all.[19]

* * *

During the cold winter months the men gathered in their tents for dinner and did their own cooking. They even had to purchase their own stoves. After dinner they smoked their pipes, played games, wrote letters, and reminisced of home. Morale fluctuated depending on numerous factors: weather, news, and temperament. "Some of the boys made a talk this morning," Samuel Kirkpatrick wrote home, "and said if this world was a bull that Camp Curtis would be the ass hole." During the day they often traveled into town or roamed the countryside. Sometimes wealthy secesh farmers offered them a home-cooked meal. As the war progressed, foraging became a significant source of food for the large armies of the Civil War as they marched across the countryside. Depending on the army or the regiment, soldiers were even encouraged to live off the land as much as possible. During one particularly successful forage, recorded Henry Twining, they brought back "five bee hives, four sheep, six geese, six chickens, and two axes."[20]

The abundance of food and lack of drilling produced the predictable results. "I am fat as a hog I weigh a bout 150 pounds," William H. Cope informed his father. William was constantly reassuring his father, who had already lost his wife, that things were going to be fine. The most pressing thing to worry about was "getting fat dear father, we have great times eating...." The war would be over soon and all William would have to show for it was added girth, he assured his father.[21]

Head surgeon Henry Strong described in a letter home to his wife what the men did to "kill ennui." In his tent was a fellow officer who wrote poetry. Calvin C. Barnes, also a surgeon, was "flat on his back on the cot reading [Shakespeare]." Steward Henry W. Turner was "smoking, [but] that's his way," said Henry. "I am writing to a mighty likely little woman." Along with writing home to family and friends, soldiers of the Eleventh wrote home to local newspapers as "correspondents." Every regiment had soldiers acting as correspondents for newspapers back home and this sometimes led to squabbling between them. This was the case with the Eleventh and Eighth regiments that spent several weeks debating who was the better regiment. By the end each had declared victory.[22]

Christmas was a lonely time for soldiers far away from home and loved ones. Most of the men of Eleventh regiment had now served 90 days or more. Though their spirits were generally good, winter was starting to take its toll, and their thoughts turned to home and past holidays. "We had a fine Christmas," Robert Sherrill told his aunt and uncle, "oh we had lots of good things to eat. I wish you a mery new years." "I wish you a Merry Christmas," Henry wrote Hattie on Christmas day. "I tell you, Hat, I wish I was up there today to have a sleigh ride.... We could have a visit to your house so the old rocking chair should not be alone but here I am down to the foot of the hill living on hard crackers and coffee, by gosh ... it was just one year ago today that I remember well when we sat side by side and heard the music from the sleigh bells but that day has passed and gone...." Henry must have been feeling melancholy, for he strayed from his customary informal signature and signed this letter "Yours Truly, H.H. Twining."[23]

Winter also brought disease. Jesse Mather was one of the first to get sick. Measles and mumps started to appear, and by February the regiment was ravaged by disease. Samuel Kirkpatrick was out four days the last week of January. They were now in Victoria at Camp Harris. Before he became sick, Samuel noted the outbreak of disease: "There is some few cases of measles and mumps, but the doctors has good luck so far." But the illnesses took their toll on camp morale: "One day the boys is in good spirits and the next they are dull." The regiment surgeon noted, about the same time, that in one company alone (Captain Whittlesey's company E) there were 10 cases of measles.[24]

In his official report to the surgeon general, Henry Strong complimented the habits of the regiment "as ... cleanliness is above the medium" and that "Drunkenness ... is hardly known." He also noted that the regiment's overall "Morality & good habits are the general rule." His report continued:

> The average Sickness in hospital and mortality in my regiment has been light thus far. Only those cases absolutely requiring it have been admitted into hospital. We have a larger proportion Sick in quarters of cararrhus, diarrhoea acutus. I account for this from the fact that most of my regiment were taken from rural districts & rural homes. Such a change of diet, habits of life, sleeping on the ground, poorly cooked food are the immediate causes.... Allow me to suggest that 20 to 22 men in a Sibley tent is too many for their comfort & health....[25]

He was not entirely wrong in commenting on the fact that these men were from a rural area, but they were not becoming sick simply because of the change in habits, though that certainly played a role. They were also experiencing exposure to diseases that they probably had never been in contact with before. Being farmers and frontiersmen, they spent months isolated on their farms where some diseases (such as measles and mumps) might not have reached. A study by John Robertson that appeared in a 2001 issue of the *Journal of Interdisciplinary History* suggests that disease and illness effected rural soldiers in greater numbers than their urban counterparts.[26]

Guarding a railroad and wandering for hours looking for secesh spies only occupied so much of their time. "It looks now as if we would never be in a battle," Samuel wrote home to his parents. "There has been more men died with sickness this winter than would have fallen in battle." Helping to keep the situation tolerable were the people of Wisconsin, who donated thousands of pounds of hospital stores, medicines, and clothing for their soldiers. The U.S. Sanitary Commission sent Reverend H.A. Reid and his wife as agents for Wisconsin, overseeing the distribution of goods. It was noted that 46 different "Soldiers Aid Societies" were operational in Wisconsin, along with "123 boxes of supplies received." Henry P. Strong mentioned in one correspondence home, "We have comforters, pillows, drawers, shirts, socks, dressing gowns for almost any emergency. Thanks to the ladies of Wisconsin." Women's clubs and organizations dutifully sent supplies to their state's soldiers throughout the war. But soon the distribution of the goods seemed to break down and accusations that Mr. and Mrs. Reid were selling and using the goods for their own purposes began to surface. Angry soldiers, including surgeon Henry Strong, sent several reports home complaining of corruption. One soldier claimed that the Reids "have lived here several months on articles that were sent here for the sick." They also received a substantial salary rumored to be in the "$1,500" range. It did not take long before Mr. and Mrs. Reid were replaced.[27]

Back in November 1861, Robert Sherrill's uncle, John Dunlap, informed him he was considering enlisting. Despite the hardships of camp life, Robert was enthusiastic. "Some of the boys dont like soldiering but I like it rite well," Robert told him. "You talked of inlisting if you take a notion come & inlist in our company." Robert mentioned several times in his letters that he thought John should join up. Also serving in Robert's company was his Aunt Caroline's brother, James Dain. The two were inseparable, "same as brothers," Robert told his aunt. They enlisted together, were assigned to the same company, shared the same tent and, when the weather was cold, shared the same blanket. Caroline and John had three daughters, Emma, Adda, and Marion, and John likely had mixed feelings about leaving his family and the farm behind. By the New Year, though, John had decided he was ready to go, telling Robert he'd sign up in the spring, after he'd planted his crop. Like so many others, John was sure he would be gone only a few months and would be home in time for harvest. "Glad you said you thought you would enlist in the spring," wrote Robert back to his uncle. But "I think you will not get a chance." Robert didn't think the war would last much longer.[28]

Captain Luther A. Whittlesey (Craig Johnson Collection).

Indeed, many of the men thought the war would soon be over. "If I am alive and well I shall expect to land on the shores of Wisconsin before the fourth of July," said Charles A. Stevens, "unless I conclude to continue the soldiers life after the war is over." William H. Cope shared with his father a rumor that they would be "disbanded by the first of January," but confessed that they would be lucky to "get away by June." To get through this monotonous and tedious time, the men wrote home with their predictions on when the war would be over. Not many, if any, had a clue of what was in store for them. Thomas Cope was worried about his only son and the farm. As he was without much help he had concerns about making the mortgage payments. "Father I want you to write how you get a long," insisted William, aware of his father's concerns. "Keep up good spirits for I think I shall be home in the spring." That would be perfect timing to prepare for the planting the next year and would surely ease his father's mind.[29]

* * *

In early 1862, the Eleventh was still scattered all along the Iron Mountain Railroad line, from Meremec River to Cole's Bridge. "Our Regt. is strung from St. Louis down to big river bridge we aint had a shot at secesh yet," wrote Jesse Mather to his sister. Jesse's company was particularly bored, not having seen many bushwhackers or spies in their area. His frustration was obvious. "I was on guard last night and it raned and thoundered and lightened it was rather mudy." Jesse and his older brother Oliver had signed up to see action, not to march in mud and guard a railroad.[30]

The men were also getting to know their colonel, who was proving to be a good leader and had the respect of his men. "I wish you could see Colonel Harris on his thorough bred charger," wrote one soldier back home to his local newspaper, "you would say at once he was Cromwell or Bonaparte. He is altogether a military man, and if an opportunity presents itself, he will make his mark." He went on to describe the officers as strict military men, and he was glad for it: "Our Lieut. Colonel [Charles A. Wood] is half horse and half alligator." Captain Jesse Miller of Company D, who was described as a "brick," was unanimously revered by his men. "I will give one dollar to see the man that does not love him," the soldier declared. "Where bravery will reap its reward [during battle], in which case we have the best of confidence in Col Harris, he is cool and determined in the society of his regiment, which is the true character of a brave man in battle." In any army, officers could gain respect only by displaying courage in battle. This was especially true during the Civil War, when courage, honor, duty, and justice played paramount roles in how people and soldiers were judged. The regiment had high praise for their colonel without seeing him in battle, as his demeanor and charisma gave them great hope that he would be a good leader.[31]

In February 1862, a report circulated back home that the regiment was "demoralized." But letters such as the one Samuel wrote on the 7th of February, while stationed in Victoria, seemed to contradict that newspaper report:

> It is purty cool to day. The snow has all gone off and it is as ruff as an old bear's ass. Last night there was about a dozen of the boys went to a dance. They returned this morning and said they had a good time. I think that you would like to live here very well. It is the most like home of any place that I have seen. The folks is very good to us. There is a shoemakers girl that thinks that I am all right. No sense. I have been sick. She waited on me first rate you bet. The folks talk about the soldiers having hard times but it is not so. The soldiers most of them has a better time than if they was at home.

Of all the soldiers in the regiment, Samuel's writing most reflected his personality. Observant and inquisitive, he had charm and wit, a lively sense of humor, and an unmistakable playfulness. His fellow Farmers Guards from Mineral Point called him "curious," and it stuck. Samuel even signed off a letter or two as "Curious Kirkpatrick." And he was curious. Cities and farms caught his attention. "I am learning something evry day," he wrote. Samuel was also a charming lady's man. He mentions several outings with local women. Family friend and fellow soldier Abraham Barret revealed in one of his letters that one night Samuel convinced several local girls at a dance that he was a "Major — Major Curious and they call him that now."[32]

Samuel was dedicated to the cause, and soldiering seemed to suit him. He was very loyal to his regiment, but more so to his company and his captain, Luther H. Whittlesey. "I like our Captain first rate and I vow to stick to him till the last," he declared one cold winter night while writing home. The motivation for these young men to stick together is not hard to imagine. Many were with childhood friends and oftentimes fought alongside brothers, nephews, and cousins. This was true for both the North and South and may have been a reason why the fighting sometimes escalated to brutal proportions, and why regiment after regiment could march on toward certain destruction.[33]

Soldiering was a good fit for Robert Sherrill as well. He was strong and rugged, and had so far avoided the ravages of disease. He often declared, "Soldering is not hard work at all." Even guard duty was easy, he told his uncle: "If you think you can stand it to be on guard evry third nite you can suit your self about it." Though Robert would find soldiering hard work later, for now it was an adventure he rather enjoyed.[34]

Very few of the soldiers wrote much about the carnage of battle, or at least few of those letters have survived. Samuel did make an interesting comment in one of his letters, telling his family they got the news of the regiment's action faster than he could report it, so why should he bother writing about it? Writing ten letters in January alone, Samuel began to question the necessity of such correspondence without much to tell. "Well must quit this nonsense," he declared, "for I am afraid you will get tired of reading."[35]

What the men wanted, or at least talked about, was getting in the fight. As rumors swirled that they were heading here or there but never came to pass, spirits would sink. "Whooray for the union there is an expedition filing out at Pilot Knob about fourty or fifty miles from here, there is cannons, baggage wagons or something of the kind goes by here on the cars most every day," wrote Charles A. Stevens excitedly to his brother one afternoon. "For that expetition there was four hundred mules that went by here yesterday on the cars for the same expetition. I expect that we will go with that expetition or at least that is the talk." By February comments from regiment correspondents home reflected the common theme of frustration. The war was going to end soon and the men were "spoiling for a fight.... If it is necessary to have fighting done, and we think it is, all of the boys would rather do it speedily." Another soldier, who signed his correspondence with the pseudonym "Monterey," deplored that the United States government did not have "confidence enough in its own strength." A six-hundred-thousand-man army was greater than any other "power" on earth, he believed — an army large enough to "insatiate the appetite of Napoleon." Yet, Monterey did not trust the talk of a quick war: "No, we've got to fight before this war is ended.... Here we are 600,000 strong, fully armed ... panting for the fray."[36]

On February 8, 1862, the officers of the regiment gathered for an oyster supper at the commissary's warehouse. For weeks they had been planning a special event for their colonel. As a sign of their devotion, during a special ceremony, they presented Colonel Harris with a "splendid gilt Scabbard & a Sash" which cost them $300, a very large sum. Colonel Harris would carry the sword and scabbard throughout the war. "Nearly all the officers came together & had a merry time," wrote Henry P. Strong, who made the presentation. Strong greatly admired his colonel, as most of the men did, and expressed his admiration often in his letters and other correspondence. Upon receiving the gift, it was recorded, Colonel Harris was deeply moved and told his officers, "Let us by our energy, courage, daring and patriotism, gain the praise of our countrymen and the fear of our enemies."[37]

* * *

The day they enlisted, October 14, 1861, Jesse and Oliver Mather had to quietly dress before the sun came up. Anxious, excited, and nervous all at once, the brothers gingerly tiptoed past their younger brother's room to their older sister Sarah's room and quietly woke her to bid her farewell. They had to hurry before their father awoke to start his daily routine. Oliver was happy to have his younger brother with him, but knew it was a great responsibility. If Jesse did not come back it would surely haunt him the rest of his life. They had three brothers, Henry (17), who would stay home and help their father with the farm, Samuel (12) and Howard (10).

The majority of Jesse and Oliver's letters home were addressed to their sister. They had volunteered without their parent's blessing, and their father (Mathew) in particular was upset with the boys. There was much talk about the hardship their father faced when they did not make it back for the next harvest. Throughout their letters, the boys asked many questions about the harvest and their father. But they remembered their mother, Caroline, as well. Jesse sent the words of a song to her not long after running away:

Mother, Can I Go.

I am writing to you, mother, knowing well what you will say,
When you read with tearful fondness all I write to you to-day;
Knowing well the flame of ardor on a loyal mother's part,
That will kindle with each impulse, with each throbbing of your heart.

I have heard my country calling for her sons that still are true;
I have loved that country, mother, only next to God and you;
And my soul is springing forward to resist her bitter foe:
Can I go, my dearest mother? tell me, mother, can I go?

From the battered walls of Sumter, from the wild waves of the sea,
I have heard her cry for succor, as the voice of God to me;
In prosperity I loved her — in her days of dark distress,
With your spirit in me, mother, could I love that country less?[38]

In December Oliver wrote home to Sarah informing her that Jesse was sick — one of the first in the regiment — but that he should be okay. No doubt that first line left a lump in her throat, but Oliver continued:

> We have had very pleasant weather here the nights are cool and frosty we have not seen but three or four days of bad weather since we enlisted. The drum has just beat for church but I cant go on account of finishing this letter I shant write much but I dont expect you to follow my example for you have better chances to write but one thing I can tell you that we know what we see but we dont know what we hear for we hear so much that it goes in at one ear and out at the other.[39]

Sarah was very attentive, and faithfully answered their letters as fast as she could (none have survived). Oliver made sure to watch out for Jesse as much as he could. They bunked together, ate together, and each made sure to report back to their big sister whenever the other misbehaved. "I will answer to the letter that you wrote to Jesse as he is engaged in some other kind of bisness," revealed Oliver. "I will not mention it but he is well at present." Jesse was most likely gambling with some of the boys in another tent. Oliver made sure to comfort Sarah and let her know they were well. "We have pretty good times here" was a common phrase. Oliver (like many Victorian era soldiers) was fond of poetry as well, and sometimes scribbled a few lines on the back of his letters or under his signature:

> Our banner glory is waving on high
> Its stars are as those of the eleventh
> And its stripes like the mingling hues of the sky
> When the morning is blushing in heaven

Oliver frowned on some of the behavior of his fellow soldiers, and did not appear to care for foraging, which sometimes turned into out–and–out stealing. "Three of our boys have been arrested and taken to Sulphur Springs for trial they stole the key out of a door of the grocery," he bemoaned, "and then went after night and took such things as they could conceal." Pleased that they were caught, he continued: "I think they are a disgrace to their company and captain I will not call any names." Reassuring his sister that his regiment was still in God's good graces, he let it be known that the local residents thought "we are the best regiment that has been here at least behave the best."[40]

It was still winter, but Oliver was already worried about the next harvest. "If I said that I would be back in the spring but if I dont come this spring," he said, "I will sometime I dont think it far distant." The boys truly believed they would be back by the next harvest. Oliver concluded his letter by asking his sister to "give my love to Father and mother and all the rest of the folks ... and keep a share for yourself."[41]

* * *

In January, General Curtis formed the Army of the Southwest (about 12,000 strong) in Rolla, and launched a campaign to push Price from southwest Missouri. By February he had forced Price and his tattered army of about 7,000 Missourians into Arkansas and the Boston Mountains. But the Confederates would not continue to retreat much longer. The new commander of the Trans-Mississippi region for the Rebels was the flamboyant General Earl Van Dorn, who was determined not only to make a stand, but also to go on the offensive and retake lost territory. "I must have St Louis—then huzza," he wrote to his wife. He intended to whip the Federal army and restore Southern pride. "Soldiers! Behold your leader," he called out to his men. "He comes to show you the way to glory and immortal renown…." Van Dorn got his chance at the battle of Pea Ridge in early March.[42]

Though for the men of the Eleventh Wisconsin the winter and spring of 1862 seemed like wasted time, the Union enjoyed one victory after another. On February 6, the combined army–navy force led by Grant and Foote took Fort Henry on the Tennessee River. The Confederacy had built forts Henry and Donelson at a point where the Cumberland and Tennessee rivers squeezed together, south of the Kentucky and Tennessee border. Taking these forts opened up Tennessee and offered the Union all kinds of opportunities for continued offensive action. Not pausing to celebrate his victory, Grant pushed on with his 27,000 men to Fort Donelson, quickly enveloping the fort and its 14,000 defenders. After two days of intense fighting the situation became hopeless, and the garrison asked for terms for surrender. Upon receiving Grant's serene reply, "No terms except unconditional and immediate surrender," the fort surrendered immediately. This stunning victory reverberated through the Union and the Confederacy. As he would prove again and again, Grant was a man of action and few words. Eventually Lincoln would discover that these qualities were what he needed in the eastern theater, where talk superseded action.[43]

Victories for the North continued throughout February. Buell finally took his Army of the Ohio on the offensive and captured Nashville on February 25. The rivers were becoming Unionized, with gunboats sailing all the way to Florence, Alabama. The North was now threatening some of the most important areas of the Confederacy, where vital iron and agricultural production took place. Newspapers throughout the North celebrated the success of its armies with enthusiastic headlines: "Glorious News!" "Marvelous!" "Brilliant!" By March no one believed the war would last past July. For the Confederacy, the outlook was disconcerting. The *Richmond Enquirer* and the *Dispatch* agreed, reporting that "the enemy have

Major General Samuel R. Curtis (Library of Congress).

shown a daring that has taken us by surprise," and the surrender of Fort Donelson produced a "staggering blow."[44]

On Friday, February 7, the telegraph operator for General Curtis received news of Grant's victory at Fort Henry. All that afternoon men anxiously awaited the particulars, and information slowly trickled in. At roll call Samuel Kirkpatrick, James Dain, Henry Oettiker, Robert Sherrill, and the rest of the Farmers Guards were called to attention by their captain, Luther Whittlesey, who asked that they "give three cheers" for the victory. "After cheering the captain remarked he had his whiskey," wrote Robert Sherrill home to his aunt and uncle. It did not take long for a celebration to commence. "We went to the tavern and got our regular wine we had a splendid time of it over the victory gained."[45]

The avalanche of success for the Union was capped off by Curtis's routing of Van Dorn at Pea Ridge on the 7th and 8th of March. Van Dorn had conceived a brilliant plan to swing around on Curtis and take him from the rear. Though Curtis had the advantage of position, since his men were able to dig in, Van Dorn had superior numbers (17,000 against 10,500), which made Curtis uneasy. This uneasiness likely won the battle. Curtis was constantly alert and on edge. Getting wind of Von Dorn's movement, Curtis turned his army 180 degrees for a surprise attack. After some hard fighting he routed the Confederates from the field, and the victory secured Missouri for the Union for the rest of the war. With Missouri locked down, it was time to secure Arkansas, with as much of the Mississippi River as possible.[46]

* * *

About this time the Eleventh Wisconsin was assigned to Brigadier General Frederick Steele's army. Though their health and morale were improving, many still suffered and death from sickness was a constant. Henry Twining wrote home to Hattie with news. "I cannot write to you as I always have before this that all is well," he said. "But one near and dear friend Johnny O. is dead. He died at Pilot Knob on the 2nd of March.... He had the measles and he got pretty near well of them and was taken with the typhoid fever which caused his death.... He told the doctor to bid his mother good-bye for him." Henry went on to list others, including himself, who were ill or just recovering.[47]

Henry also reported that in February "there was not but 35 out of 95 of our Co. that were reported fit for duty." They blamed the poor conditions and Missouri weather, warm one day and cold the next. Henry also blamed the water, and hoped they would soon move out. As March approached, the surgeon noted that the regiment was regaining its health. "Our sick are growing beautifully less in numbers now," declared Henry Strong. "We have lost only one man this month & him by pneumonia following measles," which was almost always fatal, he noted. At this point in the war his company had lost 13 men "by accident & disease," he reported. "Considering the number we have had Sick I think this a good record."[48]

After a winter with absolutely no progress for the Eleventh Wisconsin, the boys were starting to question what was happening. Rumors spread that the war would not last much longer. They heard reports and read newspaper articles about the success the Union enjoyed, but they'd seen no evidence and as they had not yet been in a fight, the men were becoming frustrated.

General Halleck issued the following order on March 8, 1862:

> The District of Southeastern Missouri is added to that of Saint Louis. This order will in no way interfere with the command of Brig. Gen. F. Steele. Brigadier-General Schofield will immediately take measures, in consultation with Col. George Thorn, aide-de-camp and chief of topographical engineers, to guard the Iron Mountain Railroad bridges with Lieutenant-Colonel Fischer's battalion and such militia force as may be necessary, relieving from duty the Eleventh Wisconsin.[49]

Orders to move out were most likely received with thunderous cheers and applause. They were finally done guarding the railroad. Thaddeus Rice wrote home to his sister on March 9 while the regiment was stationed at Sulphur Springs, Missouri: "We don't hav eny truble here, I don't think we will [get the] chance to try our guns at the rebbles. It has been the warmest winter that I ever saw. I think that we will be hom by harvest next." The war was going well, with Union armies victorious in the West. "I think secesh will have to dance where ever we will find them now," wrote Robert Sherrill to his uncle.[50]

On March 12 the regiment moved out, but not to pursue Price and Van Dorn and their shattered army, as many in the regiment had hoped. Instead, they were to join a massive patrol along the Missouri–Arkansas border, mainly to protect Missouri and Springfield in case Price came back. They were a glorified guard unit again.[51]

PILOT KNOB, Mo., March 23rd, 1862.

Maj. Gen. H. W. HALLECK, U.S.A.:

GENERAL: The Eleventh Wisconsin Infantry and the Sixteenth Ohio Battery marched from here this morning to join the advance at Doniphan or Pitman's Ferry. Three squadrons of the Fifth Illinois Cavalry are waiting here for the return of their baggage wagons, which were sent forward with supplies, the supply train not being sufficient to keep the troops in advance provisioned. The other three squadrons of that regiment are at Greenville, having been sent as escorts to trains and as guard to the depot. I have detailed the Thirteenth Illinois Cavalry, four squadrons, under Colonel Bell, to guard the depot at this point and at Greenville, or wherever it may be established, and to escort trains between these points. The squadron of Illinois Cavalry, under Captain Dodson (Dodson's and Huntley's troop), I shall take with me into the field.[52]

Steele's army had enough firepower for anything that could be mustered against them in Arkansas. Seventy-five mules and horses towed two 12-pounder howitzers and four 6-pounders. The Eleventh Wisconsin was part of the Second Brigade, commanded by Colonel Charles E. Hovey. Steele's command consisted of about 8,000 men as it moved south in order to join forces with Curtis.[53]

* * *

A few days before they headed out, William H. Cope received a letter from his frantic father informing him that he had fallen behind on the mortgage payment. His father had a plan, but wanted William's approval as both were invested in the success of the farm and livestock. "Father you say you want my permission a bout selling the cattle as pay for the morgage," William wrote. The problem was that the cattle were also financed, and there would still be payments due on them. William, stuck in the middle of a war, had to help his father figure out what to do. It wasn't that Thomas Cope didn't know what to do, but that he wanted it to be a decision that he and his son made together. They were all each other had. William's idea was a risky one, but probably the only one. "If you sold them the best way," he wrote, "would be to pay the morgage off and as fast as I got my pay, I will send it home...." And then Thomas could pay "part down" and get the cattle back.[54]

"We are joined to Steel's Brigade," wrote Samuel Kirkpatrick, "and it is a splendid Brigade." Word spread that they would be traveling some distance: "Now we have a chance to try our selves a marching. The boys is in good spirits and keen to start.... If you don't get a letter for 3 or 4 weeks you ain't to get uneasy but you can write as usually for we can get and send the mail whenever the supplies teams comes in." The regiment seemed pleased with Steele, who in turn seemed to take a liking to the Eleventh Wisconsin. "General Steele ... though but little known thus far in the war, is a fine officer," wrote a correspondent. After reviewing the regiment for the first time it was noted that "Gen. Steele said to Col. Harris ...

that he had the finest regiment of volunteers he had seen...." This sentiment was confirmed by a surgeon with the Ninth Illinois Cavalry, who noted in his journal, "[The] Wisconsin Eleventh is a crack Regt, & has better music than any other," after seeing them near Reeves Station on the Black River.[55]

* * *

Oliver Mather took a moment to scribble a quick letter home before marching commenced. Rumors had them marching to an eventual fight that could not possibly be far away, and Oliver must have been nervous. "This probably will be the last letter you will ever get from me but I hope not," he wrote Sarah. "We are goin start for Greenville tomorrow morning our advance guard started ahead this afternoon.... We will make some of the secesh at Pokehontus smell hell or they will us." Oliver was ready for a fight. He wanted to know how he would handle battle, but was overwhelmed with excitement and doubt. "My head is so thick that I cant think much so I wont write much," he told her, "but we are going to see some of the country if nothing happens...."[56]

Pitman's Ferry was the starting point for Steele's southward advance, aimed for Pocahontas, Bird's Point, and eventually White River at Jacksonport on the 10th of May. By the 25th they reached Batesville and joined with General Curtis's army. By all accounts the march was hard. "Of all the God forsaken countries," wrote the drummer boy for the Eleventh, "this is the worst." The men suffered from scarcity of food and the animals from want of forage. These were some of the harshest conditions the regiment would see. As they made these first extended marches the Eleventh Wisconsin soon realized that they had to travel lighter, and "extra blankets, drawers, and other shirts and things, lined the sides of the road for miles." The correspondent also noted that pretty much "every man threw away something of value." They were moving with only what they needed.[57]

The country was so sparsely settled that it was impossible to obtain sustenance by foraging, and pretty much all supplies had to be transported from Pilot Knob. "We went through a swamp for miles, no road, and water up to the knees," the drummer boy continued. "Not a living thing did we see but frogs." They were on half rations since leaving the Black River. But they were also happy to finally be moving, and hopes soared that they might actually get to fight. We "stand it bully," he determined. "The plan," he surmised, "is to form a junction with Curtis and go to Memphis or Corinth." This would most likely mean a fight, in his estimation.[58]

One Sunday, as the regiment camped and relaxed along the river, the gunboat *Essex* came meandering along. The men lined the shore and began to shout and cheer as they waved their hats. In acknowledgement the boat "fired a shell into the air up the river that burst in mid air & a splendid sight it was," recorded Henry Strong. The band was nearby practicing and immediately "struck up the Star Spangled Banner." The boat slowed and continued to present its fireworks. "She fired another shell" and another as the band continued to play. Then "she fired an 8 or 10 pound ball up Stream that Struck the water at a distance of 1½ miles & Skipped along the water" until out of sight. The boat was beautiful, he thought, "covered over with flags of nearly every devise." Within minutes it was gone and the men returned to their campfires.[59]

"We left Pilot Knob last Sunday morning and marched thirteen miles and stoped for the night," wrote Oliver Mather. "Our teams did not come so far so we had to sleep without our tents." The weather was pleasant so it was no hardship for the night. Although the days were warm, the nights were still cool in April and May. But it did not take long for the conditions to change. On June 10, while in Batesville, Samuel Kirkpatrick wrote to his father that he was doing fine and felt "hardy." But he could tell something was up. Thousands of soldiers were

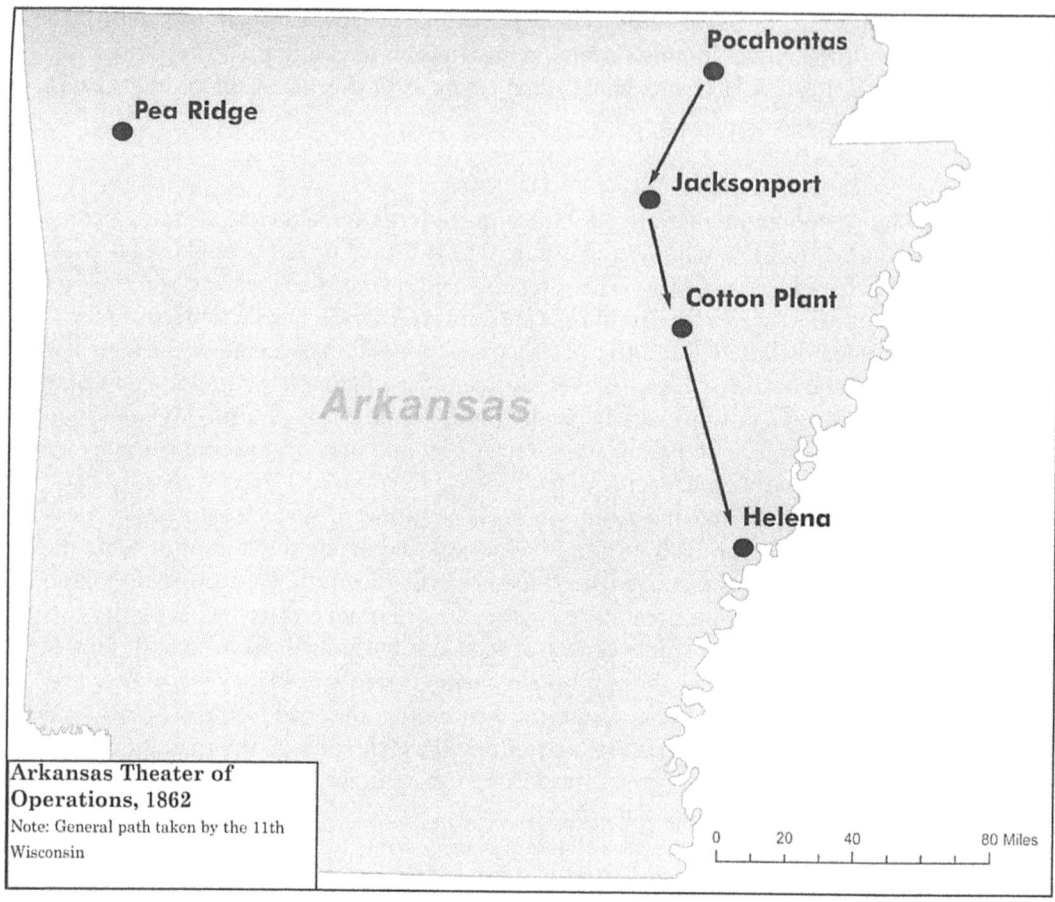

Arkansas Theater of Operations, 1862
Note: General path taken by the 11th Wisconsin

gathering for some kind of movement. "What they are all coming here for I don't know," he wrote. "We thought that we would be attacked but that is not so."[60]

The march was more difficult than most had imagined it would be. "Since we left Black River," Samuel noted, "we have marched over 150 miles.... We have had some pretty hard times on our march." The only thing that kept them focused was the "expectation of a fite," but the Rebels would not oblige. The only enemy army in the area was significantly smaller and retreated in the face of Steele and Curtis as they continued their march. There was talk that Johnny Reb would make a stand in Jacksonport, and Samuel hoped to go there.[61]

The most interesting development in June, as far as the men in the Eleventh were concerned, was the discovery of some of the largest farms they had ever seen. "There is some very large plantations down here," wrote Samuel. "On them big farms generally you will see from 25 to 30 blacks." This was likely his first encounter with slavery — surely it was his first plantation — and Curious Kirkpatrick wanted to investigate. He met the owner of one particularly large plantation, whose name was also Kirkpatrick, and "asked him where he was from and he said Tennessee and lived here 16 years." He was rich by Samuel's estimate because he had a lot of property, as well as "80 negroes that goes in the field." Later that evening, while Samuel and some others were foraging, they came upon a plantation and decided to "get dinner." When they entered, "the family got up from the dinner ... invited us to set up and have some." They, of course, first asked if the family was secesh. The answer would always be no, but they still had to ask. This time, however, some-

thing different happened. The lady of the house suddenly burst into tears and told them that her only son was in the Confederate Army. They stood up to leave, knowing that fraternizing with the enemy was not allowed, and as they left the mother stood on the porch, still crying, and shouted to them as they walked away, begging them to "Please, spare my son!!!"[62]

Arkansas, like most of the United States before the war, was a rural state dominated by agriculture and, by the 1860s, cotton farming. The land was rich near the Mississippi and the alluvial plain, as well as in the Arkansas River Valley. In these regions plantations began to flourish by the 1850s. Very few people could afford slaves; most farmed land for themselves. But large plantations developed and soon dominated much of the fertile landscape. Marching across Arkansas was not an easy task. The numerous waterways became the only major transportation routes that could be depended on, but Confederate guerrillas and bushwhackers targeted them. Roads in Arkansas were poor and rarely kept up when not near the plantations. The river and creek valleys were the best routes for travel, but they were easy to blockade by Rebels slowing down an advancing army.[63]

At the front of General Curtis's forces, the Eleventh Wisconsin left Batesville on the 22nd of June and stopped at Jackson, at the foot of the Black and White rivers. The men marched on, sometimes through strange wildernesses with cypress swamps infested with malaria. More and more in their ranks would get sick and die. During their march Samuel took time to write a quick note home, with mounting frustration. "We are now no nearer a fite than we was a month ago," he lamented. "Some of the boys is in a great way about going home. They think the war will soon be over but there is none of them that knows anything about it." He was right, of course.[64]

Frustration was once again mounting for many in the regiment. These were farmers, and spring meant only one thing. "There are about thirty prisoners in the guard house here that would be glad to go home," Oliver Mather noted to his sister, "and stay home some of them have farms and would like to be putting in their crops if they stay much longer it will be to late to put in any crop this year." His thoughts also turned to home, to his own family farm and his father and younger brother, who were left to do it all. Robert Sherrill had also left a family farm. He asked his uncle to pass on a message: "You tell my daddy that I am afraid the paymaster will not get around in time to get the money to him [in time]." He wrapped up his letter by expressing his hope that "the crops will be good."[65]

Though very few men in the regiment had fired a shot at anything other than one of their own, they were not far from their first engagement, and, for them, the beginning of the real war.

CHAPTER FOUR

1862 — In This Land of Rebeldom

"I have seated myself to write a few lines to let you know how I am getting along in this land of Rebeldom," wrote Oliver Mather to his sister, Sarah. The cotton fields, plantations, swamps, and the warm Southern spring air reminded him that he was far from home. Oliver had never seen a spring quite like this: "The thermometer stood at one hundred and eight degrees." But back home it was still chilly. "It is nothing but wilderness between here and the Knob," Oliver recounted. "Once in a while you find a farm and half of them are deserted on account of the Rebellion." Rebeldom was thus far an odd and sometimes God-forsaken place, as far as most of the boys were concerned.[1]

"I once more in the land of secession set my old bones to work to scribble off a few lines in order to let you know how I am prospering," wrote Charles A. Stevens, in one of his many letters home. "I am getting along as well as could be expected here in the state of Misery [intentional misspelling of Missouri on his part] and gaining by degrees every day and I hope when these few lines reach the great city of String Ville they will find you all up and adjusting, also enjoying good health." Charles had been sick during the winter and lost 35 pounds but was feeling better. Things were starting to get interesting, he said, as skirmishes became an almost daily occurrence. "I heard last night there was plenty of Rebels pretty near by and that there was eight of our men killed by them," Charles noted. "The men that was killed belonged to one of the cavalry regts." As of yet, the regiment had not lost a man "killed in action."[2]

"I have no idea of how long the war is to last," wrote Henry Strong home to his wife, Sarah. "The rebels are a curious people. They may take to guerrilla warfare or retreat to the cotton States & prolong there through the warm weather into the winter or they may quit at once."[3]

As General Curtis continued to push his army towards what he hoped were fresh supplies, the retreating Rebels constantly threw up obstacles and harassed his advance. Curtis protected his flank and front with cavalry expeditions of several hundred men. "They have thus far been successful," he reported in late May. At their front was a Confederate army of unknown strength. After his defeat at Pea Ridge, Confederate general Van Dorn retired his army from Arkansas and back across the Mississippi to Corinth, which provided an opportunity for Curtis to take the state's capital, Little Rock. There were also reports of another force, perhaps as large as 8,000, north of Curtis near White River. "The report seems to be incredible," Curtis lamented, "but should be looked after." Perhaps as many as 20,000 of the enemy were spread out across Arkansas and, if mobilized, would provide a serious threat to Curtis's army.[4]

As of May 1862 the Confederate forces in Arkansas were under the command of Major General Thomas Hindman, an unhinged, extremely efficient, organized, aggressive leader willing to do whatever it took to get the job done. When Van Dorn left the state to join up with General Albery Sidney Johnston's army in April, Arkansas was left virtually defenseless.

The governor of Arkansas complained bitterly and the Confederacy responded by sending Hindman. When he arrived he found a dire military situation. "I found here almost nothing," he grumbled. "Nearly everything of value was taken away by General Van Dorn." With this he ruthlessly began to organize anything and everything. He declared martial law, conscripted whoever he could find into the army, and unflinchingly executed deserters. He also instituted and authorized guerrilla warfare, encouraging the people of the state to organize into small units and harass the invading Yankees. On June 17, 1862, he issued "General Orders Number 17."[5]

> For the more effectual annoyance of the enemy upon our rivers and in our mountains and woods all citizens of this district who are not subject to conscription are called upon to organize themselves.... [Their] duty will be to cut off Federal pickets, scouts, foraging parties, and trains, and to kill pilots and others on gunboats and transports, attacking them day and night, using the greatest vigor in their movements.

The results would ultimately prove to be tragic for most of the state. In 1862, as Curtis and the Eleventh Wisconsin descended deeper into Arkansas, the harassment proved effective, and by 1865 the state was overrun by looting and pillaging bandits who robbed and killed without mercy.[6]

"My foraging parties occasionally meet straggling bands," said Curtis, "but find no large Rebel force." But the Rebels were out there, as confirmed by the daily skirmishes involving patrols and expeditions. Much-needed supplies could not get through, and Curtis's army increased its foraging to survive. "I leave nothing for man or brute in the country passed over by my army," he informed his superiors, "except a little saving to feed the poor, which will hardly save them from suffering. I am sure no Rebel army will find subsistence in Southern Missouri or Northern Arkansas." Curtis's march across Arkansas has been recognized by historians as the earliest appearance of "hard war," better known as "total war," in which the civilian population of the occupied state was, for the first time, purposely affected and targeted by a hostile army. Foraging was commenced in earnest. Atrocities were no doubt committed as guerrillas and bushwhackers continued to assault Federal troops, causing tempers and passions to rise. But it wasn't only the Federal army that laid waste to the landscape. Confederate bushwhackers and guerrillas brutally targeted suspected Union sympathizers and burned cotton wherever they found it, causing civilian morale to "plummet" throughout the state. The combined effect, according to one historian, was economic "collapse, social upheaval," and the general "collapse of social institutions." In an era of extreme belief systems and rigid values such as chivalry, honor, and justice, this was as total as war could get.[7]

The only thing people had enough of in this region was suffering. "Women and children are houseless," wrote a soldier with the Second Wisconsin Cavalry, "with little to eat or wear." As the invaders descended into Rebeldom, locals fled before them, taking only what they could carry or haul away. Sometimes mass panic ensued when a Union army unexpectedly appeared on the horizon. Entire towns were deserted. "There was not a single inhabitant," Curtis wrote after entering the small community of Forsyth, "containing only thirty dwelling houses" and not one occupied. Even large communities became ghost towns. Located near the confluence of the Black and White rivers, Jacksonport was a prospering community before the war, with over 1,000 inhabitants and "large and well finished buildings." But when Curtis and his men entered the city, "barely a dozen families" could be found. Deserted plantations were expected, but the men found nearly abandoned communities eerie and unnerving. Curtis concluded that "the innocent suffer with the guilty, and it cannot be avoided." There can be little doubt that the cultural values each man possessed were shaken to the core both during this time and as the war progressed. There was an ongoing readjustment of belief sys-

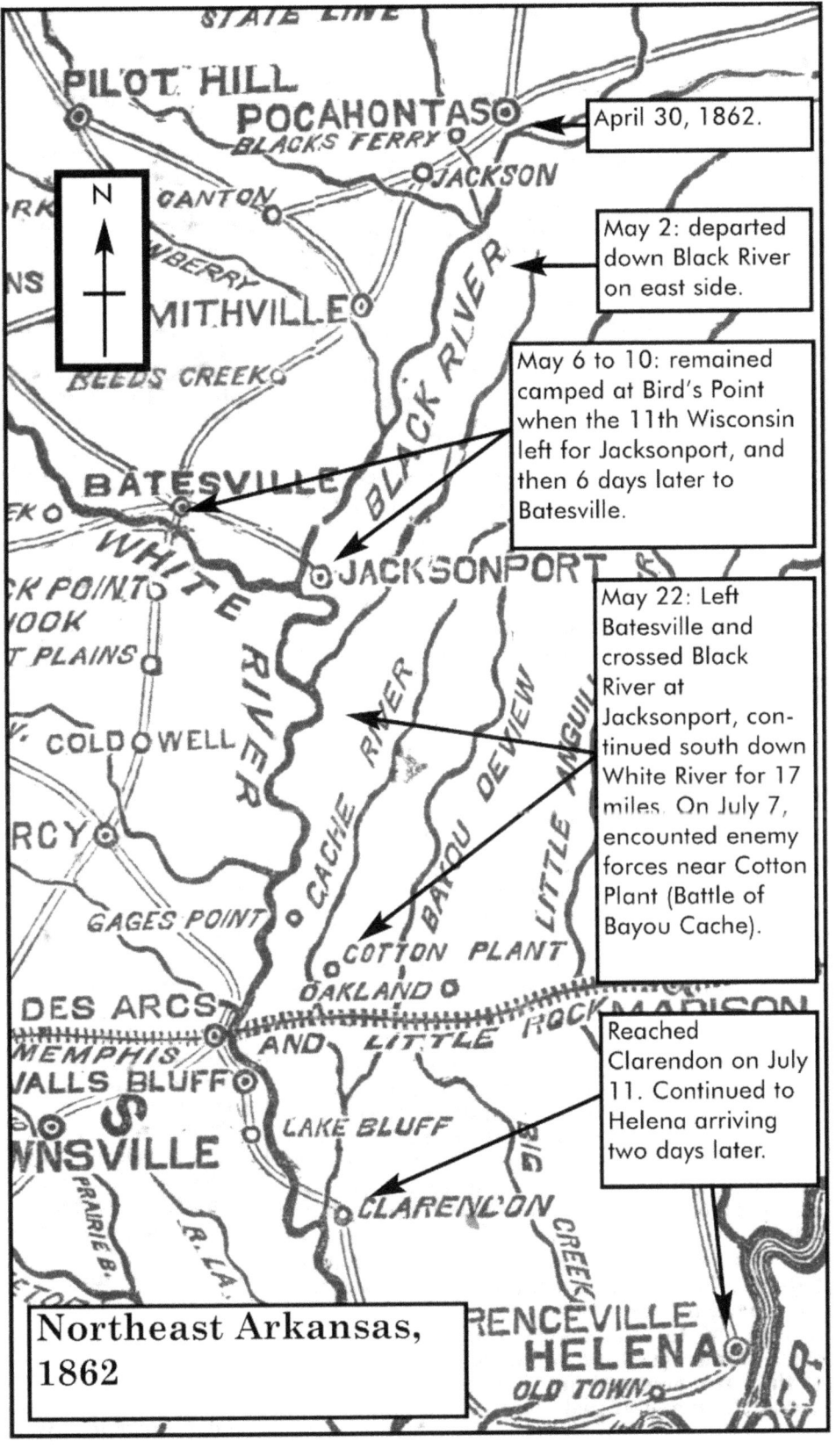

tems and values. This is best represented by a correspondent from the Eleventh regiment who wrote home in August that they "went back to the Old Testament doctrine" of warfare. The distinction between noncombatant and combatant at times became blurred. He referred to the women in Arkansas as "she Devils" and said that every one of them, including children, should be removed and "hungry flames set upon" their homes. This declaration occurred after the brutal lynching of several Union soldiers by bushwhackers. He finished his tirade, stating bluntly, "Hereafter, temper the warfare with more justice, and less mercy. We must crush these rebels, though we have to descend to their arena of fighting to accomplish it."[8]

"Everywhere we have been I have found the women almost invariably rabid, bitter Secessionists," wrote Henry Strong. "When we marched through town yesterday I saw but two handkerchiefs out waving, most of the fair Sex were either Sullen, Scolding, or crying with Vexation." It was not unusual for Southern women to be more vocal and "vicious" than the men. Southern women were, in a sense, on the frontlines of the "hard war" and often suffered as much as the men away from home fighting. "The women folks here did not cry so much," wrote one regiment correspondent home. But they did have "very hard stories to tell about boys stealing their chickens, taking their eggs without paying for them." A journalist traveling in Curtis's army noted about this time that "Jacksonport is the meanest secession town yet visited.... The women are still more rabid than the men. They jeered, hooted and waved their brooms."[9]

But it was not only local civilians who suffered. "The 11th [regiment] has recently suffered very much from sickness," reported the *Janesville Daily Gazette*. Disease and sickness still ravaged the regiment. And they were now on half rations due to the supply problems. "We have had a purty hard time of it," Samuel Kirkpatrick told his family, "for the last 4 weeks marching on half rations and poor water and sleeping out at night without our blankets...."[10]

Lyman O. Bennet was a cartographer with Curtis's army and kept a diary that detailed the difficulties endured during their toilsome march: "The march over the hills has been cold and cheerless—the clouds drifting almost to the mountain tops, threatening each hour to drench the earth with their ever charged burden of water." Rain poured down on the men all through April and into May. A Missouri soldier wrote to his wife that they were "now marching from one place to another ... just to keep our horses and mules alive. The forage is so scant that we cannot stay in a place more than two or three days."[11]

* * *

Curtis continued to have a supply problem. "Supplies ... could not be procured or transported by land fast enough to allow a rapid movement with my entire army," he reported back to Halleck. "To go beyond Jacksonport doubling my supply trains will be necessary if I have to depend on wagons." Curtis hoped to use boats to bring supplies to Jacksonport, where they could easily get them. Getting supplies from someplace like Rolla would be dangerous. But all options were dangerous at this point. As Curtis advanced he submerged his army deeper into enemy territory and risked being attacked by a larger force, or finding himself surrounded with the possibility of starvation if supplies could not be maintained. Equally aware of the potential for disaster that Curtis faced, Hindman knew he had to muster enough men to create a formidable force, and that meant stalling the Union army's march to give him time. For Curtis, it would all be worth it if he could take Little Rock, the prize he desperately wanted.[12]

A naval gunboat expedition, along with infantry, was sent down White River with the intention of securing it and opening up a supply line for Curtis. Colonel Graham Fitch commanded the Forty-sixth Indiana Infantry. However, the expedition met with disaster when it came upon two enemy batteries protecting the river. Fitch landed his men below the batteries and worked his way towards the enemy. Meanwhile the gunboat *Mound City*, just minutes into the assault, was hit by a shot from a sixty-four pound Parrot gun that plunged into the "steam chest" (drum) releasing a "scalding steam" that blasted through the boat, killing many and wounding most. Those who could jumped, but some were too incapacitated to swim and drowned. The infantry did manage to storm the battery and take it without much of a fight, but the gunboats could not continue. The *Mound City* left 48 dead and according to a witness, "the poor creatures were scalded in every imaginable manner and degree." Unfortunately the expedition would ultimately fail to join with Curtis, as his supply problems would continue.[13]

In late June, General Steele issued a disheartening report: "Our forage train was attacked this afternoon," not far from his headquarters near Village Creek. The failure to open up an effective supply line, combined with an earlier order from Halleck for ten infantry regiments to Cape Girardeau (for the upcoming movement on Corinth and Van Dorn), all but ended Curtis's ability to take the state capital. Without the extra troops (which reduced his command from about 20,000 to around 10,000) and fresh supplies, his plans fell apart. Knowing the supplies could not come to him, Curtis decided the only option was to go to them. On June 24 he abandoned his line of communication with Springfield (Missouri), concentrated his army as best he could, and commenced marching down the east bank of the White River for Clarendon. For the first time in the Civil War, an army abandoned its lines of supply, and lived exclusively off the land.[14]

Word reached Hindman that the Union army was moving down White River, and he recognized an opportunity. Cache River presented a natural obstacle, with the only crossing point at James's Ferry. Hindman believed he could get his army there first and force Curtis to attack his soon-to-be fortified position. Hindman was sure he could "strike the Federals a mighty blow" and perhaps even reverse the course of the war in the Trans-Mississippi. "Hold the line at Cache River if at all possible," Hindman told his scattered band of soldiers harassing the Union army. With haste they descended on James's Ferry.[15]

* * *

Jesse Mather wrote home to Sarah. "I received your letter today and was glad to hear from you and to know that you ower well," he told her. "Swain* is out on extraguard to day and I am on home guard we have been paid since we came hear and Swain sent 10 dolars in a leter." Jesse was concerned the money would not make it; he heard some of the soldier's letters with money in them never arrived home. But this was not his real concern. "I want you to write how father and Henry ar making it this summer and how many acres of wheat they soad and how mutch corn they have planted." He and Oliver were still not communicating directly with their father or mother. "I guess father will have to cut his grain with out us to help him this harvest." Without a reaper, a field of 50 acres would take one man 20 days to cradle. Like so many others, Jesse and Oliver had been sure they'd be home for the harvest.[16]

Oliver wrote to Sarah to let her know "we have not been in any engagement yet." He thought their advance was moving too slowly and was too costly. Advanced guards encountered the enemy almost daily. "Our advance drove back the Rebel pickets," he told her. "It has been reported that the Rebels are going to make a stand." But they knew neither where nor when. So far, all the enemy offered was a single volley before running off. "Our advance

---

*Swain was Oliver's middle name and was what everyone in his family called him.

had shirmishes nearly evry day but for all we marched along killing more ... of the bushwackers."[17]

Curtis was taking his army on a forced march, and the situation was nearing calamity. "During this period," wrote Henry Twining, "Erwin C. Griffith [of company C] ... did not survive the fatigues of a forced march." Henry's letters now regularly contained information about those who were sick, recovering, or dead. Most were his friends, some close friends, and his depressed state was evident: "We made his soldier's grave fifty-five miles south of Jacksonport, and six miles north east of White River, in the wild woods of Arkansas." Henry hoped Erwin's family would be able to recover his body. After the fighting, families were allowed to travel down and recover the remains of loved ones. In another shallow grave Henry helped bury another soldier, one he did not know well: "The sighing of the cane that stand sentinel around their grave, fell upon our ears not unlike the dirge-like music of a funeral choir." Emotions stirred in these men as they buried more and more of their comrades. They had traveled hundreds of miles, done everything asked of them, and had only death to show for it. Not death from battle, which perhaps they could reason with and say something had been achieved, but death from sickness, disease, and accidents. And their only achievement was a secured railroad and a couple dozen captured secesh bushwhackers. "As we consigned their bodies to mother earth," Henry eloquently continued, "the beautiful lines of Moore came vividly to our recollection—

> We carved not a line, we raised not a stone,
> But we left them alone in their glory."[18]

But they were starting to question what "glory" they had seen. Spirits were as low as they had been throughout the winter as even some of the officers were expressing doubts about the situation. "It has taken personal Solicitation several times to '*Stand by one another to the end*' [his emphasis], to prevent half the officers from resigning," wrote Henry Strong. "All discipline is fast fading from view, harmony is a thing that was, every man is like an enraged porcupine, quills sticking out in all directions." Henry declared that the men were on edge and he truly did not know what would happen. But one thing he knew was certain: "No biographical sketch will ever recount our names in connection with this war. No history of Wisconsin will ever notice us more than to say that we defended & held Sulphur Springs and other 'important points.' Our men have died of disease & have been killed, Yet no one writes their names down as 'heroes & patriots' in the great cause of national liberty."[19]

"We have not yet had an opportunity of proving our courage," wrote an unknown Eleventh Wisconsin soldier home to his local newspaper, "but we hope to do something more for our country soon." His prediction was that the war would end in about a year. His friends agreed, but, "all are willing to wait till it is finished in such a manner as to crush the rebellion entirely." May and June had not been good to the Eleventh Wisconsin, and Surgeon Strong and many of his fellow officers hoped July would not be more of the same: marching, disease, and hunger with no tangible results.[20]

* * *

Facing Curtis and the disheartened Eleventh Wisconsin as they pushed on were several thousand Confederates, consisting of Texas Rangers and Arkansas troops. They harassed the Federals' advance daily, hoping to stall it, force them back, or perhaps even incite mass panic as supplies dwindled. The Eleventh was near the front of the advance, along with the Third Iowa Cavalry and the Thirty-third Illinois Infantry.[21]

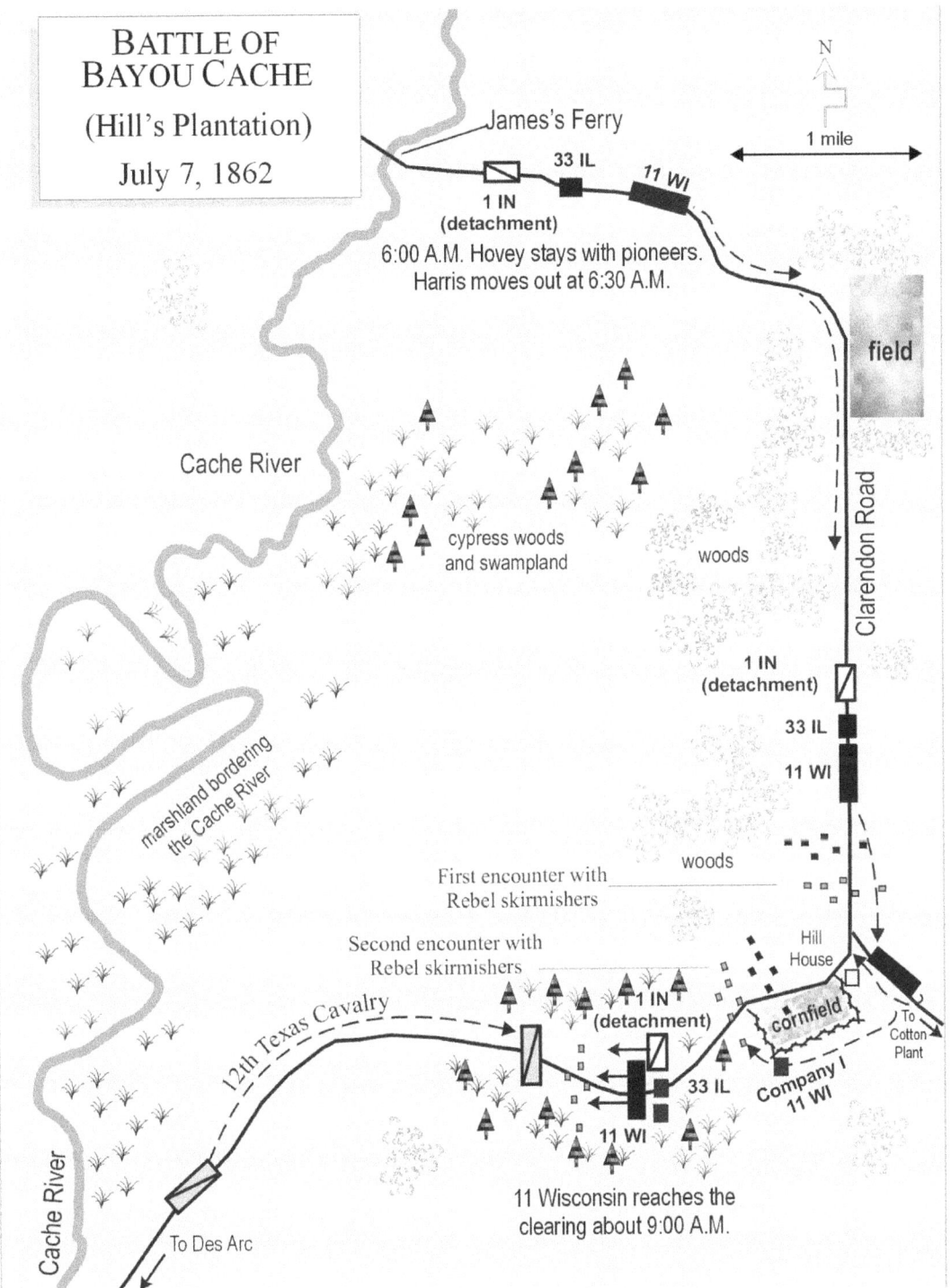

On July 5 Henry Twining was part of an advanced scouting patrol of several companies that came across an enemy camp 15 miles south of Augusta. They left at 3 o'clock in the morning "when the vanguard encountered Rebel pickets." After a brief skirmish, "in which one Rebel was killed and one taken prisoner," the rest fled and it could be heard "Curtis is upon us." According to Henry, they encountered nearly a thousand Confederates that day. The rest of the scouting party found the enemy trying to retreat on boats, so they brought up cannons and fired at them. "We saw three bodies of dead Rebels float from one ferry-boat," Henry later recalled.[22]

Encounters with the enemy increased as they continued down Clarendon Road. During the afternoon on July 7, the Third Iowa Cavalry at the very front of the column came upon a formidable barricade near the Cache River. The impassible barricade consisted of large fallen trees on the road, which was surrounded by a thick bottomland woods. Combing the nearby forest, the cavalry stumbled upon a squad of Rebels. After a brief engagement they overpowered them, killing several and taking 11 prisoners. A pioneer crew started cutting through the barricade, but the entire army had to halt for the night on the west side of the river. That afternoon one of their men wandered off to the river and never came back. They organized a search party and found him dead, "shot through the head by a guerrilla concealed in the swamp."[23]

The Confederates frequently picked areas along the Union's path to drop trees that "required a road to be cut through them before the army could pass." Then, while they spent crucial hours cutting through the fallen timber, "[the Rebels] would fire on them from concealed positions." Though easily suppressed, day after day the Rebels injured and killed many men and, perhaps most significantly, wounded the men's morale. By now their mood was at a fever pitch. "I have come to the conclusion," wrote a Wisconsin cavalryman, seething with anger, "that to put down the Rebellion ... we must fight the Rebels on their own terms—take no prisoners, but shoot down every man we find in arms against us."[24]

Night shots rang out as Confederate bushwhackers probed their lines. Scouts were sent to the east side of the river but had to first wade across before entering the forest. By morning the Union army was strung out along Clarendon Road, waiting for the barricade to be completely cleared. Earlier in the morning Colonel Harris selected four companies (D, G, H, and I) from his regiment to move out. Harris was to cross to the east side of the river, lead a reconnaissance in their front to secure the river, and then continue for a distance down Clarendon Road. Along with the Eleventh Wisconsin were four companies of the Thirty-third Illinois Infantry, and one small cannon from the First Indiana Cavalry. In overall command was Colonel Charles E. Hovey, commanding the Second Brigade. After wading across the river and establishing a defensive position, Hovey ordered Harris to continue down the road, taking with him most of the men and the cannon. In all, a little less than 400 men moved out under the command of Colonel Harris, who was "directed to move in advance of the column, and ascertain the position and force of the enemy front."[25]

* * *

Harris led his men out of camp at 6 o'clock in the morning, with Company D of the Eleventh Wisconsin deployed as skirmishers. Captain Jesse Miller commanded Company D, known as the "Richland County Plowboys," as they were made up entirely of farmers and farm laborers. First Lieutenant Jerome Chesebro commanded Company I. Both companies were at the advance of the march. Two rivers ran parallel, north and south, near the Clarendon road. White River lay to the west, with Cache River to the east and another small river called Bayou De View east of the Cache.[26]

After several miles they encountered six Rebel cavalrymen at Hill's Plantation. A brief exchange of fire dispersed the Rebels, and as usual they retreated, heading southwest towards Des Arc. Here we encounter the first of many conflicting reports. According to Hovey, Harris and his men, as ordered by him, headed down the southeast road towards Bayou De View. The southwest road led beyond the Cache River to Des Arc on the White River. However, Hovey was not with the men at this time. He was still back at James's Ferry overseeing the clearing of the fallen trees. Eleventh Wisconsin surgeon Henry P. Strong was with the leading elements of the regiment and witnessed the events. He reported that once they dispersed the Rebels around Hill's Plantation, they stopped as a quick meal was eaten. This was sometime around eight in the morning. They also confiscated some things from the plantation, which was still occupied by the wife of the owner, Lieutenant Colonel Hill, who probably was involved in the upcoming fight. After a brief stop they headed down the southeast road towards Cotton Plant, but before doing so they "reconnoitered the woods [that surrounded the road] for some distance around." Harris was a cautious and prudent soldier.[27]

Meanwhile Lieutenant Colonel William F. Wood of the First Indiana Cavalry moved toward Bayou De View under orders to secure the bridge. They arrived just in time to save it from destruction; the Confederates had started a fire at the north end. Once again, Rebel pickets fired and then fled. Wood later estimated that as many as 500 Rebels were around Bayou De View.[28]

It was at least an hour since Harris moved out when Hovey mounted his horse and left James's Ferry in search of him. A soldier with the column documented that Hovey "came dashing down the road at full speed" and informed Harris that "the secesh had come up to [Hill's] house and taken two of our boys prisoner." When Hovey found Harris he ordered him to "hasten down the Des Arc road" in search of their captured comrade.*

Harris immediately detached Company I, led by Lieutenant Chesebro, around the woods behind Hill's house, with instructions to follow the road running south in hopes of intercepting the Rebel guerrillas. Meanwhile, Harris moved out with the rest of the main column. He returned to Hill's house and continued down the southwest road. Hovey does not tell us where he goes or what he does while Harris heads down Des Arc Road. Chesebro led his company around south of the house where he "met the column" near the southwest road at the end of a cornfield. They were still in the cornfield, where it bordered the woods, when "the enemy was seen coming north" up the Des Arc Road.[29]

As Company I approached the road, Rebel cavalry could be seen in their front and on their right and left in the brush. Harris sent companies D and I forward as skirmishers to disperse the enemy. Company I spread out across the road and along the cornfield at the southwest corner, just behind Company D; Harris and Adjutant Lincoln rode on horseback between the skirmishers and the main column. Along with them were six men from the First Indiana Cavalry manning the small steel gun commanded by Lieutenant C.A. Denneman. The two companies of the Thirty-third Illinois deployed in line of battle across the road an undetermined distance from the cornfield and were commanded by Lieutenant Colonel Charles E. Lippencott. Two companies of the Thirty-third remained with Hovey around Hill's house.[30]

At this point Harris continued through a wetland clearing surrounded by woods and containing Indian mounds. Near a turn in the road that at the same time was rising up in elevation the road sank into a swampy cypress woods. At about this time, Rebel cavalry appeared (perhaps as many as 20) and the two sides exchanged gunfire. Company D was furthest ahead, held their ground, and returned fire, unseating several cavalrymen. The enemy then fell back, as had been their pattern throughout the campaign.[31]

Harris probably believed that they had encountered only a small group of Rebels, and ordered his men to continue on. What he certainly was not aware of were the 2,000 Confed-

---

*Hovey sent his entire reconnaissance party hastily down an unreconnoitered road that was surrounded by cypress woods and swamps in an area crawling with enemy cavalry. Hovey's order exposed his entire command for one or two men. A noble deed, but also one worthy of scrutiny, yet thus far not one historian has addressed this. Instead they offer excuses. One historian suggests that Hovey would not have given such an order and instead contends that he must have ordered Harris to "turn back and drive the rebels away from the army's line of advance." (William L. Shea, "The Confederate Defeat at Cache River," The Arkansas Historical Quarterly 52 no. 2 (Summer 1993).

erates, comprised of Texas Cavalry and Arkansas troops led by Brigadier General Albert Rust, who were now filling the woods in his front. Earlier that day Rust told the local citizens that they would "cut to pieces" the enemy and drive them back. As word reached Rust that the advanced guard had encountered the enemy at the edge of the cornfield, he was quickly rushing his men forward.[32]

A young Texas farmer, David Carey Nance, was with the leading elements of William H. Parson's Twelfth Texas Cavalry, whom the Eleventh Wisconsin had just run into. According to Nance, who was a part of an advanced skirmish guard, the closest support was another guard of about 50 cavalrymen several hundred yards behind them. Nance and about twenty other men were surprised to run into the Wisconsin skirmishers (Company D) and as a result suffered casualties. Nance himself was hit several times by extremely accurate fire and miraculously managed to survive; he was later captured, but was able to escape. There was an initial clash and then the two groups drifted apart. Nance makes no note of an ambush in waiting for the Eleventh. The Confederates were just as surprised as the Federals.[33]

According to some members of the Eleventh regiment, Harris "caught a glimpse of the Rebels through the green foliage." Surgeon Henry Strong wrote later that "Lieut. N.R. Done, of Co. I, came up … [and] stated the rebel force was large." Done might have been wounded and come looking for Strong to receive medical attention. After the encounter, Harris continued down the road to the end of the clearing. Henry goes on to state, "I learned from him that their force consisted of two regiments of Texan Rangers, mounted, and one conscript regiment of Arkansas infantry."[34]

Rebel scouts had galloped back after the first encounter at Hill's house to inform the Twelfth Texas Cavalry, only about a half-mile away, that their advance guard had encountered the enemy. With this information they were on the move towards the field. Behind them were the Seventeenth and then the Sixteenth Texas Cavalry, along with some Arkansas infantry; all were now in haste to the battlefield.[35]

As Company D approached the far side of the clearing a "murderous" fire was unleashed. The Confederates "were drawn up in a line of battle," wrote Henry Twining, "and were ready to receive our boys." The woods indeed came alive as buckshot sprayed everywhere. It would have been immediately obvious to Harris and his men that they had encountered more than a half-dozen scouts. Several of his men were injured. Harris ordered his men down and the cannon to fire away, but it was not sufficient. Still the firing continued. Companies G and H moved forward to join the others in a skirmish line. With the additional men and superior firepower they held their ground as "each man in the advance fired from five to twenty rounds," reported a witness.* Fire from all around them quickly began to intensify as more and more of Parson's Texas Rangers flowed in. At some point Harris ordered his men to fasten bayonets, which would later prove to be a wise decision.[36]

The initial volley was most likely the 50-member advance guard combined with the advanced skirmish line and possibly some elements of Parson's Twelfth Cavalry. The surrounding terrain was not easy for cavalry to maneuver through and it seems unlikely that in a matter of minutes all 1200 men of the Twelfth Texas Cavalry could dash to the front and deploy in full force in an ambush. As one historian noted, the battle was more of a "meeting engagement" and not an ambush. The 60 or so Rangers poured significant fire into the skirmishers of Company D, and probably wounded many. But their fire was ineffective because they lacked proper weapons. Most of the rebel soldiers were armed only with what they brought from home; some with only squirrel rifles and single barrel shotguns. Even with such

---

*In order to fire twenty rounds, they would have needed a minimum of 10 minutes, or an average of 2 shots per minute.

poor weapons, had there been 1200 or so cavalry waiting in an ambush, as Hovey claimed in his official report, the unsuspecting Eleventh Wisconsin would have been decimated despite the poor quality of Confederate arms and the cover provided by the dense woods. Had they then charged immediately, as Hovey claimed, Harris's small line would have most likely been consumed. There would have been more than the reported two dozen or so wounded and killed in this opening salvo.[37]

By all accounts, as the Eleventh Wisconsin advanced it received a heavy fire, but it's not clear how many were wounded and how badly. "Several of our men were wounded at the first fire," wrote Surgeon Henry Strong. "None were killed until some time later." According to Hovey, when he arrived, "the woods swarmed with Rebels and the firing was sharp." What is clear is that the Rebels had the upper hand and were intent on making a stand for a change. But what is not clear is when exactly Hovey did arrive and whether his descriptions of these early stages of the fight were given to him by someone else.[38]

Henry Twining said that after deploying, "Our boys marched up firm and steady heedless of the death dealing missles of the enemy." By his account they came upon the Rebels and fired into them, and "Our boys could distinctly see the secesh fall from their saddles." After advancing a quarter of a mile, Twining surmised, Colonel Harris, "fearing an ambush ... gave orders for a retrograde movement." Robert Sherrill noted, "our boys marched rite up to them when they got with in 70 yards they [Rebels] commenced firing before our men could get in line of battle they kept up a perpetual volley." But neither Henry nor Robert were on the battlefield and both were describing the events based on what they were told.[39]

For perhaps as long as twenty minutes the two sides exchanged fire as more and more Texas Rangers joined the fight. Company I was dispersed partially in the words and on the road and might have only been saved by the heroics of Lieutenant Chesebro, who, "seizing a rifle and revolver from a wounded enemy," fired with "deadly precision" and unhorsed many of the enemy. After the initial onslaught all was quiet for a moment as a smoky haze settled in on the field. The woods then came alive with the most hideous, and surely unnerving, yells and hollers. Then out of the brush and cypress forest charged a large contingent of Texas Rangers, perhaps Parson's entire Twelfth Cavalry.[40]

This first charge was "*repulsed* [his emphasis] at the point of the bayonet," recorded surgeon Henry Strong, who was present during the battle. Miller and Chesebro's men "stood, each and all, and fought," but the situation was quickly becoming untenable as all around them the enemy swarmed the woods. An order was given for them to fall back, which was mistaken for a general retreat and caused "some little confusion." As parts of the regiment broke and ran, Harris and Adjutant David Lincoln turned their horses around and overtook the fleeing men. Once upon them Harris ordered a halt. He called out to his men, "Don't never show your faces again if you run." The men responded and continued to retreat hastily, but in relative good order. After rallying his men Harris was wounded three times along his right shoulder, arm and leg.[41]

Charles Brackett was a surgeon with the Ninth Illinois Cavalry, who were also a part of Curtis's army. Brackett was on the battlefield after the fight and helped with the wounded. He also knew Henry Strong and probably received information from him. He made the following entry into his journal not long after the battle:

> Most of the wounded & killed were of the 11th Wisconsin that bore the heaviest of the fray. Two Cos of that Regt held sixteen hundred Texan Cavalry at bay for a long time.[42]

Companies D and I took the brunt of the counterattack, but held their ground for a period of time. What we may never know, and what Hovey and the others not present could not have known, is how Harris and his men performed and what really happened during those first 10 to 20 intense minutes. According to published accounts of the battle, "Col. C.L. Harris ... with elements of the 11th Wisconsin, 33rd Illinois, and the 1st Indiana Cavalry ... blundered into an ambuscade." Clearly there is evidence to suggest that this may not have been the case, and that if there was a blunder, it might lie with Colonel Hovey and his order that sent Colonel Harris and his men hastily down the Des Arc Road.[43]

The Thirty-third Illinois was not standing idly by during the 10 minutes since the opening shots. Most likely at least one of the two companies waiting anxiously behind ventured out to see what was happening. According to reports, Capt. Potter and his company (A), hearing the opening shots, moved out and joined their Wisconsin comrades. They met up with the Eleventh Wisconsin, which was moving back under the pressure of cavalry and dismounted cavalry. "The little field piece ... was ripping canister into the advancing column," but still they were forced back. At about this point the First Indiana crew and its steel cannon were in dire shape. Seeing that they required help, Potter and his company aided Lieutenant Denneman and his battered unit, even staving off a Confederate attempt to capture the gun.[44]

Hovey was not idle, nor was he present during those opening minutes of fighting. Elliott and Way, in their regimental history of the Thirty-third Illinois, mentioned several charges taking place before Hovey reached the field. We know from Eleventh Wisconsin correspondence that Mrs. Hill was home and that the Federal troops searched the grounds and confiscated things. Negroes might have even tipped Hovey off to the captured Federal soldiers that resulted in his order for Harris to hasten down the road. It would not have taken Hovey 20 minutes to cover the half-mile to a mile distance to the battlefield. So the issue is when he first became aware of the firing. Hovey could have been in the house speaking with Mrs. Hill and simply did not hear the opening gunfire until the cannon started. Depending on wind conditions and direction, and given that the fighting was taking place in a dense cypress woods, he might not have heard the fighting for some time.[45]

As Harris and the Eleventh retreated, hoping to get back to where the Thirty-third Illinois was deployed, a second charge came, this time a larger one of between 1,500 and 2,000 men, according to Private McCarthy of Company D, who was wounded during the fight. At least one of the other Texas Ranger regiments was now actively engaged with Harris's Federal column. The Confederates were deployed on both sides of the road, forming a V, with the Eleventh Wisconsin desperately trying to get out of the center. One soldier noted that it might have been their frantic and hurried retreat that saved them from being enveloped.[46]

As Harris and his men frantically dragged their wounded away and tried not to be overrun, there were two options: they could continue to retreat in a state of disarray and confusion, which could prove not only deadly but would also reflect badly on Harris and his regiment and perhaps result in lesser assignments for some time, or Harris and his officers could rally the men, regroup, and stand their ground.[47]

"At this moment," wrote Henry Twining, "Col. Harris could be seen riding up and down the lines, brandishing his sword in the air...." Harris rallied his men. After dropping back an undetermined distance, he deployed his men in fighting order back to where the Thirty-third Illinois was already lined up. Calvin Alling noted that Harris had his men "under cover," using some big cypress trees for protection. He added that this decision was a "good arrangement" since the men were "all woodsmen and marksmen." Surgeon Henry Strong would later note that many of the bodies of the Texans he examined in front of the Eleventh Wisconsin's position were hit "through the head."[48]

Hovey now reached the field at the end of a second charge that sent everyone in flight and into the cornfield, including the two 33rd Illinois companies. Hovey probably witnessed this from a distance as he arrived with his two companies. Surgeon Strong, who was now well behind the action, mentioned "a moment's conversation with him" [Hovey] as he reached the ground. James N. Butler was a member of E Company in the 33rd Illinois and was positioned at the edge of the woods near the road with the other Illinois company. Behind them was the cornfield contained by a wooden fence. He described the retreat during the second cavalry charge: "We were not in the thickest of the fight, but we were in the thickest of the run." Men fled down the road; some jumped over the fence and into the cornfield. "The pursuing cavalry seemed to be moving at a snail's pace in comparison," he wrote. How far the men fled is not clear. "Some of us wouldn't have stopped until we crossed the Arkansas line," he continued, "if it had not been for Col. Hovey." Hovey most likely was still at Hill's house when he heard the frantic retreat and crackling gunfire echo through the cleared woods along the road. He quickly gathered up his men, mounted his horse, and dashed down the road to the cornfield. When he arrived he deployed his two companies off the road and at an angle (a perfect location) where they awaited whatever it was that forced Harris back. Hovey had his men crouch down behind the fence rail with rifles ready.[49]

As Harris, Adjutant Lincoln, and Lippencott reorganized their men, Hovey ordered his men up as the Rangers burst out of the woods along the road. "As the rebels came charging at full speed and in great force in pursuit the infantry fired," wrote Hovey in his official report. The Illinois soldiers delivered steady and accurate fire that decimated the leading elements of the Twelfth Texas Cavalry. "Riderless horses rushed wildly in all directions" after receiving their volley. The fighting continued for some time as Harris, Lincoln, and Lippencott brought forward their men and joined in repulsing the charge. After two volleys the Texans fled from the field "as suddenly as they came and in great disorder." Hovey showed up just in time, deployed his two companies perfectly, and together they saved their disorganized comrades from possible destruction. Surgeon Henry Strong wrote of this event, "Col. Harris, Adjutant Lincoln, and Lieut. Col. Lippencott, of the Thirty-third, rallied the men after the retreat, while Col. Hovey was holding them in bay in the corn field." It was the Twelfth Texas Cavalry's hasty pursuit of Harris and his men into the cornfield that resulted in the only true ambush of the day. The Rangers were completely surprised and, according to one of their survivors, they were "cut to pieces pretty badly" and it was "a wonder that most of us were not killed."[50]

Remnants of the Eleventh Wisconsin indeed helped in repulsing the second charge. Captain Wilbur F. Pelton, Company G, rallied his men, according to a correspondent on the scene, "and brought them to a bayonet charge." After a long day on the march, double-timing and even running at times, the men were exhausted by now but still able to regain their composure and reload their rifles. Harris, still on horseback, rode up and down his meager line, cheering the men on. He was bleeding heavily, his strength weakening.[51]

Harris knew he must be visible during these intense and uncertain moments. None of his men had seen any real action, and they would look to their colonel (and other officers) for encouragement. Twining documented that Harris was mounted atop his horse, Charger, riding up and down the line calling out to his men, "Well done, my brave boys, that fire caused many a Rebel to bite the dust, give them another as good." Several sources indicate that Harris, though wounded, never left the battlefield until the fighting was over. Harris' leadership undoubtedly played a large part in the outcome of the fight. But it also made him an inviting target, as he rode up and down the line in plain view of the enemy. The Texas Rangers were determined and continued the fight, though taking horrendous casualties. As one soldier noted, "[They] fought with a desperate courage, some even riding upon the very bayonets of our soldiers, but they could not stand the fire of our muskets." Robert Sherrill was told the Rebels "made some dreadful charges," but that "our men would drive them back evry time." After their attempt to overrun the bluecoats, the Rebels fell back and retreated. In the sudden quiet the men noticed that Harris was severely wounded.[52]

Fighting in unknown territory, without knowledge of reinforcements, Hovey decided it "seemed prudent ... to hold the position already chosen, which had proved to be a good one," and decided not to advance or counterattack. He extended his line in an effort to protect against an enveloping maneuver by the Confederates. Hovey also sent elements of the Eleventh Wisconsin back to the fork near Hill's Plantation to protect the cannon. This maneuver might have saved them, as part of the Seventeenth Texas Cavalry made a flanking march that would have put them in the rear of Hovey and Harris; but when they arrived (most likely somewhere near Hill's house) they saw Federal infantry "rise up at the tap of a drum over two large fields like blackbirds." With the cornfield seemingly full of Federal soldiers and Hill's house now occupied by perhaps a company of men who fell back from the fight, it gave the impression that reinforcements had arrived.[53]

* * *

Colonel Wood and his Indiana Cavalry were soon galloping toward the sounds of cannon fire coming from Hill's Plantation on Des Arc Road. Hovey had sent messengers to relay that they had been attacked by a large force and "three companies were killed." A vast exaggeration, but yet it conveyed the gravity of the situation. As Wood neared the battlefield, stragglers informed him that they had been "badly used up." Greatly concerned, he increased his speed and moments later arrived at the battlefield.[54]

Hovey could see plenty of movement in his front. The Rebels were disorganized but not yet defeated. He could see them carrying their dead and wounded away. Perhaps as much as thirty minutes elapsed before Hovey and Harris began to suspect that the enemy might be beaten. The last Hovey had heard of them was an order to "Charge on the corn field!" which never materialized. The woods, though still active, seemed to be getting calmer. "I moved down up them," wrote Hovey," extending my line till it was merely a line of skirmishers." They moved cautiously to the end of the cornfield and into the cypress woods. "Our little band advanced the enemy retreated, neither giving nor receiving more than occasional shots," wrote Surgeon Strong. Hovey ordered his men ahead perhaps a hundred yards or so when he heard cheering behind him.[55]

Surgeon Henry P. Strong years after the war, date unknown (Beloit Historical Society).

There was still a lull in the action when Wood and the First

Indiana Cavalry approached the field. "The principle part of the infantry were standing in groups on the edge of the wood," Wood stated in his official report. Wood and his men were greeted with a cheer from the exhausted infantry, who were ecstatic to have reinforcements. Hovey ordered Wood, his 200 cavalrymen, and three cannons to "pitch into" the regrouping Rangers before they mustered another attack, which he most likely feared would be more than the Federals could handle. The Indiana Cavalry moved out and found the Rebels indeed on the return. Wood then formed his line of battle and readied for a fight. With his cannons in the center, they "poured canister into their front and shell into their rear." Sensing that the enemy was displaced, he ordered his men to attack the enemy's right flank and roll them up. For another 20 minutes the battle raged on as two or three more volleys cut up the enemy "in a dreadful manner." The Rebels retreated, utterly routed from the field.[56]

Wary of falling into a counterattack, Hovey did not immediately go after the retreating enemy, but instead waited until later in the afternoon for reinforcements to arrive. By the afternoon, Curtis and Steele had their entire column on the move again as more and more men poured into the area surrounding Hill's Plantation. The Eleventh Wisconsin was deployed to aid in the pursuit of the enemy. Several companies left with Brigadier General William Benton as he pursued the Rebels some five or six miles further down the Des Arc road. During this advance the violent nature of the battle became apparent. "All along the route," wrote Hovey in his official report, "the houses [were] filled with dead and wounded. Curbstones were wet with blood, and in one case even the water was crimson with gore."[57]

The battlefield, though not large by Civil War standards, was covered with the dead and dying. "I tell you," wrote Henry Twining, "it looked hard to see the dead men on the field. We had to walk over them. They were all covered with dust so that I could hardly tell whether they were Negroes or white men."[58]

As Curtis's army gradually arrived, bringing more and more reinforcements, another force of Rebels appeared on Bayou De View Road and attacked Union pickets. With Colonel Harris out of action, Lieutenant Colonel Charles A. Wood took command of the Eleventh Wisconsin and was ordered to pursue the enemy down Bayou De View Road. They chased after the Rebels, who retreated over the river. Comfortable that the battle was over, the regiment camped for the night.[59]

By all accounts, Colonel Harris, Captain Miller, and First Lieutenant Chesebro acted bravely and led their men well. This was their first serious fight, but they kept their wits, and the regiment performed soundly. Hovey acknowledged in his report the "gallant conduct of Colonel Harris and Captain Miller." And the men of the Eleventh Wisconsin had displayed courage under fire. "No men could behave more handsomely," said Hovey.[60]

The official battle report showed more losses to the Eleventh Wisconsin than any other regiment by far: 39 wounded (out of 55) and 6 killed (out of 8 total). In all, there were 63 Federal men killed and wounded in the battle that day. The Confederates lost perhaps as many as 300 men, as the Rebels managed to "drag away" a significant number of their dead and wounded. "Already 123 of the enemy's dead have been found," recorded Hovey shortly after the battle, with an "estimate [of] their dead at more than 200." They buried the Rebels in one mass grave. "I saw one ditch, or rather hole," wrote J.C. Metcalf, "in which lay the bodies of one hundred and thirty-two poor, miserable, deluded men. I was taken to the place by a sergeant, who had assisted in burying them a few hours before." The enemy had miscalculated that day, thinking it could halt the advance of Curtis's army. It took only four regiments of infantry and some cavalry to thwart the Rebel counterattack. But the questions still remain: did Harris blunder into an ambush and was it only the heroics of Hovey and his men that saved the day, as one historian has claimed?[61]

On August 12, 1862, Hovey sent for surgeon Henry P. Strong of the Eleventh Wisconsin. When Henry appeared in his tent, Hovey confronted him about an article Henry had written, which had appeared in several newspapers, contradicting Hovey's report of the events of the battle and that of the Thirty-Third Illinois. Hovey criticized Henry's treatment of Captain Potter and his company. "I wrote the facts as I saw them," said Henry. "I was upon the field & Saw more than he did." The conversation never heated up and appeared to fizzle out once Hovey was confronted with the fact that Henry indeed saw more than he did. "He soon got over his pet [Capt. Potter] & is apparently all right again," wrote Henry after the event. "Potter is a particular pet of his & his report [concerning] Potter is untrue." Henry never mentioned a confrontation with Hovey again, and continued to speak highly of the Colonel. Henry's letter suggests that Hovey was not on the field as early as he claimed. It is clear that the early moments of the battle, perhaps as much as the first 20 minutes, were not witnessed by Hovey and that his descriptions were most likely based on those of his men or Captain Potter, who certainly embellished his exploits and those of his men.[62]

* * *

Before the battle at Bayou Cache, as the number of dead increased from disease, sickness, and accidents, it was solemnly noted that many "a poor soldier must find his last resting place in rebeldom."[63]

Chapter Five

Contraband and Cotton

"Two of our orderly sergeants were captured by the Rebels," wrote Henry Twining after the battle. The Rebels had lashed them to a tree and executed them with a "savage barbarity" that Henry and his fellow soldiers had never seen before. Both bodies were riddled with bullets, one with 13 and the other sixteen. These could have been the men Hovey ordered Harris to rescue. In another incident, a soldier from the Second Wisconsin Cavalry was captured and dragged into the woods, where bushwhackers reportedly "cut off his nose, gashed his cheek, and then cut his throat in three places." Miraculously, he managed to get away and survived.[1]

The next morning they set off on what would be one of the most brutal marches of the war for the Eleventh Wisconsin. They reached Clarendon early on the morning of July 11 and hustled down to the dock, where they were to secure supplies waiting for them on boats. The men marched swiftly in anticipation, but arrived at an empty dock. Local citizens told them the boats had left a couple of days earlier. Horses and men, exhausted and overheated, entered the river to cool off. This turned out to be deadly, as four soldiers and some horses drowned. The men were jaded and, as one cavalry soldier noted, "[the] people all left town" after their arrival.[2]

Curtis was concerned his army would begin to deteriorate. "I hear nothing of supplies," he informed Halleck. "I shall try to reach Helena." The only option was to continue the forced march for another 65 miles and hopefully make it to Helena with something resembling an army. So, without stopping to rest, Curtis ordered his men on. The column sent up a tremendous dust cloud as it marched towards its destination. They left Clarendon on the afternoon of the 11th and marched 65 miles in two days, arriving in Helena on the 13th. During their arduous journey the Rebels stripped clean the land ahead of them, placed dead cattle in watering holes, contaminated every well, and forced Curtis and his men to endure extreme hardship. Men were forced to drink from wells where the water was "the color of chocolate."[3]

The results were horrific: "men were scattered along the route in squads of 5 to 20 exhausted beyond physical endurance, they had laid down not caring whether they lived or died," wrote the regiment surgeon unable to help everyone. It took nearly a week for the entire army to arrive in Helena due to stragglers, both sick and wounded. "We were about as ragged a looking set as you ever saw," said Oliver Mather. During those two long and weary days they were "tentless, rationless, and almost destitute of water," and marched in temperatures that reached 115°F, according to one documented source. But Helena was no paradise; it was woefully unprepared to handle Curtis's army and his men still went without enough fresh water and food. It was also a breeding ground for disease due to its unhealthy condition. Before war's end, General Halleck would recommend that the United States Army abandon it as a military facility.[4]

Years later the memory of that march was still vivid in Calvin Alling's mind: it was the "longest and hardest ... march of our entire four years experience." He remembered that the sun seemed to squat right on them as it beat down unmercifully. They were unaccustomed to the heat. In one day, Alling continued, "[we] marched more than thirty miles in a boiling July sun, dust shoe-top deep, and the whole heavens filled with clouds of dust, on all the roads, and scarce a drop of water." There was "considerable loss of life as a consequence." They arrived in Helena "completely jaded and exhausted."[5]

The hardships of marching and soldiering were many. But dreaded as much as possible death were the "varmits." Regiment surgeon Henry P. Strong described in one report what the regiment faced: "Sandflies, wood ticks, scorpions, lizards, tarantulas, black snakes, Rattle Snakes, Moccasin snakes," along with the miserable cypress swamps and lowlands surrounded by dense timber. "Wood ticks are just about as large as bed bugs & twice as bad," wrote the surgeon. "They burrough into the skin and bite terrible. I make it a business to pick off from one to 6 several times a day particularly at night." But the insects sometimes burrowed too deep to dig out right away and when they were finally plucked they left behind terrible body sores. "You will see by this that Soldiering in not boys play. It is hard to see strong men drop by the wayside," he wrote home to his wife. "Sick & weary & far from home. Some babies in the regiment whimper & cry like whipped children at this rough work." The good doctor himself was not feeling well by the time they reached Helena.[6]

As one can imagine, frustration was evident in many letters home. "If any one wants to know why I dont write them tell them that ther way of sending letters only once in a while," howled Jesse Mather, "and when we get word that we can send a letter we only have time to scrabble off a few lines before this mail goes out and if they write to me I haint sure if I getting the letters." His brother, Henry, had apparently complained of the lack of correspondence from his brothers. "If Henry comes in tired after working all day just ask him how he would like to march and carry a knapsack and musket, forty rounds of cartridge canteen full of water and two days rations in your haversack and march eighteen miles in five hours through the woods and a road hotter than hell and not more than half water enough to drink and if you fall out of the rank be arrested that is what is fun." Since leaving Pilot Knob on the 23rd of March, the Eleventh regiment had been on an almost constant march through difficult terrain, were harassed constantly by the enemy, had fought a desperate battle, and for much of the time lived off little or no rations and a poor water supply. Their ranks were dwindling as men dropped from disease, sickness, and now combat.[7]

"As I rote before we have had a purty hard time of it," reflected Samuel Kirkpatrick. "Marching on half rations and poor water ... and sleeping out at nights without our blankets." Robert Sherrill wrote his uncle, John, early in July that soldiering had gotten a little rougher, and that it was not as much fun as it was before: "We have done some tremendous hard marching." He went on to describe the battle that part of the regiment had been in, and how they "helped bury a hundred and thirty two" of the enemy. But if he was trying to dissuade John from enlisting, it was too late. By the time his letter reached home, John was mustered into service with the Twenty-third Wisconsin regiment. By September, John and his regiment were sent to Covington, Kentucky, eventually participating in various expeditions against the Confederates in the north central part of the state. It would be several months before Robert heard from his uncle again.[8]

* * *

Though they had survived three months of the most difficult situations they had ever faced, Jesse and Oliver Mather could not think of much but home and the harvest. Oliver was sick and barely made it through the brutal ordeal, but Jesse was well enough to write home.

"I am glad that you had a good time the 4th for I didn't," he told Sarah. "I guess father will have to cut his grain with out us to help him this harvest." The guilt that Jesse and Oliver carried with them is understandable. The Fourth of July was the date most men had thought they surely would be home, especially in February and March, when things were going so well for the Union with Grant's victories at forts Henry and Donelson. But now they knew better. Jesse had also hoped more of his fellow Sauk County friends would join up. "I want you to write me wether they ar enlisting many around there now and wether they talk of enlisting when they get through harvesting," wrote Jesse, "and all the news that you can think of. Tell Henry to write."[9]

Oliver's thoughts also turned to home and the work that had to be done. "I think you will have to pray much for harvest help this year," he told Sarah, "for you will have to do it all yourself but never mind that...." Together the boys continued to send what little money they had home to their father, so he could hire help for the harvest. "To day we signed the pay roll and I think we will be payed of tomorrow," Oliver told his sister. "I shall send another letter to father with some money in it probably about forty dollars that is Jesse and I together."[10]

Reality was setting in for the boys of the Eleventh Wisconsin and their families. "You said that you wanted me to send you a lock of my hair," Samuel Kirkpatrick wrote home, not sure how to respond. "I will send you a lock of my hair today in this letter. I would like to be home to help you through harvest but I can't." His mother and father were starting to fear their son might never make it back to them. "Don't get skeered till I write that I am dead myself," he tried to comfort them with humor, "then you may depend on it."[11]

As was his way, Samuel took on the harshness of soldiering with a grin and a smile. While others filled their letters home with the hardships of marching, Curious Kirkpatrick dedicated only a few lines to such things, and then moved on to other more interesting tidbits. "It is a good deal pleasanter here on the banks of the Mississippi than to be way back in them old sypress swamps," he continued. "Here we see a old steamer ever one or two and nothing more looks nice than to see a nice steamboat with the stars and stripes on her." He also noted that where they were now was rich with "some splendid plantations and lots of Negroes."[12]

* * *

In May of 1861 an unexpected incident occurred at Fortress Monroe in Virginia, near the mouth of the James River. Southern slaves who had escaped bondage began to appear, asking for help, and a decision had to be made. They must either be returned to their masters or essentially freed and not returned. Fort Monroe's commander, Major General Benjamin F. Butler, decided not to return the slaves, a decision that helped set what would become a common policy. In August the United States Congress took action and passed a confiscation act that authorized the freeing of slaves. Slaves who wandered into camp or were rounded up became known as "contraband." The term quickly spread and was soon the accepted way to document such slaves. Union armies rounded up slaves as they found them and did not return them to their former masters. And any slaves who managed to escape and make it to a Union camp would be confiscated as well. "The negroes flocked to our camp at Helena," wrote one of the regiment's correspondents, "many of whom have been employed as teamsters and cooks.... Contrabands has caused some discussion among the soldiers as to what shall be done with them." What most wanted were their free papers, which emancipated them and allowed them to travel north through the Federal army if they so wished. "The citizens," he continued, "feel like the old lady in Batesville, who spoke in strong

Whenever possible, slaves escaped and entered Union lines as "contraband" of war (Library of Congress).

terms.... 'It would not be so bad if he would *sell* them,' she said, 'but when he freed them it did *nobody* any good.'"[13]

"It is nothing to see from 150 to 200 negroes on a plantation," wrote Samuel Kirkpatrick. And they would often be alone, their masters having fled before the soldiers arrived. But it would be misleading to give the impression that Union armies felt like great liberators or emancipators. Like most of the men in the Union army, very few of the men in the Eleventh Wisconsin felt they were fighting for Negroes, especially in 1862. Their perceptions and attitudes did change by war's end, though, and many came to understand the evils of slavery and its impact on African Americans.[14]

At first the men did not take kindly to the Negroes in camp. "Well ... the damned Negroes ... is in camp now," wrote Samuel. "The president says all slaves that has worked on fortifications shall be freed. Well the devils is a taken advantage of that. There is lots of them that never saw a fortification is coming in and swaring they worked on Fort Pillo* or some other fort." They fled to Union army camps not just for freedom, but for protection as well. Negroes reported having to flee due to Confederate soldiers rounding up slaves and "send-

---

*On April 12, 1864, Fort Pillow (near the Mississippi River in Tennessee, about 40 miles north of Memphis) was the scene of a brutal fight that most historians agree turned into a slaughter as Confederate general Nathan Bedford Forrest led an attack on the fort. Details remain disputed and controversial to this day. The lightly guarded fort was no match for the determined Confederates, who inflicted heavy casualties on its defenders. Occupied by 262 Negroes and 295 white soldiers, the fort suffered 231 killed, 100 wounded, and 226 captured; the vast majority of the dead and wounded were Negroes. Union sources claimed that, despite the fact that these men surrendered, Bedford's men massacred the soldiers in cold blood, burning and burying some alive. For more information see Noah Andre Trudeau, Like Men of War: Black Troops in the Civil War, 1862–1865 *(1998).*

ing them handcuffed" deeper into the South and out of reach of Federal troops. On more than one occasion members of the regiment came across Negroes begging to be rescued, having been chased and shot at. Some asked to purchase weapons for self–defense.[15]

Samuel's writings about Negroes were rarely flattering, and at times disturbing from a modern perspective: "It is got so that we have a darkey do all fatigue duty such as cooking loding the wagons and cutting new roads...." Samuel got used to the idea of having Negroes around, as long as they did the work. But he was very clear, as many were, that he was not fighting for them. When he spoke of some of his fellow Mineral Point friends not enlisting because they "will not fight to free the negroes," his tone was pointed: "If I thought that that was what we was fighting for I would lay down my old musket today. I don't think it so." Today it is hard not to take offence at what Samuel and others said about the Negroes they encountered, who were sometimes described as "brutes" and "nasty." Generally the men in the Eleventh Wisconsin wrote of defending the Constitution and their country, defeating the Rebellion and attacking those white Southerners who were the cause of their anguish. They did not see themselves as liberators for the enslaved Negroes. That perspective did change, but not until late 1863 and early 1864.[16]

The contrabands performed many tasks for Union armies as they moved, such as cooking and cleaning. Some of it was hard work, and at times dangerous. During the siege of Vicksburg, Negroes helped dig trenches near the front line during the day, when it was most dangerous. Confederate sharpshooters often attacked during the day, no doubt wounding and killing many. Did these men help willingly or were they forced? Likely many did not want to help initially, but by war's end thousands of Negroes served, fought, and died in active battle. And the boys of the Eleventh would eventually fight side by side with Negroes.

Henry P. Strong and several officers, including Captain Miller, had attended a Negro wedding that spring: "After the wedding they as usual on such occasions had a regular dance or break down. It was really amusing to see them, all colors from apparently pure white to the pure African black & all mixing together like members of the Same family." The officers mingled and had a good time. Probably none of them had ever witnessed such a wedding. The occasion prompted Henry to contemplate slavery:

> A Pure African in his present condition is better off slave than free, but when they mix so that you cannot tell a Slave from a white person as it is here in lots of cases, it makes Slavery appear hideous enough to warrant the Sacrifice of Millions of lives if necessary to wipe it out.[17]

The issue of identifying what was acceptable was linked to race, or whiteness, which for most people living in the 1860s equaled exclusivity. But by being able to identify slavery without color, the evil of such a thing became obvious to many when it was not before. But one also gets the impression that they got to know Negroes as people more than as slaves. The bride, according to Henry, had blue eyes and was "an intelligent little creature." He was, of course, sensitive to the fact that some masters often slept with female slaves of exceptional beauty.[18]

Writing in a February 9, 1862, correspondence, Chaplain James Britton noted his shock and horror after running into a "white slave.... She readily exhibited her straight hair and hazel eyes as well as white skin and red cheeks; but oh! slavery, thou bitter draught! when I asked her if she would not like to be free she carelessly replied she 'would just as lief.' Say, then, ye apologies for American slavery, what ye will for the slave system, in respect to wooly heads, and thick lips, and black skins— what dare ye say of the same system, by absolute despotism and free licentiousness in regard to Anglo Saxon skin and straight hair!" The thought of whites with only a drop of African blood being enslaved outraged many soldiers. The chaplain went on to note that this occurrence was seen often.[19]

Though the changes were gradual, attitudes softened. "The Negroes has meetins every Sunday," wrote Samuel in late 1862. "Oh lord how they dress. Nice white silk stockins. One seen the legs of them would think it was somebody. Oh gosh how they strut." By 1864 Samuel's tone had softened significantly. During one experience while visiting a schoolhouse, he was taken aback by what he saw: "There is a Negro school house agoing on ... and the best of all there is 2 nice girls for teachers." It's not known if these teachers were white or black; most likely they were white and were probably the reason old Curious Kirkpatrick came by. "One of them has her mother with her so she cooks and keeps house ... so it makes things very comfortable." He went on in his letter for several more lines: "It is great fun to hear [the Negro children] ... spelling and trying to read. They are the best on singing a song." Something was changing for Samuel as he interacted with the people he met. "I was in joking one of the school moms the other day," he wrote, confessing he made regular visits to the school. "I asked her what she intended to do with them after they was educated. She said she was a going to make Congress out of them. Pretty good I thought."[20]

"I have seen slavery, and can truly say that I love it none the better for having seen it," said another Eleventh Wisconsin soldier in his correspondence home to his local newspaper. The evidence was all around him, "enough of their guilt in their own offspring, as white as themselves and whom they doom to toil equally with the blackest Negro." Yet he still felt it was best to "leave it to them to dispose of themselves," forgetting that the war was a direct result of the South's unwillingness to allow for containment, let alone disposal of the institution. He continued to echo a constant theme for many people at the time: "Better let slavery die a natural death. Just as I finish the word *death* [his emphasis], as if for a beautiful commentary on my logic" a slave the soldier knew belonging to a local owner, Alonzo Westover, rushed into his tent. The slave was disheveled and dazed, with "a deep gash" in his head where his master had struck him. The soldier asked why his master hit him. Apparently, the Negro had "simply asked for a waistcoat to protect him from the cold" and this infuriated his owner. Yet even this turn of events was not enough to change the soldier's mind. He continued to argue that the current border states (Missouri and Kentucky) were "ere long to abolish" the institution, which would result in the creation of more border states and the continuation of the "same process."[21]

By war's end Samuel, like many others, was beginning to question how a whole race could be enslaved and what it would take to undo that. "It is strange that three or four men would rule so many," Samuel wrote to his younger brother, who had apparently asked a question about slavery. "If they would send a Negro to school every one ... but that will play out as soon as the war is over." Samuel clearly believed that slavery should end. He might even have gotten to the point where it was part of the reason why he fought; but that we'll never know. However, it is clear that he was beginning to understand how the institution of slavery made slaves and created its own social order. He was beginning to see African Americans, at the very least, as fellow human beings. It's not much by our standards, but for the 1860s it was something.[22]

* * *

It was a farmer's war, as the vast majority of the fighting was done by farmers, both North and South. The men of the Eleventh Wisconsin were predominately wheat farmers. In the South, cotton was king, and not just for Southerners. Cotton was important for the North as well, though not as important for its economy as Southerners had hoped. It didn't take long for the Federal armies to seize the cotton from abandoned plantations. Confiscated cotton was returned to St. Louis and other cities, where the government sold it to help pay for the war. Before the end of the first year of fighting, half the nation's cotton mills were shut down.

One reason the South thought the war would inflict economic hardship on the North was that about half of the nation's spindles were located in the North, primarily in Massachusetts and Rhode Island. New England employed hundreds of thousands of operatives, accounting for half the manpower nationwide. Though there were some aftershocks, the economy of the North far surpassed the South, however, and even experienced development and growth in new areas. The Northern economy held numerous advantages over that of the South. The North contained more farmland, more productive farmland, and more farmers. It doubled the cash value of the South in terms of farm machinery and livestock. It produced more wheat and corn, held a significant advantage in the number of horses and sheep. However, it was in industry where the North held the most dominant advantages and ones that would prove vital. The North produced 96 percent of the country's locomotives and firearms. The United States, before the war, held the world's largest railroad network, and the South contained not even a third of it. Immigrants flocked to Northern cities where jobs and opportunity awaited them. A much steadier currency and the support of Northern banks, along with industrial development, played a huge role in economic stabilization and growth during the war.[23]

By the summer of 1862, the Eleventh Wisconsin was stationed at Old Town, Arkansas, and was part of a large swath of Union soldiers confiscating cotton all along the Mississippi. In August Oliver Mather wrote to his sister, expressing how he felt about being in the military.[24] (Note his title, "Camp Cotton"):

Aug. 4th 1862

Camp Cotton

Dear Sister

It is with pleasure that I have seated myself to write you a few lines to let you know that we are on probationary rounds and interceding terms and in good health God only knows how long we shall be so. We are not doing much now only gathering cotton where ever we can find it and haul it to the river so the boats can get it we have had good luck so far in finding it by the help of the Negroes we find some of it out in the woods where you would not think of going with a team. I wish you could be here and go out with us to a plantation and see us ransack things first into the barn smokehouse out among the bee hives in the chickencoops and then ransack the house all through up the stairs and down into the bed rooms and evry other place that we could get into and take evry thing that we want to eat drink and wore and then steal a mule or two and take Negro or two we do most evry thing that can be thought of and more to. I cant think of any more so I will close by saying good by write soon and tell how much money you have received in all together we have sent 145 dollars but have not heard wether you have received it or not. We sent forty dollars by express from Batesville by express.... I will close good by give my love to all the folks write soon from your brother O.S. Mather.[25]

Oliver was probably being facetious when he told his sister he wished she could be there to see them ransack people's homes. He seemed not to like doing such things by the tone of his other letters. But by this point in the war in 1862, as the men began to harden some, perhaps he no longer despised such activities. Perhaps he saw it as a justifiable means to an end. This was war, after all.

The regiment remained in one area so long as there was cotton to be gotten. But not all of the cotton grabbed by Union armies made it back to the United States government. Calvin Alling later described what he believed was going on. "Here some of the regiments engaged in stealing and smuggling cotton in the name of the Government," he noted. "Notable among which was Col. C.E. Hovey* of Illinois [he was their commander during the Battle at Bayou

---

*I have not been able to substantiate Alling's claim. According to official documents, Hovey was "forced by ill health to resign from the army in the spring of 1863."

Cache] who later was dismissed from the service in disgrace, after realizing two or three hundred thousand dollars out of it." Alling went on to claim, "I saw much of these operations, and in fact, with the right wing of our regiment, was on the first cotton-stealing trip across the Mississippi, to the Harding plantation."[26]

A report to Secretary of War Stanton on October 20, 1862, noted that Army officers purposely kept regiments in cotton-rich areas where they were *purchasing* cotton from farmers and Negroes — at a very favorable price, no doubt — and then shipping it North for sale at a handsome profit. Colonel Hovey, now a general, is even mentioned by name in the report (not for stealing cotton but for exchanging a slave for cotton), which went on to state plainly, "Cotton and cotton buying was the order of the day." In September of 1862, Hovey was suddenly promoted to brigadier general, for reasons never revealed in the official records. The promotion was astonishing for someone who fought in only one minor battle, though he performed well. For reasons unknown, the United States Senate did not act upon his nomination within the statuary period and it expired on March 4, 1863.[27]

The regiment knew what was going on and often wrote about it. "A part of the Regt. and part of the 33 Ill. Regt [Hovey's regiment] has been down the river 10 miles below hear," Jesse Mather wrote to Sarah. "They have been geting cotin they got quet a lot ... about 5 miles and got ... all the cotin." They confiscated cotton wherever they could find it, and made no distinction between secesh or loyal citizen. An October 13 army correspondent to a local newspaper reported, "The citizens ... do not like Gen. Hovey, because he has taken so much cotton from them, and they say he would not be paroled if taken prisoner." The same article claimed Hovey and other soldiers from the Thirty-third Illinois exchanged 15 Negroes for thirty bales of cotton. Continuing, the correspondent noted, "This transaction has made the whole camp indignant, and the soldiers ask how many bales of cotton a soldier is worth, if a Negro is sold for two bales."[28]

"I would have written before but I hain't had time," Samuel Kirkpatrick wrote home. His family hadn't heard from him for quite some time, and must have thought he was on the march towards a fight. He continued: "We have been over in the Mississippi after cotton." Their son had volunteered to fight for his country, and thus far the majority of his time had been spent guarding railroads and supply trains, and now confiscating cotton. They must have been baffled until they read his next line: "We got 600 bales and its worth 85 dollars a bale." And this was just the tip of the iceberg; they would collect thousands of bales in 1862 and early 1863.[29]

"We went down in the state of Mississippi," said Henry Twining, "and got 1,000 bales of cotton worth $150 each. Since we have been here we have got $400,000 of cotton for the U.S. I think that is doing pretty well." A soldier with the Fourteenth Wisconsin believed they had confiscated "one million and a half of dollars" worth of cotton in the Mississippi region during the winter of 1862 and spring of 1863.[30]

A soldier writing home from the Eleventh Regiment noted that "Every city, town, village, landing, and even point at which a landing could be effected, suddenly turned into a cotton mart, and soldiers and teams were busily employed.... And whom, we ask, gets the proceeds of this cotton. Is it government?" He had his doubts. Cotton, depending on where you found it, could be grabbed for the generous price of "ten dollars a bale" and sold in St. Louis for "fifty cents a pound.... No matter! Only a few privates whose lives are nothing compared with a few bales of cotton!" Prices seemed to vary depending on who was doing the dealing.[31]

Cotton speculation did not end with the generals and colonels of the army, and it seems likely that Hovey profited. Henry P. Strong wrote home to his wife, Sarah, that "Hovey will make himself rich out of our late trip I have no doubt." Perhaps seeing an opportunity, Henry decided to get into the game: "I will tell you now that I have a few hundred dollars invested in a cotton Speculation — whether I make 3 or 4 hundred dollars, nothing or lose it all remains to be determined.... Keep mum!" And he had good reason to ask her to keep quiet; Strong most certainly did not have the required permits and could be arrested if caught. The government wanted to keep its monopoly. After asking Sarah to keep it between them he wrote, "I am dealing through Col. Hovey, I am not known for it." He purchased 4 bales at $40 per bale. It would sell for around $100 per bale in St. Louis. Henry continued to spill the beans and detailed cotton speculation: "It is bought of niggers after the people have deserted the plantation. Some has been bought as low as $8.00.... A part of it is confiscated, the balance is bought.... If I was out of the army and had a few thousand dollars I could make a small pile." Unfortunately for Henry, his attempt to turn a profit by cotton speculating ended in failure, as Federal troops seized the boat carrying his cotton and confiscated it before it made it to its destination.[32]

Sadly, small skirmishes during these cotton expeditions sometimes resulted in the death of soldiers. During the cotton-grabbing mission Henry mentioned above, he recorded that "we had a man killed and 4 wounded at one time. Our men killed 7 of the Rebels."

Henry Twining reflected on his military service thus far:

> It is nearly a year since I enlisted. It seems like a long time for me to be from home. I hope this war may end so that we may all return home once more. But I hope I shall have good health so as not to have to be furloughed or discharged for I enlisted with a proud motive, the intention of serving in a war to do what I can to put down the Rebellion, and I hope to stay in the service until it is accomplished.... There is not very much news to write so I shall have to close by hoping to hear from you soon, Your Friend, H.H. Twining.

This was Henry's last letter that has survived. As usual, he opened it by noting who was sick or injured from his company. Certainly many in the regiment were questioning why they went out day after day looking for cotton. This was not what they had signed up for; they wanted to distinguish themselves. By the end of 1862, most of the men in the regiment had had enough of army life. Henry would be among them, as both of his brothers, Aaron and John, would die of disease by year's end.[33]

All the men were homesick from time to time. Oliver S. Robinson of H Company was particularly interested in a recent family gathering his parents had written about. He wondered if anyone had mentioned his name:

> I hop you enjoyed yourself and sincerely hop father did also. Yes I know you must for elder Low was with you. Oh how I love those two persons. Mother and Father was my name mentioned out there at the association? Did you see the blind bird! Please tell me how does she appear and so on. Tell me what old Mrs. Tenny had to say about maters and things. How is Nelson Tenny, the Elders Folks and so on? Tell me all about it.[34]

With his uncle John fighting the Rebels somewhere in Kentucky, Robert Sherrill wrote to his aunt Caroline, whom he clearly respected and loved:

> Dear Aunt
> It is with pleasure that I take my pen in hand to answer your kind and welcome letter it came to hand the 6th of this month [November] it found James [her brother] and I well. We are just after haveing a great feast of chicken. We live pretty well sometimes James is on guard to day I expect to be on to morrow I expect John and the rest of the boys has lots of fun taking Secesh honest while they are on the march. I know we made the things suffer last summer marching through Arkansas I did not like any better fun than searching some of them rich old planters smoke house and some times his dwelling house they used to think a greate deal but did not say much you wanted James

and I to send you our likeness you had out to of wrote a little sooner before we left pilot knob. We have no chance at present to get it take but just as son as we get a chance to get it taken you shal have them with the greatest pleasure.... I have not heard from John since I left Helena. I am looking for a letter in evry mail from him. I have nothing more to write. Give my respects to all enquiring friends write soon directed as before.

I remain your obedient servant

Robert R. Sherril to Mrs. Caroline Dunlap[35]

On the 19th of November, John's regiment left Louisville for Memphis, Tennessee. They did not stay long, however, and continued on to Milliken's Bend, Louisiana, in December. A few weeks later Robert received a letter from John, written when John was still in Kentucky and on the march. Robert wrote a quick note to his aunt telling her that John was well, but that he had "seen some pretty hard marching to do but we have done harder marching than that." He was perhaps in his own way trying to tell her that John was doing fine and all was well.[36]

By November of 1862 the Eleventh Wisconsin had moved to Patterson, some 30 miles below Pilot Knob, on the Black River. "We have been hear ever since the first of the month but how mutch longer we will stay I do not know. A soldier does not know what moment he will be called on to leav," Jesse wrote. "Howard [his younger brother] wrote to me that you had a sewing machine. Father must be geting quite liberal since we came away." Things seemed to be getting better within the family, but there was still no communication between Jesse and Oliver and their mother and father.[37]

Just a year earlier the Eleventh Wisconsin had counted a thousand men in its ranks, but as 1862 came to a close only 621 able-bodied soldiers were present for duty.[38]

Chapter Six

1863 — A Midnight Battle

"After nearly two years of military maneuvering and strategies, the Union cause seemed to be in a baffled and doubtful situation, having experienced more downs than ups," wrote Calvin Alling after the war. Even the always upbeat Samuel Kirkpatrick was starting to have his doubts: "This war is managed mighty strange." When Samuel's parents asked if the war would end soon, his response was blunt: "I think that is a impossibility." For Samuel the war was becoming "too much show and stile," and he no longer held out hope for a speedy end.[1]

"The conspiracy against the government extends over an area of 733,144 square miles," wrote one newspaper, not to mention the 24,414 miles of shoreline, along with an interior boundary line of 7,031 miles. The Union had to invade an area the size of modern France, Germany, Italy, Spain, Portugal, and Great Britain combined. In addition, large sections of the South were unmapped: "The effort to restore the Union, which the Government entered ... was the most gigantic endeavor in the history of civil war." The North not only had to invade, but it also had to occupy the land it had conquered to secure its position — especially in the western theater. This slowed the armies down. To maneuver they had to constantly secure their rear and supply lines. Hundreds of thousands of soldiers were needed to hold and secure large areas of land. Though the Union outnumbered the South at least two to one, with so many men busy securing supplies and guarding occupied land, it was often difficult to take the offensive. And when they did move, they seemed to be going nowhere by the soldier's estimation. There were long periods of time when they did nothing but collect cotton and guard bridges or railroads.[2]

Samuel even began to doubt the outcome of the war:

> This war has not turned out as I thought it would and I hoped it would. I don't believe we will whip them now. It aint the men's falt. They dont want it to come to a close. They haint made enough money. I believe that the Southern Confederacy will be established before 2 years. It aint the Union that we are fighting for. We never hear the Union mentioned nowadays. It is something else. The minds of the private soldier is changed considerable in the last six months.[3]

The something else that Samuel referred to was President Lincoln's Emancipation Proclamation. "I do order and declare that all persons held as slaves ... shall be free," declared Lincoln. Initially written shortly after the Union victory at Antietam, some months earlier, the proclamation did not take effect until January 1, 1863. From this date forward Union armies were effectively armies of liberation.

The proclamation was denounced by antiwar Democrats throughout the Midwest as January 1863 approached. Newspapers reflecting Democratic views poisoned the public, in the eyes of many soldiers, and undermined the war effort. Most likely morale in Union armies started to plummet. But others rejoiced. "We shout for joy that we live to record this righteous decree," wrote Frederick Douglass. Lincoln's proclamation also opened the way for Negro soldiers to serve in the war, and perhaps, most important, the South's hope of European intervention faded. However, France continued to have a military presence in Mexico, which allowed the South to keep its hopes up.[4]

In south central Wisconsin newspapers such as the *Janesville Daily Gazette*, in an editorial printed on January 2, offered praise for Lincoln: "The President has kept his word. Yesterday he struck the shackles from the limbs of 3,000,000 slaves, and lifted them from the condition of chattel to that of free men and citizens, to take arms in their hands and do battle for their own freedom and the salvation of their native land."[5]

By January there were nearly a million men in the Federal army, while the Confederates could barely muster half that. Still, Union losses in late 1862, along with inept generalship in the east, caused morale to plummet throughout the North. Casualties soared to unimaginable heights in some of the war's bloodiest battles, at Shiloh, Antietam, and Fredericksburg. That it would become bloodier was inconceivable.[6]

News from the east was nothing but bad. "The times look gloomy," wrote an Iowa soldier in the Army of the Tennessee, Grant's army. "The war will never be over by fighting," said another soldier. "Nothing but a compromise will save us, I fear–." The Battle of Fredericksburg in mid December was a debacle, over 12,000 dead, wounded, or missing for the Union. It was yet another blow that appeared to bring the North to its knees. A few weeks later, along the Trans-Mississippi, one of the first movements against Vicksburg took place when Sherman moved down from Memphis to attack north of the city at Chickasaw Bayou. While Sherman marched south, Grant was to move from Oxford in the north, but the capture of one of his main supply bases at Holly Springs by Confederate general Van Dorn forced his withdrawal. Sherman ordered his final attack on the 29th of December, but even with two-to-one superiority he was easily repelled by a well-entrenched foe and forced to retreat. With his first attempt to move on Vicksburg a disaster of sorts, Northern newspapers were quick to dish out criticism. Grant's days seemed numbered.[7]

"At present things look very dark on our side," continued Samuel Kirkpatrick in his letter home. "The last dispatch that we had was that the Rebels had got the best of us at Vicksburg and another story yesterday was that Rebels was in position at Springfield, Mo. but there is so many reports a going that one don't know what to believe but one thing shure that I do believe and that is that the soldiers is a getting sick of such work and I don't think the soldiers will stand it for six months more." There was now talk of desertion. The regiment was owed pay, which some thought was intentional; men with pay and nothing to do would be up to no good, or even head home. Fortunately, very few men deserted. From the summer of 1862 to the spring of 1863, eighteen men were listed as having deserted from the regiment. "Robert Carr, who deserted sometime ago," wrote one regiment correspondent, "was soon arrested and is now in the guard house ... a disgrace to himself and his company." Most men would not risk the humiliation of deserting, both within the regiment and when they returned home. But rumors were constant and seemed to take great hold of the men. One particularly nasty rumor claiming peace had been declared spread quickly, causing many disruptions. But it was the constant sight of death, mainly from disease, that gnawed at the men. The ground near the river was unsuitable for burial due to the mud and clay. This led to them using the levees that, in the words of one Ohio soldier, "became a cast cemetery stretching for miles along the river."[8]

As the Eleventh Wisconsin had already experienced, newly formed regiments suffered heavily from disease. And with the wet, muddy, cold weather, sickness was wreaking havoc during the winter of 1863. One of the new regiments reported 352 sick out of 842 men. Some companies were reduced to less than ten able-bodied men. The 114th Ohio regiment, whom the Eleventh would get to know in the coming years, reported only 350 standing for duty, and, of those, many were reported as unfit for duty. Though the men were frustrated, the Eleventh was in fairly good health. "The health of the Company at present is purty good," reported Samuel.[9]

Major General John A. McClernand, in command of the Army of the Mississippi, organized new regiments. But diseases such as measles would run their course with devastating effect. Supply shortages also caused many to suffer and die needlessly. McClernand, realizing the gravity of the situation, urged Grant to do something: "If the new troops here could be replaced by older ones, it would be better in all respects." One of those "older" regiments was the Eleventh Wisconsin. Just a little over a month later the regiment was on the move again, and this time not for cotton or foraging but for fighting.[10]

* * *

After the battle of Shiloh in 1862, where Grant was surprised and nearly defeated but able to bounce back and drive the enemy from the field (at an extremely high cost), old rumors surfaced that he was drinking again and perhaps incompetent as a result. When politicians approached Lincoln requesting Grant's removal, he responded firmly, "I can't spare this man; he fights." Lincoln's eastern armies were reluctant to take the offensive and were usually defeated when they did engage in battle, so it's no wonder Lincoln held on so tightly to any general who had shown him results.[11]

And Grant *wanted* to fight. He wanted Vicksburg but, isolated as he was in western Tennessee, he had little hope of achieving that aim. Facing him in Mississippi was a fellow West Point graduate, and now a Confederate general, John C. Pemberton. One of those rare Northern generals who fought for the South (he married a Southern belle and spent many years in the South, which became his home), Pemberton commanded an army of about 35,000 men. Grant commanded roughly 40,000, but neither knew for sure the size of his opponent's army. There were rumors that Grant was facing a superior force. If this were the case, he could be sending his army to its destruction. Below him, Union general Nathaniel P. Banks was trying to work his men up the river from Baton Rouge. Grant was to cooperate with him as much as possible. Though he outnumbered the enemy roughly two to one, like so many other Union generals at the time, Banks was having little luck. Near Nashville, Tennessee, William S. Rosecrans and his 84,000 men were engaged with a Rebel force of about 45,000 led by General Braxton Bragg. And there were other armies scattered around protecting land and railroads.[12]

So the situation in 1863 was simple yet perplexing. Pemberton and Grant were face-to-face on the Mississippi: Grant on the west bank, Pemberton and Vicksburg on the other side. Could Grant get his entire army safely across the wide river to high ground, or would they be destroyed trying?

As he would during the entire campaign, Pemberton held the advantage of terrain. Vicksburg lay near the tip of a severe bend in the Mississippi, just below where the Yazoo River meets the Mississippi. Built atop bluffs, Vicksburg was heavily fortified. Men could not land on the eastern side of the city because of the batteries perched along the bluffs, which would sink every boat. Even if a transport got across, the men would be cut down in a turkey shoot. Ships trying to pass through to get south of the city would face a lengthy and powerful line of cannons. The east side of the river was high ground, and north of the city lay a valley that was also heavily fortified.[13]

Grant had no choice but to bring his men down the western side of the river. But this presented serious obstacles. The area bordering the river was half flooded, making it a giant, mucky levee covered with swamps, bayous, and overflowing lakes. Below the fortress were more guns perched on the high bluffs at Grand Gulf. Grant soon realized the only way to take the fortress city was by land, coming at it from the east. But how could he get his army safely to the other side of the river?[14]

There were options, none of them very appealing at a time when Northern morale was at its lowest. Recent elections had seen gains for the Democrats, and more and more newspapers were convinced the war could not be won. Grant had to take action; it was his nature — it was in his blood — and it was the only thing that could restore the morale of his army and his countrymen. To turn back to Memphis to regroup and swing east to attack Vicksburg would have essentially meant failure, and the aftereffects could have unraveled the war effort in the Midwest, not to mention that Lincoln would most likely be forced to remove Grant from command.

Grant was about to place the Union cause on his back and attempt to carry it to victory. "He fights," Lincoln had said. After meeting with Grant, Brigadier General Cadwallader C. Washburn reported that the general "looks well and feels pretty well, but feels that he has got a heavy job on his hands." Indeed he did. Sherman agreed with Grant that the only way to attack Vicksburg and have a chance was from the east, by land. Grant wired Halleck with his thoughts: "What may be necessary to reduce the place [Vicksburg] I do not yet know, but since the late rains think our troops must get below the city to be used effectively."[15]

A nervous Halleck, who had not heard from Grant in over 12 days, sent a communication reminding him that it was "very desirable that you keep us advised of your operations." There was a lot riding on Grant's operations. But Grant was busy trying to find a way to get at Vicksburg and had apparently neglected to keep his superiors informed. Halleck was focused, as Grant was, on opening up the Mississippi River. Reducing Vicksburg would accomplish that and cut off a vital supply resource to the Confederacy. Halleck continued his letter, offering praise and caution, but in the end he could not help but point out the obvious: Vicksburg capture would be the equal of "forty Richmonds. We shall omit nothing which we can do to assist you." Grant would be given his chance to succeed.[16]

Grant's early ventures to get his army east of the city involved ill-fated attempts to reroute the Mississippi River by digging a canal through the peninsula opposite Vicksburg. This could have allowed his boats to move past the fortress virtually untouched, land south of it, and drive inland. Though Grant didn't think this would work, Lincoln encouraged him to try the canal. The first attempt failed, followed by another attempt 20 miles below Vicksburg at Duckport. Grant then ordered an expedition (Yazoo Pass Expedition) to attempt to open a passageway north of the fortress. If they could get their gunboats and transports into the smaller rivers above the city, they could attack from there. In late February the expedition of troops, transports, and gunboats moved out. But it met resistance at Fort Pemberton, followed by several days of fighting that resulted in a full retreat. Though the Yazoo Pass Expedition had not gone well, it was followed by another attempt using Steele's Bayou, which also ended in failure. One Wisconsin soldier who fought along the Yazoo called it the "river of death." Taking Vicksburg from the north would be impossible, and Grant started looking for another way.[17]

Union soldiers were not the only ones disappointed by the outcome of the Yazoo expedition, noted a captain with the Twenty-eighth Wisconsin:

> During the day we passed many splendid plantations, most of them deserted by the white people, and left in the sole possession of the "colored" population, who greeted us with every demonstration they could think of — waving of hats and handkerchiefs, jumping up and down, clapping of hands, shouting, &c.— In some instances there were the whole black populations of a plantation

General Ulysses S. Grant (left) and General William T. Sherman (Library of Congress).

standing upon the bank, with their bundles, a mule or two, a bale of cotton which they had succeeded in saving from the rebels, expecting to be taken aboard. With what joy and hope they first hailed us, and with what bitter disappointment were their hearts filled, as we steamed slowly by them, can only be appreciated by an eyewitness. But we could not afford them any relief in that way.[18]

* * *

By mid March 1863, Grant was no closer than he'd been in January, increasing the whispers of his incompetence back in Washington. Some claimed Grant was a drunkard and would make a debacle of the Vicksburg campaign. Some thought he already had. Washburn sent back another report, and this time he held no punches, writing that the campaign was "badly managed." He told his brother, a United States congressman, "I fear a calamity before Vicksburg. All Grant's schemes have failed. He knows he has got to do something or off goes his head. My impressions is that he intends to attack in front."[19]

Instead of removing Grant, Lincoln and Secretary of War Stanton sent Charles A. Dana, who was to spy on Grant and report back. Grant got wind of it, but cared little; he had nothing to hide. It did not take long for Dana to report that Grant was fine, but his situation wasn't. By spring 1863 the nature of the war had changed. There would be no compromised peace as long as Lincoln was in office. But the conflict had changed militarily as well, when the "application" of warfare became "recognizably hard war" in nature.[20]

Halleck sent out a correspondence outlining the situation: "The character of the war has very much changed within the last year…. We must conquer the Rebels or be conquered by them." This seemed to invigorate Grant, who was becoming more confident. Grant was an aggressive leader and now he could take the fight to the South. To do this he had to take some risks, and he knew it. He was about to cut loose from his supply and communications base, divide his army, and push south along the west bank of Mississippi. The navy would run the batteries of Vicksburg and meet up with Grant well below the fortress to ferry them across. It was bold, but was it prudent? When Grant shared his plan with his commanders, the response was not encouraging. Even his friend and confidant, Sherman, had serious doubts.[21]

* * *

"Last Sunday morning the Ram 'Queen of the West' ran down past Vicksburg," wrote James K. Newton of the Fourteenth Wisconsin regiment in early February. "It seems to me if the wooden boats can run down past the batteries, that there is no need of cutting the canal for the gunboats, but they keep on digging."[22]

What Lieutenant Newton observed did not go unnoticed by Grant. Neither did the observance that the old rules of warfare might not apply anymore, rules such as *Thou must have supply and communication lines at all times.* Foraging in desolate places like Arkansas rarely offered the opportunity to cut loose and roam the country at will. Curtis learned this the hard way. But in Mississippi there were ample opportunities to subsist off the land. The territory was rich and lush. "We took possession of two of the largest plantations I have seen yet," noted one soldier, "[with] all the Chickens Turkeys Geese pigs and cattle we wanted to eat." Taking these factors into consideration, Grant's move down the river to cross it, leaving his supply and communication lines behind, though risky, was looking more and more like his only real chance.[23]

Usually there would be foraging parties who were designated to search the areas around the various Union camps. Officers were also involved and in the case of the Eleventh Wisconsin, their colonel. "Hogs run wild in the woods here [Missouri]," wrote Henry P. Strong home to his wife. "Every hog is a 'wild hog' of course & in soldier parlance a 'slow deer' and very few escape alive…. Col. Harris & myself were standing together & the men aimed at the hogs … but did not hit them. The col. in a low tone said you shoot with your pistol and see if you can hit one." He did and was successful, much to the delight of comrades who "cried out 'bully!'"[24]

* * *

In February, the Eleventh Wisconsin was still stationed in Missouri, but was ordered again to move out towards the Mississippi. Though long marches were nothing new, the men sensed a difference this time. The march was rapid with a sense of urgency that was exciting. Samuel Kirkpatrick wrote home to his parents:

> I never knew what it was to soldier till we took this last march. I have seen the time that I would give a quarter for hard crackers but they were not to be had. This is the place for a boy to get his teeth cut. I have all ways got along very well for the reason that I did not forget that bit of advice that you gave me that morning that we went to Washburn in the buggy together. Dear Father I often think of that morning one thing that I have been mighty lucky in and that is good health and I thank God for it. This was an awful thing any way you can take it.[25]

Though the marching was hard, it was no harder than their forced march after the fight at Bayou Cache. What had changed, however, was the will to go on. They were giving up inside, in their hearts and minds, and they believed things would not get any better. Curious Kirkpatrick had lost his sense of humor and his spirit. Writing home to his younger brother John he was somber: "Well … this soldering is a purty ruff thing."[26]

But Robert Sherrill was still upbeat. Though he acknowledged that marching was difficult, he amazingly still felt that soldiering was "good times." He had yet to see any real action, and was getting used to the marching. He did receive bad news, though. His aunt's daughter, Emma, had passed away. "I heard little Emma was dead," he wrote to her, "I am very sorry." Robert was also beginning to get a little worried about John, whom he had not heard from "for a long time." He then asked Caroline to write him often. "Tell me all the news you need not be afraid to talk to me tell me the news just the same is if I was there to talk to you." He had time to write only a couple of paragraphs; the regiment was on the march.[27]

The Eleventh Wisconsin headed for the Mississippi River, traveling 40 miles to St. Genevieve on the 11th of March. After a few days they traveled downstream to Memphis, arriving on the 17th. While in St. Genevieve, Samuel wrote home with sad news of his dear friend Frank, who was left behind at the Ironton military hospital. "I hated to leave him behind for I dont think he will live," wrote Samuel. He then sent a letter to Frank's family, informing them of his condition and urging them to come to their son before it was too late. But no one knew what was wrong with Frank. "It was hard to tell what was the matter.... His heart seemed to be broken." Though they had not fought any major battles, they had nonetheless been under constant threat for many months, marched several thousand miles, and had weekly and sometimes daily skirmishes. As a result, Frank was likely suffering from battle fatigue. "He would sit around and never say a word unless some body would speak to him," wrote Samuel. The toll of the war seemed too high even for Samuel at this moment. "We have served near half our time now and to look back it looks like a long while to be parted from ones friends...." And Frank was not the only ill soldier. By the end of the march the regiment was down to 526 men present for duty.[28]

The Eleventh Wisconsin arrived at Milliken's Bend, Louisiana, on the 22nd of March. Just less than 30 days before, the regiment was stuck in "snow storms" and the isolation of winter. Now they were further south and the climate change suited them. It was spring and the "peach trees [were] red with blossoms, and roses and violets in bloom." The color and warmth of spring had a positive effect on the men.[29]

Grant was concentrating his Army of the Tennessee for the offensive, and Milliken's Bend was a major gathering point before making the move south on the west bank of the Mississippi. The Eleventh Wisconsin was now part of Grant's Army of the Tennessee. Colonel Harris and his lads were members of Second Brigade, Fourteenth Division (commanded by Brigadier General Eugene A. Carr), in the Thirteenth Army Corps led by McClernand. Their own Colonel Harris was to command the brigade, but he was severely weakened with dysentery and many wondered how long he would be able to command. The other regiments in their brigade were the Twenty-first, Twenty-second, and Twenty-third Iowa regiments.[30]

William Charleton was mustered into Company B as a first sergeant on November 8, 1861. He earned the rank of first lieutenant before being mustered out of service in 1865. William, born in Ireland in 1831, came to the United States with his parents when he was a young boy and settled in Dane County. William was well liked within his company, as the letters written to him by comrades and superiors are consistent in their admiration and love for him. William's caring nature did not end with the war. In March 1882 he offered testimony on behalf of one of his men who was seeking a pension for disability as a result of his wartime service. It was not uncommon for comrades in arms to stay in touch and help one another years after the war.[31]

In March of 1863 William Charleton's mother Constantia wrote, "Not having received a letter from you today I feel very uneasy about you but I trust in God you are enjoying good health." She had not heard from him for some time and wanted him to know she had sent him a new watch, socks, and stamps—three essentials for a soldier on the march. Constantia then did what most family members felt obligated to do; she reported to William the rumors and developments from home: who was getting married, who was acting peculiarly, who had given birth, and who was supportive of the war and who was not. In particular she mentioned the latest developments in the local newspapers:

> The letter you wrote to Captain Oakley was published in the journal and the copperheads is mad about it John Driesbach gave it to you in the meeting Tuesday night and Mr. Close took up the cause for you Jessie Miller wrote a letter some time ago ... and Mr. Flick got it published in the patriot he talked about Close and Wilson and William Drake in it and said when he got home he would knock any man shanty down that would say a black man was as good as a white man some one in the 12 regiment wrote an answer to his and sent it to the editor of the journal saying be was sorry the two regiments was so far apart or he would give Jess a chance to knock his shanty down....[32]

By April 6, William's mother and sister had finally received word from him. "I am sorry to hear you caught a cold but I trust in God that this time you feel much better." She continued echoing her firm belief in God's protection and that it "will save you from sickness and protect you from all your enemies." She then reaffirmed her request that if he became ill, he should come home where he could get proper care.[33]

William's sister Mary reported back to him, on his request, about the recruitment of replacement soldiers for the regiment. The draft would take effect in July of 1863. "You wish to know how the conscription act takes up here it does not take well there is a great many thinks the people will resist draft but I suppose it wont help them if they do...."[34]

"I wrote you a few lines when we first came here and should of wrote more but I did not feel like writing any," said Oliver Mather to his sister. "God I was tired we had marched so long and so far and I thought I would write and let you know that we were well and alive." There was a calm among the men. They perhaps felt they were about to experience war on a scale they could not imagine. Were they eager for the fight, or too worn out and demoralized to really care?[35]

* * *

The Mississippi River was a mile wide in some places, making it difficult to find safe passage across. The terrain beyond the western shore across from Vicksburg, where the Eleventh Wisconsin was slowly making its way south, was inhospitable. It was a swampy bottomland filled with stagnant algae water and infested with malaria-breeding mosquitoes (and the men had no repellent). Throughout March and April the Thirteenth Army Corps cut roads and built makeshift bridges from Milliken's Bend to New Carthage, just south of Vicksburg on the western side. They eventually cut their way to Hard Times, directly across from Grand Gulf, which was where Grant wanted to ferry his army across the river.[36]

When Grant finalized his plans with United States Navy admiral David D. Porter, he was pleasantly surprised by Porter's receptiveness. Grant was asking Porter to expose a large part of his navy to possible destruction. If the convoy of ships that were to "run" the guns at Vicksburg got hung up, the large cannons would sink or disable them. But Porter agreed to the plan, and told Grant he would need until April to ready seven armored gunboats for the first run. There were to be several runs, which would include transports. Sherman, on the other hand, was not so sure the plan would work and conveyed his misgivings. "I confess I don't like this roundabout project," he said, "but we must support Grant in whatever he undertakes." Sherman was always loyal to Grant, but he was worried, to say the least: "I feel in its

Grant attempted to dig canals in order to bypass Vicksburg but failed. Sketch by H. Lovie, *Frank Leslie's Famous Leaders and Battle Scenes of the Civil War*, edited by Louis S. Moat (New York, 1896).

success less confidence than in any similar undertaking of the war." This gloomy correspondence home was written as he was leaving Milliken's Bend with his men.[37]

By April 16, Porter and his seven armored gunboats (and three transports) were ready. This was intended to be a "run." Even if the boats did not move swiftly, they would benefit from the current and hopefully the cover of darkness. For added protection the men laid hay bales and sandbags to protect the transports' machinery, boilers and pilothouses. Hoping to slip by the fortress undetected, Porter and his small fleet departed around 11 o'clock in the evening, with Grant and his family watching at a safe distance. All lights and lanterns were put out, the engines were warmed up, and slowly they meandered downstream and out of sight. But within minutes, as the caravan reached Vicksburg, "all hell broke loose."[38]

Grant sat with his wife and smoked a cigar as he watched the action. He reportedly neither moved nor (barely) spoke, and was visibly shaken by the sights and sounds coming from the river. Though Porter agreed to the run, Grant must have believed his career was on the line. And because of the distance, he couldn't really tell what was happening. Were the boats still moving? Did something terrible happen? Soon the renewal of darkness and silence indicated the boats had made it past the first set of guns. Farther downstream another set of Confederate batteries belched fire and flame, presumably at the still-meandering caravan. Were they simply mopping up the fleet, or was the run actually succeeding? Grant could stand it no longer, and set out on horseback to get firsthand knowledge of the results.[39]

All of the gunboats and all but one of the transports made it relatively unscathed. Grant returned to Milliken's Bend invigorated. His plan was in motion and nothing, he hoped, could stop him now. By the end of April, McClernand had most of his men spread out along the 30-plus mile makeshift road to New Carthage. Sherman, meanwhile, moved north to Young's Point above Vicksburg, where his primary objective was to confuse Confederate general Pemberton as to Grant's real plan. If Pemberton emptied Vicksburg of its garrison to attack Grant, Sherman could attempt another action and try to capture the city from the north. Everything was indeed in motion.[40]

While Porter's ships were making their run, the Eleventh Wisconsin, still part of McClernand's Thirteenth Army Corps, was making its way to New Carthage. It was slow going as they fought off Rebel patrols and maneuvered over bayous and swamps. At times the advance slowed to a crawl. But supplies were not a problem. The men came across "rich plantations" filled with "Turkeys, Geese, ducks, Pitches, Sheep, Cattle, Sugar, Molasses, Salt Hams," and "everything you could think of." They would have full bellies, at the very least.[41]

At one point during the road construction, floating bridges were required. These citizen soldiers constructed floating bridges of 300 feet or more, sometimes bridging distances of 1,000 feet. "The bridges were soon built of such material as could be found," said Grant, "[and] so substantial were they that not a single mishap occurred.... The ingenuity of the Yankee Soldier was equal to any emergency." His men were frontiersman from Iowa and Wisconsin, pioneers who built barns, constructed houses, cleared forests for farmland, and knew how to overcome, in their own way, any number of obstacles back home on their family farms. They knew how to approach a problem and, without instruction, figure it out.[42]

"The river was at its highest," wrote Calvin Alling, "our only road was to follow the levees in their zigzag lines." They moved as quickly as they could, but conditions were not ideal, for "the ceaseless and hurried tread of the troops by day and night along the narrow tops of the levees," he continued, "often so wet and slippery as to require an acrobat's skill to keep from skidding into the water."[43]

If Pemberton grasped the seriousness of Grant's downstream movement, he would only have to shift a significant number of his men south of Vicksburg and crush Grant before his bridgehead could be properly established on Pemberton's side of the river. But Pemberton seemed to have been puzzled by the recent activity. Sherman was still camped to his north, Federal cavalry had done serious damage in his rear with raids, and now to his south he had to know Federal troops were massing.[44]

Grant did not know what Pemberton might do. What he did know, just a few weeks before Porter made his run, were persistent rumors of a large force (perhaps as much as 75,000) making its way to Mississippi gathered from various regions in the south, including Richmond, Charleston, Savannah, and even Mobile, in an effort to reinforce Johnston. Though Grant likely dismissed the idea of so large of a force coming to Vicksburg, it had to be unnerving as he waited to make his move to the eastern side of the Mississippi. Halleck, as usual, was worried and sent several telegrams expressing his concerns, warning Grant not to divide his army and that "nothing must be neglected to insure success." There was a lot riding on this campaign. If Grant's landing force ran into any sizable Confederate army, they would be thrown back into the river with severe casualties, and this would most likely result in the failure of his campaign and possibly his career.[45]

* * *

As the regiment joined the buildup opposite Vicksburg, Robert Sherrill wrote home to his aunt that her brother was very sick: "I am well but not with pleasure to let you know that James Dain is sick he took sick about the first of this month with the typhoid fever." Robert spent a few days taking care of James, but was ordered back to the regiment. James was too weak even to read a letter from his father, so Robert had to read it to him. ("I do not wish to alarm you at all but laying all jokes aside he was dangerously ill.... I have not heard from him since.") James was taken upriver to Memphis on the hospital boat. But there was good news. While Robert was writing his letter a figure appeared in his tent's entrance; standing there was John Dunlap. His regiment would also be involved in the Vicksburg campaign. John and Robert shared dinner, exchanged stories and news, and took a long walk. "He is well he looks first rate," Robert assured his aunt. At dusk the two parted company and returned to their regiments. "I would like to come home on furlough mighty well," said Robert, "but I suppose there is no chance probably there might be a chance after Vicksburg is taken."[46]

"I presume you have heard of our great wonders that we have wrought long before this so I will not try to write any thing about it for you know that I dont like to write very well and dont write much of the best," wrote Oliver Mather. "So I will close by saying good by hoping these few lines will find you enjoying the richess of blessings give my love to mother and father and all the rest of the folks and keep a share for your self O.S. Mather." Oliver and Jesse still seemed to be at odds with their father over their enlistment. They were on the verge of missing yet another harvest. How many more would they miss?[47]

Before heading to Milliken's Bend, Jesse wrote home pondering if he and his brother would ever get the chance to fight in a major battle. "We have been now in the servace 18 months, we have seen every thing but fighting and that haint our falt for we could not catch them rebles [as] we have martched all over gods creation," he said. "I think that we will have more fighting to do if this thing dont close but I hope it will close so we wont have to do any more fighting." The pull of emotions between wanting to distinguish themselves in battle and just go home without seeing the war up close, having had enough of the marching and pointless meandering through one state after another, was powerful. "I think it will last a good while yet the way it is going." Jesse didn't think the war was every going to end. "Well I must close hope these few lines will find you well give my respects to all ... write as soon as you get this good by."[48]

But morale increased as the regiments moved south towards New Carthage. They were moving, and they knew it was "on to Vicksburg," and that would mean fighting. They'd had their fill of contraband and cotton. "I never felt better in my life than I do to day," Samuel expressed his joy with their movement. "But it is hard to tell how long it will last. Death is uncertain to all."[49]

As the Eleventh Wisconsin took its place in formation, at the head of Carr's Fourteenth Division, they met up with old friends. "All along the river we see our friends," noted Samuel. "We seen the old Eight Wis. Vol. ... 23 Wis. Vol." For mile after mile they marched and were never out of sight of other regiments; it was a massive buildup of men and materiel.[50]

As usual, Curious Kirkpatrick was taking note of his surroundings. "I thought I had seen lots of fine plantations in Arksansaw ... they ain't but a garden spot to the places here. The houses here that they have for their Negroes is better than half the white folks has in the North," Samuel declared. "It is nothing to see from five hundred to 1000 darkies on one plantation here." His fascination with southern plantations never ceased during the war. Closing his letter, he took note that they were getting ready for offensive action: "I understand that we are a going to Vicksburg soon. We have troops all the way up and down the river from here to Vicksburg.... I think we can take it by siege and not lose so many lives as to take it by storm." Samuel sensed what could be in store for them if taking Vicksburg turned into an all-out assault.[51]

General Carr submitted his report on his division's movement thus far, at the business end of McClernand's advance:

> My division left Milliken's Bend April 12, and proceeded to Perkins' Plantation, on the Mississippi, below Vicksburg, where it arrived on the 23d, having been engaged in making and repairing roads, repairing levees, making, getting together, and navigating boats of different kinds. Distance from Milliken's Bend to Perkins' plantation, 30 miles.
> On the night of April 27, we embarked on steamboats and barges, and the next day moved down the river and disembarked at Hard Times. That evening we marched 2 miles across to a point on the Louisiana side, below Grand Gulf.
> The next morning (April 30) we re-embarked and moved down river to Bruinsburg....[52]

In order to get behind Grand Gulf (on the Mississippi), Carr's division landed well below Vicksburg, at the mouth of the Bayou Pierre near Bruinsburg.

"We have been very busy this week a moving. We are now 30 miles below Vicksburg," wrote Samuel. This would be his last letter as they advanced. "The lines was cut and we had to go by water.... General McClernand was a talking to us yesterday," he said, "and said we had lots of work before us and bloody work too." Then he quoted the general: "We have a lot of brave boys here and I know you can take it," said McClernand. "Lay hold of it, my brave boys, and then we are all right." For some reason the frankness of their general was not alarming. The men were somber, not fearful. It was their turn to fight and they knew it. "The health of the Reg. is good. We haint got a man in the hospital," wrote Samuel of the situation as they moved out. A few weeks before, Samuel had recorded that the regiment had been reviewed by Carr: "He louded we looked splendid and the old Col. said that our Co. [company] looked the best...." The soldiers of the Eleventh Wisconsin were starting to feel confident again. "The boys is in a great way about the fight. They all seem keen for it." With that news, Samuel signed off and headed out, not sure what would become of him or his fellow soldiers.[53]

* * *

The Eleventh Wisconsin regiment was a part of the leading elements of three divisions—some 17,000 men—who would touch ground first near Bruinsburg on the eastern shore of the Mississippi. They were the first in their brigade to touch ground on April 30. Grant wanted McClernand to get to Port Gibson and secure the bridges across Bayou Pierre before the Rebels destroyed them. McClernand placed Carr and his division in the lead. After reaching shore, Carr placed Colonel Harris' Second Brigade in the lead, followed by the Twenty-first, Twenty-second, and Twenty-third Iowa infantries. "I was one of the first to step ashore," wrote Calvin Alling. As they ascended the bottomland along the river to the plateau above, all eyes were on the bluffs: "Within thirty minutes we were in line and on the march northeast towards Port Gibson."[54]

Luckily they did not meet resistance at this point. If they had, it could have proved fatal to Grant's plans. Still well below high ground at the base of a ridge, they would have made easy targets. The march up the bluffs and inland was toilsome in the hot afternoon sun; hoping the enemy had not detected their movements, the men moved as quickly as the terrain allowed. Once atop the bluffs, "The whole army could be seen for miles, worming its way over that vast flat country with the bayonets gleaming in the sunshine," wrote an Iowa soldier in the Twenty-second regiment (Lawler's brigade) once he reached the plateau.[55]

Commanding the Confederates in this area was Brigadier General John S. Bowen, who was aware that Federal soldiers were landing on his side of the river. He sent a warning to Pemberton: "Three thousand Federals were at Bethel Church, 10 miles from Port Gibson, at 3 P.M., advancing. They are still landing at Bruinsburg." He reported that he was "vastly" outnumbered, but would prepare a defense.[56]

Bowen instructed Brigadier General Martin E. Green to deploy his men west of Port Gibson, which placed them in a strong defensive position straddling the old Magnolia Church ridge. It was covered with trees and brush, lying just before a fork in the main road that would undoubtedly be the chosen route of the Union advance. The crucial bridges were in his control.[57]

Colonel Harris had suffered from dysentery for weeks and was in a severely weakened state from the rigorous marching. He had led his men up the bluffs and when ordered to move out to Port Gibson, Harris, though struggling, led them again. However, around 10:00 P.M., exhaustion overcame him, and he had to remove himself from command of Second Brigade. "I was called upon to take command," wrote Colonel Stone of the Twenty-second Iowa Infantry. "My instructions were to reach Port Gibson at as early an hour as possible, and occupy the several bridges across Bayou Pierre at that place." Colonel William M. Stone would prove to be a solid leader, and eventually became governor of Iowa after his distinguished service.[58]

Carr's Thirteenth Division steadily filled the eastern side of the Mississippi as thousands of men swarmed up the bluffs. By the next day (May 1) 17,000 men were across the river and moving towards Port Gibson. As Second Brigade was ordered out in the advance, Stone placed a fellow Hawkeye regiment, the Twenty-first Iowa, at the lead as advance guard, along with a howitzer, followed by the Eleventh Wisconsin and the Twenty-second and Twenty-third Iowa regiments.[59]

Port Gibson stood at the junction of several important roads. Two roads exited north, along with a railroad that reached Grand Gulf. The Bruinsburg and Rodney roads led from Bruinsburg, converging into one just outside of Port Gibson. The roads going north reached as far as Vicksburg and Jackson, the state capital. By taking Port Gibson Grant would force the evacuation of Grand Gulf (which Porter and his fleet had failed to reduce the night before), just north of Bruinsburg on the Mississippi River. As McClernand had no reliable maps, it took some time for him to ascertain where the roads led. This was remedied when a runaway slave was found and kindly clarified the situation. After this brief stop he sent Second Brigade

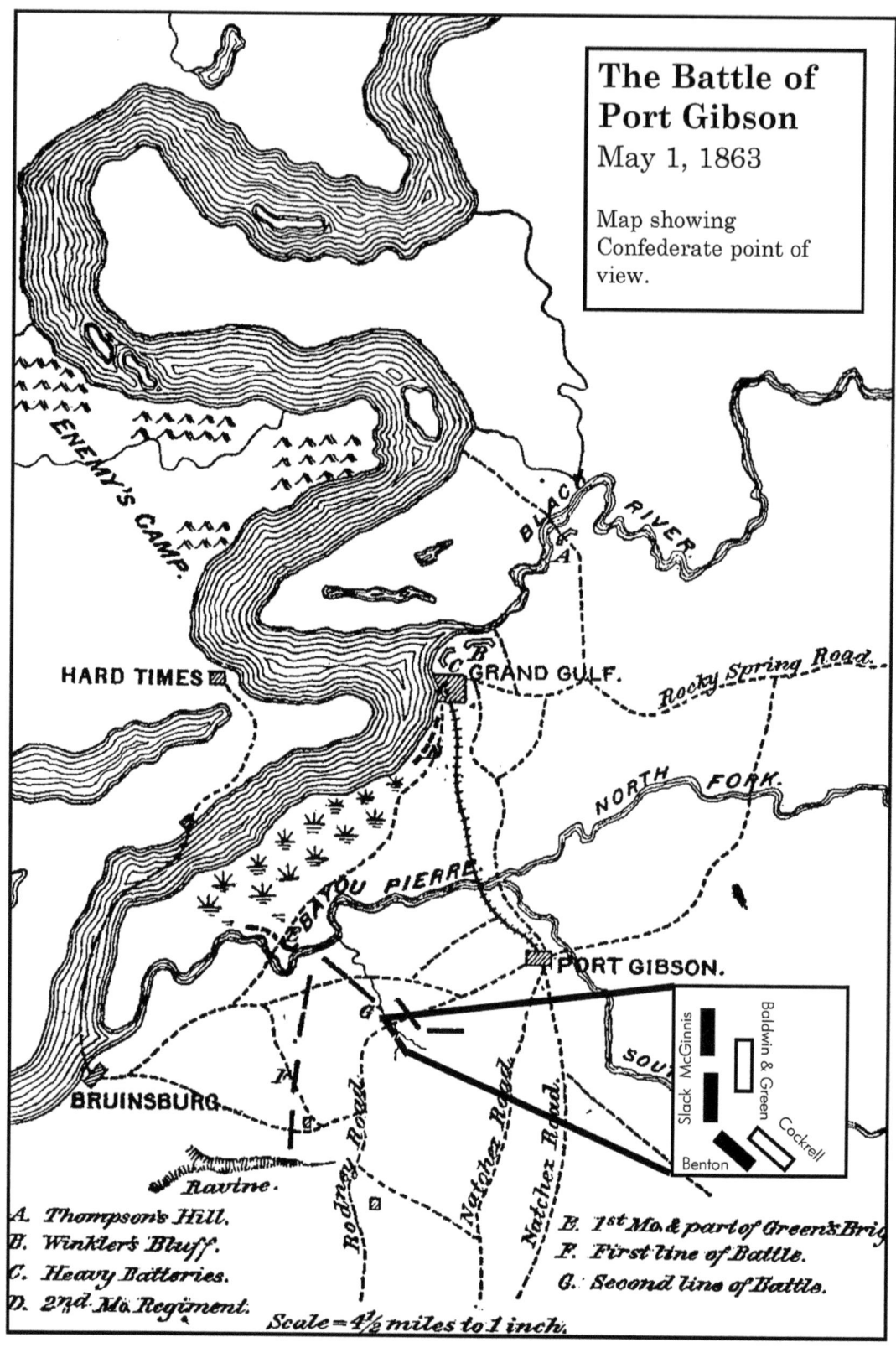

Confederate map showing general placement of Union troops during the battle (Library of Congress).

Six. 1863 — A Midnight Battle

down Rodney Road in a southeasterly direction, before it turned steadily northeast to Port Gibson. It was dark and the terrain surrounding the roads was inhospitable.[60]

Earlier that evening (Confederate) General Green's Second Brigade reached Port Gibson, then headed about 2 miles and a half west of town where they settled on a strong position near the junction of the Rodney and Bruinsburg roads along the Magnolia Church ridge. With about 1000 men (his returns showed 775 engaged) belonging to fragments of the Sixth Mississippi, Twenty-first Arkansas, Fifteenth Arkansas, Twelfth Arkansas sharpshooters, and some artillery, they dug in "on the crest of a hill running diagonally across the road." Green then deployed skirmishers and ordered his men to "sleep on their arms" and await the enemy. Later on that night Green received reinforcements when Brigadier General Edward D. Tracy and his brigade of Alabama troops reached Port Gibson at about 10:00 P.M., bolstering Confederate strength to about 2,500. [61]

The Eleventh Wisconsin, along with Second Brigade, headed up Rodney Road towards a possible ambush. But Stone was moving cautiously, with two Iowa companies as skirmishers deployed out in front. Rodney Road meandered along gorges and ravines, surrounded by thick timber, underbrush, and cane that made travel difficult and nerve-wracking. Though the sky was clear and moonlight illuminated the road, an enemy regiment could be waiting in ambush in the brush just off the road and not be seen until it was too late. Around midnight, having traveled close to 12 miles, Stone's advance was fired on about four miles southwest of Port Gibson, near Magnolia Church.[62]

Not far behind them the First Brigade was on the move, pushing on in the darkness. "As we pass along an old darkey gives us his blessing, but fears there will be few of us ever to return," wrote Charles A. Hobbs of the Ninety-ninth Illinois regiment. The men were unnerved; Grant wasn't the only one who heard rumors of a large Confederate force coming to Vicksburg. Hobbs recalled that the moon was "shining above us and the road ... romantic in the extreme." All night the army was on the move, with wagons rattling forward in the moonlight.[63]

Stone's skirmishers returned fire before the Rebels fell back, after hitting them with a quick volley. Stone immediately deployed his regiments in line of battle and pressed on. "I became satisfied that we had not yet reached the immediate vicinity of the enemy's main force," he wrote later. Once at the church Second Brigade was met with a "tremendous volley" that dropped many men. The enemy, posted on the ridge along the road to the right and left, delivered continuous fire, but still Stone pressed his men on until they were forced to stop. By now the entire brigade joined in the fight. Said Calvin Alling, "A strong picket force near Magnolia Hills, a half mile further on, were greeted by fire from a battery directly in front, causing a sudden halt."[64]

"The Brigade was immediately formed in line of battle," wrote Eleventh Wisconsin regimental historian James McMyler, "Capt. L.H. Whittlesey ... and Capt R.E. Jackson," being the first to deploy their companies. In Jackson's company (F), brothers Jesse and Oliver Mather quickly formed their line with the rest. Then the trees and brush came alive as Confederate gunshots whizzed by, causing branches to lurch and snap. But the Federals could not tell what direction the fire came from. Suddenly gunfire filled the air. Like lightning flashes, explosions illuminated the road and woods. Enemy silhouettes flashed into sight and were gone, followed by shots fired at empty spaces. Men maneuvered like ghosts, hunting an enemy they could never quite see. As the fight heated up they were pinned down, returning fire as best they could. Men sat up and quickly fired before throwing themselves back to the ground to reload. By now six guns from the Confederate Hudson battery zeroed in on their position and began firing. All hell was breaking loose like never before for the men of the Eleventh Wisconsin.[65]

Samuel Kirkpatrick had been promoted to sergeant, so as the shots rang out this night he helped organize the line, often having to stand to give instructions and exposing himself to enemy fire. In his company were Calvin Alling and Henry Oettiker. Henry and Samuel had become friends, even mentioning each other in letters home. Not far from Henry was Barney Callahan, a resident of Willow Springs born and raised in Ireland. A little further down the line was Stephen Hoskin from England, Martin Latch from Germany, and Thomas J. Jones from South Wales. All called America home and were willing to fight and die for it. As the battle intensified men were wounded and Samuel tried to get to them, but the darkness made it difficult. Davis Reese, a private, was severely wounded and called out for help as he lay in the darkness.[66]

Meanwhile, not far from Rodney Road, William P. Benton of First Brigade could hear the sounds of cannon fire in the distance. Not long afterward he received orders to hurry his guns to the front to support Second Brigade. Benton ordered the First Indiana Battery to head "at a full run" up Rodney Road. Arriving in minutes to a ridge at the rear, where the First Iowa battery was already returning Rebel fire, they deployed and engaged the enemy's cannons. The midnight battle turned into an artillery duel. Throughout the night the two armies fired at one another, attempting to zero in on the opposing battery's muzzle flashes. Men who were lying on their backs watched the shells whiz overhead while skirmishers moved forward, attempting to probe enemy lines. The gunfire was broken only by occasional screams and cries for help from the wounded. "The extreme darkness, the screaming and bursting of shells, and the rattle of grape through fences and timber," said Colonel Stone, "conspired to render the scene presented by this midnight battle one of the most terrific grandeur."[67]

The battle raged on until 3 o'clock in the morning, when all was quiet. Still in position, the Eleventh Wisconsin and other Iowa regiments were ordered to "lay on their arms" and be ready for daylight, when they would "meet the Rebel infantry face to face in bloody combat." Few men slept that night.[68]

* * *

Rodney Road was a most inhospitable place to fight a battle, with its thick timber, underbrush, and canebrakes, and sporadic fenced-in fields not large enough for more than a few regiments to maneuver in. As Grant reported later, the fighting took place "over the most broken country I'd ever saw." Though the midnight battle was effective in frightening the hell out of the men, it had produced no strategic results. At daylight it became evident to McClernand and Grant that concentrating their forces was impossible. The fighting was to take place along the two roads leading to Port Gibson, and the terrain would limit effective cooperation and communication between the two halves of the army slugging it out with well-positioned Confederates.[69]

Perhaps as early as 5:00 A.M. McClernand had reached the area. Benton, commanding First Brigade, recalled his encounter with the general: "[He] came dashing to the front, asking a thousand questions as to the position and strength of the enemy, the roads, and the general topography of the ground, and, with matchless energy, proceeded to verify every statement by a personal investigation." McClernand sent First Brigade down Rodney Road towards the front. Also rushing to Magnolia Church was Brigadier General Peter J. Osterhaus' Ninth Division. When the First Brigade reached the fork in the road they could see Shafer's house, which would be a landmark throughout the battle. Reinforcements started to arrive and were sent either northwest to Bruinsburg Road or southwest to Rodney Road. Union soldiers began exploring the ravines around the area, looking for Rebel skirmishers. They encountered sporadic resistance, but were able to drive back "the stubborn enemy at the point of the bayonet several hundred yards." Throughout the day most regiments had bayonets fastened at all times. With the thick forests and underbrush, they sometimes had no more than 30 yards' warning of a Rebel company charging upon them with "bayonet's glistening." Like small bands of hunters, each army moved out in search of the other.[70]

Carr's division engaged the enemy around 7 o'clock in the morning, supported by Brigadier General Alvin P. Hovey's division. By now Rebel cannons were again shelling the Magnolia Church ridge, where the Eleventh Wisconsin was deployed. Both their right and left were occupied by elements of Carr's division, leaving the Eleventh in the middle "ordered by General Carr to hold ... in readiness to charge the enemy lines." Regiments that had not done so were ordered to fasten bayonets. The front now stretched out, north and west, for nearly a mile through the thick and tumultuous terrain.[71]

"The smoke of preliminary skirmishing hung in long wreaths over the fields and woods, and warmed and reddened in the morning sunlight like a halo," wrote the historian of the Forty-second Ohio regiment, who took part in the action.

Major General John A. McClernand (Library of Congress).

"The trees were in full leaf, and the thickets and canebreaks that filled the ravines were dense masses of fresh, green foliage." As they passed General Carr heading for the front he called out, "A good day for a fight," and then rode away.[72]

"I kept the enemy employed with my Second Brigade and tow batteries," wrote Carr in his official report. During this time he moved Benton's First Brigade down to the right of the road with orders to "press" on the enemy's left flank. The terrain made the going difficult, but Benton was able to get his men through and engage the enemy. "Now came the 'tug of war,'" with each side trying to pull the other off balance.[73]

It soon became apparent that the enemy was trying to expose Benton's brigade, at the extreme right of Carr's division. "For at least two hours," Benton noted, "[they] fought ... giving volley for volley." During this intense fight McClernand received Benton's plea for reinforcements, and ordered General Hovey to support him. Hovey immediately sent his First Brigade, commanded by Brigadier General George F. McGinnis, down the ravine to support Benton. Hovey then ordered Colonel James R. Slack to take his Second Brigade up the center to support Benton's left flank, where it joined Rodney Road and Magnolia Church. Upon reaching the front where the Eleventh Wisconsin was positioned, they received "severe fire" from the enemy.[74]

By now regiments and brigades of Hovey's Twelfth Division and Carr's Fourteenth were intertwined along the convoluted mile-long front. Hovey's First and Second brigades became heatedly involved with the enemy, allowing the Eleventh Wisconsin and the rest of Stone's Second Brigade some reprieve as they readied in the center to make a "charge" when called on.[75]

At about ten o'clock Stone realized that Benton's left flank was wavering: "At this junction I moved my brigade forward in double lines of battalions for the purposes of charging upon the advancing columns of the enemy." The Eleventh Wisconsin, along with the rest of the brigade, moved out. They could see an open field in the distance, with a Rebel line building at the far side. They had to cross a "deep hollow" of thick underbrush, which probably concealed their movement until they reached the field. There they stood their ground against the advancing foe and "opened our fire upon them with such rapidity and precision that, unable to resist it, they soon broke and retreated in utter confusion," wrote Stone.[76]

Hovey was not a commander who waited in the rear for reports. After spurring his brigades into motion, he rode to the front for a first-hand appraisal of the situation. "As I rode down the road [Rodney Road] towards the front and middle of my line," he wrote in his official report, "I met Captain Klauss, First Indiana Battery, who had been gallantly fighting the Rebel batteries." Klauss pointed out the location of the Rebel battery, which was now within reach of Hovey's infantry. Hovey galloped to the Thirty-fourth Indiana regiment, commanded by Colonel Cameron, which was in line along a fence at the edge of the field. The enemy line and battery was about 200 yards away. Hovey gave the order to charge the battery, with the Fifty-sixth Ohio to support the advance. Cameron ordered the men to fix bayonets and with "loud shouts," doing their best imitation of a Rebel Yell, they swiftly advanced. They staggered not more than a hundred yards when they received direct shots from the cannons. The fire was so intense the Hoosiers were forced to the ground, lying flat on their stomachs for several minutes waiting for a break in the action. When the lull came they sprang to their feet and charged. In the distance Hovey could see their "bright bayonets … glittering in the sun." Sensing that he could increase his advantage, Hovey shouted "forward" as several more regiments sprang to their feet and charged the Rebel lines. After several minutes of hard fighting they had forced the enemy back, taking several hundred prisoners and capturing the guns and a stand of colors.[77]

All along the line each brigade rapidly advanced in a wave of blue, swarming over ravines and ditches, smashing through thick underbrush, and charging across fields. As if in a race to be first upon the enemy, they advanced "with the wildest enthusiasm," wrote Benton, "the men of my brigade vying with their friends of Hovey's division who should first reach the enemy."[78]

Meanwhile, back near Bruinsburg Road to the north, other Union soldiers were also engaged in serious battle. General Osterhaus, having received reinforcements from Brigadier General John E. Smith's Third Division, was driving back the Rebels near Bayou Pierre. Using three brigades, the Union Army attempted to punch through the Rebels and force their disseverment. When the fighting intensified, the Confederate lines were smashed and they were forced to give way. After some intense fighting west of Port Gibson the Rebels were in retreat, but not yet defeated.[79]

Confederates were in full retreat east of Magnolia Church as well, when they came upon reinforcements setting up on a hill about one and a half miles from the original line. General William E. Baldwin's brigade of Mississippi and Louisiana troops was just itching to get into the fray. Bowen ordered General Green's men to fall in line with Baldwin's troops and form along their far left, hidden in a creek bed, where they waited for the Union advance.[80]

In the distance they heard cheers, hoots, and hollers. Hundreds of men in blue lined Rodney Road, waving hats and thrusting muskets into the air, their bayonets glistening in the afternoon sun. "The wildest enthusiasm prevailed," wrote Hovey, "as Major Generals Grant and McClernand rode down our lines." But Grant was not in a celebratory mood, and immediately ordered Hovey to continue to press the enemy and turn their retreat into a rout.[81]

Not far from Rodney Road, the Eleventh Wisconsin could hear the cheers. Samuel Kirkpatrick checked his fellow Mineral Point boys, taking a quick head count. He found Henry Oettiker and gave him a pat on the back. Further down the line Henry Twining, Oliver and Jesse Mather, and Robert Sherrill congratulated friends and comrades on their apparent victory. But they soon noticed the aftermath of the fight. "The dead and wounded of the enemy lay thickly scattered over the ground," wrote Stone afterwards. "We remained but a few minutes on the victorious field." Stone moved out with his brigade toward the retreating Rebels. In the lead he placed, once again, the Eleventh Wisconsin.[82]

They climbed first to a plateau and then to a ravine at the base of a hill covered with thick timber. After about a mile they were fired upon. Sergeant Kirkpatrick formed his company in line of battle. With sword in hand, he gave instructions as bullets whizzed by, some dropping several men around him. His voice was steady as he called out to his men. Neither Robert Sherrill nor Henry Oettiker noticed as they reloaded their guns; but they could no longer hear Samuel's voice.[83]

Stone rushed to the front, where he found the Eleventh Wisconsin under intense fire from the enemy. "I saw at once that the enemy had been strongly re-enforced and were determined to make another stand," he later wrote. They were on high ground at the crest of a hill, using the thick tree line as cover, "commanding the entire ground over which we were compelled to approach." Stone ordered his men to form up, and as soon as his artillery was in place, attacked the Rebels with a "spirited" fire. He was hoping to rush the enemy and force their withdrawal, this time pressing on to try and rout them. But Confederate artillery returned fire, hitting Stone's line. Taking direct fire from both cannon and Rebel infantry, Stone knew they needed help before charging again. The battle erupted again as Hovey's men moved up and engaged the Rebel batteries, which were now decidedly outgunned. "The battle raged with terrific fury along our lines," said Stone. The Rebels tried yet another counterattack, but again were driven back under hellish fire. Soon the fighting died down, save for the artillery.[84]

After another hour of artillery fire, the Confederates realized they were facing impossible odds and began to withdraw from the field. Green knew he risked being cut off and destroyed if his flank was turned or his line broken. Using a ravine, he quickly pulled his men from the line and retreated from Port Gibson. The battle took the lives of 131 men, with another 719 wounded and 25 missing. Stone's Second Brigade suffered 101 dead and wounded. The Eleventh Wisconsin lost two men, with 23 wounded. McGinnis' brigade was hit hardest, with 221 dead and wounded.[85]

Grant was essentially dividing his army, which was a risky thing to do. Pemberton didn't know if Grant planned to attack Vicksburg from the north or the south, thus allowing Grant to get most of his army across the river before taking on a Confederate force of unknown strength. But there was far more to Grant's plan than a Mississippi gunboat run and roundabout marches through swamps and bayous. He also needed to avoid Confederate general Joseph E. Johnston and his army, who were reportedly lingering nearby in case Vicksburg was attacked. By keeping Pemberton guessing, Grant hoped to not allow the Confederates time to mass an army and meet him head-on. Pemberton might have been convinced the action below Vicksburg was a feint, and not the real threat. But most likely he knew that Grant was coming up from below. However, temporarily dividing Union forces and making feints north of Vicksburg meant Pemberton had to keep his eye on both north and south fronts. Grant could then swing Sherman back down and around and come at the Confederates with a unified force. Even the average soldier understood the value of dividing the army. "Thereby weakening the afore said place and strengthening the other place so that an attack on both places simultaneously," wrote Oliver S. Robinson home, explaining what they were doing, "will insure the fall of both so one cannot assist the other." Divide and conquer was Grant's plan throughout the Vicksburg campaign.[86]

Chapter Seven

Champion Hill

Though slightly wounded and momentarily dazed, Samuel Kirkpatrick was able to regain his composure and finish the battle at Port Gibson. Afterwards, he wrote a quick note home informing his parents that he was okay. "I got a slight wound on the side of the face and a small nick out of my left ear, but it is well now," he told them. But there was no time for reflection. Early the next morning the Eleventh Wisconsin was on the move again.[1]

It was no secret that McClernand wanted Grant's command. A former Democratic congressman from Illinois, he was ambitious and wanted to be the first to take Vicksburg. Which is precisely why he and Grant did not get along. McClernand had lobbied with Secretary Stanton and President Lincoln for the command, but was refused. When Grant learned McClernand would command one of his corps, he protested, calling McClernand "unmanageable and incompetent." Grant was privately planning to remove McClernand from command when the opportunity presented itself. His army moved too slowly, his officers were undisciplined, and he never did anything to Grant's liking.[2]

Grant ordered McClernand to "renew the attack at early dawn and if possible push the enemy from the field or capture him." The next morning they reached Port Gibson and found it devoid of enemies and nearly abandoned save for "finding arms and clothing scattered in every direction, it soon became evident that the rebels had left." They soon reached the Bayou Pierre bridge, but the Rebels had burned it, leaving it almost completely destroyed. Again McClernand's pioneers were put into action, swiftly building a bridge using "materials ... obtained by tearing down the [nearby] buildings, cotton-gins, &c., in the vicinity." By mid-afternoon they were on the move again, and McClernand was able to reach eight miles past Port Gibson before dark.[3]

By the next day, General McPherson's corps was leading the advance. Bowen abandoned Grand Gulf on May 2 and pulled back towards Vicksburg. On May 4 McPherson reached Willow Springs, heading in a northeasterly direction towards Rocky Springs.

Grant arrived at Grand Gulf and stayed the night. He noted the "health and spirits" of his army and probably rested in comfort knowing that everything was going as well as could be expected. He noted in a communication to Halleck that his men had "marched as much by night as by day, through mud and rain, without tents or much other baggage, and on irregular rations, without a complaint, and with less straggling than I have ever before witnessed."[4]

Grant believed the Confederates were "badly beaten" and demoralized at this point. However, though Pemberton was probably licking his wounds, he was not defeated. He was on the alert, having moved his command from the state capital (Jackson) to the security of Vicksburg. Pemberton was probably relieved when Sherman withdrew from the north, but still perplexed as to Grant's intentions.[5]

Pemberton sent a flurry of communications to his subordinate commanders giving instructions, to Richmond pleading for reinforcements, and to General Johnston asking for help. Vicksburg and Jackson were connected by a railroad, a very key railroad, as it turns out. Capturing Jackson would cut Pemberton off from communication with the Confederacy. Pemberton didn't know if Grant intended to strike below him at Warrenton, or hit his communication lines at Jackson or perhaps at the Big Black River.[6]

Though the state's capital might have to be abandoned, Vicksburg could not be. At least that's the impression Pemberton got when Jefferson Davis wrote him after Port Gibson: "Hold[ing] both Vicksburg and Port Hudson is necessary to a connection with Trans-Mississippi." Giving Vicksburg to the Federals would be giving up control of the Mississippi and would essentially "sever" the Confederacy. But Pemberton was still optimistic as he wired Davis: "With cavalry in Northern Mississippi and re-enforcements promised, think we will be all right." But he would attack only if the opportunity presented itself as Grant extended his line. Then he would strike at Grant's weakest point and defeat him. Pemberton believed Grant could not live off the land for long. If he could prevent him from gaining a foothold above Vicksburg on the east side of the river, for the purpose of resupplying his army, Grant would have no choice but to withdraw.[7]

Grant was also in good spirits and wanted to convey this to his army. So on May 6 Grant issued General Order number 32, with instructions that every commander read it to his men:

> Soldiers of the Army of the Tennessee! Once more I thank you for adding another victory to the long list of those previously won by your valor and endurance. The triumph gained over the enemy near Port Gibson, on the 1st instant, is one of the most important of the war. The capture of five cannon and more than 1,000 prisoners, the possession of Grand Gulf, and a firm foothold upon the highlands between the Big Black and Bayou Pierre, from whence we threaten the whole line of the enemy, are among the fruits of this brilliant achievement.[8]

Grant was an aggressive commander. The only thing that concerned him was the location of the enemy army, its strength, and how to get at it. What he knew at this time was that Pemberton had maybe 25,000 men with him at Vicksburg to use for an offensive, while leaving perhaps another six or seven thousand to garrison the defenses. At Jackson, intelligence reports estimated an undermanned force of no more than 10,000 defenders. At Port Hudson they had another 10,000 troops commanded by Major General Frank Gardner. And now reports were coming in that reinforcements were on their way, but how many and from where he did not know. Grant wanted to strike quickly, take out Jackson, and then turn on Vicksburg before reinforcements could join Pemberton there. He contacted his Corps commanders and advised them of his plans.[9]

At 8:15 P.M. on May 11, Grant sent McClernand his orders:

> CAYUGA, Miss., May 11, 1863 — 8:15 P.M.
> Maj. Gen. JOHN A. McCLERNAND, Comdg. Thirteenth Army Corps:
>
> In accordance with my verbal instructions this afternoon, you will move your command at daylight to-morrow on the Auburn and Edwards Station road, and, if practicable, a part of one division by the road to the westward of the one just mentioned. Move cautiously, but rapidly as convenient, and so that your entire corps will arrive on the Fourteen-Mile Creek simultaneously and in a compact line. It is also important that your corps reach the creek at or about the time that Sherman's does, he having to move only about 7 miles.
>
> I shall pass to the front early to-morrow, and go to Raymond if I can from that place. I shall return on the road to a convenient point for headquarters in the vicinity of Fourteen-Mile Creek.
> U.S. GRANT.[10]

On May 12, with Sherman moving up at the tail end, Grant moved out with about 35,000 men, advancing up the eastern side of the Mississippi, and he would soon have 42,000. They moved in a northeasterly direction, heading for Fourteen Mile Creek, threatening both Vicksburg and Jackson. Grant had McPherson moving up the Big Black River, on the east bank, still heading in a northeasterly direction away from Warrenton on the Mississippi. Sherman would support McPherson's movement should they run into a significant Confederate force. Once reaching Fourteen Mile Creek, where it intersected the Big Black, McPherson would turn hard right and head straight at Jackson, the state capital, with Sherman protecting his flank. McClernand would then continue with his corps, having rested for a few days east of Port Gibson, and move up along the Big Black River. As he did so he would become the left wing of Grant's advance, with McPherson at the right wing as he moved on Jackson, and Sherman eventually settling in the middle, providing support to either. It was a strong movement that would be difficult for Pemberton to take on without the aid of reinforcements. But there were concerns. Grant's army moved with only 2 days' rations. This was taking a serious risk as he awaited his supply train. Though he was counting on foraging, it would not be a feast for all regiments.[11]

On the 14th Pemberton wired Confederate General Johnston, who was now in Jackson. He arrived on the 13th after an arduous three-day train ride to find only 6,000 men defending the capital. Facing 25,000 advancing Federals, he had no choice but to withdraw. Pemberton told Johnston that he was preparing to leave Vicksburg with a force of 17,000 men. Pemberton wanted to try and "cut [the] enemy's communications" and force them to attack him. But he seemed unsure how to do that. He did know that McClernand's corps seemed to be headed for Edwards Station. That might have provided a good opportunity, but Pemberton was moving slowly and cautiously, and this would cost him. Johnston wanted Pemberton to join him in one united army, meet Grant on a field of their own choice, and defeat him. One thing was clear to Johnston, however, and that was the hopeless situation around Jackson. He would have to abandon the city.[12]

* * *

A Wisconsin soldier belonging to Sherman's Fifteenth Army Corps noted as he departed from Port Gibson that the Eleventh Wisconsin was staying put: "We then pressed on, passing on our way ... 11th and 23rd Wisconsin regiments." Grant instructed McClernand to turn towards Bolton Station. This placed him away from Jackson; instead of being in the advance, he was now in the rear. Meanwhile, McPherson and Sherman advanced on Jackson. But he soon realized that once Jackson fell, he would be closest to Vicksburg and once again at the advance of the attack. As McPherson neared Raymond on May 12, his advanced guard made contact with an enemy force of unknown strength. Thinking perhaps Pemberton had marched from Vicksburg to give battle, McPherson readied for the attack. Instead of Pemberton, however, the Union army ran into a single brigade of about 4,000 men led by Brigadier General John Gregg. After a short engagement, McPherson's men entered Raymond around 5 o'clock and stopped for the night, camping in and around the town.[13]

The next day, McPherson reached the rail line in Clinton that ran from Vicksburg to Jackson. They were now only nine miles from the capital. They tore up as much of the railroad around Clinton as they could while waiting for Sherman to catch up to help them take Jackson. A steady hard rain on the morning of the 14th slowed, but did not stop, McPherson's movement as his corps crept up to Jackson, due east of Clinton. The roads were slippery and then miry, a combination that slowed their movement considerably. McClernand's corps reached Raymond and headed northwest towards Bolton Depot, eight miles west of Clinton along the same railroad. Slogging along, they reached the outskirts of Jackson before noon.

With a break in the weather an attack was ordered. There was only a small garrison left behind, including a detachment of artillery. There was a short fight that did not amount to much, and within a couple hours they were inside the capital. The men in blue were jubilant as they entered the city. "Got to Jackson today about noon & camped in a beautiful grove in the suburbs of the city. The advance had another fight here yesterday. Dont know how many lost on either side," wrote a soldier with the Fourth Iowa cavalry, which was also moving up with Sherman's corps. "This is one of the most beautiful cities I have seen in the South."[14]

Unfortunately, not every soldier appreciated the beauty of the city. Excitement grew into outright pillaging and, in some cases, despicable acts, until officers got control of their men; some officers were unfortunately the instigators. Grant and Sherman allowed some latitude for their armies to forage, but the scene in Jackson that afternoon, by some accounts, crossed the line. But Grant had not come to Jackson to protect the people there, though he did have an obligation to restrain his men as much as possible. He was there to bring an enemy to its knees. He ordered that all "foundries, machine shops, warehouses, factories, arsenals, and public stores" be confiscated and burned to the ground. The nature of the war had indeed changed.[15]

"We were sent to a place seven miles from Jackson, where we camped the night that Gen. Grant occupied the capital," Otis* of the Eleventh Wisconsin wrote home to a local newspaper. The next day they were ordered to move towards Edwards Station, where a large enemy force was reportedly gathering.[16]

* * *

A bit of luck helped ease Grant's concerns about what Pemberton was doing; little did he know that it wasn't much of anything. A spy delivered some interesting news to McPherson and Grant. "[I] learned that General Johnston," wrote Grant later in his official report, "had ordered Pemberton preremptorily to march out from the direction of Vicksburg and attack our rear." To do this, Pemberton would have to swing southeast to cut the line near Clinton. The message indicated that Pemberton would be moving with his army, as many as 25,000 men by some reports. Grant wasted no time turning west in the hope of hitting Pemberton before he could unite with Johnston's troops near Clinton, if that was indeed the plan. Leaving Sherman and his men in Jackson to finish neutralizing the city, the rest of Grant's army marched quickly, hoping to hit the Confederates at the most opportune time.[17]

Johnston wanted Pemberton to come and meet him, allowing the two armies to unite to take Grant on with a force large enough to stop him. But by the time Pemberton finally left Vicksburg to do just that, Johnston had inexplicably changed his mind and was not on his way to Clinton. He sent a message to Pemberton, but it would arrive too late. Two armies totaling over 40,000 men were converging, with only one aware that the other was out there. On the 15th, part of McClernand's corps reached a point near Bolton Station and camped for the night. By now he had reports of enemy movement ahead of him, but could not completely ascertain what was happening. In the advance was A.P. Hovey's Twelfth Division, with McGinnis commanding First Brigade and Slack leading Second Brigade, both of which had fought at Port Gibson.[18]

Three roads led into Edwards Station from Bolton. McClernand's army advanced on the morning of the 16th using all three roads: one at the top (extreme north), one in the middle, and one below, south of the others. Hovey's division moved along the north road (called the "Clinton/Vicksburg Road" in official reports, but also known as the Jackson Road), Oster-

---

*"Otis" appears to be a pseudonym, because the article does not list a last name.

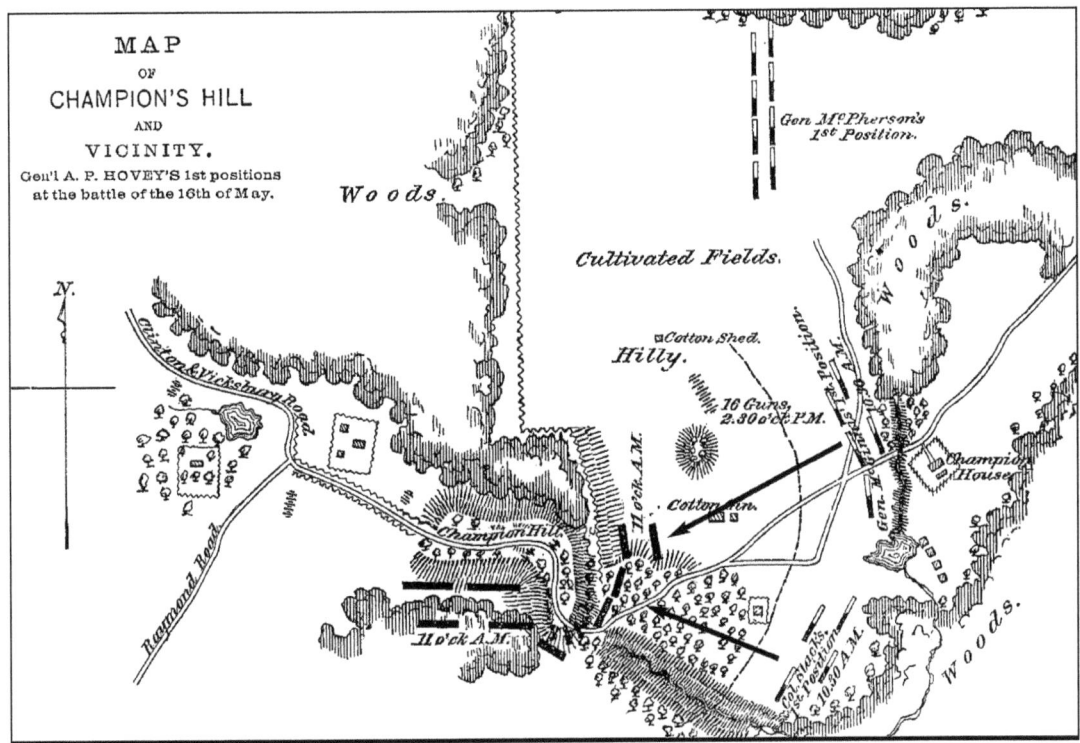

The Battle of Champion Hill was named for the owners of a nearby plantation (Library of Congress).

haus and Carr took the middle road, and on the south road was Smith's division. Hovey's division was at the lead, forming the point of their advance. According to Osterhaus, Hovey's advance was a mile above him, while Smith was "at least" four miles away in the center. Coming up fast behind Hovey, on the north road, was part of McPherson's corps. All three roads ran near Champion Hill, converging before reaching Edwards Station.[19]

McGinnis' brigade was deployed as skirmishers at the very advance of Hovey's column. That morning Hovey sent a squad of cavalry on a reconnaissance in their front. Around 10 o'clock in the morning they arrived at Champion Hill, where they discovered an enemy force of undetermined strength positioned on the crest of the hill, commanding the area for miles around.[20]

Pemberton had been warned of an advancing Union army. He quickly placed Major General Carter L. Stevenson's division on Champion Hill with excellent cover, in view of anything coming up the Clinton/Vicksburg Road directly from Bolton, the northernmost road Hovey traveled. South of there, and still on high ground along a ridge, Pemberton placed Bowen (from Port Gibson) and Major General William W. Loring's divisions. They were perfectly placed to catch Osterhaus and Smith as they came up the roads. Pemberton had lucked into a strong defensive position.[21]

Champion Hill rose as high as 100 feet. Surrounding it were timbered and tangled ravines, gullies, and dense woods, making it a nasty place for a battle. But before attempting to scale the ridges and rising hill that faced them, Hovey's advanced guard had to first cross a large field completely exposed to Rebel cannons perched high on the hill. As shots rang out in the distance, Hovey was off toward the front, riding as fast as he could.[22]

McGinnis ordered skirmishers to advance while he organized his line of battle. Hovey arrived and ordered him to advance his line in an effort to "feel the enemy." By now his skirmishers were exchanging fire with the Rebel pickets in what he described as "sharp and rapid firing." McGinnis' line began its advance over the open field, but after 500 yards intense fire from Rebel cannons opened on them, throwing volley after volley of canister and grapeshot at them. "The men were ordered to lie down until we had time to inform ourselves more accurately in regard to the enemy's position and the nature of the ground over which we had to move," McGinnis wrote afterward.[23]

Hovey also ordered Colonel Slack's brigade, positioned on the left side of the road and opposite the field where McGinnis advanced, to move out. An entanglement of underbrush and vines and the ravines impeded their advance, but they pushed on and reached the crest of the hill, where they were greeted by heavy enemy fire. "Then the battle began with great fury," wrote Slack, "the men loading and firing as they advanced, and unfalteringly receiving a most deadly fire from the enemy." Hoping to flush the Rebels from their cover on the hillside, Slack continued to push his men forward, determined to reach the enemy battery several hundred yards away. The battle raged on as Slack heroically advanced his brigade under harsh conditions. The trees and brush came alive as fire from both directions shattered and sometimes downed small trees. Men were dropping constantly, leaving "the ground ... literally covered with dead and wounded."[24]

While Hovey (and soon McPherson) engaged the enemy, McClernand followed his order from Grant, which was clear in his mind. He was to seek out the enemy, but without bringing on an engagement unless he felt he was ready for it. What neither of the generals anticipated were the delays in their communications in reaching the other. McClernand inquired to Grant around 9:45 A.M., "Shall I hold, or bring on an engagement?" Then he waited. He was not willing to start a fight that his commander was not ready for; this would surely bring on Grant's wrath. Grant's 10:15 A.M. order to McClernand to advance would not reach him for several hours. Neither Grant, Sherman, nor McPherson liked McClernand, and he knew this, and their communication as a result suffered. The terrain did not help the situation either, as delays were caused by the lack of sufficient roads, open roads and open terrain. Though he could hear the distant sounds of cannon fire, which should have alerted him that the battle was already started, McClernand could not be certain what was happening, and therefore he did nothing until ordered to do so. But then it was too late.[25]

Though the Eleventh Wisconsin could also hear firing in the distance and see the rising smoke drift away in the breeze, they knew not when or if they would engage the enemy. McClernand kept most of Carr's division back while he inspected the enemy line. The men tried uneasily to rest. Some cleaned their rifles, while others made a quick meal. Though their distance from the fighting might keep them out of it altogether, the men were still tense, knowing they could be called on at any moment. Samuel Kirkpatrick smoked his pipe and walked among his men, making small talk.[26]

* * *

Though taking murderous fire from the enemy, McGinnis knew he had to get his brigade moving again. The order was given and his men jumped to their feet and again advanced with "bayonets fixed, slowly, cautiously, and in excellent order." As they neared the base of the hill the Rebel battery opened fire, causing every man to hit the ground in fear. Dirt and brush were thrown into the air. Sometimes direct hits sent men and body parts flying. Still determined to move up the hill, the brigade waited until the battery reloaded and then jumped once more to their feet and charged up the hill. McGinnis later described the advance:

> The whole line moved forward as one man, and so suddenly and apparently so unexpected to the Rebels was the movement, that, after a desperate conflict of five minutes, in which bayonets and

butts of muskets were freely used, the battery of four guns was in our possession, and a whole brigade in support was fleeing before us, and a large number of them taken prisoners.

Having captured the Rebel battery and pushed the Rebel line back several hundred yards, for a brief moment they thought the battle was won. But men all along Hovey's line were hotly engaged with the enemy. Hovey was aggressive and continued to press his commanders to advance, sustaining heavy casualties.[27]

Realizing his left flank was being pushed back, Pemberton tried to shift men facing McClernand's force in the south (his center and right flank) to the north to reinforce his men there. He did so just as his flank faltered in the face of Hovey's advancing lines. Both McGinnis and Slack, who only minutes before took the Rebel cannons in their front, were counterattacked by Confederate reinforcements and pushed back down the hill several hundred yards, yielding their captured guns. Hovey sent requests to Grant and McPherson for reinforcements. General Grant and McPherson arrived to find Hovey hanging on by a thread.[28]

Moving into position to support Hovey's right flank was Major General John A. Logan's division. Logan was in a perfect position to roll up Pemberton's exposed left flank. But by the time Logan considered doing just that, a messenger arrived from Grant ordering him to come back around and reinforce Hovey. Meanwhile, Pemberton was having trouble getting Loring, on the right flank, to move as ordered and come to the aid of his left flank. For some time Confederate and Union counterattacks moved up and down the hill, fighting at times in hand-to-hand combat. The wounded and dying were often left out in the open, exposed to enemy gunfire. "At this time my whole division, including reserves," wrote Hovey in his official report, "had for more than one hour been actively engaged, and my only hope of support was from other commands."[29]

McGinnis' men were exhausted, having advanced and retreated, sometimes on the run, for over an hour. They were also badly cut up. "Seeing that we were largely outnumbered, having every confidence in the valor of the First Brigade, and yet fearing they would be overwhelmed," wrote McGinnis, "I started messengers to General Hovey, informing him of the state of affairs and asking for assistance." Hovey decided he had only two options: attack up the hill yet again in hopes of routing the enemy for good, or pull back and lick his wounds.[30]

Further south Slack's brigade was faring no better, having also been forced back down the hill. They had charged and taken ground, only to be repelled. Slack was contemplating retiring from the field when a battery not far in the distance, near McGinnis' position, opened up on the Confederates. When the fighting was over Slack would describe the action as "unequal, terrible, and the most sanguinary conflict, which, in point of terrific fierceness and stubborn persistency, finds but few parallels in the history of civilized warfare."[31]

When Hovey ordered another advance, McGinnis wondered if his men were physically able to comply. They had just pulled back in the face of another furious Rebel counterattack and were about to leave their captured enemy guns behind when reinforcements arrived. McGinnis vividly recalled the dire situation:

> Having driven the enemy before us, and fought over the same ground three different times, after having been engaged in a continual conflict for nearly three hours, our ammunition being nearly exhausted, many of the men being entirely out, having fired 80 rounds, and relying upon what they could get from the boxes of the dead and wounded, and being overwhelmed by numbers, the First Brigade began to fall back, not in disorder and confusion, but in good order, step by step, contesting every inch of ground. As we neared the ground upon which the batteries had been captured, and from which the enemy had been driven in the morning, just as it appeared to every one that the guns would again fall into the hands of the Rebels, we were greeted by the shouts of the long promised re-enforcements.[32]

With the support of newly placed artillery from Brigadier General Marcellus Crocker's division, Hovey ordered another attack. They advanced in force and the equally exhausted Rebels gave way, falling further and further back until they were out of range. A soldier in Logan's division described that action: "We arrived at the center of the line in the hottest of the fire, and had orders to immediately fix bayonets and to charge." Logan found the Rebels giving ground all along the line: "Such a yell you never heard in your life as our boys gave when they went at them ... right at the thickest of them, breaking their center and ... putting the whole [enemy] line to a hasty retreat. We lost inside of ten minutes, ten killed and 28 wounded...." As Logan's men swept up the hill, McGinnis' men regrouped and joined in the charge that routed the Rebels from the hill.[33]

Though victorious, Hovey's division was shattered, having left one-third of its men lying dead or wounded on Champion Hill. It took well into the next day to recover the wounded and bury the dead. Some wounded spent the night alone, without water, before they were found. Grant later commented on the bravery of Hovey and his men, calling them "good troops."[34]

The sun sank lower in the blood red sky and the men of the Eleventh Wisconsin were probably convinced they had avoided the battle, when the order was given for them to advance. Grant was more than frustrated with McClernand when he ordered him to pursue the retreating Pemberton. McClernand's inaction must have dumbfounded General Carr of the Thirteenth Division, as he moved out at dusk at the advance of the pursuit. Carr was a veteran of Pea Ridge and his men were battle tested and proven. To hold back and not engage the enemy must have bordered on cowardice in his mind. They moved out at the double quick, rounding up Rebel stragglers and sending them to the rear as they pushed on. They reached Edwards at 8 o'clock and rescued from fire several train carloads of ammunition and provisions that the retreating Confederates could not take with them. Thus ended the battle at Champion Hill, one of the most intense fights ever fought, and some of the bloodiest hours of fighting in the west during the Civil War.[35]

The victory was complete, and for Pemberton the defeat was staggering. Within a few hours he lost 3,800 men and 27 guns, and was now in a full retreat that would not stop until Vicksburg.

CHAPTER EIGHT

Vicksburg — Through the Mouth of Hell

Colonel Harris was no longer in command of Second Brigade due to illness, but he was back in command of the Eleventh Wisconsin. Though still suffering from dysentery, he wanted to be with his men as they pushed on to Vicksburg. Colonel Stone, commanding Second Brigade up to Champion Hill, was also suffering from dysentery and severely weakened. Following Harris' example before the midnight battle outside of Port Gibson, Stone removed himself from command of the brigade.[1]

Pemberton retreated to the Big Black River, a point only twelve miles from the gates of Vicksburg. It was here, he knew, that he would have to make a stand or retreat into the city and face a siege, the worst prospect. But he chose the field well again. The west bank of the river was a bluff that allowed for perfect firing position. A few hundred yards east of the river the Confederates dug in around the open end of a horseshoe-shaped area, with the river at their back and fields in their front. Federal troops would exit the woods and face a field several hundred yards in width, completely covered by artillery positioned on the bluffs across the river. It would be a killing field. The northern section was particularly well defended, with a four-foot-deep swampy area that would have to be crossed to get at the rifle pits. The Rebels also built parapets with bales of cotton along their nearly mile-long entrenchment. Because of the horseshoe-shaped path of the river, it would be virtually impossible for the Federal army to flank them. Any assault would have to be right at them and should prove to be a suicide mission. Reviewing the defenses, Pemberton felt he could stall Grant's advance, in the hopes that Loring's division could rejoin him or perhaps Johnston would come to his aid.[2]

Sherman's corps left early in the morning from Jackson so as to arrive at a point north of both McClernand and McPherson, at Bridgeport on the Big Black River. Once there, Sherman's army would be eleven miles above them where he was in a perfect position to flank the enemy. Grant wanted McClernand to push on to the Big Black River and wait for the rest of the army to come up. Once massed, Sherman's corps could swing the anvil down from the south and crush Pemberton, if he indeed was going to make a final stand at the river as reported.[3]

South of Sherman was McClernand's corps, led by Carr's brigade in the advance, followed by McPherson, moving along the Vicksburg/Clinton railroad to where it bridged the Big Black River. McClernand was pushing his men hard, most likely embarrassed by his lack of action the day before at Champion Hill. With Carr's division above him on the north side of the railroad and Osterhaus below him on the south side, McClernand was prepared to hit the enemy on two fronts simultaneously. By the time McClernand reached the Big Black and deployed his men, Grant arrived on the scene and discovered that the advantage of terrain, once again, benefited Pemberton. He knew a frontal attack would be costly. With Sherman crossing north of them at Bridgeport, Grant decided to stay the course and "hold" the enemy where he was, and wait for Sherman's movement. Grant wanted to smash Pemberton's army and obliterate him before he reached Vicksburg.[4]

Early that morning as the leading elements of McClernand's corps reached the Big Black River, First Lieutenant Hiram J. Lewis of Company K (Eleventh Wisconsin) noted that "It was a beautiful Sunday morning," but unfortunately he knew it would be wasted, as "an army is no respector of days and the work of death soon began."[5]

* * *

He stood six feet three inches tall and weighed as much as two average-sized men put together. He was a giant, and by all accounts a "stout" man, so large his sword belt did not fit him. Brigadier General Michael K. Lawler was truly one of the most colorful and intriguing characters of the Civil War. He now commanded General Carr's Second Brigade, replacing Colonel Stone. Secretary of War Charles Dana once said of Lawler, "He is as brave as a lion, and has as much brains." For good or bad, the Eleventh Wisconsin Volunteer Regiment was now under Lawler's command. A gruff Irishman with undeniable wit and charm, he was known for his simple adage, "If you see a head, hit it." This probably summed up his entire understanding of military strategy. He was a man of fearless action, and little else.[6]

General Carr ordered Lawler's brigade to move in on the extreme right, guarding the right flank of his division. Lawler sent Colonel Harris and the Eleventh Wisconsin regiment ahead through thick woods. Harris deployed companies A and F as skirmishers. Suddenly cannon shots whistled overhead. The men momentarily ducked, but then went about their business. The rest of the brigade — the Twenty-first, Twenty-second, and Twenty-third Iowa regiments— moved out and followed the Eleventh Wisconsin as they made their way to a clearing just north of the opposing Rebel rifle pits, at the far end of a wide field. As Lawler reached the edge of the wooded area, on the right-most flank of Carr's division, he found himself facing a deep field bordered by a swampy lowland, nestled in front of an entrenched enemy line. Although hunkered down behind makeshift cotton bales and logs, there were still plenty of heads to hit, with enemy lines continuing a mile or so to his left and out of sight. To his right was the river, which could not be waded.[7]

By late afternoon all four regiments were strung out along the tree line, with skirmishers posted at the edge of the clearing. Sharpshooters engaged their butternut counterparts with sporadic fire but few results. As the afternoon progressed, the sun and humidity-choked air made the

Brigadier General Michael K. Lawler (Special Collections Research Center, Morris Library, Southern Illinois University Carbondale).

men uncomfortable. At about 3 o'clock Lawler walked his line and conferred with his subordinates, impatiently waiting on what he hoped would be an order to attack the enemy. The men sweated profusely in the hot, sticky air, dodging enemy gunfire and occasionally returning it in kind.

Lawler peeled off his sweat-drenched jacket and flung it down in frustration. He stood for a moment in his untucked checkered shirt and double-seated cavalryman's breeches. His iron scabbard and sword were flung over his shoulder and "dangling from his side," and as he took a few steps the spurs on his heels jingled. He unbuttoned his collar and peered across the field at the Rebel line, seemingly taunting him to come at them.[8]

His line continued to return fire sporadically, but it served only to waste ammunition. Taunts of "You missed me, Billy Yank!" and "I'll get you, Johnny Reb!" rang across the field. They were just wasting time. Lawler's frustration continued to grow. But at last a scout informed him that a floodplain depression in the field might allow his men to approach the enemy with some cover. With this new piece of information, and sensing Lawler's frustration, Colonel Kinsman of the Twenty-third Iowa approached and proposed that his regiment fix bayonets and charge the enemy. Lawler readily agreed, but instead of one regiment, he decided to send his whole brigade. He was tired of waiting around.[9]

A small battery of guns from the First Wisconsin deployed at the edge of another clearing would provide some covering fire for the assault. They also had additional support from two regiments of Indiana troops. Realizing that he needed some kind of diversion to draw attention away from his real point of attack, Lawler ordered two companies of Hoosiers to advance as skirmishers in hopes of distracting the Rebels.[10]

Colonel Harris moved down his line, telling his "brave lads" to cast off their knapsacks and blankets, and to "fix bayonets" in preparation for the charge. Sergeant Samuel Kirkpatrick passed the order along to his Farmers Guards as word spread that a "bloody battle was anticipated." Hearing that they were to charge, Henry Twining and the rest of Company C quickly removed their knapsacks and fastened their bayonets. Drenched in sweat, they removed their wool jackets in order to lighten their load. Brothers Oliver and Jesse Mather stood side by side, as usual, looking nervously across the field and to the swamp below. A line of rifle pits with hundreds—thousands—of Rebel soldiers just itching to get a shot at them was all they could see. Stray bullets continued to whiz by as Lawler's troops formed their battle line.[11]

For the most part, it would be a surprise attack. Most of Lawler's men would emerge from the woods and rush across the wide field, taking fire most of the way. Each regiment was staggered along the tree line, the farther down the greater the distance to travel. For the Eleventh Wisconsin, second from the end, their initial starting point was 500 yards away. Luckily they would get to move closer (several hundred yards) before charging. It was discovered that there was a gap between two adjacent rifle pits. This presented an opportunity if they acted swiftly. Using the floodplain, they would charge obliquely across the field, taking fire from two sides (right and front) in an attempt to enter the end of the rifle pit below the swamp. There the men would have to wade through the muddy swamp, with rifles raised to their shoulders, then climb the small embankment and attack the rifle pits, taking direct fire from the enemy all the while.[12]

Lawler inspected his men, giving nods of approval. Just a few days before, during the battle at Champion Hill, the general was brusque when a stray bullet caused one young soldier next to him to duck. "Don't dodge!" he said. "Don't you know when you hear the bullets they have already passed!" Lawler unsheathed his sword, holding it by his side, nostrils flaring as he took several deep breaths. About this time, Samuel Kirkpatrick noticed a rider galloping up to his position. Captain Whittlesey had been acting as division quartermaster

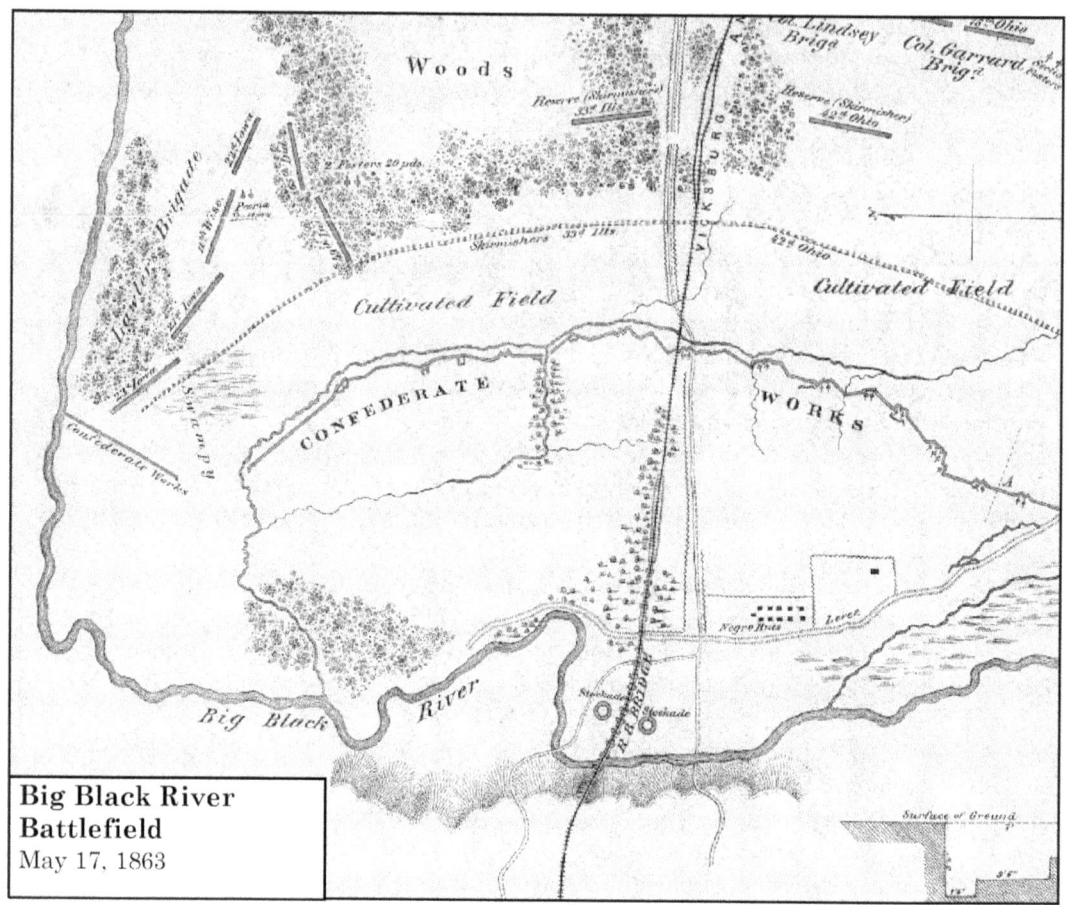

Lawler's Brigade (top left) and the Eleventh Wisconsin regiment (Library of Congress).

when he heard the Eleventh Wisconsin was once again on the front line. He found a horse and dashed off in hopes of making it in time. "Here he came in a lope on his horse," said Samuel, "and took his place in front of our Co. and said 'Come on boys, follow me.'" Just then the artillery opened up with spirited fire to aid their advance.[13]

The companies that were to lead the charge were formed "with bayonets fixed" and the order was given to "charge!" Colonel Kinsman and his fierce regiment of Hawkeyes led the way, bursting out of the woods yelling and screaming as they charged across the field in what one reporter who witnessed the event later called "the most perilous and ludicrous" act he had ever witnessed.[14]

* * *

About this time, General Grant received an urgent message via courier that he mistook as being from Halleck. This confused communication seemed to ask that he withdraw and return to Grand Gulf to support General Nathaniel Banks' movement south of him.* He handed the message back with a quizzical grimace, when in the distance he heard cheering and the sounds of cannon fire coming from Lawler's position, followed by the crackling of

---

**The messenger (General William Dwight) was from General Banks, not Halleck.*

gunfire. Something was happening. "See that charge!" Grant told the courier, "I think it is too late to abandon this campaign." And with that he galloped off toward the fighting.[15]

All along the line, dumfounded Federal troops watched as Lawler's crazed hoard of bluecoats emerged from the woods and dashed across the field to their certain destruction. Had an order been given to charge? What were they doing? Men looked around nervously, wondering if they too should charge. Not far down the line, the colonel of the Ninety-ninth Illinois regiment perched in the hot sun along his tree line, sweating it out in frustration, just as Lawler had. But he stood and cheered in delirious admiration as the wave of blue descended from the woods. Then, turning to his men with sword drawn, he shouted, "Boys, it's getting too damned hot here. Let's go for the cussed Rebels!" Regiments here and there began to emerge from the woods, charging straight at the Confederates. This was going to be a slaughter.[16]

Back on the battlefield was Lawler, swinging his cavalryman's broadsword and "yelling mightily." The Rebel rifle pits came alive in one simultaneous cloud of bursting fire. Rifle balls sliced up Kinsman's regiment in short order, with Kinsman himself falling. Lawler was behind him and saw the colonel go down: "Struggling to his feet, he staggered a few paces to the front, cheered forward his men, and fell again." Numerous shots went clean through, mortally wounding him. "A murderous fire of shot and shell" slowed the advance, but did not stop it as "these brave men dashed on."[17]

Though reports suggest there was a floodplain that provided cover and allowed Lawler to move up close to the Confederate position, several eye witness reports, like this one from First Lieutenant Hiram J. Lewis, suggest otherwise:

> There was an open field of 3/5 of a mile to pass over offering nothing to shield us from the bullets of the enemy. Nothing could be seen of the rebels but their hands as they raised to shoot.... It was the greatest foot race I ever witnessed.[18]

Having crossed the wide field, leaving more than a hundred dead or wounded, the men plunged into the swamp. A second group stopped at its edge and, before entering, fired a volley into the Confederate line, providing momentary cover for those wading across.

With rifles above their heads, the first wave of men took direct shots, likely killing many instantly. Still they pressed on. But by now something strange was happening. The intensity of the fire seemed to diminish. Writing later, the Eleventh Wisconsin regimental historian noted that the attack was indeed so "sudden and unlooked-for that the Rebel fire was not given with such destruction" as they had expected. What they, and Lawler, did not realize was that Pemberton's army was not only hopelessly outnumbered, but demoralized. When the charge was made, and the mile-long wave of blue emerged from the woods, many Rebels decided they had seen enough. The Missouri and Arkansas troops facing Lawler managed only one or two hasty volleys before fleeing. "Our troops were completely surprised," said a soldier with the Twenty-first Arkansas. "[They] were really surrounded before they knew it."[19]

But it was the frustration and aggressiveness of Lawler that exposed the Confederates this day. As they rushed up to the rifle pits a short but fierce fight took place, hand-to-hand, with many men dying by the bayonet. At this point the Rebels were falling back in great numbers, and in some places in a full retreat. Lawler grabbed Colonel Harris and ordered the Eleventh Wisconsin to hurry across another field of 200 yards to the Big Black River bridge and cut off their escape. "The movement was successful," Lawler later wrote. With his sword in the air, Harris led his men across the field, taking more shots from Confederate soldiers near the bridge, which was on fire. Within a couple of minutes they reached the railroad tracks and discovered a swarm of Confederates retreating towards them, some running for their lives. "A score of extemporized white flags rose along the lines and the works were yielded without further resistance," noted McMyler, the regimental historian. The Eleventh Wisconsin cut off General Green's First Missouri infantry, and reported that they "surrendered to a man," which was an exaggeration. Private Roswell Clark of Company F had the honor of capturing their flag, which the regiment sent home a few months later and presented to the governor.[20]

Grant arrived just in time to watch Lawler and his crazy brigade of Iowa and Wisconsin pioneers "flounder" across the field. The general was so moved by the bravery he saw that he later complimented Lawler, saying, "When it comes to just plain hard fighting I would rather trust old Mike Lawler than any of them." Lawler's brigade rounded up 1,700 prisoners, "chiefly collected by the Eleventh Wisconsin," 18 guns, and four stands of enemy colors, of which the Eleventh Wisconsin collected one. "It is, perhaps, worthy of remark," noted Lawler in his official report, "that more men were captured by my brigade than I had men in the charge." Treading a fine line between bravery and stupidity, Lawler's bold, courageous, and perhaps reckless charge should have gone down in the annals of the Civil War as one of the more gutsy and irrational acts of the war. Did Lawler get lucky or was it a brilliant tactical move? Had the Confederate troops facing him that day had any fight left in them, the outcome might have been far different.[21]

Unfortunately for the Eleventh Wisconsin, this was not their last charge of the war, nor was it their last under General Lawler's command.

* * *

Standing solemnly on the other side of the river, Pemberton was devastated as his whole line collapsed and fell back. Men frantically tried to swim the river (some drowning) while others ran over the bridge as it burned and crumbled. He had lost two battles in two days and half of the army he had with him in the field. Not long after the battle Pemberton received a note from Johnston: "If, therefore, you are invested in Vicksburg you must ultimately surrender. Under such circumstances, instead of losing both troops and place, we must, if possible, save the troops. If it is not too late, evacuate Vicksburg and its dependences and march to the northeast" to join with Johnston's army.[22]

Pemberton was now isolated and cut off from Johnston, who showed no signs of coming to his aid. Conflicted by two orders, one from Confederate president Davis that he hold Vicksburg at all costs, and now Johnston (who was his superior) telling him to evacuate, Pemberton turned his horse around and left the Big Black River, demoralized. Riding with Pemberton as he retreated to Vicksburg was a Confederate officer. They had ridden some time when Pemberton turned to him and said, "Just thirty years ago I began my military career by receiving my appointment to a cadetship at the U.S. Military Academy; and today — the same date — that career is ended in disaster and disgrace." The officer tried to encourage Pemberton, saying that Johnston would come to their aid once the promised reinforcements from the east arrived. But Pemberton was inconsolable as he galloped out of sight.[23]

Standing over the rifle pits that only moments ago were occupied by the enemy, Lawler turned to face the field they had just crossed, which was littered with several hundred of his men, dead, dying, and wounded. The Eleventh Wisconsin suffered 35 casualties, including a captain, Daniel E. Hough of Company A. The smoke and setting sun lent a reddish glow to the horizon. Lawler praised the men standing near him whose "courage" and "steadiness" were "due the glory of the brilliant and decisive victory of Big Black Bridge."[24]

For the rest of the day they collected discarded weapons and ammunition. Some regiment members went immediately back to the field to see to the wounded and help bury the dead. Kinsman's Twenty-third Iowa regiment suffered greatly, losing 101 men. They were so dismantled that they were sent back with the prisoners by order of General Grant. Engineers were already at work on the bridge by the evening of the 17th, and by the next morning the army was once again on the move, heading west towards Vicksburg. They camped another night before McClernand's corps moved towards the fortress city.[25]

"The following morning we started for V [Vicksburg]," wrote Hiram J. Lewis of Company K, "and took up our position opposite the rebel works at 2 pm." The march was toilsome and hot: "We suffered greatly." They had enough water, but were running out of rations, and no supply line to replenish them. "We have now been on half rations for nearly a month and have worked, fought or been on the march most of the time night and day," yet he had not "heard a man murmur."[26]

But the supply situation had to be taken care of and soon, and Grant knew it. What he didn't know was how lucky he was about to get. By now Sherman had reached Haines Bluff and the Yazoo River north of Vicksburg, and found it unoccupied. This was a minor miracle; Grant now had a passage north of the city from which to quickly bring supplies to his men, some who were nearly out of food. As Sherman worked his way down from Haines Bluff, McPherson and McClernand reached the outer defenses of the city on the 19th of May. In all, about 42,000 men were now investing the city and its 28,000 defenders (including the divisions manning the defenses). Pemberton was again in good spirits, convinced he could hold out until reinforcements arrived.[27]

* * *

On the 19th of May the Eleventh Wisconsin was camped southeast of Vicksburg when Sherman's corps launched an attack north of the city. The attack was supposed to involve both McPherson and McClernand's corps, but it was uncoordinated and poorly planned. Jesse and Oliver Mather could hear the muffled sounds of cannon fire and the crackling of rifles as they made dinner. If the men stood up and looked into the distance they could see the smoke drift with the wind north of them. All three of Grant's corps were squeezing the Rebel fortifications around the city, with Sherman in the north, McPherson in the center, and McClernand in the south. "We have them entirely surrounded, our army being entrenched on all the surrounding hills, from 200 to 1,000 yards from their line of forts and rifle pits, and our gunboats on the river," wrote a soldier with the Seventy-sixth Ohio regiment.[28]

Back home, reports from Vicksburg were appearing daily in the local newspapers. "The 11th [Wisconsin Regiment] is on the side of a hill five hundred yards from the Rebel works, and protected from their rifle balls by some earthworks thrown up on the crest of the hill," wrote one correspondent. Families all over the state anxiously awaited reports from the 12 regiments taking part in the siege of Vicksburg.[29]

Word spread that the assault on Vicksburg had ended badly on the 19th; some brigades were badly torn up, but Grant was undeterred. He believed Pemberton's army was defeated and, most important, psychologically beaten. Grant also believed the attack had failed because of poor preparation and planning, something he vowed would not happen again. However, Grant was not aware of the renewed confidence the Confederate army had experienced. Grant could no longer outmaneuver the Rebel army and defeat them in the field, and the idea of having their backs to the wall inspired many to fight to the last. But most likely, they now understood they had the advantage of being behind the heavily defended earthworks and fortresses of the city. Pemberton's army also seemed to think that Johnston would surely come to their aid.[30]

Pemberton was perhaps as surprised as anyone by the relative ease with which his men literally bounced Sherman's corps back from Vicksburg's walls during the May 19 assault. He sent a message back to Richmond reporting on May 19 to Jefferson Davis, "Our men have considerably recovered their morale." However confident he might have felt, he knew that it was only a matter of time: "Unless a large force is sent at once to relieve it, Vicksburg must before long fall."[31]

Vicksburg's outer defenses were strong. About a mile outside the city a "rude crescent" afforded the Confederates a "commanding" position for their network of "redoubts, redans, lunettes and field works, connecting them by rifle-pits so as to give a continuous line of defense" all the way around the half-circle, from north to south, ending at both ends on the Mississippi River. At the top of crests, slopes, and hills the semicircular defensive perimeter consisted of "irregular ... ridges on which they were situated." The defensive line was jagged and required troops to attack at sharp angles exposed to fire from more than one direction. Redoubts (forts) were strategically placed at distances "varying from 75 to 500 yards" apart and "connected by lines of simple trench or rifle-pit." In front of the rifle pits were steep ravines filled with tangled brush and abatis.* In short, the area in front of the fortifications was another well-constructed killing field. As the chief engineers of the Army of the Tennessee noted in their official report, Vicksburg owed "much of its strength to the difficult ground, obstructed by fallen trees in its front, which rendered rapidity of movement and ensemble in an assault impossible." When Grant ordered his attacks, each brigade, each regiment, would at times be operating by itself and exposed to a massive line of fire.[32]

As one historian noted, like a medieval siege the Federal army would need fifteen-foot, and at some places twenty-foot, high ladders to assault the Rebel line. Beyond the fortifications, the Army of the Tennessee could see occupied buildings and houses perched on the hill; they were eager to get at them.[33]

On the night of the 21st of May, Grant decided the time had come to attack again. This time all three corps would move in unison at precisely ten o'clock in the morning, after a naval bombardment by Admiral Porter. According to Shelby Foote, this was the first synchronized attack in modern warfare. That night Grant rode nearly his entire line, giving encouragement while personally inspecting the situation. His men were full of confidence and determination. As Grant returned to his headquarters that night, he felt certain of victory.[34]

* * *

In McClernand's front was the focus of his attack, Railroad Redoubt, known to the Rebels as Fort Beauregard. Sitting on half an acre, the earthwork rested on the Southern Mississippi Railroad track. Its walls were 20 feet high and surrounded by a ditch 15 feet wide and ten feet deep. Rifle pits ran along the high ground on either side, stretching out to the next fortification. In Sherman's front, like everywhere else, were abatis-filled gullies and hollows, but also several roads that could be used to avoid some of these hazards. His corps' primary objective was Stockade Redan and its surrounding area. McPherson's corps faced the ominous "Great Redoubt" along with a smaller earthwork, which together presented perhaps the toughest challenge. McPherson's men would use Jackson Road to get closer to the walls and assault them, before having to scale the gullies and ditches below — anything to get the men quickly to the earthworks while taking the least amount of fire.[35]

During the Vicksburg campaign, Oliver S. Robinson of Company H wrote home, "Mother, I send you a ballad of verses which I found in an old hymbook knowing you would prize it so much." To his father and brothers he wrote, "I send you my best wishes. But I have

---

*An obstacle made by laying felled trees on top of each other with branches, sometimes sharpened, facing the enemy.

forgotten to tell you I am just as hardy as a man can be." The soldiers wrote home as often as they could, reassuring their loved ones that they were well and in good spirits. "I sit down this fine day to let you know that I am still harty," wrote Samuel Kirkpatrick in April, "I wish I was there...."[36]

When word spread that there would be an assault on the fortifications, the men of the Eleventh Wisconsin were solemn as they moved under cover of darkness to their launching point for the attack. All along the Federal lines, last minute letters were written, with instructions given to comrades if they should fall in battle. Valuables such as "watches, rings, pictures" were given to the those who would not see action, with specific orders to send to loved ones if the soldier did not return. Others tried to comfort their friends who feared the bloody work to come. "Comrade W. came to me and with emotion confessed that he had a presentiment that he would be killed," wrote a soldier in the Thirty-third Illinois, "and requested me to take charge of his few effects and forward them.... I tried to cheer him up...." Luckily both men would make it through the upcoming day. Few slept much that night. They knew what they were facing and that a terrible fight was about to take place.[37]

"Shells from friend and foe were continually bursting over our heads," wrote Hiram J. Lewis, "musket balls falling thick and fast, making it lively but not pleasant."[38]

* * *

Two days before the attack, General Lawler (perhaps on orders from Grant) asked for volunteers to reconnoiter the defenses in his area. He wanted a few men to get as close to the Rebel works as possible. He asked for ten volunteers, but got only eight. One of them was Corporal James M. Sanford of Company B in the Eleventh Wisconsin regiment. "Our orders were to go up and find out how deep the ditch was," recalled James 47 years later. They were required to "bring back a piece of dirt" as evidence of their success. Surprisingly, said James, "Grant had promised that the man who did the most to help capture Vicksburg" would receive a "commission," and James badly wanted it.[39]

Under cover of darkness the eight men crawled out of their trenches and slithered their way through the ravine and small ditches leading up to the outer rim of the Rebel earthwork. Through the abatis they went, working their way to the fort as quietly as possible. "We crawled through the rebel picket line but could not get to the ditch," recalled James. There were dozens of Confederate soldiers working on it, and they feared capture. "We spent the whole night and had to return without accomplishing our end."

But James was not to be deterred. The next day he and his friend, Daniel Cook, set out by daylight to see if they could get close enough to the large ditch. It took them several hours of slow progress "creeping through the brush," but they managed to get close to the ditch. "While trying to discern the depth of the ditch, the rebels fired a full volley" on them. Daniel Cook took a direct hit while one shot grazed James' face, "spoiling my chin hairs ... so close as to draw blood." Somehow he managed to drag his friend back to the safety of their line. Daniel survived and was discharged from service because of his wounds. Though exhausted, James remained undeterred.

"I took Corporal Cook back to the hospital and then went and reported to General Lawler," he remembered. "He asked if there was any way I could find out the depth of that ditch?" This was important information, because if it were too deep to climb out of, the ditch would become a grave for all who entered. James told the general he would try again, but this time he wanted some covering fire. "I told him to have the men understand not to shoot me." This way, James thought, he would be able to "charge on the works," spot the ditch, and then sprint back. With the aid of some sharpshooters, James made it to the ditch, determined its depth, and then froze. Once at the ditch, he realized he had outrun his covering fire, and to get back would require all his remaining strength. "I made the run of my life," he said, and arrived unscathed back at the Union line.

He reported that the ditch was only three feet deep and the Rebels were still busy trying to deepen and widen it. Other parts of the ditch (it was miles long) were deeper, but at that particular location it was shallow. By this time James knew the safest route to the Rebel earthworks: "I knew the ground better than anyone else in the command." A series of banks and ravines could be used as cover to get up to the ditch, James reported to General Lawler. Seeing that James, this brave young corporal, was exhausted, Lawler offered him the comfort of his tent for a nap. James happily accepted, sleeping soundly until he was woken. "When I awoke, General Grant, after asking a few further questions as to the lay of the land, told me I had done my share and I could go to the rear." James had won his commission. But the assault on the fort began, and James dashed off for the front in search of his regiment. "Knowing the ground as I did, I was able to catch up."

James M. Sanford was hit during the attack. A cannon shot of grape* was fired in his direction, and "one of these grape-shot[s] struck me on the fourth rib on the right side and carried me over one hundred feet to the rear." It threw him into a ravine, where he was found during the night and taken away. He was carried to a hospital, "but really it was more of a dissecting ranch," he observed, "where they were sawing off arms and legs and throwing them into a hole." The doctor took one look at James, who must have been a bloody mess, and said, "Lay him out there on the ground. We can't do anything for him. He'll soon be out of his misery." James tried to speak, but his chest hurt too much and his emphatic response of "No!" was not heard.

The next day the same doctor walked by James, who was lying somewhere on the ground, and exclaimed, "Sanford, are you alive?" Indeed he was. "But I was so choked up with blood," said James, "that I could not speak." They placed him in a bed and had a nurse look after him, along with a Negro boy, who diligently kept flies off his chest and wounded abdomen. Sometime thereafter General Grant came to visit the wounded. He apparently inquired about James and the commission he had been nominated for. But the doctor, still thinking James would die, told the general not to bother. "There is no use recommending him. He cannot live." And with that, General Grant was gone.[40]

* * *

Those who did manage to doze off on the night of May 21 snapped awake during a tremendous volley of cannon fire. The fireworks came from barrowed 8- and 9-inch guns from Admiral Porter's fleet along with 13-inch mortars fired from six mortar boats anchored behind DeSoto Point. Cannon fire thundered overhead and into the city throughout the night. The soldiers hoped terrible damage was being done, thus making their work that much easier. But the intense barrage of the combined naval and artillery fire was more for show than anything. Mortar fire from the boats was limited in distance and woefully inaccurate. It has also been argued that Grant was utterly unprepared for a siege, let alone a long one, and did not have enough of the 13-inch mortars that would have aided his men as they encroached upon Confederate entrenchments. This led to the improvised creation of wooden mortars that were put in use and by most accounts worked effectively. But Grant hoped, at the very least, that this display of force would encourage his men and further demoralize the enemy.

---

*Similar to canister, grapeshot consisted of metal balls, but unlike canister that fired 76 balls, a round of grapeshot consisted of nine or so balls and they were usually not packed in cans.

Eight. Vicksburg— Through the Mouth of Hell

Siege of Vicksburg; Sketch by F.B. Schell, *Frank Leslie's Famous Leaders and Battle Scenes of the Civil War*, edited by Louis S. Moat (New York, 1896).

The impact the cannon fire had on the walls, rifle pits, and earthworks for the most part was minimal. The barrage was nearly continuous the entire night and morning. Then about 10 o'clock it suddenly stopped. Lieutenant Colonel Wood and captains Miller and Whittlesey readied their men.[41]

However, during the days leading up to the assault, McClernand's guns had done some damage knocking out Confederate batteries and possibly even accounting for some destruction to the outer wall of the Railroad Redoubt. When Federal rifled artillery was accurate, it could and did penetrate the inadequate fourteen-foot parapets constructed by the Confederates. During the upcoming assault, McClernand's forty-five guns would pound Rebel defenses unmercifully.[42]

Crouched in their trenches infantrymen nervously waited for the signal. Henry Twining, brothers Oliver and Jesse, Robert Sherrill, and all the rest would have agreed with Cornelius Du Bois of the Thirty-third Illinois who was not far down the trench from them when he wrote after the war, "As we looked across the valley in front and beheld the great fort and formidable earthworks, I, for one, must confess I could not see any prospect of success in the assault."[43] The order was given to fasten bayonets. Then Colonel Harris waved his sword in the air: "Forward, my brave lads, forward…. Charge!"[44]

They sprang from their trench, yelling as they charged over the uneven ground. Samuel Kirkpatrick and his Farmers Guards rushed on with a roar of fearful excitement. The men let out a wild roar as they lunged from the trench and hustled up and down the embankment. As they reached the crest of the hill a wall of "shot, shell, canister, grape and musketry" greeted them, "which thinned our ranks terribly." "Every man moved with firmness but with doubt," recalled Hiram J. Lewis of Company K. Some simply concentrated on getting over the hump and down into the ravine as fast as they could. Off and on they caught glimpses of the most hideous and wicked-looking fortifications they had ever seen. The sky was choked with a smoky haze, and a series of twisted and mangled obstructions lined ravines and ditches below. In the near distance, atop hills and breastworks, tattered Confederate flags flapped in the breeze. The men must have felt as though they were entering the depths of some strange hellish land.[45]

Attack of the Federal Forces on the Confederate works during the siege of Vicksburg, May 22, 1863; Sketch by F.B. Schell, *Frank Leslie's Famous Leaders and Battle Scenes of the Civil War*, edited by Louis S. Moat (New York, 1896).

Standing on the Confederate line atop one of the forts at that very moment was Brigadier General Stephen D. Lee. He was enjoying the sudden quiet when:

> As if by magic every gun and rifle stopped firing. The silence was almost appalling. Suddenly there seemed to spring almost from the bowels of the earth dense masses of Federal troops, in numerous columns of attack, and with loud cheers and huzzahs, they rushed forward at a run with bayonets fixed, not firing a shot, headed for every salient along the Confederate lines.[46]

For just the briefest of moments Rebel soldiers in rifle pits and atop the walls of their fortifications stood in awe as the earth opened up and released its blue demons upon them. The Texas and Alabama troops facing Carr's brigade (including the Eleventh Wisconsin) knew they were in for the fight of their lives.[47]

Charging alongside them was Colonel Stone's Twenty-second Iowa regiment, who were given the task of assaulting Fort Beauregard head-on while the Eleventh Wisconsin attacked the rifle pits on their left. The Twenty-first Iowa regiment followed closely behind, supporting Stone, with the Ninety-seventh Illinois supporting the Eleventh. As Stone and Harris' men reached the crest of the hill, just in front of the deep ravine, Rebel rifle pits on the opposite side welcomed them with "a terrible fire from … [the] front and on both flanks," sweeping away rows of men with "fearful execution." But the Union men did not stop to shoot or attempt to shoot while on the run, for it would not matter against a well-entrenched enemy occupying high ground. This was a mad dash to, hopefully, a safe place from which to fire.[48]

Major Salue G. Van Anda of the Twenty-first Iowa watched in horror as "officers and men fell on every side." The men could not run all the way across the 100 yards separating them and the Rebel works. There were too many obstacles to overcome while taking fire. "Down into the abatis of felled timber and brush we went," wrote one soldier from Illinois. "Still up the hill we pressed, through the brambles and brush, over the dead and dying...." The descent took perhaps as long as a half an hour until what remained of the men were on the other side. Once there, the Iowa troops attempted to storm the Railroad Redoubt by crawling up its slope, tying desperately to get a foothold. The Eleventh Wisconsin, along with their Illinois supporters, dashed to the left of the redoubt, charging the rifle pits as a hail of gunfire poured down on them.[49]

Once at the outer rim of the fort, the Iowa regiment charged the Rebel rifle pit and, in hand-to-hand fighting, overpowered the Texas soldiers. Now the Iowa troops had to scale earthwork walls 20 feet high to get inside Railroad Redoubt and assault it. Sergeant Joseph Griffith noticed that artillery fire had punctured the redoubt, and that they might be able to get in that way. Taking 12 men with him, he managed to climb to the hole and get inside the fort. A short firefight was followed by intense hand-to-hand combat, and soon the Stars and Stripes was planted atop the fort, after Griffith and his men chased off the remaining sharpshooters.[50]

Action intensified all around the redoubt into a "tornado of iron on our left, a hurricane of shot on our right. We passed through the mouth of hell. Every third man fell, either killed or wounded," a soldier from the Twenty-first Iowa recalled. After half an hour of fighting, the Eleventh Wisconsin finally reached the other side of the ravine and the hill beyond. Ascending the hillside they continued to take fire nonstop, but "up, up [they] struggled, over logs, into ditches, clinging here to a bush to keep from falling backwards, and there to a thorny bramble." Things were not going well for the Eleventh Wisconsin and Ninety-seventh Illinois.[51]

* * *

Not long into the assault Grant and Sherman realized it was failing badly. For nearly two hours reports came back that all along McPherson and Sherman's line their assault was repulsed. Grant was over a mile from McClernand's position and did not know the situation there, but feared it was more of the same. Here and there individual brigades managed to cut their way into a fort or a section of the rifle pits, only to be expelled at a bloody toll. As Grant surveyed the situation, all he could see were bluecoats gathered in ditches and huddled in ravines, desperately trying to find cover and, in some instances, digging their own foxholes with bayonets, shovels, and, sometimes, fingernails. The Confederates had no shortage of targets and they lit the fuses of their 12-inch shells and rolled them into the ditches and gullies below, attempting to blow up groups of Union soldiers. Just as Grant was about to order a withdrawal, a message came in from McClernand stating that he had "part possession of two forts, and the stars and stripes are floating over them." He wanted reinforcements to exploit his advantage and if the other corps could make "a vigorous push ... all along the line," he might be able to make a breakthrough. Though Grant was skeptical, he decided to continue the assault.[52]

McClernand did indeed have a temporary hold on the Railroad Redoubt and another smaller fort, but it was tenuous at best. Griffith, though planting the flag atop the fort, could not hold it as the Rebels furiously counterattacked his dwindling company of men. Realizing it was hopeless, he and the few others who were still alive abandoned the fort and returned to the rifle pit below the fort to rejoin their comrades. But the flag fluttered above the redoubt for another hour or so before the Confederates removed it. Flags from the Seventy-seventh and 130th Illinois, as well as the Forty-eighth Ohio, would also go up for a time.[53]

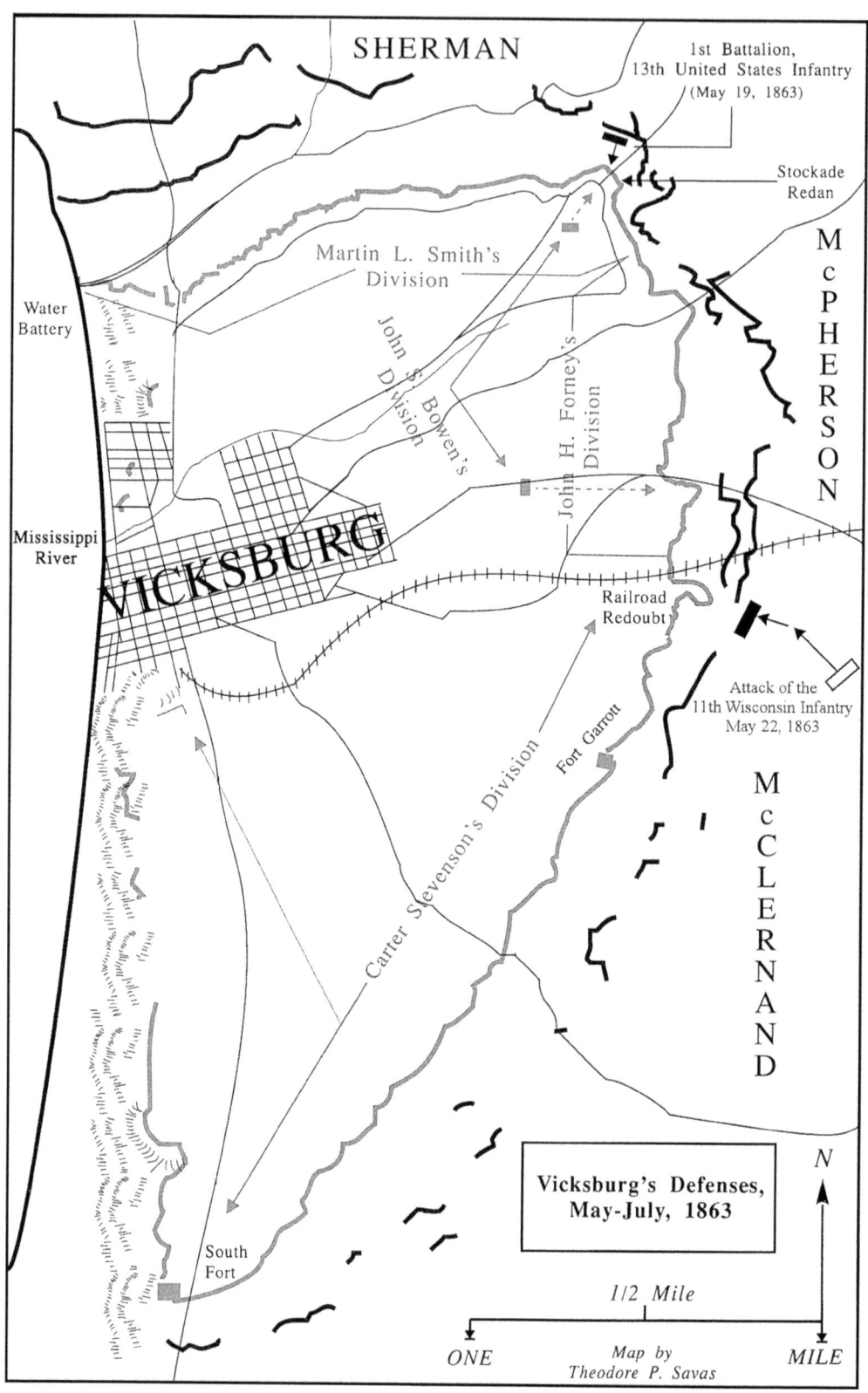

Vicksburg defenses.

The Eleventh Wisconsin found little cover along the ravine. With no other options, Harris led his men into the next ditch, where they fortunately found cover. After an hour of intense fighting they stopped to rest, exhausted and bloodied. They could advance no further. Though some reinforcements had arrived — the 130th Illinois and Forty-Eighth Ohio, along with a Kentucky regiment — Carr could not get the advantage in and around the fort. The intensity of the battle subsided towards mid afternoon. McClernand kept his men engaged, hoping for more of a demonstration by McPherson on his immediate right, along with more reinforcements. "No re-enforcements, however, could be spared us during the forenoon, and until late in the afternoon our position remained the same," wrote Lawler in his official report.[54]

At sunset Union soldiers were pinned down all along the ravine and around the fort when a furious counterattack by the Rebels successfully dislodged the Hawkeyes from the fort. They fell back to the crest of a hill near the ravine and found cover. "A heavy fire was kept up from both sides until dark," Lawler continued in his report. At about 8 o'clock McClernand admitted that his attack, too, had failed, and gave the order to withdraw.[55]

With cover of darkness, Colonel Harris led his men out of the ravine and through the gullies and ditches, up the hill, and back to the safety of their line. Samuel Kirkpatrick had lost more of his men, but how many he did not yet know. Though exhausted, they did get back and also managed to bring some of their wounded. Most companies were able to drag off their wounded, but many were left behind, out of reach. During the chaos of the battle Jesse was separated from Oliver, and by the time he returned was frantically searching for him. Companies were intertwined and mixed up, and would not be reorganized until morning. Jesse searched for Oliver, but could not find him. He was missing, probably still out there somewhere in the entanglements of a ravine, and most likely in need of help. All night Jesse sat peering into the distance, helplessly listening to the moans and cries from the hundreds of wounded soldiers who were not recovered. The sights of the day were horrific for all the men, and now the sounds of the night were equally horrifying.[56]

* * *

Two days later Grant had still not asked for a truce to collect his dead and recover his wounded. Perhaps a thousand or more men littered the ground for miles along the rifle pits and ditches and around the forts. "The stench of the dead, whose bodies were swollen grotesquely, and the cries of the wounded, who suffered the added torment of thirst, were intolerable to the men who had shot them down," wrote historian Shelby Foote. Still, Grant refused to show any weakness, and to request a truce was showing weakness in his mind. After three days Pemberton demanded a truce, "in the name of humanity," so that Grant could "remove your dead and dying men." Before dusk Union soldiers once again emerged from the "bowels" of the earth, but this time to bury their dead and recover the wounded that had managed to survive their injuries and nearly three days without water or help. There weren't many. After a few hours the men slowly returned to their trenches, and the firing commenced immediately.[57]

Miraculously, Oliver was still alive when Jesse found him in the hospital, and for the most part doing well. But the hospitals were unsanitary to say the least. "I tell you Mattie it is such sights as are to seen at the Hospitals that makes ones Heart sick and makes him wish that the cruel war was ended and that we could all return to our peaceful happy homes," wrote a Wisconsin soldier after visiting one hospital outside of Vicksburg. No one realized that infection resulted from exposure to bacteria. Doctors never bothered to wash their hands. The only treatment for bullet wounds that broke or shattered bones was amputation. Being sent to the hospital was more often than not a death sentence. One surgeon after the war recalled, "We operated in old blood-stained and often pus-stained coats, we used undisinfected instruments from undisinfected plush lined cases." If an instrument fell on the floor it was picked up and doused in a basin of blood and pus-ridden water and used as if it were clean. The mortality rate for Union soldiers struck in the chest by a gunshot was "62 percent of all cases" and for abdominal wounds "no less than 87 percent." Compared with World War II, where aseptic procedures were the norm, only 3 percent of all wounded soldiers died. The most dangerous place for a soldier during the Civil War might have been the field hospitals, which is why Civil War soldiers dreaded getting wounded and being sent to the hospitals.[58]

Jesse wrote home, as many did, telling his family that they were all right. "Family, by now I'm sure you have heard the news..." were typical opening lines to the letters the men wrote. It wasn't until later in the week that most of the letters were sent home. "We have done a good deal of marching and fighting and we are now lying close to Vicksburg and the big guns are booming away day and night," wrote one soldier. "Our forces made a charge on the forts and got up close to them but could not get in.... It was a Murderous thing and many a hundred good and brave men yielded up there lives on that day." Before anyone could get a letter home, Wisconsin newspapers already reported the dead and wounded.[59]

"The ... 11th Wisconsin was concerned in the famous charge upon the entrenchments at Black River Bridge, which resulted so gloriously," wrote a correspondent with *The Chicago Tribune* on May 22. "To-day they led the charge and gallantly did they do it. The regiment is decimated. I do not dare to say how many are killed and wounded." They were to have official reports on the dead and wounded by the next day. That evening families across Wisconsin worried and slept little as they waited for the next day's report.[60]

By now the Eleventh Wisconsin had gained a measure of respect from newspapers. "The 11th is always brave; it has a reputation which cannot be called in question," one article said. Wisconsin was well represented in Grant's army, and thousands of her sons were shedding blood in its service. In the charge it was reported, "the 11th, 14th, and 17th Wisconsin regiments ... are noted for their gallantry." The *Chicago Tribune* correspondent went on to describe the charge that had taken place:

> Slowly at first, then quickening into a run, they crossed the crest of the hill under a murderous fire from the earthworks, and a double charge of grape and canister from the Rebel artillery. No mortal man could withstand the terrible tempest, and they were forced to fall on their faces and let it pass by.... A charge was again made, and they succeeded in getting close to the ditch surrounding the works, and planting their banners there.[61]

Every day families huddled around newspapers and read the reports out loud. Most could not help but be overwhelmed at the thought of how difficult the fighting was for their loved ones. Mothers, fathers, daughters, sisters, and brothers were all on edge, waiting for the official report of the dead and wounded. On May 29, Sarah Mather picked up the paper and read the headline "List of Killed and Wounded." Quickly she found "11th Wisconsin," then "Company F," and the world must have stood still and all sounds faded but the beating of her heart when she read "O. S. Mather" had been wounded but had "since died." Every family in every town across Wisconsin nervously searched through the lists, praying they would not recognize many names. But by now that was impossible. Oliver S. Robinson was also wounded, in the thigh, and though still alive when the report above came out, he later died of infection.[62]

"We will have the town yet," wrote First Lieutenant Hiram J. Lewis, "it is only a question of time." Though repulsed in their assault, the men still had desire to "see this thing through."

Hiram marveled that through five battles he had yet to receive so much as a "scratch." Surely an exaggeration, but he was indeed one of the lucky ones not to have been hit. "I believe this is the best army in the world," he continued. "Gen. Carr is proud of his command and well he may be."[63]

Carr's Fourteenth Brigade, Second Division, lost more men that day than any other in Grant's army. With 368 casualties, Lawler's command was shattered. The Eleventh Wisconsin lost 91 men, the Twenty-first Iowa lost 113, and the Twenty-second Iowa suffered severely, with 164 men lost. It was the bloodiest day the Eleventh Wisconsin had seen.[64]

* * *

Samuel Kirkpatrick wrote home on the 28th of May and reported that he was wounded, but not severely, and was fine.

> Dear Father, mother, brothers and sisters:
> I sit down today to write you a few lines to let you know that I am well. We have been fighting all this month so that we had no chance to write. The first of the month we had a fight at Port Gibson and I got a slight wound, but it is well now. We have been in several purty rough fights in this month but I aint got time to write you the perticklers but the biggest fight was last Friday. Grant charged on their fortifications but the ground was so rough that he could no nothing. We are fortifying ourselves now ever night.... On Sunday they came out with a flag of truce to bury the dead and then we went over to see them. We talked all afternoon with them. We told them that we was a going to have that place but they thought not.[65]

Though there was time to write the particulars, few soldiers could bear the thought of reliving the experience. And they did not want their families to relive it with them. Perhaps the men thought better of sending home the particulars of battle, to spare their loved ones the worry and stress of reading their descriptions. A few days later, by moonlight, Samuel wrote another letter home to his family. "I sit down on the battlefield to let you know that I am still spared." Federal artillery was still shelling the city day and night. "We have lost killed and wounded one hundred and seven men out of our co," he wrote. "John killed dead on the field. William Jones died. John Stevens (brother of Filo Stevens) dead. Grant Andrews died of wounds. Newton died of wounds. Sergeant Prisk wounded.... Still we all have great faith in God. No more at this time." To have gone on about the hows and the whys would have been fruitless.[66]

The citizens of Vicksburg were also suffering. Numerous diaries have survived from those trapped inside; one was written by Dora Miller. About a week after Grant's ill-fated attack on the city, she questioned whether they should continue the struggle:

> May 28th.— Since that day the regular siege has continued. We are utterly cut off from the world, surrounded by a circle of fire. Would it be wise like the scorpion to sting ourselves to death? The fiery shower of shells goes on day and night. Every man has to carry a pass in his pocket. People do nothing but eat what they can get, sleep when they can, and dodge the shells. There are three intervals when the shelling stops, either for the guns to cool or for the gunner's meals, I suppose,— about eight in the morning, and the same in the evening, and at noon. In that time we have both to prepare and eat ours. Clothing cannot be washed or anything else done. On the 19th and 22d, when the assaults were made on the lines, I watched the soldiers cooking on the green opposite. The half-spent balls coming all the way from those lines were flying so thick that they were obliged to dodge at every turn. At all the caves I could see from my high perch, people were sitting, eating their poor suppers at the cave doors, ready to plunge in again. As the first shell again flew they dived, and not a human being was visible. The sharp crackle of musketry-firing was a strong contrast to the scream of the bombs. I think all the dogs and cats must be killed, or starved, we don't see any more pitiful animals prowling around.[67]

The citizens of the city were forced into cellars and shelters to avoid the nearly constant shelling. Many sought reprieve by digging caves in which to hide in the sides of hills. The hardships of the siege were taking their toll, on citizens and soldiers alike. Outside the city Federal troops continued to dig in, build more artillery batteries, and advance their lines closer each day to the Rebels. As they did so, sharpshooters were deployed in the trenches to pick off anyone who dared poke his head up. Sharpshooters on both sides spent a lot of time harassing the other, though not much damage was done. But the effect of the constant threat of being shot was significant. "The enemy is not much damaged by them [sharpshooters]," wrote a Wisconsin soldier, "however it seems to scare them more than any thing else." The artillery shells constantly barraged the city and its outer fortifications, according to this soldier. "Does not seem to do them much damage either only to knock down their breastworks and they can build them up as fast as we knock them down."[68]

At night soldiers gathered on hilltops at a safe distance to watch the fireworks. "It's a pretty sight," he continued, "to see the shells from the mortars going up higher and higher until they look as though they were clear up among the stars." Some disappeared in the distance and then "burst high in the air scattering pieces of shell in every direction and without doubt dealing death to the inhabitants." This seemed good fun until a few of them thought they "could hear the screams of women and children." Soon they sat in somber silence and watched with uncertain thoughts.[69]

Calvin Alling agreed that the sight of the bombardment of the city gave the boys of the Eleventh Wisconsin "a fine fireworks display, and as the shell revolved continuously and slowly, we saw the burning fuse-light." The constant roar of the shells being delivered, often overhead and into the city, resembled that of "an approaching railway train." After the war, Alling remembered the terror of this bombardment and that the "terrific sharp crack of the bursting shells, together with the weird hiss, roar, shriek, and crash of their fragments and contents, like many unearthly demons, were enough to terrorize the stoutest head within these beleaguered lines." The men hoped and prayed that the fortress would capitulate, for the sake of both sides. By June 11 only 465 men from the Eleventh Wisconsin were present for duty.[70]

The daily routine of dodging bullets, along with the continuous cannonading, became monotonous for everyone. Complacency, however, could lead to death. The lines were now close together; at some points just a few dozen yards separated Rebel rifle pits and Federal trenches. A well-placed sharpshooter could kill several men before being rooted out. "One of them made a button-hole in my coat where it was not needed," wrote Calvin Alling. One afternoon Captain Jesse Miller performed a demonstration to "test the accuracy of the enemy's fire," in what he hoped would be motivation for his men to stay down. He took a soldier's hat and placed it on a "ramrod" and then lifted it to "just visible above the loose earth" and within moments "zip! Through the hat would go a rifle ball thus showing the vigilance of the enemy and the necessity for our caution." Close calls were rare. Sharpshooters took advantage whenever someone offered himself as an easy target. Samuel Kirkpatrick's Farmers Guards were one of the companies that performed sharpshooting duty for the regiment. "We sharp shoot all day and at night we post our pickets," he wrote home one afternoon. "Our Co. was sharp shooting today and Oliver Phelps was killed. He did not speak a word. We got a pine box and buried him very nice." Oliver was one of four brothers who served in the regiment.[71]

To work on their trenches in relative safety, and in an effort to dig as close to the Confederate rifle pits as possible, Union soldiers used what were called "sap" rollers to protect the diggers at the head of the trench. At intervals these trenchers had to dig toward the enemy earthwork, and this was when they were most vulnerable. After the war Captain Miller described what this was like:

> A sap roller was constructed of three empty barrels surrounded by bundles of cane closely bound with wire; three layers of these bundles covering the barrels, and again bound with telegraph wire. This was rolled up the hill in front of the men as a protection while digging.[72]

As these rollers allowed the trenches to get closer and closer, the Rebels inside the fort began finding creative ways to stop the progress. Miller noted that their work "had a very irritating effect upon those inside the fort." Forced to act, they tried to burn and blow up as many of the rollers as possible: "Lighting a short fuse to a round shell, they would set it rolling down grade against our roller." The Confederates were able to disable three rollers, "but anticipating this, we were always prepared with a fresh [one]," said Captain Miller.[73]

With their trenches getting closer by the day, Federal and Confederate pickets sometimes bumped into each other at night. Usually this meant someone was taken prisoner. But even though they had spent weeks trying to kill each other, Federal "pickets and the Rebel pickets [were] getting very friendly," declared Samuel in a letter. In the darkness a whistle was heard: "We answer him and he preposes to leave his arms and meet half way and have a talk. Then we meet and spend an hour or two talking." Samuel told his parents they should believe him, even though it sounded like a "big story." Johnny Reb was "very glad to get some hard bread the boys gave them." After sharing a few stories, "trading knives and canteens," the men would separate, disappear into the darkness, and once again return to being enemies. Samuel said that after one such encounter they were sharpshooting again a few days later when "[Thomas Satterlee] while shooting through a port hole was mortally wounded in the head.... He was a splendid soldier and the Co. misses him a great deal." Sadly Samuel noted how hardened the men were now: "It is no more to us to see a dead man than it would be to you to see a dead dog. We are a getting ust to it."[74]

Captain Miller made an arrangement with Captain Vick of the Thirty-first Alabama regiment, positioned near the Eleventh Wisconsin. They had dug far enough to get to a ridge south of the fort, but on one side it was occupied by Rebel pickets. "To gain possession of it without bringing on an engagement" was his goal one night when he ran into the Rebel captain:

> I had reached the picket who challenged ["Who are you?"], and I answered, "Captain Miller, 11th Wisconsin." Reply, "What are you doing there?" Answer, "On picket, who are you?" Answer, "Captain Vick, Thirty-first Alabama." Upon this I made him a proposition to compromise peaceably the matter of possession and meet half way. After consulting with his men, he accepted ... and then and there arranged for the placing of his pickets just in front at a short distance from ours, with instructions there should be no firing or contention, unless in case of a general movement.[75]

As historians have noted, regardless of which side they fought on, Civil War soldiers shared a strange bond during and after the war. They fought hard, sometimes viciously, against each other, but when the moment was right they were able to meet and talk as if friends. After the war there would be reunions where soldiers from both sides would gather and discuss battles lost and won, and comrades who had fallen.

* * *

By mid June reinforcements swelled Grant's force to over 70,000 men. He was able to surround the fortress city and still send Sherman's army back to the Big Black River to keep a watchful eye for any Confederate reinforcements. While Grant's numbers increased, Pemberton's decreased. Pemberton knew that his only hope was to "cut" his way out, but he also knew that he could not afford to do so. They would have to be rescued. But Johnston was not willing to attempt any movement until he had more men. Dejected, Pemberton made a delusional proposal, suggesting Johnston make a feint and try to bluff Grant away from Vicksburg, since Grant had no idea as to the strength Johnston's army. Johnston, of course, scoffed at the idea.[76]

Another development by the end of June was the removal of McClernand from command. The May 22 attack was a blunder, over 3,000 dead, injured or missing, and though McClernand's men did most of the fighting and dying that day, someone had to be blamed. Historians tend to point out that McClernand was trying to seek some kind of glory and this cost lives. Perhaps, but McClernand truly believed he could have achieved success had he been given more men and more support. It was arguably Sherman and McPherson who failed. McClernand's main problem seems to be his arrogance and his big mouth, as he never knew when to shut it. This left him disliked not only by Grant but also by McPherson and Sherman, who called him "a dirty dog" and "so envious and selfish that he cannot harmonize with any where he does not command." On June 18, Major General E.O.C. Ord replaced McClernand as corps commander.[77]

As Federal trenches crept closer to Rebel forts and rifle pits, someone came up with the seemingly brilliant plan of digging tunnels underneath the forts and breastworks, and igniting mines. On June 25, after a month of digging, a tunnel was completed under the Third Louisiana Redan. The Federals carefully laid 2,200 pounds of powder carried 400 yards in individual grain sacks deep inside the tunnel. Everything was ready by 2:00 P.M. with a 3:00 P.M. launch. Three o'clock came and went and nothing happened. Grant was even on hand to watch. At 3:30, the explosion sent debris hundreds of feet into the air. The blast caused a breach through which hundreds of Union soldiers from the Forty-fifth Illinois poured. The crater was twelve feet deep and forty wide. The fighting was helter-skelter as men fought it out with clubs, rifle butts, and bayonets. The melee was a free-for-all of hand-to-hand combat, point blank executions, and struggles to the death with bayonets and bare hands. The fighting lasted through the night as regiments circulated in and out relieving their comrades when possible. The fight lasted well into the next day until it was called off by Grant at 5:00 P.M. The fort, filled with the dead and dying, was greatly reduced and part of it was in Union hands.[78]

The Federals kept digging tunnels and on July 1 another explosion at the fort blew off yet more of the breastwork and sent dirt and debris flying everywhere. Men on both sides ducked and dove for cover. When the Federals reemerged from their trenches they found a dazed Negro cook lying on the ground. Dumbfounded, they realized he had been blown out of the Rebel fortification and into their trench, miraculously almost unscathed. A soldier on hand recalled how "one Negro was thrown 150 feet." The Negro's name was Abraham and he became a celebrity of sorts. For the rest of the siege he was known as "America's first aeronaut." Abraham finished the war working for the Union Army as a cook.[79]

By the end of June, Johnston had 31,000 men and was slowly making his way towards the Union rear near the Big Black River, which he reached on July 1. What he found when he got there was Sherman waiting for him. Johnston was hoping to strike by the end of the first week of July. In an impromptu war council Pemberton's generals informed him of the bleak situation. The men were too weak and in no physical shape to continue. In addition, their lines were close to being breached by Federal trenches, and if attacked in force, would almost surely give way. Pemberton realized he had but one option.[80]

One of Pemberton's commanders summed up the situation best:

Fight in the Crater after the explosion on June 27, 1863. (Author's Collection, sketch by F. B. Schell).

From shortness of rations, and greatly more from a confinement of forty-five days to the trenches, under the summer sun of a debilitating climate, few, if any, of the men are in their ordinary health and vigor. I am disposed to believe that perhaps one in five of those now reported for "duty in the trenches" would, under different and favorable circumstances, be receiving medical treatment; and I have less hesitation in declaring it as my opinion that of this number, for "duty in the trenches," 50 per cent.[81]

On July 3 white flags were raised atop the Rebel fortifications and Pemberton sent word to Grant that he wanted to meet and talk. That afternoon the two generals met briefly. Grant decided the terms should be fair enough to compel Pemberton to accept, thereby avoiding his scheduled assault that was to take place on July 6, one that would most likely be bloody. That night the ceasefire remained. Rebel soldiers took advantage of the peace and quiet and wandered out from their lines to trade and talk with Billy Yank. As one historian noted, "brothers met, and any quantity of cousins. It was a strange scene."[82]

First Lieutenant of Company K Hiram J. Lewis observed, "Death-like silence reigns, not a gun having been fired sine the mortar boats ceased at 12." The quiet was a relief after 43 days of fighting. Many of the men took advantage of the quiet and quickly fell asleep, as it was not uncommon to go "36 consecutive hours without sleep." The siege was not only exhausting for the people trapped in Vicksburg, but for the soldiers investing the place. "Our whole army is badly worn out," Hiram admitted.[83]

By July 4 the terms were set and agreed upon. Grant had toyed with two options: accept the 30,000 Rebels as prisoners of war and ship them north to POW camps; or parole them, still as prisoners of war, but allow them to return home without their weapons. Paroling the men was a risk, but it was common knowledge that very few parolees returned to active service. Most went home eagerly to their farms and families. This way the men became the South's problem, and not theirs. To ship all those men north would have been a logistical nightmare, not to mention costly. History has shown that Grant was right. Very few of the paroled men returned to active duty. Shortly after the terms were signed, Grant and his army took possession of Vicksburg. All of the Confederate soldiers had to remain while the parole paperwork was completed. The Federals also brought in food and supplies to the starving people who had been trapped inside for nearly two months.[84]

Halleck sent Grant a wire shortly after his victory on July 7: "It gives me great pleasure to inform you that you have been appointed major general in the Regular Army, to rank from July 4, the date of your capture of Vicksburg." Though some were already criticizing Grant for paroling the Rebel soldiers at Vicksburg, Lincoln called his siege of Vicksburg "one of the most brilliant in the world."[85]

* * *

Surgeon Henry P. Strong was sick, suffering from dysentery and fatigue. Well before Vicksburg had surrendered, his wife, Sarah, was urging him to resign and come home. Henry wanted to wait until Vicksburg fell, something he thought would be the beginning of the end for the Confederacy. At that point he felt "my work is done" and he could resign knowing that he had done all he could. "I am of the opinion," he wrote on July 1, "that we are on the eve of great events but in what particular way they are to come about I am at a loss to know." Once Vicksburg fell, he noted, "The Confederacy is now cut in twain and in the east they are driven into the Seabaord states. From where will the support for their army now come?"[86]

General Joseph E. Johnston (Library of Congress).

By July 7, Henry documented his deteriorating condition. "The increasing heat is depressing to me, I can feel it now day by day," he wrote in one of his last letters. "Dysentery has given me a Severe time...." He felt that if he stayed he would surely die. He approached General Carr and asked if he would approve his resignation. "Are you in earnest?" Carr asked. "Yes, Sir," Henry replied. "My mission is accomplished and I want to go." Carr mulled over Henry's words. "I will do so, then," he said. Lieutenant Colonel Whittlesey, in Colonel Harris' absence, would also sign off on the resignation as the commanding officer of the Eleventh Wisconsin. He did so, adding, "I beg leave to add that for nearly two years Surg. Strong has been in the Service he has Served with distinguished zeal and professional ability." Henry still needed the approval of Hammond Med, Thirteenth Army Corps, who at first denied it, telling Henry he "could not spare" him. Henry persisted and eventually gained his approval. The final approval would rest with General Grant.[87]

Days passed as Henry waited his signoff; all the while his health continued to decline. He even made a personal visit to Grant's headquarters, but the general was too busy to see him. Though disappointed, he was impressed with Grant. "He is very busy and will not see any one unless upon very important business," Henry jotted down in a letter. Reflecting on what he had seen of Grant during 1863 he wrote, "I now believe Grant has the most comprehensive military mind combined with the power to comprehend and carry details of any man in the country." Henry was a keen observer and he possessed a strategic understanding of warfare that is impressive for someone not actively engaged in military matters. His writing gained him a bit of fame, and he was offered numerous jobs to become a correspondent for various newspapers, including the *Chicago Tribune*.[88]

Henry was hospital bound as the Eleventh Wisconsin left Vicksburg. Whittlesey wrote to him on the 8th of July: "I am truly sorry my dear friend that your health renders your resignation expedient. Few Surgeons of Regiments can bring to their office the professional skill and the gentlemanly character & manner that make an officer most agreeable. These you possess in an eminent degree and you know that I do not say this to flatter you."[89]

Luckily for Henry, Special Order No. 192, Extract 11, on July 16, 1863, stated, "The Resignation of Surgeon H.P. Strong ... is hereby accepted to take effect this day ... by order of Major General U.S. Grant." The doctor's good friend Whittlesey had possibly found a way to make an appeal to Grant and succeed in gaining his acceptance.[90]

Henry, still in the hospital, wrote his last letter to Sarah before heading home:

> I have yet failed to find the chivalry of the South during all my travels. It certainly cannot be among the men who carry muskets. They are so ignorant about matters involved in this struggle that any one can see they are but machines worked at the will of designing men. Ask one what he is fighting for and he is as likely to say "I don't know" as anything: he may say that he is fighting for their liberties, or fighting abolitionists perhaps, but no one has any thing like a comprehensive view of affairs.[91]

Henry returned to Beloit and after recovering he continued his medical practice.

* * *

"Dear Parents it would have done you good to hear us cheer," wrote Samuel Kirkpatrick. "It was the best feeling fourth to me that I ever enjoyd." Though the months leading up to the Vicksburg campaign were filled with doubt, the men were now victorious and feeling well. "The 4th will be a bigger day now than ever especially amongst Grant's army."[92]

It was one of the most decisive victories of the war. Grant had effectively eliminated around 47,000 (37,000 prisoners, and another 10,000 killed or wounded during the campaign) enemy soldiers from the South, along with 172 cannons and arms and munitions for 60,000 more soldiers. The cost by comparison was manageable, with less than 10,000 men lost. The fall of Vicksburg, along with General Lee's disastrous defeat near Gettysburg on July 3, proved a staggering blow the Confederacy would never recover from.[93]

Chapter Nine

1864 — Bivouacked in the Sand

Even though it had ended in victory, the Vicksburg siege cost the Eleventh Wisconsin dearly. In May alone the regiment had 104 casualties—12 killed and 92 wounded. On July 6 Jesse responded to an urgent letter from his mother, the first he had received from her:[1]

Dear Mother,

I received your kind letter about a week ago and was hapy to hear from you and to know that you ower getting along so well. Mother I was not with Swain when he died I was with him the day before till 4 o'clock and when I left him he was doing very well as well as could be expected. I did not think him very dangerous when I left him he said that he felt first rate. He was not with strangers for their was some of the boys their taking care of our wounded. I saw Swain after he was dead and after he was buried I got a board and had his name, age and time of his death and what Co and Regt. and state he belonged to and got it out on their and putt it up to the head of his grave so that it could be found. After so mutch hard fighting and sacrificing so many lives we have succeeded in getting Vicksburg we got with it 25000 prisoners, 30000 stands of arms and 200 pieces of artillery. Vicksburg surrendered the 4th day of July about 10 o'clock. Our regt. has gon back to black river I didn't go with I dont know how long they will be gon but I guess not more than a week. The weather is very warm hear now it is a good deal warmer than I wished it wer. Mother I should like to see you very mutch and hope that it wont be long till I will be permited to see you. Well I must close hope these few lines will find you well and all the rest of them I want you to write as often as convenient. good by

Jesse Mather[2]

Jesse had been permitted to stay with Oliver when the regiment headed to Jackson with Sherman's men to hunt Johnston. Jesse buried Oliver's body and placed a marker above it so it could be recovered and taken home for a family burial. While Jesse was seeing to Oliver, the Eleventh Wisconsin helped recapture Jackson, as Sherman tried everything to get Johnston to stand and fight.

Jesse was not the only one with bad news. "I have painful news for … your Brother is dead," wrote Robert Sherrill home to his aunt, Caroline. "I am very sory for the poor fellow the whole Co. joines in mourning the loss of our friend and brother." Robert was grief-stricken and was shouldering the blame: "I tryed my best to get to go and take care of him but it was imposible. Dear Aunt you must not think I was the means of getting your Brother in the service…." Robert's self defense was probably not needed, but he rambled on as if trying to convince himself. "James Dain was to high minded to stay at home and see the greatest part of his neighbor boys going." He grieved James' death like the loss of a brother. "It is true me and James enlisted to gether and stuck to gether as long as it was possible." Robert's grief was compounded by the additional news that "John is sick in the hospital…. He looks very bad." This letter must have produced a river of emotions for Caroline. She had written Robert about a bad dream she had one night. Robert acknowledged it as a "sign of bad news." But he felt if John could survive the next few weeks, he would "get well and get his discharge."

The war had lost its luster for Robert. "Caroline we have had a pretty rough time of late plenty of fighting we have been fighting here over a month a greate many of our brave men fell...." He wrote another letter a couple of weeks later, telling her he was ready for the war to end. "I hope we may soon end this war with out any more blood shed." But it was Caroline who was to suffer most, when word reached her that John was dead. Within the span of four months she had lost a daughter, a brother, and now her husband.³

* * *

The Eleventh Wisconsin did not get the needed rest they deserved after the fall of Vicksburg; instead they headed out with Sherman towards Jackson on his expedition, as Confederate general Johnston's army had retaken the city. After a couple of weeks of fighting, the Rebels withdrew once more from the capital. William H. Cope of Company I observed, most likely expressing the sentiments of many, "I think the way the war is conducted now on our side the rebellion will soon be ended."⁴

Though the North was victorious again on two fronts, partisan politics still swirled in the Northern states. "You wrote something about the democrats and the republicans a having meetings," wrote Samuel Kirkpatrick. "They do more harm than good. If they know when they are well off they will hold their tongues. This tongue fighting is played out. The copperheads* of the North needs the war in their own states. Let the Southern army go into Wis. and see what they think. A army is what ruins a state. Now you can look at this state before the army came here. The people was ritch but now they are worth nothing but their land." Like most soldiers, Samuel's emotions ran high whenever he read or heard about politicians or members of the press and their ideological blathering. The time for words was over, for most of the men were fighting and dying on distant battlefields. All they wanted was a quick end to the war. In March the officers of the regiment held a meeting and passed several resolutions in response to the "bitter partisan spirit" which was becoming, in their opinion, "dangerous, malicious and revengeful in our State and elsewhere." The resolution called for their "friends neighbors" to "lay aside all party jealousness and animosities."⁵

Jesse was back with his regiment when he received another letter from home, this time from his younger brother, Howard. "I was very glad to hear from you but sory to hear you was not well but am in hopes that you ar well by this time," Jesse replied. "I was glad to hear that evry thing looks so well you must have a prety good flock of turkeys and chickens. I should like to be their to help you eat some of them this fall and maybe I will but don't know. I mean to try and cum home if I can."⁶

* * *

By August, the Eleventh Wisconsin had left Mississippi—after taking part in the Jackson Expedition—and were headed downriver to Carrollton, Louisiana. From there they went further south to Brashear City on Berwick Bay, west of New Orleans and the terminus of the Great Western Railroad. When they arrived they were greeted by "Hordes of men, women and children ... eagerly offering for sale, in almost every language, everything eatable that could be carried in a cart or basket—fish, fruit, cakes and pies." The prices were agreeable and it was not long before "every man had a banana in one hand and a piece of pie in the other." For some men, it was the first time in months that they "had had a fair chance at pie." Louisiana was a pleasant experience upon their arrival. Colonel Harris had taken another

---

*Antiwar Democrats wore copper penny lapels and were nicknamed "Copperheads," but the name was also in reference to the Copperhead snake.

leave of absence due to illness, but by September was back in command of the Eleventh and Second Brigade, which was still part of the First Division, Thirteenth Army Corps, commanded by Ord.[7]

Louisiana offered Curious Kirkpatrick more things to marvel at. When they entered Carrollton he wrote home, very impressed: "They have the best roads in this country I ever saw. The roads here is made of oyster shells. They make a splendid road. You can get fresh oysters here and fresh lobsters and you can get as large a fish as you can carry for 50 cents." Samuel wrote home at least once a week, documenting his travels for them. These letters must have been greeted with excitement by his brothers and sisters, for Samuel was taking them along on his journey to these new and interesting places they had only read about. Samuel faithfully and patiently answered everyone's questions, resulting in some very long letters. "There [on the Mississippi] I seen some of the finest buildings I ever saw all along the river. There was splendid sugar plantations—the largest I ever saw far a head of cotton plantations." The further south he traveled, the bigger and wealthier things were.[8]

They were camped only six miles or some from New Orleans, wrote William H. Cope, and he agreed with Samuel: "[It] is the richest country and the plesant that I have seen [in the] South I have seen several orange trees and trees loaded with fruit and many courious plants that I dont know thar name yet." As farmers the men always reported back what kinds of vegetation they observed. Farming was, of course, never far from their minds: "Thar chef crop here is rice and sugar cane they rase some corn the land is very low and is now level with the river." Rebeldom continued to amaze and surprise.[9]

While in Louisiana, Calvin Alling "saw for the first time an alligator" and it was a big one, "some ten or twelve feet long." As they traveled down the Mississippi, Alling agreed with Samuel that it was a "very picturesque scene." They were led by five gunboats from Admiral Porter's fleet. Calvin counted 15 or 16 transport steamers. He and several others went up to the top deck to admire the splendid view, "as though soaring up in the air, and we were able to look over the tops of the houses. It was grand, beyond all description."[10]

Replacements were starting to replenish the Eleventh Wisconsin ranks, and Samuel was not impressed with the new recruits. "Our Reg. stands the hot weather fine but some of the new Reg. dieing off like sheep. The old Reg. stands the heat the best. They have more get up about them. Some of the new Reg. will lay in their tents day after day and all they think of is getting home. There seems to be no life in them a tall." The fact of the matter was that Congress initiated the draft in 1863 to get the manpower the North needed. This left it up to each individual county to draw the names of eligible men to be drafted into service. The more territory the Federals controlled, the more men it needed for offensive action while also securing the land they'd already taken. These replacements were looked down on by most of the veterans. Many of these new soldiers were unmotivated and deserved the scrutiny, but a few would earn the respect of the veterans, once they had proved themselves in battle.[11]

Riots were often inspired by rumors and lies about the draft in newspaper editorials. Newspapers such as the *New York World*, *Baltimore Gazette* and *Philadelphia Evening Journal* were all suspended by the government for "extension of aid or comfort to the enemy." Some even printed false reports of President Lincoln calling for hundreds of thousands more draftees than he had. Though a civil war was raging, with the survival of the country at stake, some newspapers used sensationalism to further their own agendas and circulations.[12]

* * *

By now the men of Grant's western army were being hailed as heroes. "When we went to New Orleans they asked us if we belong to Grant's army and we said yes," wrote Samuel.

"They said we was the men to have the praise not the Eastern men." After the fall of Vicksburg, spirits soared among the men. These hardened veterans had cut their teeth more than once in battle. General Johnston warned Richmond to be leery of Grant and his men who, in his opinion, were "worth double the number of northeastern troops."[13]

Though victorious and now celebrated, Grant's army split shortly after the fall of Vicksburg, with some of the men going east, some south to Louisiana (including the Eleventh Wisconsin) and some staying put. Major General Nathaniel Banks was charged with getting western Louisiana secured for the Union, and was unfortunately having a rough go. He took Port Hudson successfully, but Confederates were still moving freely on his western flank. Strangely, after Vicksburg Grant was in a kind of limbo with really nothing to do while he recovered from minor injuries after taking a spill from his horse. All war fronts had generals taking on the enemy, but in Grant's area the enemy was either destroyed, captured, or on the run. So he went to New Orleans to see General Banks, where the two of them discussed a possible move on Mobile, Alabama.[14]

* * *

By September the Wisconsin state flag the regiment carried into battle was "worn & torn" and "unfit for further service," as the regiment reported back home to the governor. They would require a new one. The National flag was still okay except for the "bullet holes" and a large cut from a "fragment of a shell" during their charge at Big Black River. It was their hope to have "new colors" before their next engagement.[15]

Samuel's younger brothers inquired constantly about army life. "Well John this soldiering is purty ruff thing but it ain't killed me yet," Samuel replied. "The old 11 Wis. Vol. has been in 7 fights and has never had to retreat yet and I hope we will never have to." A few weeks later Samuel continued his dialogue with John. Samuel was a good soldier and felt his brothers would be as well, so he encouraged his younger brother. "Well John this is a great place for a soldier. I wish you was here with me for we have such fine times. I know it would sute you." Samuel was concerned that his younger brother not "get like David Baret," who apparently was "turning out ... bad." It seems John had not taken a liking to schoolwork, and when Samuel found out he wrote a stern letter. "Well John I must say a few words to you and that is mind your parents. You may think you know best but when you grow up you will see the need of it then.... You must not forget that there is nothing like a good education."[16]

It was September 2, and the Eleventh Wisconsin was camped near Carrollton, a lush and beautiful place. "I wish we would be aloud to stop here until our time is up," declared Samuel. But orders soon arrived for the regiment to be ready to march, "to leave our knapsacks and our tents behind and only take our oil cloth and one blanket." The men knew what that meant; they had some hard marching ahead of them. "I cant say where we are a going but the general opinion is that we are a going to Mobile," wrote Samuel. The weather was cool and pleasant, so he had hopes the marching would be tolerable.[17]

But before they left, a grand review was ordered, with a surprise for the men. "General Grant came in front of the lines," recorded Samuel. The men immediately began cheering, pumping their rifles into the air and waving their hats in acknowledgement. Then they paraded past their beloved general, brigade after brigade, thousands of men. As a tribute, Banks had banners made with the names of the battles fought and won during the Vicksburg campaign. "It was a stirring moment for them and him," wrote one historian. As they marched by him and out of sight, Grant and his western soldiers parted ways, never to fight together again. "I don't know but I fear we will not fare so well now as we did when we was under General Grant," said Samuel. "General Banks no doubt is a good man but I haint got the confidence in him that I have in Grant." Samuel's sentiment was unfortunately prophetic, for Banks would never appreciate or understand the steadiness and toughness of his new troops, especially when the fighting got tough.[18]

They were not to go to Mobile just yet. A few weeks later they were on the march, a part of what was called the "Second Teche Expedition." It was early October before the mail train caught up to them and the regiment was able to send letters home. "We are steering for Texas as fast as we can. The first day we marched 15 miles and the second 12 miles and the third 16 and today 10 miles," said Samuel home in a quick letter. By October 6 they were in New Iberia, a prairie-like region with large sugarcane plantations. When they stopped for the night the men set off on a massive foraging expedition to the large nearby plantations. They brought back everything they could carry: cows, "hogs, turkeys, chickens." They hauled it back "by the wagon load." Then they were at St. Martinsville, and then on the move again, marching 31 miles in one day. "On the 23d in the midst of a cold drenching rain, we broke camp, and marched to Carrion Brow Bayou ... next day marched twelve miles," then another 12 miles and another. On October 29 and 30 they "marched 35 miles through mud knee deep, and heavy rain." All this and then they were back at New Iberia. "I don't think there was ever a Reg. that left the state [Wisconsin] that has done any more marching than we have," wrote an exhausted Samuel.[19]

During the campaign they followed the Nineteenth Army corps as it chased Rebels around the state. They traveled "215 miles over bad roads, experiencing cold, wet, and stormy weather," and yet fought in no battles. During the campaign "the men suffered severely from exposure." It wasn't until November that they headed out for Texas, first by rail and then by boat. Landing at St. Joseph Island (located between Aransas Bay in Texas and the Gulf of Mexico), they "bivouacked in the sand" on the south end. The boys took off their boots, rolled up their pants, and waded in the clear blue water. It was good fun. But the fun didn't last long. That night a severe storm hit them with driving wind and rain. Without tents, they had only their rubber blankets for cover. The island had no reliable wood supply, so there were few fires to dry themselves off. They would try to dig holes for shelter, only to have the sand drift in and fill them back up in a matter of minutes. The water was also bad and nearly impossible to drink. The storm continued for days, the wind blowing furiously. The regiment historian noted that the wind was "blowing a perfect hurricane." The men suffered from exposure, and some were injured.[20]

By the end of November they were on the march yet again through "deep sand," and one that would prove to be a "toilsome march." Without much wood or drinking water, they kept on the move, marching along the beach and camping on "sand hills." By December 2 they reached Fort Esperanza. Though part of the invasion of Texas, they took no part in the fighting. A battle took place on November 23 before they arrived, at Cedar Bayou. And when Union forces reached the fort on November 27, a two-day battle ensued. But by the time the Eleventh Wisconsin arrived the Rebels had evacuated the fort. A few days later the regiment moved to nearby Decrows Point, on the Peninsula. There "for the first time since September 3d ... [they] pitched tents." Having traveled from the farmlands of Wisconsin to a desert near the ocean, they must have felt they had reached the end of the world; but at least it would prove to be a warm winter.[21]

They still had problems with the water. "The wells on the main land is bitter and soapy," said Calvin Alling. "Curiously enough, the water from the wells dug within a few rods of the surf is fairly good, fresh, cool, and sweet." The men had time to walk the shoreline, barefoot in the soft sand, and collect driftwood for campfires. "This is the greatest place for shells that I ever saw," wrote Samuel to his brothers. "All kinds of little shells. If I had a chance I would

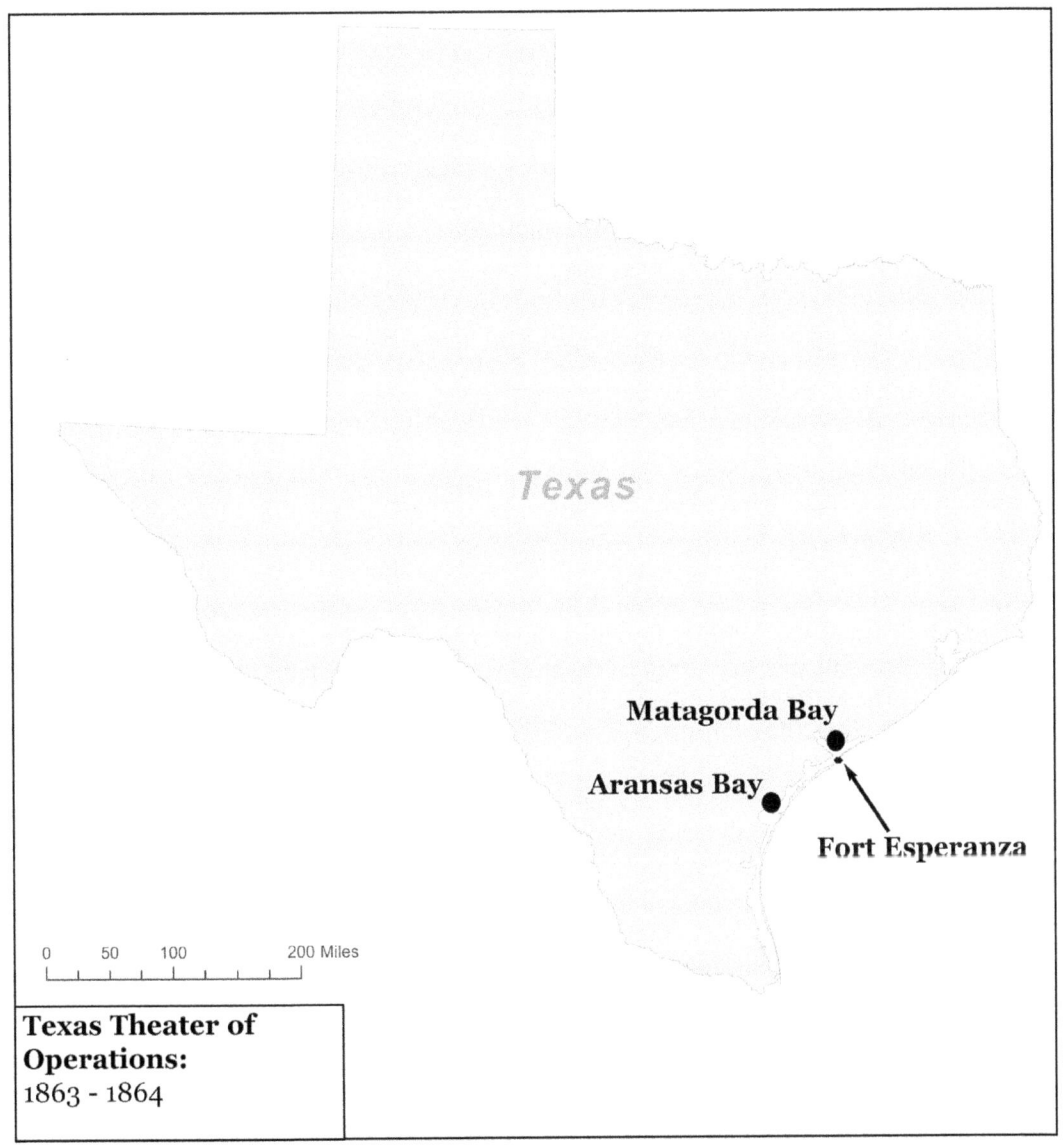

Texas theater of operations.

like to send you a little box of the nicest ones." But as far as Samuel was concerned, the lack of good drinking water and wood aside, the weather "beats any winter ... that I ever saw yet." He reckoned he would like to move there after the war. "It haint rained here for 15 months — only what they call a little sea mist." Except when the occasional "Northerner" blew through, it was paradise.[22]

William H. Cope wrote home to his father reassuring him they were doing well and that "the wether is fine and like spring I like the climate first rate a good deal beter then [home] ... and fine wether most of the time the boys here has grate time[s]...." Families back home in Wisconsin must have been amazed by the descriptions and stories sent home by the boys and men of the Eleventh regiment.[23]

* * *

While his comrades marched in the sand, Jesse Mather was still in Mississippi at the military hospital in Jackson. He was not feeling well, and probably depressed. He had received more bad news: his younger brother, Henry, had died. The family was reeling, heartbroken. Jesse took up his pen and wrote his mother, who was worried about him. She wanted him to come home, but he knew that was not possible. In a few weeks he would head out to rejoin the regiment. His writing became scribbled, his sentences and words fractured; he was struggling:

> Dear Mother … I am sory that you ar feeling so bad you musent let any thing trouble you keep up good spirits and not wory about me I will do the best that I can and try to cum home and see you as soon as I can. As Swain and Henry have departed from us never to return again. You must not let it wory you. They ar don with the trials and troubles of this world. They ar beter off than we ar we still have trials and troubles to contend with. We must trust in him who forgiveth all our inquities. And who healeth all our diseases.[24]

His mother's trepidation at this point in the war was normal. Families were troubled more than ever as the fighting continued month after month, year after year, with seemingly no end in sight. Letters from home asked questions the men were not sure they could answer. "You wished me to write you about how I felt at being shot in the battle," wrote one Wisconsin soldier. As they approached the battlefield each man had to deal with a wide swing of emotions. Then as the fighting started and their friends (and sometimes family members) standing next to them started dying, "I can tell you it is no very pleasant thing," the soldier continued. The bullets started flying, hissing by, seemingly swarming around each soldier's head and shoulders. The "shells come whizzing screaming and tearing through them like some angry spirit seeking revenge."[25]

It was the waiting period before a fight that drove men crazy, noted one soldier: "A man's heart is put in a flutter by the suspense." A historian who spent years studying Civil War soldiers' descriptions of battle concluded that because they were broken down into companies regionally, it made them a "band of brothers whose mutual dependence and mutual support create the cohesion necessary to function as a fighting unit." Going into battle caused physical changes, of course. The release of adrenalin into the bloodstream produced a "jolt" that powered the soldier, producing a state of either fear or rage. The men would yell and scream as they fought, sometimes not even knowing they were doing so, because it helped release the tension and anxiety. But being together with familiar and often friendly faces, many could find some calm in the midst of the storm.[26]

The Eleventh Wisconsin was hopeful they had seen the last of their days as fighting soldiers; they probably thought the odds were in their favor. But the Union cause had received another blow in mid–September during the disastrous battle of Chickamauga. It was the largest battle to take place in the western theater and saw Federal forces (Army of the Cumberland), led by the incompetent Major General William Rosecrans, utterly defeated and nearly routed had it not been for Major Gen. George H. Thomas, who earned the nickname "Rock of Chickamauga" due to his fierce defense of Horseshoe Ridge. Despite losing over 15,000 dead, wounded and missing, it could have been much worse. With its victory the Confederate army showed it still had plenty of bite in the western theater. Still, as 1864 approached the North felt optimistic about ending the war soon.[27]

* * *

By October Lincoln had appointed Grant commander of all Union forces in the west. Almost immediately, Grant replaced Rosecrans with Major General George H. Thomas, who had saved the Union army from disaster during its crushing defeat at Chickamauga. Grant also assigned Sherman to succeed him as commander of the Army of the Tennessee. "Our army has a great faith in Grant," wrote Samuel. "The men cant be whipped if they have good generals." By December the Eleventh Wisconsin was as relaxed as it had been at any point in the war. They were far away from the fighting. "Some thinks they will not fite atall in this state," said Samuel, and that was alright by him. They had seen enough of war and would be happy never to see another battle. But emotions ran high when letters from home reported that some of the young men now of age were refusing to be drafted. "I think that a man that is a feared to risk his life in defense of his country is not much of a man," Samuel replied.[28]

They were still stationed in Matagorda Bay, Texas. They spent their days on patrol, looking for Rebels. When ships came in they helped unload them by rowing small boats out to the vessels. One afternoon Calvin Alling and three other men were out on one of these small boats. Amateur sailors, they had only been boating on the ocean for a few weeks. No one had noticed that "the tide runs in during the day, and begins rushing out about sundown, however we did not consider this fact, from ignorance." As they were returning they noticed the pier light was not getting any closer, and an officer in the group, realizing "we were going out to sea," became "completely unnerved," and started shouting, "We're lost, we're lost!" Calvin pushed the sergeant out of the way and took hold of the rudder, telling the others to "pull for your lives." It was getting dark and if they were indeed heading out to sea they would never be rescued. Luckily there was also a pike pole long enough to barely touch bottom, and they managed to push their way back into shallower water and to the pier. "The suspense was terrible," wrote Calvin. "I shall never forget it."[29]

Though once again the only significant threat to their well being was themselves, they did not mind it a bit. They spent their free time hunting for seashells, taking baths in the ocean, and in the evening visiting with the local women in town. They became fishermen and learned to catch oysters, crabs, and enormous fish. Samuel noted that all the local men and boys were gone fighting, leaving some lonely women to whom he was more than willing to offer a comforting shoulder. Every night men strolled along the shore at sunset during high tide as the ocean roared in.[30]

Chapter Ten

Damn the Torpedoes!

In early 1864, General Grant and his staff gathered round a table inside an old log cabin and partook of a modest meal before retiring outside near a campfire for coffee and tea. Grant took his usual spot and eased back, even appearing to relax. He crossed his legs and puffed generously on his cigar. He watched the flames consuming a log in the fire. After a few moments, he slowly sat up and waited for quiet.[1]

"I look upon the line for this army to secure in its next campaign to be that from Chattanooga to Mobile, Atlanta and Montgomery, being the important intermediate points," said Grant. "I look upon the Tennessee River and Mobile as being the most practicable points from which to start and to hold as bases of supplies after the line is secured." He considered Mobile and Alabama as important strategic objectives in his desire to end the war as quickly as possible. After his success toppling Vicksburg, Grant had proposed a move on Mobile but was refused by Halleck who, along with President Lincoln, wanted a campaign west of the Mississippi.[2]

"It would have been an easy thing to capture Mobile," said Grant years later. The strategic value of Mobile alone should have made it a priority, not to mention the negative effect that taking the city would have had on the morale of the South. Alabama was virtually untouched by the war, a fact no more evident than in Mobile, which its residents considered the "Paris of the Confederacy." With Mobile as a base easily supplied by sea, Grant could "throw" troops at the "interior to operate" at will against the enemy.[3]

Grant abandoned the strategy of taking and holding land in hopes of somehow forcing the South to capitulate. Instead, he and Sherman decided to take the war to the South, in particular the Deep South, with a "raiding" strategy. "It is my design," Grant wrote Sherman in April 1864, "if the enemy keep quiet and allow me to take the initiative in the spring campaign to work all parts of the army together and somewhat toward a common center." Grant believed if the South could be "pressed" as much as possible, if given "no peace," then the end could not be "distant."[4]

By May, two western campaigns ended badly. Instead of a move on Mobile in the spring of 1864, General Banks, commander of the Department of the Gulf, was instructed by Halleck to make a move west of the Mississippi via a combined naval and military operation along the Red River.[5]

It was hoped that the Red River campaign would secure Louisiana and perhaps gain back control of Arkansas. It would also eliminate any potential French intervention by way of Mexico. Though at this point in the conflict it was highly unlikely, it was still a threat as far as the Union high command was concerned. The plan called for an attack on Shreveport from the north and south. Banks in the south would work his way up along the Red River with his force of 30,000 veterans, while General Frederick Steele and his force of 10,000 worked its way down from Arkansas in the north. The expedition got underway on

General Edward R.S. Canby (left) and Admiral David Glasglow Farragut (Library of Congress).

March 10 and by May it was in full retreat, with 4,000 causalities. The turning point came when Banks' army of seasoned veterans was halted and defeated on April 9 at the battle of Mansfield by a smaller Confederate force under the command of Major General Richard Taylor. After the campaign, Banks was relieved of command and General Edward R.S. Canby took charge of the newly formed Military Division of West Mississippi. Canby was an interesting choice, as he lacked the experience such a position seemed to demand. However, the Kentucky-born Canby was regarded as a prudent soldier, which was apparently what the position required.[6]

When Canby took command, the overall situation in the Trans-Mississippi was unstable. The department was vast — the largest in the Union — stretching from Missouri to the Gulf and from Florida to Texas. A majority of its forces were spread out in forts and garrisons to protect the rivers and railways from raids and guerilla operations. Canby took immediate action in organization and administrative matters, as this was his strength. He instructed Steele to concentrate his forces and abandon all positions not essential for maintaining his current position. He also gave indication that he was not going to sit on anything, and told Steele to "be in readiness for offensive movements."[7]

Canby also designated Vicksburg as his supply depot and consolidation point for future troop movements. He ordered Major General H.W. Slocum, in command at Vicksburg, to be ready with enough supplies to accommodate 40,000 men. From Vicksburg troops could be moved swiftly north, south, east, or west. Canby also requested more engineers and began work on railroads needed to "render our own force as mobile as that of the Rebels." By concentrating his forces, he could gain more flexibility for offensive action. Protection of Sherman's rear and communications was also a priority that would occupy a significant amount of Canby's time over the coming months.[8]

* * *

In January 1864, Grant received information from a refugee imprisoned for a time in Mobile. According to the informant, Mobile was virtually defenseless, with only 3,000 to 4,000 men to protect it. The condition of these troops was also in question, as it was claimed that at nearby Selma, "there is [only] a company of boys and old men."[9]

The plan that Grant and Sherman envisioned could have had a lethal effect on the war. While Sherman marched on Atlanta, Canby would overtake the nearly defenseless Mobile and march on Selma and northern Alabama, still untouched by the ravages of war. Selma was a key munitions manufacturer for the South, holding a "large and extensive arsenal." Sherman also saw the capture of Mobile as a maneuver to secure his rear as he took on Confederate general Johnston and headed towards the "interior of the enemy's country," at Grant's orders. In order to cut off its port, Admiral David Glasglow Farragut was also pushing for a combined naval and military move on the forts that protected the Bay.[10]

On June 4, 1864, in an attempt to get momentum for an assault on Mobile, Sherman, in an apparent effort to influence Halleck to support his plan, sent several communications. He simultaneously contacted Generals A.J. Smith and Canby, suggesting to each a movement on Mobile. His correspondences called for a relatively small force of "6,000 to 10,000" men led by A.J. Smith (who just happened to have such a force under his command) to be sent with Farragut to assault Mobile. In a communication with Admiral Porter, Sherman exclaimed, "there is no one there [Mobile]." Porter agreed, replying, "I think now is the time to go to Mobile." When Sherman wired Canby, suggesting Smith's movement, he hoped all bases were covered. It's obvious Sherman had reservations that contacting Canby alone would be enough.[11]

Yet both Sherman and Grant believed Mobile was there for the taking. "I know from prisoners taken that all the troops in Alabama are here with Johnston, and he is calling for every man from the southwest." Grant, always on Sherman's side, also pressed the issue with Halleck, urging him to authorize a movement. He proposed that taking Mobile would help Sherman defeat Johnston and "secure for him a base of supplies after his work is done."[12]

* * *

After dinner on June 6, Sherman sent a telegraph to Halleck. Around 7 o'clock, hoping to see some progress, he inquired, "Has the movement on Mobile been ordered?" Playing possum, he continued: "Canby telegraphs me that he can spare General A.J. Smith. All I ask is the co–operation of Farragut's fleet." One can only imagine the smile that greeted Halleck's reply later that evening—"Operations on Mobile has been suggested to General Canby"—then the frown—"A.J. Smith has been sent to Memphis to break up Forrest's [Nathan Bedford] operations on your line of supplies."[13]

Then finally, just after midnight, Halleck telegraphed Canby: "General Grant suggests that, if troops can be spared," a force should be sent to Mobile. Halleck knew Canby was somewhat overwhelmed with various issues. Canby had a huge logistical, fleecing, policing, and organizational job facing him. In Missouri there was trouble with guerrillas, not to mention Arkansas and Kirby Smith. All along the Mississippi raiders were throwing up blockades and assaulting ships, and in Mississippi and West Tennessee Forrest was proving difficult, if not impossible, to contain. The final comment in Halleck's midnight message made his intentions clear: "Perhaps the security of Sherman's rear and prevention of raids into Missouri will absorb all your spare forces."[14]

Halleck was not asking a question. He was ever so subtly encouraging Canby's tendency toward paralysis by over-analysis. He didn't want him to move on Mobile yet. Halleck knew that another Red River-type disaster would threaten Lincoln's reelection during his 1864 campaign. What if a move on Mobile ended badly? Canby was put in command because he was overtly cautious, which is exactly what Halleck wanted, even if the general was sometimes debilitated strategically to the point of indecision. The always prudent Canby would take significant offensive action only when success was almost certain. It would have been a bold move to take a small force of 10,000 troops and attack Mobile and its surrounding forts in the summer of 1864.

Not long after Halleck's midnight message, Canby was still apparently considering offensive action. He went to sea and visited Farragut, parked with his fleet off Mobile Bay as he prepared for the inevitable assault on the forts protecting the bay's entrance. An important meeting was about to take place, one that could decide the future of Mobile in 1864.

* * *

If there was any momentum building for Grant and Sherman's Mobile plans, it came crashing down on the 10th of June 1864, near Guntown, Mississippi. There, General Samuel D. Sturgis and his army (nearly 8,000 strong) were utterly outmaneuvered and outfought by a much smaller force of 4,800 led by Confederate general Nathan Bedford Forrest. By all accounts the fighting was vicious. Forrest caught Sturgis with his army strung out, and defeated his cavalry and infantry piecemeal. The defeat was so decisive that within 48 hours various reports on Forrest's movements, strength, and direction convinced Major General Cadwallader C. Washburn that Forrest had a force possibly as large as 15,000. In response, he felt troops should be sent to Mobile, where he believed Forrest might be heading.[15]

By June 14 even Sherman admitted, "Under the circumstances, the expedition to Mobile should not be attempted." A.J. Smith and his men would indeed be needed to subdue Forrest. Sherman then telegraphed Secretary of War Stanton in Washington; seething with anger, he wrote, "Forrest is the very devil." His frustration grew with each word: "I will order them [A.J. Smith] to make up a force and go out and follow Forrest to the death, [even] if it costs 10,000 lives and breaks the treasury."[16]

Forrest's smashing defeat of Sturgis sent a mini tidal wave through the entire Trans-Mississippi region. Commanding generals refused to give up forces to Canby for fear of being caught off guard. Enemy troop movements and strength were unusually exaggerated. But most importantly, Grant and Sherman would not be able to prod and push Canby or Halleck for an immediate move on Mobile.

* * *

Canby had just returned from his visit with Farragut when word of Sturgis' defeat reached him. Both concluded that Mobile was formidable enough to require a force "greater than General Sherman indicates." Canby informed Halleck that he did not feel comfortable making any kind of move until he could "send a force twice as great" so as to not "endanger anything." If there was an aggressive bone in Canby's body, Forrest's handling of Sturgis broke it. He would not risk a thing.[17]

Canby went to see Farragut in an effort to obtain firsthand information on fortifications and enemy strength; he believed Farragut to be the best source for such information. But Farragut had spent the better part of his last six years on the water, and his health was "giving way." He himself admitted that "the last six months have been a severe drag upon me, and I want rest, if it is to be had." He saw his work to be "at an end." He was now in his early sixties, and his body was breaking down under the stress and workload.[18]

He also suffered from vertigo and fainting spells, and even to his men he appeared fragile. Farragut was a spent man, having endured four grueling years at sea in the service of his country during war. Emotionally and physically taxed, he was not interested in helping the army assault Mobile, and said so himself: "I never was in favor of taking Mobile." Taking the city directly would have been most difficult for his fleet, because the bay protecting it was "bristling with ... batteries and shielded by ... torpedo-laden waters."[19]

Canby's lack of military experience was the root cause of his indecision and overtly cautious approach to Mobile. He graduated from West Point with the rank of second lieutenant. During the Mexican war he saw action in the battles of Cerro Gordo, Contreras, Churubusco, and Belen Gate. He ascended to lieutenant colonel during this time. In 1861 he was appointed colonel of the Nineteenth Infantry and put in command of the Department of New Mexico, where he proved himself defending an invasion by Confederate general Henry H. Sibley. Canby was able to "block his advance, control supply lines, and ultimately force the Confederates to retreat to Texas."[20]

But he had acted mostly as an "adviser," and worked "behind a desk" for the bulk of the war. In July of 1864 he was assigned to New York City, where riots protesting the draft broke out. At one point Negroes were dragged out into street and "lynched." It was a dreadful situation, and by all accounts Canby took command and was decisive. But this was hardly a military command of distinction. Canby was a lawyer, an "astute" officer with an intense desire to learn. He was a bookworm whose best asset, as Grant later confirmed, was as a "staff officer," not as a commander. Canby, by most accounts, was a humble man and was therefore likely aware of his own deficiencies.[21]

* * *

It was December, and the regiment was still camped out on the peninsula enjoying the warm weather. Jesse Mather was back with his company. His mother and sister had hoped he would get to go home, but it was not to be:

Dear Mother
  I have seated myself to write you a few lines in answer to your kind leter that came to hand some time ago I am well at present and hope these few lines will find you the same. We ar having nice pleasant weather hear now we ar camped right on the edge of the bay.... Some of the boys say that this is an island and sum of them say it is a peinsula. I dont know whitch it is and dont know as I care. You thought that I wouldent go back to the regt again I thought that I wouldent go back their for a while, but I got minding well and the Doctor wouldent give me a furlow and so I thought that I would go to the regt. I have stood it first rate since I came back we have been on the go about all the time since I got back, though we have been on the boats the most of the time and that is not very hard moving that way we have martched about 50 miles since we came around hear and had to cary every thing that we had or else throw it away and had to cary five days rastions in our havesacks. I don't expect to com home now till my time is out you must not wory about me but keep up good spirits I haven't got a great while longer to serve and if my life is spared I will com home as soon as I can and see you. Well I will close for this time hoping to hear from you soon again by way of letter. I remain your affectionate son.[22]

However, most of the men were not fixated on being back home anymore. They were used to being away from family and friends, and what concerned them most was the war. They were far away from the bloody battlefields in the east and that was good. They were also far away from the cold Wisconsin winter, and felt they had found a kind of paradise. It had its drawbacks, but for the most part it was better than their other options. By January 1864 the regiment had moved to Indianola. They were still on the Gulf of Mexico, but now they had houses to live in, since the town was abandoned by the time they arrived. Though it could get cold at times, it was still paradise for these former wheat farmers.

German immigrants founded Indianola in 1844. By the time the Civil War broke out, it was challenging Galveston as Texas' top port city. The war would ruin the place. But Samuel Kirkpatrick didn't care; they now had a "splendid two story house" to live in. Slowly the townsfolk filtered back and this, too, was all right by Samuel, who was having a "great time here with the girls and widows." But the big news was their reenlistment. Their three years were nearly up and they had to decide if they wanted to reenlist as veterans. Though they had experienced several skirmishes with Rebel cavalry since arriving at Indianola, Samuel thought reenlistment was as "good business as a single man can go in to." Those who did so received a reenlistment bounty (sometimes several hundred dollars) and were granted a veteran furlough, which meant they could go home for 30 days before reenlisting. For Samuel, it was also about patriotism: "I want to see the old stripes and stars aflote over all and then I will be satisfied to come home to live and if it fails I want to fail with it but I think the war will be over before three more years rolls around."[23]

Jesse wasn't sure what to do. He had lost two brothers and was encouraged by his family to come home. "I don't think that I will go those that do go will go back to the state and have 30 days furlow and maybe stay the summer," he wrote. "I am in hopes that this war will close before my time is out. I dont think it will last a great while longer. I think that there is as good a prospect for it not to...." Jesse and Oliver had volunteered because they wanted to fight the rebellion. They had probably made promises to each other should one be killed, or at the very least discussed the possibility. Jesse was torn between wanting to reenlist and wanting to go home at the end of the three years.[24]

Beyond Indianola was a vast prairie full of cattle. Beef was plentiful, and small herds sometimes wandered into town. They weren't the only thing that wandered in. Near dusk on the 9th of January, Rebel cavalry, about two or three hundred strong, appeared northwest of town. Quickly the Eleventh Wisconsin deployed Company A as skirmishers while the rest of the regiment formed up in line of battle. But the Rebels had no intention of fighting. A few shots were fired from long range and then they were out of sight. Colonel Harris took a couple of companies and followed them several miles out of town before heading back for the night. Off and on during the month Rebels would appear on the horizon; sometimes they would fire a shot or two, but then drift away into the night. Why did they keep coming back? What did they want?[25]

Samuel barely noticed, for he was too busy fraternizing with the women. The town was devoid of men, with only boys and old men left. The local women were apparently lonely (their husbands and boyfriends may very well have been those who appeared sometimes in the evening!) and it was Samuel's prediction that if they remained there much longer, "there will be lots of wedens." By February, Samuel reported that nearly 300 of the boys were reenlisting. "I can get 17 dolars a month and bord and cloths and $400 and 2 dollars bounty," wrote Samuel. The pay was good for "soldering in peace" he declared. He was pretty much convinced that he had seen the worst and perhaps the last of the war. That three-fourths of the regiment reenlisted speaks volumes for their determination to see the war through to the end.[26]

For the most part these were good times, and love was in the air. Letters from the single men to their parents mentioned their loneliness. Samuel wrote to one friend who had missed out on the chance to marry his sweetheart when she married someone else. Apparently the poor fellow had his chance, "but he thought he could do as he pleased," wrote Samuel. "Love is some thing that no one ought to fool with." By the end of winter Samuel took note that "several of the boys has got married since they came here." Love was indeed in the air.[27]

* * *

By March 1864 the regiment was back in Wisconsin and reunited with friends and family. Before being allowed to leave on furlough they were reviewed by Governor Lewis. The parade ground was lined with people as the Eleventh Wisconsin marched in column before forming in line and coming to a halt. Colonel Harris gave back the regiment flag they had carried away nearly three years before. It was tattered and worn and in such bad shape that it was retired and a new one issued. Though no doubt people were proud to see their sons and husbands return, it had to be strange to count only 300 or so of the original 1,029 that had enlisted. "The regiment presented a fine appearance, and were highly complimented for their neatness and soldier-like appearance," wrote James McMyler, the regimental historian. What else was there to say? These were not the same jovial and innocent young men who had marched off to war so enthusiastically. These were battle-hardened veterans. The looks on their faces, the scars both visible and hidden, told no lies. They were forever changed. But that afternoon they managed to let their guard down, just a little, as they were discharged from service and allowed 30 days rest "in the enjoyment of their friends" until April 23, when they were to rendezvous at Camp Washburn in Milwaukee.[28]

Private Jesse Mather after the war, age unknown (Author's Collection).

"The joy of meeting kindred and friends after so long an absence," wrote Calvin Alling years later, "the soldier boys were feted, and nothing was too good, or left undone that could be done for their comfort and pleasure." Calvin thought the time right for marriage, and on April 4, 1864, he married in what he described as a "very quiet and pretty wedding." The time flew by for everyone, and the "parties, receptions, and the many kindnesses shown" surprised the men. Calvin recalled after the war, "Everybody seemed to be our friends." Calvin took his new bride home and introduced her to his family. He was not the only one in the regiment who married. Samuel Kirkpatrick was wed on April 16 at a hotel in Mineral Point. His wife, Caroline, is never mentioned in his letters. Whether she was a longtime sweetheart is not known. It was a joyous time for those who had returned, and no doubt there were even more weddings.[29]

Jesse Mather did not reenlist. He needed to get home. His family had lost two sons and his father needed help with the harvest. In his last letter home in late 1864, Jesse told his sister:

> The time is not far distant, when I hope to see you again I am waiting the time to come as patiently as possible I think we will start from hear the 1st of Oct. if they do I will get up their about the time my time is out after you get this you needent write any more till you hear from me probably when you do it will be by the word of mouth I will close this time hoping that I will soon see you good by with love to all. Receive this from your affectionate Brother.[30]

Jesse returned home and helped his father with the harvest. Within three years he married, bought his own land, and had a son. His wife, Lottie, bore him five children—four sons and a daughter. He never again left Sauk County, Wisconsin. Jesse died there on August 26, 1924, at the age of 79.[31]

William H. Cope also did not reenlist. He returned home to help his father with the farm. It is not known if their plan to sell the cattle was instigated. Shortly after returning home William married Margaret, an immigrant from Scotland whose family migrated to Wisconsin from New York. In 1870 they had twins, a boy and a girl, and by 1880 the Copes had moved to Mount Morris, Wisconsin. Thomas Cope, William's father, was also listed on the census report as a member of William's household.

* * *

It would be Navy Secretary Gideon Welles who finally got an attack on Mobile to materialize. He wanted Farragut to take action and Farragut wanted one last shot at glory before his health gave way. Confederate blockade runners from Mobile to Havana were still operating and had to be dealt with. In August 1864, a joint military and naval operation hit Mobile Bay. There was still a chance that another pressure point could be applied to the South. The forts protecting the mouth of Mobile Bay were little match for Farragut's fleet after it had finished the meager Confederate navy, spurred on by the Admiral's now famous words: "Damn the torpedoes, full steam ahead!"

Perhaps most importantly, however, the men manning these forts, including their leaders, lacked the desire and commitment to defend them. The first fort to fall, Fort Powell, offered little resistance before it was evacuated. As for the other forts, Gaines and Morgan, Confederate major general Dabney Herndon Maury, in charge of defending Mobile, thought they would be "stubborn" in their resistance. He even wired Richmond telling Jefferson Davis as much. But they were also being assaulted by land. Canby allowed a force of about 2,000 troops under the command of General Gordon Granger to take part.[32]

But the forts would not hold. On August 8, 1864, just as his first message of optimism was received in Richmond, Maury was forced to send another telegram. "It is painfully humiliating to announce the shameful surrender of Fort Gaines.... This powerful work was provisioned for six months and with a garrison of 600 men." Disheartened, he then asked, "Can you spare any good infantry?"[33]

When Federal troops marched into Fort Gaines after its surrender, Canby wrote Halleck that the fort was taken with "47 [46] commissioned officers and 818 enlisted men, with its armament, 26 guns intact, and provisions for twelve months," and that it had "surrendered unconditionally." Maury in his official report stated that the fort could have "long withstood an attack"[34]

This report was significant. When the fort surrendered it was still in fighting shape, had plenty of armament and provisions, and could have withstood more attacks. Most significant of all, inside the fort was the Twenty-first Alabama, which consisted mostly of boys and old men, confirming that the Confederacy in Alabama was but a shell of its former self.[35]

The final fort protecting Mobile bay was Fort Morgan, now exposed and an easy target for Farragut's fleet. On August 23, 1864, the inevitable occurred. At half past six in the morning, a white flag was raised and the fort was unionized. Granger's force, now at 4,000, suffered only one killed and seven wounded. The Confederate army protecting Mobile had proven itself incompetent, unprepared, outmanned and, in the end, lacking the will to fight. Yet Canby and Farragut failed to recognize this and capture Mobile's defenses, which could have easily been accomplished. Maury admitted as much, reporting, "Mobile is henceforth liable to attack."[36]

By this time Maury was a nervous wreck, believing a major attack was on the way. He constantly requested reinforcements and overestimated the intentions and size of Canby's forces. "Canby has been with Farragut," wrote Maury. "His army lies near here." In August, just before the attack, Maury reported that the "total number of men now under arms in the whole district is about 6,000, about 1,000 of whom have been under fire, and a large portion are citizens of the place. The city has probably more women and children in it than at any time since the war began."[37]

Of Maury's 5,000 or 6,000, Farragut had to know that many were "boys" and "local troops." Yet he reported back after the capture of Fort Morgan, "I consider an army of twenty or thirty thousand men necessary to take the city of Mobile and almost as many to hold." Nothing during the entire month of August should have given Farragut or Canby anything but encouragement to strike Mobile quickly, while the iron was hot. Another consideration was not to bother with the city of Mobile itself. By August it was a closed port, and taking the city directly was not necessary; bypassing it would have been easy. Mobile would never hold out as long as Vicksburg.[38]

In mid August Canby was informed that a Rebel deserter claimed there was a force of "8,000 to 9,000" defending Mobile and its vicinity, comprised mostly of "boys and old men." Assuming Canby took this deserter's information at face value, which he should not have, he must have recognized a trend. The army Maury had, whatever its size (5,000 to 9,000), was mostly conscripts, boys, and old men, and from examples of their defense of Forts Gaines, Morgan, and Powell, morale was low. Nonetheless, Canby had heard enough and capitulated to his nerves. No significant offensive action was to be made "until we have a larger land force than can [now] be spared."[39]

The day before the Rebel deserter ran to Canby's waiting arms, a telegram arrived from Sherman, who was in Atlanta. It read: "Convey to Admiral Farragut my admiration of the bold and successful passage of the Mobile forts." Was this a subtle jab at Canby from Sherman? We know Sherman believed it would not take much to bypass Mobile and secure the region. He was confident enough to send Halleck a letter telling him as much.[40]

But it was not to be. Writing Grant in response to Sherman's letter, Halleck echoed Canby: "I think Sherman has entirely overestimated Granger's forces and underestimated the difficulty of passing Mobile and ascending the Alabama some 150 or 200 miles." As the dominos fell in 1864, it is difficult not to see Farragut and Canby as the impetus behind the crash. The planned expedition on Mobile with A.J. Smith's army fell apart when Forrest crushed Sturgis, which was unfortunate. But when the possibility of taking Mobile presented itself, or at the very least opening up another front in Alabama after Farragut and Granger's victories, Canby was quick to quash any talk of a larger movement: "I have only a reserve force of 12,000 men, in addition to 5,000 at Mobile." His main concern, and a legitimate one, was the possible threat of Kirby Smith west of the Mississippi. Canby believed Smith's army was now "reorganized and considerably strengthened, and will [not] remain comparatively idle much longer." But it would. The war southwest of the Mississippi, for all practical purposes, was winding down by the end of 1864.[41]

In August Canby wrote meekly to Farragut: "Permit me to add the expression of my regret that I have not at present the means of co–operation that would give the most perfect results of your glorious operation." But was this really the case? Canby's reserve force of 12,000 men needs to be considered. Almost 2,000 of the 5,000 men he sent to Mobile were from Texas, not from his reserves. In the returns of the Military Division of West Mississippi for the month of July 1864, there is no mention of a specific reserve among the 114,000 aggregate total listed, which isn't in itself unusual. In March 1864 there was a more detailed return. New

Orleans and its surrounding area was shown to have about 29,000 men for defense. In a report filed in June by Major George B. Drake from the Office of Chief Engineer, Department of the Gulf, Drake clearly states that a "total force" of only "12,000 men" was required to defend the city and its vicinity. It's unlikely Canby had 29,000 in the area, but he had to have something close to that number. Did he have another 9,000 troops to spare from New Orleans? He might have had additional men to send, on top of his reserves. In hindsight, there was an opportunity for a quick strike on Mobile. It would have been a bold move, but one Canby was unwilling to make.[42]

By opening another front in Alabama, from which Grant could have "thrown" troops into the heart of the South, Canby could have forced an already depleted Confederacy into making some hard decisions, the results of which will never be known. Unfortunately, Canby's lack of conviction, military skill and strategy would cost the Eleventh Wisconsin and thousands of other Federal soldiers dearly during the final days of the war.

Chapter Eleven

1865 — Down on the Bayou

It was a "rainy and gloomy" day as the Eleventh Wisconsin prepared to leave for Chicago on April 24. By the time they reached Memphis, newspaper headlines read "Disaster in Banks Department." General Banks' Red River Campaign ended in disaster. Though his ranks swelled with Grant's veterans, his leadership and generalship reflected that of McDowell in 1862, not Grant in 1863. Since Grant's successful Vicksburg campaign and General Meade's defeat of Lee at Gettysburg, the North had seen little if any real progress in the war. Just the week before, reports had come in concerning the "Massacre at Fort Pillow," where 221 Negro and white soldiers had been brutally killed. A large Rebel cavalry force under the command of Nathan Bedford Forrest attacked the fort, which was poorly defended, and once inside executed and perhaps even tortured many of the defenders. News of the atrocity swept across the North, followed by cries for revenge. An editorial in the *Janesville Weekly Gazette* put it most eloquently:

> If the colored man is so magnanimous as to shoulder his musket and bare his breast for the defense of the liberty of a race that has never treated him to anything better than the auction block and the overseer's lash — if, in return for selling his wife and children into abject and hopeless slavery, he is generous enough to risk his life in defense of ours, is not the government bound by every consideration of duty and obligation to render him the same protection that it does to the white? The black race of America exhibits a magnanimity and a forgiving spirit towards their lifelong enemies that has had no parallel since the world began.[1]

Though not everyone agreed with this profound statement, there was a changing of attitude toward Negroes that continued after the war. An investigation into the Fort Pillow incident was ordered and a congressional subcommittee was formed to oversee the proceedings. But until the war was won, there was little that could be done.

By April 1864, around 136,000 veterans had reenlisted in the Federal army, and the vast majority were the "fierce-fighting western men" Grant had led to triumph the year before. Back east in the Army of the Potomac, where morale was once again low, only 27,000 reenlisted. Even the offer of a $400 bounty, plus whatever bonus states or counties came up with, was not enough. The eastern soldier had seen a long line of obtuse leadership that bled the army dry, and without much to show for it. The list was long: McDowell, McClellan, Pope, Burnside, Hooker, and Meade. President Lincoln knew what he had to do. Grant was placed in command of all Union armies and was lieutenant general. He was only the second general since George Washington to hold such a rank, the other being Winfield Scott (1786–1866).[2]

On April 29, the Eleventh Wisconsin Volunteer Regiment reached Memphis and was assigned to Major General Washburn's command. By May 1 they were marching with General Sturgis and his expedition through west Tennessee and Northwest Mississippi in an attempt to sweep the area clean of Forrest's Rebel cavalry. The expedition failed to engage Forrest in a major battle, though, resulting in only minor skirmishes and heavy marching.

"This campaign was a very severe one," wrote McMyler of the Eleventh Wisconsin. "The weather was extremely hot and the men were not prepared for it. Coming directly from home without army shoes, they suffered severely from blistered feet."[3]

The regiment was eventually sent back to Louisiana and its bayous. The rainy coastal country where they were stationed contained marshes, fertile delta lands, rolling pine hills, and prairies. The Mississippi River dominated the many waterways, but there were other rivers and slow-moving bayous threading the coast. In places slow streams formed large stagnant pools. Mosquitoes, alligators, and crawfish were plentiful. The air was also thick with humidity and the water tasted stale compared to the crisp spring water the men had enjoyed only weeks ago in Wisconsin.

Robert Sherrill and Caroline had by now resumed their letter exchanges. "I take this oppertunity of writing you a few lines to let you know that your letter of the 19th instant came to my hands yesterday...." Robert had also reenlisted, though the somber and defeated tone of his letters in late 1863 and early 1864 gave the impression he was ready to stop fighting. Whatever his reasons for reenlisting, the old Robert was returning in his letters: "All quiet along our lines except a little cavelry skirmishes one took place yesterday...." During this letter Robert included a strange comment: "I believe I could tell you somethings if I was a mind to. That is some thing that was told me not intimating as though I knew anything personally only what was told me." He then signed his letter "yours truly."[4]

The regiment's health was good and its numbers replenished somewhat. It now numbered "about 600 men fit for duty," wrote Samuel Kirkpatrick, and he was fairly accurate; the Eleventh Wisconsin reported 561 present for duty. Their mission was simple: guard the Great Western Railroad and sweep the nearby bayous and swamps in search of renegade Rebels and deserters hiding out on isolated plantations and in backwoods cabins. The regiment historian, James McMyler, described their activities at this time:

> The Regiment has been engaged in all kinds of duties, building fortifications and performing Picket, Guard and Provost duty. In addition to this, we have frequently been called upon to go aboard the gunboats stationed here, and aid in reconnoitering up the Teche and many other bayous which are connected with Berwick Bay. The picket duty has been of a very serious nature, and the line picketed by the Regiment very extensive, extending in a circuitous rout four miles north and five miles south of this place. Much sickness has prevailed in the Regiment during the summer months, caused by the low swampy lands surrounding. Being between the lower Mississippi and the Gulf Coast, the country is thickly interspersed with narrow deep bayous running in every conceivable direction, whose banks are lined with a thick foliage mostly cypress, and filled with a very dark-colored poisonous water which is drained from the many cypress swamps so noted in this Southern country, causing malaria in its worst form.[5]

Most of the men made the best of it. "At this post in the big cypress timber, we had great times," said Calvin Alling, "quarreling with the mosquitoes, eating blackberries, which were abundant, fishing, scouting...." They were after small bands of Confederate bushwhackers, which was not too dangerous, and that was all right by the Federals. They were still far away from the bloody battlefields in the east, where thousands were dying in the Wilderness, near Spotsylvania Courthouse and outside Petersburg. Grant continued to press Lee, hitting him again and again in what would be the bloodiest year of the war.[6]

* * *

Ithamar Stowe Chaffee was one of the new guys to help bolster the Eleventh Wisconsin's ranks, which were depleted to less than 600 active for duty. Ithamar was 37 years old, married, and listed his occupation as a farmer. He was mustered into service in October 1864, and joined the regiment in early November as a member of H Company. Upon his arrival one of his first duties was to vote, documenting that "Lincoln received 512 votes and McClalland received 82" from the Eleventh Wisconsin. The success of Sherman around Atlanta during the second half of 1864 all but guaranteed Lincoln's reelection, which was anything but a lock before Sherman's victory.[7]

"Dear Aunt, I received your welcome letter a few days ago.... I am happy to say that the seventeenth of October finds R.R.S all rite side up with care and I hope these few lines may find you all enjoying the same great blessings." Robert Sherrill was one of the lucky ones, seemingly resistant to the heat, humidity, and stale, malaria-infested water the men were forced to drink. "I have escaped sickness," he wrote. "I should judge it is kind of lonesome since this last call for I understand that all the men is gone on it." Caroline had told Robert about a wonderful picnic she and daughters Adda and Marion enjoyed. "As for me," he continued, "I am taking the world as easy as I can." For the first time in a long time, Robert felt good. Then the letter turned to Robert's social life, and the single ladies in town. "I am acquainted with a very few young ladies here," he assured her, though some were "very sociable." "What did you mean in your letter by saying that you hoped that I would not get insulted by receiving a letter from you? I hope you will explain your self in your next." Whatever the explanation, it was getting late in the evening:

> A serenading band of musick came in on the train this evening. It is playing now it is a delightful piece of musick and a splendid band playing it. I wish you could hear it. I will have to postpone writing for a few minutes to go and listen to it.... They have quit now so I will procede now with my letter it is now half past eight the camp is all quietness and I am a lonely wanderer sitting in my tent all by my self trying to scribble of a few lines to my friends I feel thankful to think I am able to do so. I consider myself very lucky.[8]

* * *

"Today I got a pass to go to New Orleans tomorrow and return Sunday," wrote William Henry Oettiker* in his diary in early 1865. "Friday and in the eavening I went to the theater and saw a young elephant and also the first ones I ever saw." He spent several days in the city and was apparently fascinated with the elephants. He spent "all day buying all sorts of stuff to take out to the regiment. I spent 50$ today and in the evening I went to the sircus again it was the same things over." After two days of rest and relaxation, Henry was on his way back to the regiment when "I had my pocketbook and 25$ stole by one of the Indiana boys but got it by mutch trouble again." Though not a particularly big fellow, Henry was tough, and most likely fisticuffs were involved.[9]

The regiment was strung out along the railroad in southwest Louisiana. Most of them, like Oettiker, had it pretty good stationed in Brashear City. Others, like Calvin Alling and Samuel Kirkpatrick, had it much tougher out in the bayous at isolated locations. Calvin recalled one patrol where they were after some Rebels hiding out in the swamps. They had "orders to lie in ambush on the bank" in the water and wait for Rebel boats to come by. He continued:

> In about a half hour alligators began to put in an appearance. Four immense great "crocodiles" that were judged by all to be not less than twenty-four feet long, rose up in the water on the opposite side from us. After eyeing us for perhaps twenty or thirty minutes, finding we did not move, they began towards us, to the middle of the stream, which was some fifty feet wide, where they halted perhaps ten or fifteen minutes.

**He was called "Henry Oettiker" by most accounts.*

They sat motionless another hour as the alligators began to move down the bank. But it was a nerve-racking experience; they "could have struck" the alligators with a "ten foot pole." The monsters settled into the water, where they held underwater with "only one eye and the knot on their snout" visible, then slowly the eyes and snouts disappeared under the water. "Never did the men so much long to disobey orders," said Calvin.[10]

Back in Brashear City, things were not as exciting. Henry Oettiker chronicled the monotony of daily army life for most of the regiment.

Wednesday, January 25, 1865
Releaved from guard this morning. Drew clothing I drew a fore of coats. No noose of note has occured today only Battellion drill this afternoon and dress parrade. Wether cold, frost and windy.

Thursday, January 26, 1865
On fatigue on the parripet [parapet] until 3 this afternoon and then we had to go on Battellion drill and dress parrade in the eavening. No noose of any importance has occured on this post today. Wether cold clear.

Friday, January 27, 1865
No noose on this post today I was at work all day fixing ower coats. I got a letter from home with two dollars in it. A short drill this afternoon. Wether cloudy and some rane.

Saturday, January 28, 1865
At work building barracks fore of us built ower shanty today by hard work. The Regiment has almost all of them in barracks now. No noose of any importance. Wether cold.

Sunday, January 29, 1865
On guard at the boat landing today one oyster boat come in loaded with oysters. No noose in camp today about piece. Wether cold and cloudy.

Monday, January 30, 1865
The Company is at work building some more barracks. Still more letters and noose about piece. I was at work all day. Wether cloudy and stormy looking and cool.

It rained off and on throughout January and February, turning the roads into thick sticky mud. The daily routine bored the men dreadfully, especially the replacements, and at times they made poor decisions. One soldier was to serve "two years with out pay for getting drunk & loading of his gun and calling the Colonel a son of a bitch," wrote Henry. Joseph Hillier of A Company filled his diary with notes on the weather, which he wasn't taking a liking to. The mud made an impression on him; several days in a row he mentioned how deep it was, as he marched through it on guard duty. Samuel Kirkpatrick thought life was great. "All we have to do is guard a bridge," he said. "It is as good as I ever had." It took the veterans to realize this was the good life.[11]

The Eleventh wasn't the only regiment stationed in this area. Along with them, among others, was the Ninety-third U.S. Colored regiment. They were stationed at Brashear City and Berwick until June 1865. "Releaved from guard this morning by Negroes at 10 and the cussing the poor cuffies got was not few," wrote Henry, because they were apparently late. As they had seen, the love bug can hit a regiment isolated from family and friends, and it was no different for the Ninety-third. Henry wrote in his diary that "thare was 35 of them [in the Negro regiment] got married today" in New Orleans.

The weather was changing, and the warm Southern spring air was welcomed by all. But the companies scattered throughout the swamps of Louisiana could only take so much. "We have been in the swamp long enough," declared Samuel Kirkpatrick after five months on the bayou. Even the veterans had their breaking point. The weather was especially hard on the new recruits, fresh from the Midwest. The regiment lamented that it took a draft to get others to join up and fight for their country, and they were equally disgusted with the draftees once they arrived. What some of the veterans did not understand was that these men had not necessarily dodged the war because of cowardice. Many were merely trying to support families.[12]

* * *

Another one of the new regiment members was John W. Kennedy from Bloom City, Richland County. The father of four children, two sons and two daughters, and husband to Mary Ann Kennedy, he owned a small farm with a few head of cattle and other livestock. He joined the regiment in January 1864. It was particularly difficult for him to leave his wife and children. John wanted more than anything to be with his family, but would not turn his back on his country when called upon. He was placed in Company D and sent to Bayou Louis, a very inhospitable place. But his mind, as it always would be, was back home with the farm, the harvest, and his family.

"You must do the best you can with your crop this summer," John wrote home to his wife in the spring. "But I dont want you nor the little boys to work to hard." He then told her if the crop failed to sell the cattle in the fall. They would bring in a good price and would save them the added cost of purchasing feed. He closed his letter asking her to write him often about how the crop was faring.[13]

John's letters home focused almost exclusively on his wife and children. He inquired constantly about their health, and worried about the upcoming harvest and what his wife should do if things did not go well. He wrote often, sometimes several letters a week. After receiving a letter from his children, one of his first letters, he wrote home with mixed emotions: "I was realy glad to hear from you that you was all well and prosper as it was the best news I could hear just now for I am aweful home sic." John, like so many others, wanted no part of the war, but he understood it was his duty.[14]

By September things were not going well for his wife or the farm. The crop turned out badly, which was probably not a great surprise. But he could not have anticipated her solution to their financial problems. Mary was raising four young children and tending to a farm, a feat that would have made anyone long for a change. She thought it best that they sell the farm, since it seemed hopeless that she could handle it alone. She had found a nice little home near town that she thought would be better suited to raising a family while he was gone. "Now I don't want you to talk about bying it let alone by it," John wrote home somewhat frantically in a short letter. He also asked her how his horse was and if it was being tended to properly. His distance from home, both physically and emotionally, seemed to get the best of him at times.

In December, John wrote home to his wife:

> I take my pen in hand this morning to answer your kind letter of the 15th of Nov which gave me mutch pleasure to hear from you again & to hear that you was all well it found me in good health & in fine spirits for the papers last evening stated that the Rebel congress was in a perfect confusion about half of them wants to come back in to the union again & old grant & gen Sherman is a moving forward with great success.[15]

John was in good spirits, thinking the war would soon come to an end. He predicted an end by the spring of 1865, and that seemed manageable to him. He could make it that long and his family could too. John had sent money to help Mary, but according to her last letter it had not yet arrived:

> Now I wrote to you every week since that time & I sent you my price for ower farm in 3 or 4 letters but for fear that you do not get them I will give it in this my price for the farm is one thou-

sand dollars or for the stock that you have mentioned & the farm twelve hundred & 50 dollars & no less not if any person wants to buy it at that prices you can write to me & I will get a good deed made & I will sign it & send it to you direct.

The farm was too much for her to handle alone. They had an offer on the table, and Mary wanted to take it. But John also knew that moving to a house in town would not be as easy as she perhaps thought. He wrote again:

You seem ancious for me to take that offer ... and let you move close to town to live now mother I know what it would cost to do that suppose that you would have to buy your wood & flower & meat & all that you would have to live upon & pay house rent & do without a cow.... What do you think that it would cost in a year to do without a sheep to. I would rather that you would stay on the farm if you did not tend one acre of it but cut the medow & paster the balance until I come home it is easy to get rid of a home but it is not so very easy to get one if we have not got the money.

This was his longest letter to Mary, with several pages of random thoughts. One can sense the conflict John undoubtedly had between allowing his wife to sell the farm and move somewhere convenient, or asking that she hold on until he got back. Then his thoughts turned to his children and how worried he was that they stay out of the cold and avoid getting sick. He would be heartbroken if anything happened to them. He asked her to have the boys pile the firewood close to the house during the day when it was warm, so they would not have to go far during the cold nights. He continued:

I love all of the children & I want you to tell them all to be good children & mind what is told them to do & to be good & learn there book all they can. I want you mother to be kind to them & learn them to be kind to each other & do not let them make use of bad words.

The holidays were hard on all the men, and for new recruits such as John it was their first Christmas away from their families. By now John was desperate; he didn't want to lose the farm. "I do wish that the war would come to a close soon or we would get paid off soon," he said, "so that you could get my pay from Madison God knows that I want you to have it as bad as I ever wanted any thing in my life...." He was stuck in the middle of nowhere and felt hopeless. The army was behind on their pay and his farm hung in the balance.[16]

By February 1865, John and his wife had not yet sold the farm. But Mary was so worried she was not sleeping. Apparently an accident on a nearby farm claimed the life of a young child whose father was also away fighting the war. John tried to comfort her and calm her fears. "I suspect that you take trouble to your self more than you need," he said. His wife was overwhelmed, and there didn't seem to be anyone who could help. We can only imagine the hardships she faced trying to constantly overcome her fears, raise her family, and struggle to keep their farm operating. But John had a plan to save the farm. What little pay he was making was not "enough to do any good" by sending it home, as he had been doing. They needed to make money in chunks. He wanted her to send him as much money as she could:

And I will buy clothing with it & double my money in six months now mother you must not be afeared that I will spend it foolishly for any thing for I am stinyger now than I ever was for I want to have a nice pile of money to bring home with me when I come.

He thought he could make a couple hundred dollars and that would be enough do pay off the loans. It was a gamble, but one worth taking. There were most likely several reasons for his decision to take a chance like this. He hadn't seen any real action and they were nowhere near the fighting, and the war was winding down. Grant was moving in on Lee, and Sherman had finished up his "March to the Sea" and all but exposed the South as a beaten country. There were no downsides in John's mind. So they took the chance. She sent him all the money she had.

On February 23, 1865, John wrote with news:

> My Dear Wife I take my pen in hand to write a few to you to let you know that I am well & in fine spirits. Well mother I thought that I would not write to you until in the morning for I have not got a letter from you this week but I have to write to night or not write to you from Brashear City for it is 8 oclock & I have just come in my tent from role call & the order come for us to pack up in the morning to leave this place & mother I cant tell you where we are a going to we are a going to Orleans tomorrow & then we may go to Mobeal but we cant tell mother I am a going to pack up a box of clothing in the morning & start it for home.... Mother it is nine oclock & I have nothing more to write this time to you for the boys is coming in & out so I can hardly write so I will close by sending you & all of the children my love & well wishes & asking you to write to me after so fare well for this time this from John W. Kennedy to Mary A. Kennedy his wife until death.[17]

The Eleventh Wisconsin was heading out, part of the long-anticipated Mobile expedition led by Canby. This was John's last letter. Sadly, he did not make it back to his beloved children. John was killed on April 9, 1865, as he and the rest of the regiment assaulted Fort Blakely, Alabama. Ironically, it was on this same day that Lee surrendered to Grant at Appomattox Courthouse, and for all practical purposes ended the war. The battle fought by the Eleventh Wisconsin at Fort Blakely was the last significant engagement of the Civil War. John was right. The war would be over soon; unfortunately, it was not soon enough. It is not known what happened to the money he was saving. It may very well have perished with him. Within the year Mary was forced to sell the farm and livestock, and eventually ended up in Madison alone with her four young children.*

Though the regiment's ranks had improved since March 1864, when it could count only 373 present for duty, it was still far from its full strength of 1,000 men. In an effort to recruit more soldiers, William Charleton was sent back to Wisconsin. He arrived in early fall of 1864 and was stricken ill and bedridden for several weeks. By October, William was feeling better. "I am pleased to learn your health is improving. I was afraid you were not going to be able to do your needful duty," wrote Warren W. Nye to William. He continued urging him to do his duty, "We have from six to eight men excused daily, excluding those in hospital." Nye also offered his appraisal of the political situation, "I am grateful to learn that copperheadism is dying out so fast. May it breath its last before election!!" The upcoming election was hugely important for Lincoln and the war effort. Nye believed that McClellan, Lincoln's challenger, and his Copperhead supporters were "just so blind that they cannot see they are influencing and acting opposite to what they are fighting for." Nye then made a terrible and haunting declaration, "Old Abe will be our president in the next four years 'unless sooner shot' as the boys old saying [goes]."[18]

---

*There is no grave for John that could be located in Wisconsin or Alabama. This is not unusual, as Civil War soldiers did not wear dog tags or identification. However, the attack on Fort Blakely was one of the first battles on American soil where "torpedoes," what we call landmines, were used extensively, and it is possible John was the victim of such a device, with no body for a grave.

CHAPTER TWELVE

What an Awful Destruction of Human Life

On February 26, 1865, the Eleventh Wisconsin was ordered out of the bayou to Algiers. They marched out with about 520 men fit for duty. "Our regiment at last was allowed to pull out of this hole of stagnation," wrote Calvin Alling. Their band played "Out of the Wilderness" as they marched to the train station. Men hummed and sang along, smoked their pipes, and congratulated each other on their good fortune. They boarded the train for a short ride before getting onto steamers that delivered them just below New Orleans, and they camped on the famous 1815 Battle of New Orleans battlefield where Andrew Jackson defeated the British. They were out of the wilderness at last, but where they were headed was unclear. All of the fighting was still far away, and the possibility that they would take part in the last significant battle of the war was unfathomable.[1]

Finally confident with an army 45,000 strong, General Canby set them in motion towards Alabama against Confederate general Maury and his roughly 9,000 men. In his official report Canby noted that the rainy season had delayed him, and there is ample evidence that January and February were indeed wet months. "The general plan," said Canby, "[is the] reduction of the enemy's works on the east side of Mobile Bay, the opening of the Tensas and Alabama Rivers, [then] turning on the strong works erected for the defense of Mobile, and forcing the surrender or evacuation of the city." He was not going to attempt to lay siege to the city and its strong defenses, made up of three stout trench lines, though it is likely that the defenders would have been stretched so thin that breaching the lines would not have been difficult.[2]

Grant had already lost his patience with Canby and even requested that he be replaced. "I am very much dissatisfied with General Canby," he wrote to Secretary of War Stanton. "As soon as [Major General Philip] Sheridan can be spared I shall want him to supersede Canby." Luckily for the "prudent soldier," he was finally on the move before Grant could replace him.[3]

There would be two main columns of advance. The first column, commanded by General Frederick Steele, left Pensacola with 13,000 men and made its way north, using the railroad, to hit Pollard in a feint against Montgomery. The second column of 32,000, led by Canby, gathered at Forts Gains and Morgan in Mobile Bay. The troops at Fort Gains took transports to the eastern side of Mobile Bay, landing in a smaller bay at the mouth of the Fish River well below Mobile, which lies on the west side at the northern end. The troops at Fort Morgan marched up the peninsula through the sand and magnolia trees along the coast.

The Eleventh Wisconsin was now part of the Third Brigade, Second Division, of the Sixteenth Army Corps commanded by Major General A.J. Smith. Colonel Harris was once again in command of the brigade. The Thirteenth Army Corps (General Granger in command), along with some cavalry and engineers, made up Canby's column. Steele had in his column

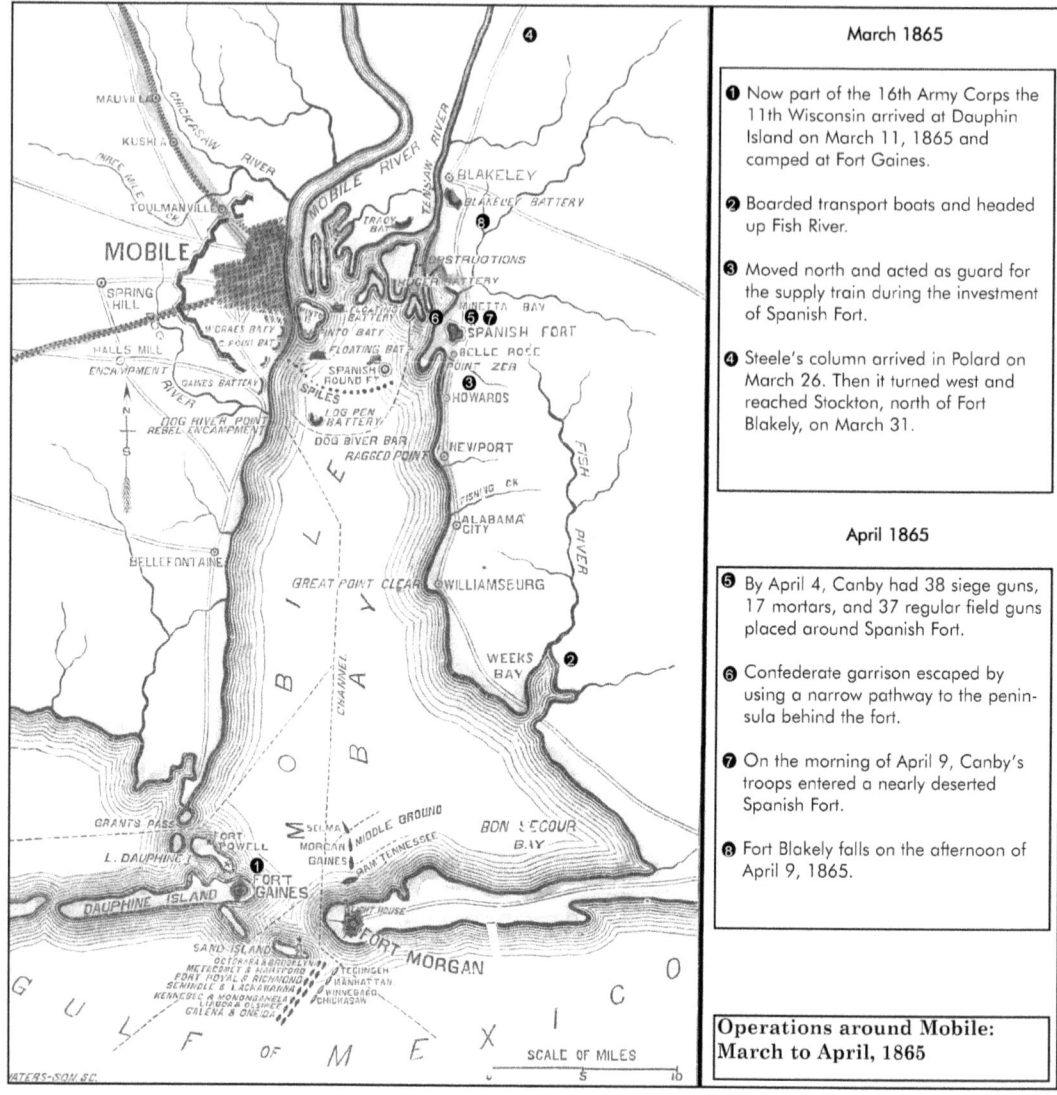

Operations around Mobile.

two brigades from the Thirteenth Corps, as well as a Negro division of 5,500 men. It was the largest gathering of Negro soldiers ever assembled during the Civil War. Among them was the Seventy-third U.S. Colored Troops (USCT), whose service record went back to 1862 when they fought as the First Regiment Louisiana Native Guards at Port Hudson. They were often a much maligned unit that suffered from poor leadership and at times brutal treatment at the hands of their white officers—once leading to a near mutiny. But now they were on their way to Mobile with redemption on their minds.[4]

* * *

By March 11 the Eleventh Wisconsin was camped near Fort Gaines on Dauphin Island, at the mouth of Mobile Bay. The men pitched their tents in the sand and relaxed for a couple of days. "Some great baseball games were played to-day," wrote Calvin Alling in his diary, "the team of the Eleventh Wisconsin being victorious over all competitors." In their brigade were four companies of the Fifty-eighth Illinois, Fifty-second Indiana, Thirty-fourth New Jersey, and 178th New York regiments.[5]

On the 17th, the Thirteenth Division was in motion toward Fish River, while a small force made demonstrations on the west bank of Mobile Bay, occupying Mon Louis Island with orders to make "as much display of force as possible." By taking the roundabout route up the eastern side of the bay, away from the city, and hitting Forts Spanish and Blakely, Canby was correct in thinking that Mobile would have to be abandoned by the Confederates. With his five-to-one manpower superiority, as well as severely outgunning the enemy, Canby was playing this by the book.[6]

"Noose in camp today that we will leave here tomorrow, the 13 army corps has left today to some plase unknown to us," wrote Henry Oettiker in his diary. The men assumed they were going to Mobile, but when they landed on the eastern side of the bay (away from Mobile), some thought they might avoid another Vicksburg-type siege. Writing a couple of weeks earlier in a letter home, one soldier said, "I *think* [his emphasis] we are intended to operate against Mobile if it is found necessary to send troops there." But no one really knew for certain, and it was hoped they could avoid the city's defenses. They did not know that their destination was two strong forts with abatis, earthworks, landmines, cannons, and an entrenched enemy. As they moved out only one thing was clear: they had landed on the correct side, because the enemy expected them on the "other side of the Bay."[7]

On the 19th of March, the Sixteenth Corps followed Granger's Thirteenth Corps along the beach on Mobile Point, over "the surf-beaten shore of the Gulf" where crushed oyster shells provided a kind of makeshift road. James Lockney of the Twenty-eighth Wisconsin, marching with Granger's corps, was on the move when he noted that they seemed far away from anything worth attacking: "The view afforded was wide & pleasing, but we could not see the object of our labors, the City [Mobile] far away at the head of the bay."[8]

They had marched for hours when "After crossing & toward noon we stopped a short time to rest, & about this time an aged Negro woman stood near the road in wonder & amazement, & as we passed she showed strange signs of joy by her actions as well as by her words."[9]

At various points during the march, slaves whose masters had run off at the sight of Federal troops came out to greet the soldiers. They shouted, "Glory, Hallelujah!! Thanks to God for the coming of the Yankees." These sights of pure elation perplexed some of the men. "She acted as if wholly unconscious, or so wrapped in the joy that seemed to fill her whole being as to be forgetful of all around her," wrote Lockney. "Many of the boys jeered & scoffed at this poor woman! I thought then she must have felt most bitterly the many cruelties of Slavery & thy joy is to me no wonder."[10]

It was a dark, gloomy, and overcast afternoon when the Eleventh Wisconsin arrived at Fish Bay. Not all of the transports had landed safely; several were stuck on sandbars and would not be freed until the next day. An ominous smoky haze turned the sky gray as they made their way inland. Earlier that day several regiments of the Thirteenth Corps started fires that blew out of control in the dry grass. Luckily a long rain that night followed by a torrential downpour the next day put the fires out.[11]

Canby's column now stretched several miles, from Fort Morgan to Dannelly's Mills and Deer Park. The heavy rain continued for several days, at times coming down so hard and fast it was "several inches deep on the high ground & knee deep in the low places." Not only was the weather bringing Canby's advance to a near standstill on the 20th and 21st of March, but the "mosquitoes are out in force," wrote Lockney. "I have never saw anything like it. They sting like bees." Giving it more thought, he knew why the insects attacked with such viciousness, for they "seem bound to have their fill of Yankee blood" and "have not been able to procure [it] until lately."[12]

By the 23rd the weather had changed, and none too soon. "This is a fine morning," wrote Joseph Hillier. After days of steady rain, the sun was a welcome sight. "The sun shins brite and warm ... heavy firing in the direction of Mobile all day." Gunboats had moved up the bay and were shelling Spanish Fort, not Mobile, in preparation for the coming siege. The Eleventh Wisconsin, along with the rest of the Sixteenth Corps, stopped for the night as parts of Granger's Thirteenth Corps reached the outskirts of Spanish Fort on March 26. Though surrounded by excitement and activity, Curious Kirkpatrick was once again admiring the scenery:

> We are camped on a beautiful high ridge. The timber is all fine. Sum of the nicest pine logs that I ever saw. We are camped in line of battle and the report is now that the Rebels is agoing to fite us here.... Old Major Canby is in command of the expedition.[13]

The Confederates had skirmishers marking Canby's advance, at times delaying it for several hours with small battles. "Hevy skirmishing on the right for a little while the enemy gave way," wrote Henry Oettiker in his diary. "Ower loss was one wounded and the Rebbles 2 killed and one wounded as for as known. The 13 army corps has come up to us today, the 27, 28 and 35 Wisconsin are also here ower Reg was at work building brestworks." As the Eleventh Wisconsin continued to fortify their position, Thirteenth Corps continued on to Spanish Fort to begin the siege.[14]

Meanwhile, Steele's column was covering more ground than Canby as it made its way towards Pollard, arriving on the 26th. The roads were still bad, and corduroy had to be laid to get the artillery and wagons moving. "We did not make but 5 miles the roads being so bad," wrote one soldier. "In one place the whole brigade turned out and made a corduroy across a swampy piece of road, about 600 yards in length, making it almost entirely out of fence rails."[15]

The rain was miserable for both man and beast. One night the ground was so flooded there was no place for the men to sleep. The next day they found the wagons sunk to their axles in the thick mud. After some work to get them on what appeared to be good ground, the horses and wagons were quickly "belly deep in the mire" again. Food was running short because of the delays, causing Steele to put his men on half rations and commence foraging. It didn't take long to realize there was not much to be had. According to a captain with the 114th Ohio regiment,

> [The land] looked to poor to sprout peas when we were in the advance we were always met before we reached the house by the tall lank jawed Swarthy looking women with their long uncombed hair and dirty whitish looking dresses the Skirts of which resembled a mill Sack with the end cut out with tears in their eyes begging of us not to rob them and their house full of Swarthy ragged looking Children it seemed to me if I was Starving I could not have taken one meal from them.[16]

But others would, and soon Steele came across houses where the women were "weeping in the most pitiful cries complaining to us and pointed to their once Scanty and now empty house and what ever become of them and their poor little pale faced Children god only knows but I Fear they were never rescued from Starvation." By the end of March some portions of Steele's column had their men on one-third rations, but still they pushed on. Brigadier General Christopher C. Andrews, commanding the Second Division, reported "the majority were suffering from hunger. The labor and exposure were enough to reduce men who were well fed." On the 29th, Steele's column was in Weatherford, and by March 31 it was north of Fort Blakely at Stockton, after practically building their own road to get there. If the weather held up they were only a day's march from investing the fort and joining Canby's column with its fresh supplies.[17]

* * *

Inside forts Spanish and Blakely, the mood of the defenders was for the most part upbeat and confident, even as the column of blue reached the outskirts of Spanish Fort. It stretched out of sight to the south as all day more and more troops poured into their front. Lieutenant Colonel James M. Williams of the Twenty-first Alabama seemed anxious for the coming assault when he wrote to his wife: "Nobody is excited half my men are working in the trenches and nearly all the other half are playing marbles before the quarters like so many school boys. If the Yankees don't come this time I will be vexed for I want to see them in front of my boys once more." Williams' regiment was down to 225 men, but they did get their chance to face the enemy when they ambushed the Eighty-first Illinois regiment just outside of Spanish Fort, killing many before disappearing into the swamp and returning to the fort. Unbeknownst to them, Major General A.J. Smith was among the troops fired upon and barely escaped injury when men around him were struck down.[18]

Though stoic, most of the men entrenched in and around Spanish Fort and Fort Blakely knew the end was near. Their ranks had dwindled from the usual death and disease, but many had also deserted, sometimes entire companies of men. Corporal D.G. Gammack of the Thirty-eighth Alabama regiment wrote to his mother from inside Fort Blakely: "Dear mother I shudder when I look to the future for it does seem to me that we shall yet be subjegated and no doubt our effects confiscated. May heaven avert the storm that now hangs over us. Where ever I turn my eyes I see nothing but desolation and destruction." The war had devastated the southern economy, even in the relatively untouched state of Alabama.[19]

"On every side we are losing ground," wrote Sergeant William Pitt Chambers, stationed in Mobile. "I very much doubt whether the morale of this army or of the citizens of the land is equal to the emergency that confronts us. All of us are weary of this ceaseless turmoil and bloodshed — we long so much for peace." Even now, as Federal troops massed across the bay, Mobile was most likely a divided city, with many of its inhabitants wanting nothing more to do with the war.[20]

* * *

The Confederacy's decision to arm slaves in 1865 was not well received. By allowing slaves to fight in the war, the South was removing the very reason for the war in the fist place. Months before, when rumors swirled throughout Mobile, one soldier from Spanish Fort wrote of his disgust: "They propose to put one Negro for two white men and make them cook, wash, and make fires for us but we would have to drill and fight side by side with the stinking things." Though Corporal Gammack did not object to the extra help, he did not consider it practicable, telling his mother, "I can't think they will make efficient soldiers as they could have nothing to induce them to fight for us and our cause." Many believed that "if we are reduced to that extremity that we must depend on the slaves for our freedom ... then why not stop the war before it goes any further." The Confederate Congress voted in favor, though, and the Negro soldier bill went into effect on March 13, 1865.[21]

As Spanish Fort was invested and the siege begun, a *Mobile Register* correspondent, writing from Fort Blakely, reported back to his fellow citizens whom he felt were not being very patriotic.

> I would like to transport over to Blakely a lot of our Royal street crackers, and let them mingle with the troops. They would first become ashamed of themselves, and then pluck up a little cour-

age and, in all probability, form a first rate opinion about our success…. The courage, pluck and spirit of the troops is as good as the most sanguine could desire. Where all behave so well and so much confidence exists, non–combatants should not doubt.[22]

There can be no doubt that the hardships endured by the citizens of Vicksburg during Grant's siege of the city — the starvation, destruction, and death — was on everyone's mind in Mobile, not to mention the fact that Petersburg was at this very moment under siege by Federal troops. When the bluecoats did not appear outside the city, a large sigh of relief was breathed on the streets. But as the investment of Spanish Fort began, many in the city must have wondered when their time would come. Day and night they could hear the sounds of cannons and guns in the distance, a constant reminder of the possibility.

* * *

As the siege of Spanish Fort began, Brigadier General Kenner Garrard's division, including the Eleventh Wisconsin, was "in an entrenched camp to cover the right and rear of the army." They spent several days digging, with "heavy firing" day and night. Granger's corps started the investment of Spanish Fort, followed by several divisions from the Sixteenth Corps, including the Eleventh Wisconsin's old divisional commander, General Eugene Carr and his Illinois and Missouri troops.[23]

Spanish Fort was garrisoned by only 2,800 troops commanded by Brigadier General Randall L. Gibson, a veteran of several battles, including Shiloh. Scouts had captured maps and drawings, and reported back that Canby was upon them with an "estimated force to be not less than 20,000 muskets strong; perhaps much larger." The Federals advanced their skirmishers and trenches, digging day and night, and soon came within striking distance of the fort. In front of them lay a 300 yard clearing of fallen trees, with a line of abatis 15 feet thick. Directly in front of the breastworks was a ditch five feet deep and up to eight feet wide. There were also batteries and redoubts, six of them in all, scattered along the line and connected by rifle pits and trenches with sharpshooters embedded. Canby had no idea how few were in the fort, because the Confederates made a very good showing once he arrived. Gibson knew he had to keep the men's morale up, so at sunset he ordered "all the batteries" to open fire "and the skirmishers and parts even of the main line to keep up a brisk fire, and all officers to observe the enemy closely, and to hold themselves in readiness for any contingency."[24]

For the first ten days Gibson's artillery, combined with his well-trained sharpshooters, was very effective in handling the Union advance and often "broke up" their working parties in "handsome style." At first there appeared to be some hope. Gibson had a fairly strong position, especially on his right where eight guns were placed on a crest of bluffs that nicely followed their line. He also had experienced artillery teams, including an elite company of New Orleans' Washington Artillery, that were effective in silencing the Union guns facing them. In the center were veteran troops from Tennessee and Alabama. While they were peppered by Federal artillery, General Orders No. 1 instructed the Spanish Fort defenders: "You must dig, dig, dig. Nothing can save us here but the spade."[25]

But day after day the Union lines kept crawling forward, "steadily digging up to our front and flanks," observed Gibson, powerless to stop it. And the Union "fleet kept up a well-directed and heavy fire." The bombardment and advanced skirmishers and sharpshooters kept the pressure on Gibson's beleaguered men. "When there was no fighting there was digging, cutting, moving ammunition, taking down and putting up heavy guns, and repairing damages, and extending the main lines." It was exhausting work for a garrison both severely undermanned and outgunned. By April 4 Canby had 38 siege guns, 17 mortars, and 37 regular field guns in place, and was pounding the Confederates unmercifully. After ten days the noose was tightening, and "it was evident, from his overwhelming resources in men and guns, that it would be impossible" to stop their "gradual advance." Gibson had but one option — to save his men.[26]

* * *

Many of the troops facing Spanish Fort were veterans of Vicksburg and were more than willing to dig trenches and wait for the eventual surrender of the garrison. Digging in was commonplace by now, and siege work for them, though not easy, was better than the alternative. "For my own part," wrote James K. Newton with the Fourteenth Wisconsin, "& I believe I speak the mind of the whole Regt ... if it were on an open field I would say charge at once for we can whip the Rebs every time." But, he noted, when facing a formidable defense with breastworks and abatis, charging the enemy was an "altogether different matter."[27]

During a siege a soldier worked long hours digging and tunneling, not to mention having to dodge sporadic gunfire from sharpshooters. But there were also mines (they called them torpedoes) to be avoided, something these men were not accustomed to. "We hear much about torpedoes which are said to be just under the surface so as to be out of view," said Lockney just before he arrived in front of Spanish Fort. They soon discovered that mines had been planted all around the surrounding area, exploding daily and killing and injuring dozens of men.[28]

Still they kept "creeping along while the [cannon] balls whistled over us, very sharp & numerous," Lockney wrote. As the Federal lines moved closer to the outer rim of Spanish Fort, nighttime became a confusing ordeal. "I thought sometimes that I saw Rebels in our front as if they were digging a pit nearer to us," he continued. So anxious were the men that they sometimes stayed up all night. "Some of us slept during the day while others watched. We found the duty very fatiguing & severe." During the day the defenders stayed well hidden. A puff of smoke after the sharpshooter fired the shot was usually all they could see.[29]

Gibson had been working on an escape route since the beginning, as he knew he would probably need it. The fort backed onto a shallow bay belonging to the Apalachee River. High grass screened the work parties as they constructed a "narrow treadway, about eighteen inches wide, which ran from a small peninsula from the left flank across the river," which would allow them to hike north and to safety. During the day weeds and moss were used to conceal the path and, although occasionally a stray artillery shell interrupted their work, it was performed completely undetected.[30]

With his artillery nearly all destroyed or disabled from heavy and accurate Federal artillery, his men exhausted and hungry, and the Federals' lines making such progress that they "will soon dig up to my main line at the rate he is advancing," Gibson decided it was time to move. On an overcast and cloudy April 8, a fierce artillery barrage hit Gibson and his beleaguered men. The plan was to pull out of the fort that night. But seeing the Federals picking up their pace, with their work crews digging in even closer, Gibson instructed his skirmishers to harass the enemy as much as possible and to take "every precaution" in order to prevent a "surprise" attack. They needed to hold on for one more day.[31]

Later in the afternoon, "just at sunset," Gibson ordered all able batteries "to open [fire], and the skirmishers and parts of the main line to keep up a brisk fire." He wanted to discourage any possible assault the damned Yankees were preparing for. He was concerned about his left flank, which was a vulnerable liability. Fearing an attack, he ordered more men to cover it. Not long afterward, Federal artillery and mortars sent a flurry of shells into the fort, concentrating on the flanks of the earthwork and silencing the Confederate batteries. The fire was intense and accurate, with shells breaching nearly all the "gopher holes" the Confederates believed were strong enough to offer protection, scattering men in every direction. A direct hit dismembered men, leaving only traces of humanity behind. "There was no shelter from these bombs," said one of the defenders afterwards, and "no defense from that fire. We had to stand and take it." Men huddled together in any nook and cranny they could find. The shelling continued for two hours, leaving Confederates dazed and confused as "soldiers staggered about, blood rushing from ears, mouths, and eyes," wrote one historian. Even from the Federal position, some thought it "impossible for any in the fort to survive."[32]

General Carr knew the enemy was reeling from the latest barrage, and ordered Colonel James L. Geddes and his Hawkeyes "to press with skirmishers" directly against the Rebel left in order to "feel their strength, ascertain the nature of the ground, and take as much as he could hold." Parts of the Eighth Iowa regiment jumped from their trenches and rushed across a hundred yards of swampy earth covered with fallen trees and into the outer line of the fort, quickly overrunning the still dazed Confederates. For 300 yards they advanced, nearly taking in Gibson's entire left flank, including the high ground.[33]

With the crackling of gunfire and cheers from the Union line, Gibson's greatest fear was materializing. His left flank was now breached and the enemy threatened to roll up his entire line and capture the fort before they could escape. If Gibson had not decided to evacuate the fort by now, which he most likely had, this breach of his line convinced him. But before he could, he had to retake or at least stabilize his flank. After a failed counterattack by about 100 Texan troops, Gibson ordered a combined assault of 200 North Carolina troops and 100 of Lieutenant Alfred G. Clark's Provost Guards. Throwing themselves at the Union position, the attack lost momentum and stalled, with Clark himself a casualty. Though he had not retaken his flank, Gibson had stabilized it and his men dug in. He was now more anxious than ever for night as the sun began to disappear on the horizon. Only a few more hours and he could attempt their escape.[34]

On the morning of April 9 the sun revealed empty Rebel rifle pits. Dumfounded, Federal troops cautiously approached the silent fort. Only remnants of the Eighteenth Alabama regiment remained, apparently sacrificed by Gibson (or somehow not informed of the escape). Some fought briefly before being overrun and surrendering. Canby had allowed his enemy to escape, a most humiliating event. As Federal troops poured into Spanish Fort, word reached them that Petersburg had fallen. Confederate President Jefferson Davis had fled Richmond and was on the run, as was General Robert E. Lee and his army. James K. Newton wrote home to his parents enthusiastically: "Don't you begin to see 'the beginning of the end'? I do." The end was indeed near.[35]

* * *

What no one knew, as Canby shifted his men north to Fort Blakely on the morning of April 9, Palm Sunday, was that 800 miles to the northeast Confederate general Lee and his disheveled band of 35,000 men had broken out of Petersburg and were on the run from Grant and his 100,000 strong. They had reached the Appomattox River on April 7, and Lee was still hopeful he could join with General Johnston's army. But it was not to be. Promised supplies for his starving army never materialized, and by the next day Grant had caught up and surrounded him. That night Grant and Lee exchanged brief communications. Grant called Lee's situation "hopeless" and seemed to almost beg for Lee to discuss terms for surrender. Grant hoped that Lee would respond to his plea and that the general would not destroy his army. Lee at first was defiant; he did not see the "hopelessness" of his situation. Grant responded, telling him that "peace being my great desire," and that his terms would be reasonable.[36]

Lee had three options: he could fight it out to the end, he could order his men to break

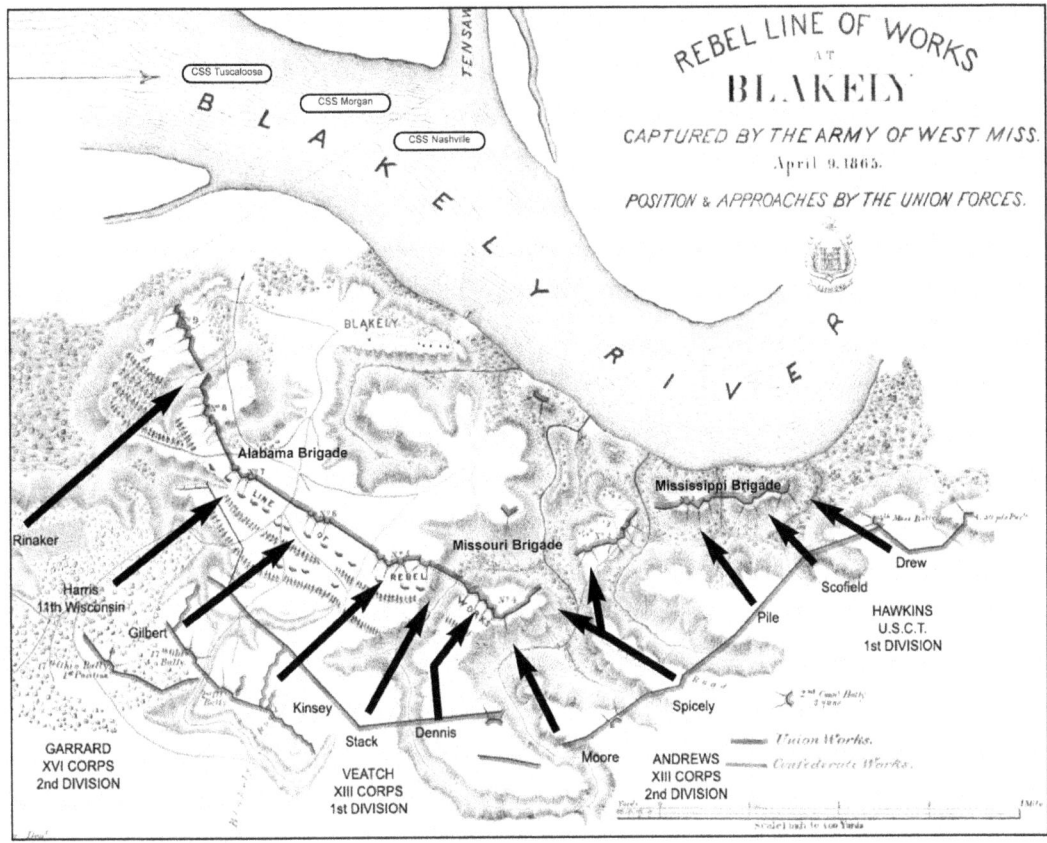

Colonel Charles L. Harris and the Eleventh Wisconsin are noted at the left (Library of Congress).

up and melt away into the mountains and continue the war as guerillas, or he could respond to Grant's plea for peace. Some wanted him to order his army to break up and continue to fight as guerilla units scattered across the country, something that would have taken months, perhaps years, to clean up and could quite possibly have threatened the future of the United States. But that was not Lee's way. He was a fierce warrior — a cunning and brilliant strategist — but he was also a man of honor. He did not believe it honorable to fight such a war. It was time to seek peace and hope for healing. They had lost, and must admit defeat. His only concerns were his men, his country, the people of Virginia, and the South.[37]

A thick fog rolled in that morning as General Lee solemnly composed his message to Grant, initiating what would be more correspondences that day, culminating in a meeting and the formal surrender of his army. As Lee rode to Appomattox Courthouse he surmised he would be taken prisoner, but hoped his men would not. Grant, too, had no intention of doing the dishonorable thing. He knew that now the war was won, how peace was achieved would be key. The two men met around half past one in the afternoon, and a most glorious peace was indeed achieved. Lee and his army, once swearing an oath to the United States and laying down their arms, were allowed to return home to their families and their farms.[38]

* * *

On that same morning the men of the Eleventh Wisconsin awoke, if they slept at all, to the news that Spanish Fort had fallen. Later that morning Federal spotters in trees reported that boatloads of Rebels were leaving Fort Blakely. These troops were from Spanish Fort and made only a brief stop before heading to Mobile, but it gave the appearance of an evacuation. Canby was now on hand and feared if he delayed any longer he would miss his opportunity to strike. By mid afternoon rumors intensified that nearly all the Confederates at Spanish Fort got away. This knowledge, combined with the unusually low amount of activity from Fort Blakely's skirmishers, did not sit well with the Negro troops occupying the extreme right of the Federal line. Brigadier General John P. Hawkins commanded their division. Brigadier General William A. Pile commanded First Brigade, made up of the Seventy-third, Eighty-second, and Eighty-sixth U.S. Colored Infantry. Colonel Hiram Scofield was in charge of Second Brigade, consisting of the Forty-seventh, Fiftieth, and Fifty-first U.S. Colored Infantry. Finally, Colonel Charles W. Drew led the Third Brigade and its three units, the Seventy-sixth, Forty-eighth, and Eighty-sixth U.S. Colored Infantry. Many of these Negro soldiers were former slaves, and most were about to see their first action. General Andrews later said that they were "burning with an impulse to do honor to their race."[39]

The Confederates were conserving ammo, convinced the Federals would not want them to escape as well and would assault quickly. By 3 o'clock in the afternoon, the rifle pits in front of Hawkins' division were for the most part silent. Colonel Henry C. Merriam commanding the Seventy-third U.S. Colored Infantry noted that his men were eager to attack before the fort emptied. "The effect upon us was very depressing," he wrote afterwards. "To me it appeared that the escape of the garrison in our front also would be simply disgraceful." A rumor circulated that perpetrators of the Fort Pillow massacre were inside the fort. Feeling that his Negro soldiers desperately wanted to take action, Merriam approached Pile with a request. He asked if his men could make a quick strike on the rifle pits in their front. Pile approved the order, officially telling Merriam that his men were simply to "feel" the enemy.[40]

In front of Fort Blakely was a clearing nearly four miles in length, forming a half circle around the outer rim of the earthwork. Trees were felled 600 to 800 yards away, with abatis laid out in two rows, and all through the area were "subterra shells," as Canby called them. Before Pile agreed to let his men advance, Canby had already made up his mind to attack before the day was over. He ordered an all-out assault on the fort at half past five that evening. Though Hawkins' division was already closer to the fort than anyone else, Pile had managed to advance his line another 140 yards on the evening of the 8th, leaving him only 700 yards from the Rebel rifle pits. At this point Scofield was still closest to the rifle pits, which lay about 600 yards from his line. On the immediate left of Hawkins' division was Andrews and his Second Division of the Thirteenth Corps, some 800 to 900 yards from the Rebel rifle pits; then Vaetch's First Division, Thirteenth Corps about 1,000 yards away; and finally Garrard's Second Division, Sixteenth Corps, a little further back at 1,100 to 1,200 yards away.[41]

Before sending his men forward, Pile ordered a small battery of cannons to fire at the last known location of the Rebel guns to determine if they were still manned. Several volleys were fired. Pile waited a few minutes with no response. Satisfied they were gone, he started anxiously for the front of his line to give the order to advance when Major General Osterhaus arrived and inquired about the cannon fire. Pile took the general with him to the head of his line, where Osterhaus examined the situation. Osterhaus authorized Pile to continue as planned before heading back to Canby to inform him of Pile's progress. At about 4 o'clock, 60 men from the Eighty-sixth and Seventy-third U.S. Colored Infantry jumped from their rifle pits and charged toward the Rebel line. As they worked their way to a ravine and the abatis below, the Rebel rifle pits, which were not evacuated, opened with an intense fire consisting of "heavy artillery and musketry" that quickly had them pinned down. Seeing this

Pile ordered five more companies to advance, with instructions to hold the ground gained—some 300 yards—and dig in.[42]

Earlier that day Colonel Scofield, commanding Second Brigade, noted that the lack of activity in the fort "caused a general belief" among his men "that the place was being evacuated" and that his Negro soldiers were anxious that the "prize was slipping through [their] fingers." As gunfire and the booming of cannons filled the air, Scofield's Negro soldiers eagerly awaited orders to advance. Scofield decided to waste no time and began advancing his lines. His men climbed out of their trenches with a cheer and pushed toward the Rebel line. The entanglements of the abatis were nasty and slowed their advance, and they too came under heavy fire, but still they pressed on. Like a chain reaction, Colonel Drew heard the eruptions of battle and the cheering from Scofield's position, and he too released his men. Only days before, a land mine had killed or wounded 15 Negroes under his command. They were eager for revenge. As they descended into the ravine, more land mines erupted, killing and wounding more of his soldiers.[43]

Henry M. Crydenwise was a captain in the Corps D'Afrique, and during the initial charge he described the early stages of the advance:

> Cautioning my men to follow me in one rank & keep close to me, I sprang over our rifle pit & away we went on a hard run for the Rebel pits. The Rebs saw us coming & swept the ground with shot, shell & tried to stop our advance, but to no purpose. Onward, still onward we went, down a slope, across a ravine filled with logs, brush, stumps & trees but these we hardly noticed. Then up a little rise & were soon in possession of the desired line. O! My God how the Rebs did sweep that line with those searching, devilish shells & it seemed that nothing could live under such a fire.[44]

As they advanced, the earth seemed to come alive with eruptions that spit the splintering fragments of exploding land mines in every direction, killing and maiming dozens of men. Lieutenant Colonel Daniel Densmore led the Sixty-eighth U.S. Colored Infantry in Drew's brigade and was near the head of their advance. Being closest to the enemy rifle pits, they came upon them quickly only to discover some abandoned. Afterwards, in his official report, Densmore noted that his men:

> ... had just reached the pits when the regiment was ordered to charge. Passing quickly beyond the rifle-pits the men of the Seventy-sixth (also charging) and Sixty-eighth Regiments became mingled amid the slashing, and to avoid the severe fire of the enemy's artillery as well as to take advantage of the open pathway along the crest of the bluff, the greater portion of them gained ground to the right and on the bluff side.[45]

They had the soldiers remove their jackets so as to maneuver through the entanglements more easily. Seeing the initial success of his men, Drew waved his hat in the air and shouted, "Forward on the enemy's works!" The men surged forward, reaching a point "within a few yards of the left of the enemy's parapet." But they were now under intense fire from the fort and three Rebel gunboats positioned in the river behind the fort. Grapeshot and canister were thick, and the wounded fell all around them. One Negro soldier recalled that the "charge was made under a terrible fire from the enemy, the men dashing forward with all their might." The firing intensified and men were forced to burrow into the ground using bayonets and small shovels.[46]

Drew continued to feed men into this hopeless situation, resulting in more causalities. After maybe 30 minutes of hard fighting, and "so reduced in numbers and exhausted," he solemnly reported afterward, "I ordered them to fall back to a ravine where they would be safe from the fire of the enemy's gun-boats." He had anticipated reinforcements during his attack and went in search of them. When he found Colonel Charles A. Gilchrist, and his Fiftieth U.S. Colored Infantry, they were preparing to dig in instead of advancing. This infuriated him. "He came up to my right, and in a very ungentlemanly and unofficer like manner," said Gilchrist, "ordered some of my companies' officers to take their companies forward." They informed Drew that General Steele had just issued orders not to advance any further, and to dig in and hold the line. This sent Drew into a frenzy. He was sure that if assaulted now, with enough men, the Rebel fort would fall. "He still continued in a perfect tirade of abuse and finally went to the rear." Officers of Negro regiments knew all too well that officers of white regiments regularly received all the credit, and no doubt this added to his frustration as he tried to get support for his assault.[47]

They were on the slope of a ravine, hidden behind fallen trees, when they realized something wasn't right. A small detachment of about 15 Negro soldiers ahead of the pack just below the fort did not receive the order to withdraw. The two officers (captains Holcomb and Norwood) in command soon realized they were cut off. Fearing a Rebel counterattack, and knowing that, if captured, as white officers of a black unit they would be executed (not to mention what would happen to the soldiers), they ordered their men to fix bayonets. They had no intention of being taken alive. There was no panic, no cries of fear. With no other alternative, they jumped from the ravine, climbed the bluff to the fort, and in hand-to-hand combat actually overtook the Rebel rifle pits in front of the fort. There, on high ground, they dug in and waited for help.[48]

* * *

Just a week earlier, Confederate general Liddell noted the approach of "Steele with his negroes," and fully exposed the race issue in its infected and raw appearance. It's not hard to see the battle that was about to take place around and in Fort Blakely as a precursor to Reconstruction. This was to be the last major battle of the Civil War, but just the latest in a racial confrontation between white and black America that would last another hundred years.[49]

The men who bravely occupied Fort Blakely watched as thousands of Negro soldiers slowly and persistently closed in on their defenses. The end was near and the situation for them, some former slave owners, was much different. For now the white defenders faced a well-armed legion of Negro soldiers just itching to get at them. These were not submissive or passive slaves. Before his men knew of Steele's arrival, Liddell informed them that the enemy they were about to face was "composed principally of negroes," former slaves. He then stressed the "importance of holding their position to the last, and with the determination never to surrender." The implication was clear.[50]

When Federal lines moved to within sight of the fort, the thought of being captured became palpable. Both sides wanted to get their licks in, though, and one Confederate soldier recalled that, during the fight, "I took deliberate aim every time I fired and must have killed $50,000 worth of Negroes that day." Two hundred years of slavery were coming down to this one battle, as both sides sought to lash out at the other before it was too late.[51]

After the 4 o'clock thrust by Drew and his Negro soldiers, Liddell reinforced the beleaguered Mississippi troops on his left with extra men. One of two things was going to happen there, he surmised, and neither was pretty. Either his men would stand and fight to the last, or panic and flee. The defenders also had another problem, besides being severely outnumbered. To fill their ranks the South had initiated conscription that allowed for pretty much anyone to fight. This led to 14- and 15-year-old boys fighting next to 50-year-old men. Brigadier General Bryan M. Thomas' Sixty-second Alabama regiment was placed on their right, and their numbers were almost exclusively made up of such conscripts. On their left were veteran troops from Missouri. An officer remarked that his men could hold their line, but he thought that "the old men and boys on our right, who had never been under fire, would get excited when the assault came, and shoot the tops of the trees off." But he would be wrong; the Alabama troops were up for a fight.[52]

The Rebels strengthened their skirmishers and rifle pits as best they could. The skirmishers in front of the fort were told to hold on as long as possible, resulting in horrendous casualties. There was much doom and gloom by this point; they knew there was no escaping the coming onslaught. But things seemed to settle down as the sun hung low in the horizon. It was nearly 5 o'clock, and perhaps the damned Yankees would wait until tomorrow. If they did, maybe the transports from Mobile would return in time to rescue them. But their answer came soon after, when an intense artillery barrage sent everyone scurrying for cover.

* * *

"The Sabbath comes in dark & gloomy," wrote William Flenner of the Seventy-sixth Illinois regiment in his diary on the morning of April 9, 1865. Flenner's regiment was part of Andrew's Thirteenth Corps and was just to the left of the Negro regiments. Though he wasn't even into his second full year of fighting, he had seen enough of war to be inspired to biblical proportions:

> Not a single sound of rejoicing breaks upon the morning air. If we are asked to sing the songs of our prosperous days we will be silent & weep as did the daughters of Isreal [sic] when they remembered Jerusalem in their captivity & hung their harps with the waters of Babylon. O Thou cruel & ungrateful demogogues surely thy mad ambition ought to be satiated with the many lives already sacrificed to the raging demon of war.[53]

The demon was about to rear its ugly head one last time for the Eleventh Wisconsin.

Just a few days before, Henry Oettiker had received some good news: "I receved my commition today as 2nd Lieutenant in the 50th Wis. Inf. I also have made applications for my discharge." In a matter of days, the day after the 9th to be exact, Henry was to head home for a furlough. From there he would join his new regiment and head west.[54]

During the afternoon all brigade commanders, including Colonel Harris of the Eleventh Wisconsin, were called to General Veatch's tent. There, orders were given to be ready for an assault that evening. It had been "decided that this division should move on the enemy's works in two lines," wrote Harris in his official report, "with a strong line of skirmishers in advance at 5:30 pm." He then returned to his line and met briefly with his company commanders. As 5 o'clock neared, most of the men relaxed and wrote letters home. They were cooking meals and smoking pipes when Jesse Miller, now a major, appeared, followed by a group of sergeants and captains. He walked the line briskly, making eye contact with as many as he could. Soon all were silent. Miller reached for his sword, grasped it for a moment, then snapped it out of its sheath and to his side. "Fall in Eleventh, we go once more!" The regiment quickly formed two lines of battle. Sergeant Samuel Kirkpatrick organized his Farmers Guards into line. Henry Twining knew what was up as he shook his head and took his place in line. Robert Sherrill was calm and collected, as usual. Henry Oettiker hurriedly put out the fire and grabbed his rifle. Calvin Alling formed into line with the others and stood at attention.[55]

Harris arranged his brigade into two lines as instructed. The first consisted of the Eleventh Wisconsin, the 178th New York, and a battalion from the Fifty-eighth Illinois regiment. The second line was occupied by the Thirty-fourth New Jersey and Fifty-second Indiana regiments, spread out one man for every two or three in front of them. While they formed their line, Harris had Major Jesse Miller send out three companies (A, F, and D) as skirmishers, with orders to "lie down" as close as possible to the Rebel rifle pits. They would only be a few hundred yards away at most. As they moved out, a "rapid and severe artillery fire commenced."[56]

Around a quarter past five, just a few hours after Robert E. Lee formally surrendered to Grant, a blue wave of 16,000 men stretching three miles began its assault. But it wasn't a thing of beauty. Official reports from the officers in command show that some brigades moved out at a quarter past five, while others did not begin their advance until half past five or even later. The uneven release might have aided in the assault's success. The center of the attack reached its destination first, while the left was just getting going. Advanced skirmishers, like the ones deployed by the Eleventh Wisconsin, were almost instantly upon the Rebels and hand-to-hand combat took place. With yells and hollers, thousands of bluecoats emerged from their lines and plunged into the ravines that led up to the fort. About a mile away from the Eleventh Wisconsin, a solider with the 114th Ohio described what he saw:

> The skirmish line had not advanced more than fifty yards, when the Rebels opened on them with grape and canister, showering it over and around them as thick as hail. During this time the Rebel infantry was not idle but gave us volley after volley, but not with the deadly effect you would suppose, as their aim was not accurate, and too high. When our skirmishers were within about one hundred yards of the Rebel works they left their outer line of rifle pits and ran for the fort like scattered sheep. We were yet laying in, or rather standing on, our advanced line of rifle pits, cheering our skirmishers on to victory or death. When the Rebels began to scale their wall, it was only by repeat commands and threats from the officers that the men could be restrained from rushing to the charge without orders. At last they could no longer be held in check, but rushed to the charge, amid the iron storm and leaden hail, to participate in the glorious victory, which we knew waited us. I never saw more cool courage displayed than was shown by both officers and men, each striving to be the first inside the works.[57]

In the path of this advance were the poor Missouri skirmishers instructed to fight to the last. William H. Kavanaugh was one of the few who survived to tell the tale. At about half past five he observed the Federals "advance on our immediate front in solid columns." Though it was as "imposing [a] sight" as he had ever seen, his "little thin line of skirmishers loaded and fired as rapidly as possible" in the face of the onslaught. As they were overrun William and a few others managed to get out of their pits and scurry back towards the fort, an exhausting run through abatis and over fallen trees as bullets whizzed by, some hitting their mark as men fell on either side. "It appeared to me that all hell had turned loose," he said later, "that every man in the U.S. was practicing on us with repeating rifles."[58]

As the scattered Union line reached within 50 yards of the fort, a thick brush fence with sharpened limbs pointing outward momentarily slowed their advance. Once past that they came to a line of "inclined pickets planted in the ground and about breast high, these also were sharpened." There were openings at certain points that one could crawl or run through, but sharpshooters hidden in the fort zeroed in on these intersections. What everyone feared the most, however, were the "torpedoes" planted in the earth. About four feet in front of the ditch surrounding the main works the Confederates had a wire stretched out about ankle high. Union soldiers rushing forward tripped over the wire and tumbled into the ditch, where they landed injured or unharmed, while others were blown to pieces by the land mines.[59]

During the weeks leading up to the assault, the land mines continued to go off sporadically. The Union soldiers were horrified by the death and injury their comrades sustained. "I think that we should retaliate against them for such infernal work it is worse than barbarism," declared one soldier. The days leading up to the assault witnessed numerous discharges of land mines. "The first day 4 or 5 horses were killed by them and two or three men wounded," wrote a soldier with the Nineteenth Iowa regiment. The sporadic and deadly detonations kept the men unnerved, and by the time they were ordered to attack many were out for blood.[60]

As the Union attack quickly rolled up the Rebel skirmishers in the middle, fleeing butternut soldiers rushed back to the earthwork fort, and the Union soldiers had to be repeatedly restrained from charging the fort. Everyone inside and outside of Fort Blakely knew the war was nearly "played out," and the men knew this might be their last chance to strike at the enemy (while it was still legal). Emotions ran high, sending some men into a frenzy. Some wanted simply to spill more blood, but many wanted revenge. They wanted retribution for their years of sacrifice, and to avenge the loss of friends and comrades. These men, for these few moments, hated each other more than ever before. All believed they were correcting the injustice that had been brought upon them. In this last gasp of the Civil War, the demon would not die without a fierce fight.[61]

Without doubt the most vicious fighting took place on the Confederate left, where the Negro division was now charging on the heels of the rest of the advance. The Mississippi troops opposing them faced not only overwhelming odds but also the desire of every Negro soldier to lay some deed of retribution upon the altar of slavery. As the center of the Federal attack reached the minefields, Hawkins was finally reinforced by more Negro regiments and quickly joined in the attack, "taking up the yell" as they charged. They rushed forward against the strongest fortifications and the deepest minefield, and faced the most and best men the Confederates could muster. The Negro army swooped over the earthwork in front of the fort in what one reporter on hand described later as a dark "cloud of wrath" that "bore down upon the foe."[62]

Most had never seen action and had never had the chance to avenge the injustices they had suffered. Emotions must have run high. Moments before their attack, a colonel noted that those Negro regiments held back in reserve "wept" and were overtaken by their emotions when the realization they would not be attacking set in. The blood-curdling screech of the horde as it rushed upon the enemy caused many Confederate troops, some battle-hardened veterans, to turn and run toward the middle of the fort to be captured by white soldiers, hoping to avoid the inevitable.[63]

Many of the Rebels had no intention of running, and did not look kindly on being captured, believing they would most likely not survive anyway. Confederates cheered in the distance as a land mine sent a half dozen Negro troops into the air, killing several. Pockets of Rebels fought to the last. "Several of the confederates, with muskets, remained outside the works, refused to surrender," wrote one soldier, "and maintained a cool and desperate struggle till they fell." As they were overrun they were shot, clubbed, and bayoneted. The Negro soldiers poured over the parapet and into the fort, and according to one officer they could not contain their enthusiasm. It "was unbound," he wrote, "and they manifested their joy in every conceivable manner." It was a carnage.[64]

* * *

As the fighting on the Confederate left disintegrated into a brutal and bloody affair, Samuel Kirkpatrick, Robert Sherrill, Calvin Alling, Henry Twining, Henry Oettiker, and the rest of the Eleventh Wisconsin had already worked their way up to the fort while taking heavy fire and dodging land mines. Comrades began to fall, some dying.

Colonel Harris placed the regiment in the front line (there were two lines of battle). Brigade commanders sometimes placed their own regiments at the head of an attack for two reasons: to avoid being accused of protecting their own men, and because they knew them best and trusted them most. Having been instructed to crawl to the outermost position half an hour earlier and lie down, the advanced skirmishers were the first to spring up and charge the rifle pits. The rest of the regiment quickly followed and worked their way through the usual lines of abatis and fallen timber. Land mines exploded and cannon fire ripped into them as they charged, dropping many before they reached the rifle pits. Major Jesse Miller was near the front, urging his men on as they rushed forward "with a yell and made for the enemy's works" directly in front of them while taking a "murderous fire" from cannons mounted on parapets. The skirmishers were the first to reach the Rebel rifle pits and crawl up the earthwork embankment, many dying by the bayonet.[65]

Angus R. McDonald, a lieutenant in Company A, was part of the advanced skirmishers for the Eleventh. Angus was described as "a very large and powerful man, and brave almost to temerity." He was one of the first to set foot inside the Rebel fort. Though the Mississippi troops facing the Negro division by and large scattered when attacked, the Alabama soldiers McDonald and the rest of the regiment encountered were up to the fight. One of the soldiers fighting in that area later said that the Rebels "fought like devils." McDonald slid over the hump of the earthwork and jumped into the fort, brandishing his sword. He took on several Alabama troops and ordered them to surrender. Several obeyed and threw up their hands. Several more bluecoats appeared and jumped into the fort. But nearby a Confederate officer with a dozen men was approaching and shouted, "No quarter to the damned Yankees!" They opened fire, downing both Yankee and Rebel soldiers. McDonald was saved by using a fallen Rebel as cover, but was not unscathed, suffering a gunshot wound through the thigh. Quickly an attacker was upon McDonald with a bayonet and stuck him several times, until Sergeant Daniel B. Moore grabbed a Confederate rifle and shot the attacker dead. Moore would receive the Medal of Honor for his actions. McDonald survived and became a hero in the regiment. After only 15 minutes, the Eleventh Wisconsin's colors were planted atop the Rebel works, but fighting further down the line was just heating up.[66]

Angus R. McDonald (Wisconsin Veterans Museum).

A soldier with the Thirty-second Iowa, charging to the right of Harris' brigade, wrote afterwards that they were forced down to the ground, crawling at various points, over "numerous torpedoes planted in our way up to the fort." While they made their way through "various obstructions" they took steady and at times heavy fire. As they reached the parapet housing "a great big cannon," the cannon fired several times "with disastrous effect, killing 14 of our men in one discharge." It was a gruesome business. Land mines discharged, blowing men and earth into the air and dropping them, mangled. Cannon fire blasted through groups of men, killing and maiming dozens at a time.[67]

The fighting in front of the fort raged on as pockets of Confederates fought their desperate struggle till the end. Hawkins' men had almost completely engulfed the Rebel's left flank, save for one group of brave Mississippians whose commanding officer was later reported to have shouted, "Lay low and mow the ground — the damned Niggers are coming!" And they obeyed, taking countless Negro soldiers with them to the grave. But in no time hundreds of Mississippians scrambled to the center and rear of the fort. The screams of "Remember Fort Pillow!" from the Negro troops sent the Confederates into a panic as they tried desperately to escape. They were soon joined by fleeing Alabama and Missouri troops. Some reached the banks of the river and tried to swim across, while others ripped planks from the wharf to use as floats. The river was soon filled with the frantic splashing of Rebels trying to escape; some could not swim. Not far behind them hundreds of bluecoats stopped at the river's edge and opened fire. Negro soldiers rounded up the Rebels who did not make it to the water. Confederate gunboats nearby could not provide covering fire as the two armies intermixed along the shore. They were able to rescue some, recorded the commander of one of the boats, "but many were drowned, some killed in the water and some on the shore, and the rest surrendered." Few Rebels made it downstream or to the other side.[68]

What happened next is unclear, but it cannot be denied that some Negro soldiers went about executing Confederates who had surrendered or were attempting to do so. One white officer later claimed that when the Negro soldiers "caught sight of the retreating [Confederates] ... the very devil could not hold them.... Their eyes glittered like serpents and with yells & howls like hungry wolves" they attacked. They clubbed and bayoneted prisoners and were only restrained by threats from white officers, one of whom was killed while trying to intervene. It is not known exactly how many they killed, but one officer noted, "The niggers did not take a prisoner, they killed all they took to a man." After a few minutes, order was restored.[69]

But all was not chaos. Within this hour of fury humanity still existed. What is most astonishing was that the gesture came from a former slave. One Negro soldier came across his former master among the prisoners, and instead of offering him the bayonet, he offered him his canteen. "They appeared happy to meet," wrote a witness, "and drank from the same canteen." By far most of the comments in diaries, reports, and letters by those who fought on this day offered praise for the Negro soldiers. White officers and fellow soldiers seemed genuinely impressed with their black counterparts. "The Negro brigade fought like tigers," wrote one soldier from Iowa. Though he did say that the Negroes were angry and some had to be restrained, he asked simply, "Who can blame them?" The comments continued from generals to colonels. General Andrews noted that his colored troops "fought nobly." But perhaps most impressive was a comment given decades later by a veteran of an Illinois regiment. In his memoir he wrote that, though it wasn't "even remotely" related to his own war story, it "would be a pleasure to tell of the magnificent courage of the colored troops in this engagement."[70]

Iowa troops arriving from Spanish Fort after the assault inspected the fortifications around Blakely and were amazed that the attack succeeded. "How men could charge over such lines of defense," wrote one Hawkeye, "we, ourselves not wholly ignorant of warfare, could not imagine." They continued down the earthwork until encountering the Negro division where they inexplicably found even stouter defenses. They approached one Negro soldier, standing near the fort, who had taken part in the assault. They asked the "powerfully built" soldier, "How on earth men could ever have charged over that most formidable abatis[?]" The Negro soldier's "eyes glistened" and he said, "Nebber knowed dat ar brush-pile was dar!" They were indeed "burning" with such a desire to do justice that nothing could have stood in their way. That same Iowa soldier later noted that whenever the captured Alabama soldiers and Negroes were in the same vicinity "There [still] seemed to be some old grudge to settle."[71]

The Eleventh Wisconsin had made its last charge of the Civil War. They captured over 300 prisoners, numerous guns, ammunition, and horses. They lost 61 men, 15 of them killed. As the wounded were collected and the fort secured, men gathered in groups to smoke their pipes and speak of their heroics. William Flenner found a quite place to rest and record an entry into his diary. His thoughts most likely summed up what most of the men felt that night:[72]

> Now the roar of musketry & artillery ceased.... The thick smoke of battle has cleared away. The moan of a dying soldier comes up from the ditch. A wounded man is calling for water to slake his burning thirst. Listen again & hear the shrieks of the wounded a way back on the field among the brush who fell in the first of the charge.... O God how horrible is the scene of battle upon this Sabbath evening. What an awful destruction of human life has followed the track over which we passed. Ah, the thought of these changes is painful to endure. Men are slaughtered by wholesale & though I am among the fortunate who have passed through the dreadful conflict safely & though feel proud satisfaction swell my breast at the truth I participated in the charge & helped win so brilliant an achievement as the capture of this Rebel stronghold yet there is a pang of grief at the thought of the fallen.[73]

CHAPTER THIRTEEN

Back Home and to the Frontier

Upon receiving official word of General Lee's surrender, Wisconsin, like every other Union state, rejoiced that the long and bloody war was finally coming to an end. "On the receipt of the news of the fall of Richmond," wrote a Menasha resident, "and the capture of Jefferson Davis, the town was alive with crowds of people and with demonstrations of joy, the blowing of horns, the clanging of bells, the firing of anvils, and the shouting of the people." The spectacle was such that he declared, "I never expect to see such a demonstration again."[1]

As Wisconsin communities geared up for main street celebrations, the men of the Eleventh Wisconsin were still facing several thousand armed Confederates in Alabama. The war was not over for them just yet. It would take until May for General Canby to negotiate terms of surrender with General Taylor, who commanded the Department of Alabama, Mississippi, and Louisiana for the Confederacy. Back in Madison, on April 12, residents and politicians once again gathered near Capital Square. The *Journal* reprinted the highlights of a speech given by a resident of Madison, Mr. Cassody, who said of these victories:

> [They] had been won partly in consequence of the motives that inspired our soldiers. Other soldiers might fight as the tools of despotism or the spoils of victory, but the American soldiers fought because they loved their country.[2]

But celebrations were short-lived when it was learned that President Lincoln had been shot on April 14, while enjoying the play *Our American Cousin*. Accompanying him at Ford's Theater that night was his wife, Mary Todd Lincoln, Major Henry R. Rathbone, and Major Rathbone's fiancée. On the way to the theater Lincoln told his wife that he had never felt better in his life. While the play was in progress John Wilkes Booth approached the presidential box, aimed, and fired his Derringer pistol. The president slumped forward, unconscious. Rathbone tried but failed to grab Booth as he jumped from the balcony and fled the theater. Lincoln was rushed across the street to a boardinghouse, where nine hours later, at 7:22 A.M. on April 15, he died.

* * *

Henry Oettiker was on his way up the Mississippi River when he received news of Lincoln's death. He stopped at Vicksburg, found the city abuzz, and noted it in his diary. Henry was about to become a second lieutenant in the Fiftieth Wisconsin regiment and was on his way home to be mustered into service. By April 1865, the Fiftieth Wisconsin was one of only two Wisconsin regiments, the other being the Fourth Cavalry, in the field. By April 22 he was in Cairo, then on a train to Chicago and on to Madison by the 24th. The next day, "I was musterd 2 Lt of Co. K of the 50th Wis but did not get my pay and perhaps wont till tomorrow. Baut a suit today, sword and sash & belt for 62 [dollars]." He was to become an officer and seemed excited at the prospect of continuing his military service. A few days later he was at home and finally able to rest. By May 1 Henry had spent the better part of two days at home resting. That evening he ventured out, recording later, "I visited Melvins and a grate many friends came to see me."[3]

* * *

Back in Alabama, the Eleventh Wisconsin was stationed at Montgomery. "We have good times here now," said Samuel Kirkpatrick in one of his last letters home. It was May 12, and the war was pretty much over. Camped three miles north of the city, the regiment was stationed in the middle of a popular return route for Confederate soldiers. "Old General Lee's and Johnson's men is still coming into the city," he wrote. "We can see from 100 to 300 come in ever day." These men were looking for transportation to Texas, Louisiana, and other states. "The most of them says that they was whipped and that long ago and others say they are agoing to stop awhile to get beter redy." But most were friendly and some were probably a little scared, desperately trying to get home to their farms and families, not knowing what was left to return to.[4]

By July the regiment was in Mobile on provost guard duty. It was their hope they would soon be returning home. Before their arrival on May 25, more than half the town was burned to the ground when an arsenal caught fire, exploding as artillery shells, mines, canisters, and gunpowder ignited. A local paper described the carnage: "bursting shells, flying timbers, bales of cotton, horses, men, women, and children co-mingled and mangled into one immense mass." Three hundred people lost their lives. What is remarkable is that Calvin Alling insisted in his memoirs that as late as July, when they arrived, parts of Mobile were still smoldering.

In his last letter home Samuel Kirkpatrick noted that many of the new recruits were sick, again. The weather was warm and humid, and disease was making its usual rounds. "Some old fellows I fell sory for and there is more of them that mite have come out in sixty one," wrote Samuel. "They thought that ther home was the safest and so it was. But if all had thought that where would we be to day — standing on but little free soil." In the end, perhaps, it was about freedom after all — freedom from a rebellion, and even maybe that of a whole race.[5]

By August the regiment was more than anxious to go home, noted Calvin Alling. "A delegation of ten," he noted, "one from each company, called on Colonel Harris, urging that we may be discharged as soon as possible." They didn't have to wait much longer. On September 4, 1865, the regiment was mustered out of service and ordered back to Madison to be disbanded.[6]

By the 16th they were in St. Louis, and without stopping they boarded a train and reached Madison by the 18th at about 10 o'clock in the morning. There they were "enthusiastically received" by Governor Lewis, city authorities, and many citizens, friends, and family. That night they were quartered in Camp Randall. Most likely it was an odd feeling to spend one last night in the place where it all began so long ago. The next day they signed their payrolls and were officially disbanded.[7]

That night Calvin Alling made an entry into his diary: "10 pm, I am again with my dear wife, at her home. She is well, but wearied with anxious waiting, waiting, waiting. It is all over now, and we will rest." Indeed he did. For three days Calvin made no entries in his diary. Then on September 22, 1865, he made his last entry of the war:

> Started to-day on foot for my father's home, twenty-miles north, in Sylvan township, Richland County, Wisconsin. My wife essayed to "go a piece" with me, which was very elastic, covering the whole distance; so for the last fifteen miles, I procured a horse and side-saddle for her. We found everyone well, and rejoiced at our return, after an absence of four years, one month, and twenty days.[8]

The men of the Eleventh Wisconsin Veteran Volunteer Regiment were finally home for good, after traveling 9,000 miles, 3,500 of them on the march. The official record of the dead at war's end stood at 348 men lost, 262 of them to disease.⁹

Regiment Vital Statistics:

Original Strength: 1,029.

Gain by recruits in 1863, 72; in 1864, 263; in 1865, 24; by substitutes, 62; by draft in 1865, 147; veteran reenlistments, 363; total: 1,965.

Loss: by death, 348; deserted, 25; transferred, 9; discharged, 19; mustered out, 1,264.

* * *

Samuel Kirkpatrick returned to farming after the war, but did not stay in Wisconsin. He was too much the explorer and his curiosity kept him (and his wife) on the move not only to various places in Wisconsin but also outside the state, to Nebraska and Colorado. Samuel most likely explored other states, but these were the only ones listed as residences in his pension applications. Samuel and his wife, Caroline, had five children. An 1880 census shows Samuel returned to Wisconsin and settled down near Mifflin, having purchased some farmland. Samuel died in Platteville, Wisconsin, on July 29, 1911, at the age of 70. Caroline survived him until 1926.¹⁰

William Henry Oettiker in 1906 (Author's Collection).

Calvin Alling and his wife, Emmaretta, bought 80 acres of farmland in Richland County right after the war and had two children, one of whom died in infancy. A few years later they sold their land and moved to Grant County where they had a son, Aaron, who would also join the army and unfortunately die in Arizona in 1895 during peacetime maneuvers. By 1880 Calvin and his wife had moved again, this time out of state to Bloomington, Illinois. There they had another child, a daughter, who also died during infancy. Still restless, they headed west and ended up in Kansas, outside Wichita, after a short stint in Texas. There they had two sons who lived to adulthood. Calvin remained in Kansas until his death in 1928, at the age of 88.¹¹

The hero of Fort Blakely, Angus McDonald, was born in Scotland in 1832. Angus and his brother Allen were among the first settlers of Mazomanie, where they built one of the town's first hotels. After the war they donated the property to a church next door, and it became a parochial school. Angus was promoted to captain after the war and was in charge of the local armory. He left town for Milwaukee, where he became a shopkeeper. Angus passed away on April 14, 1879, and it was reported that "his death was not unlooked for [as] some months ago the Captain was taken with paralysis." He was bedridden and had lost the sight in one of his eyes. He most likely suffered a stroke. By all accounts his funeral was well attended. His body was delivered from Madison back home to Mazomanie, where he was buried with "the old flag wrapped around him in the midst of weeping friends, the mortal remains of the heroic soldier were lowered in the grave by those who had followed him on many fields of battle."¹²

James Sanford, who survived several dangerous missions around Vicksburg and took direct fire from a cannon, ended up in Kearney, Nebraska, after the war, where he bought some land to farm. His wife, Jennie, bore him two sons and a daughter. On his deathbed in November of 1910, he dictated to his children a short autobiography that included his unbelievable story. He passed away on December 7, 1910, at the age of 74.[13]

Left and above: Henry Twining's brothers: Aaron and Harrison, both died of disease during the war. Unfortunately no picture of Henry has been located (Marc and Beth Storch Collection).

According to an 1880 U.S. Census report, Robert Sherrill moved to Iowa, where he bought land near Indian Creek in Mills County. He married Martha Hodgin, and together they raised four children — two daughters and two sons. Unfortunately, from 1890 to 1920 no census or pension reports produced entries pertaining to Robert or Martha Sherrill.

Henry H. Twining never married Hattie Perkins, but interestingly enough he married a Miss Hattie Miller. After the war he left Wisconsin and bought land in Kansas. Unfortunately, Henry disappears from census until 1920, when we find that he retired to Franklin, Kansas, with Hattie. They apparently had no children. In 1925 Hattie applied for Henry's pension after his death.

By 1880, Surgeon Henry P. Strong had established himself as one of Beloit's most prominent citizens; he was elected mayor five times (1864–66, 1868, 1869). He owned a home large

---

Opposite top left: Henry Luneburg of Company B (Marc and Beth Storch Collection). *Opposite top right:* Lavander Harris of Company I (Marc and Beth Storch Collection). *Opposite bottom left:* William Devine of Company F (Marc and Beth Storch Collection). *Opposite bottom right:* Seldon Huntley of Company C (Marc and Beth Storch Collection).

enough to house a staff of servants and housekeepers (eight of them), as well as a mother in-law, and two sons: Harry (14) and Russell (11). Just a few years after he returned from the war he became secretary of the State Board of Health of Wisconsin (Wisconsin State Medical Society) and was elected president in June 1870. The years before his death were spent on his extensive stock farm of Kentucky thoroughbred horses; on a warm summer morning, June 20, 1883, Henry died suddenly. His funeral was attended by nearly the entire city. Because he was once director of public schools, Beloit named a school after him, the Strong school, located near City Park.[14]

Colonel Charles L. Harris had studied law before the war and was a prominent citizen of Madison. He was ambitious and, for the regiment's good fortune, a good leader. After the war Colonel Harris headed west, like many other Civil War veterans, and settled in Cedar County, Nebraska, where he worked as a lawyer and a merchant. Interestingly, his loyal and trustworthy captain, Jesse Miller, followed him to Nebraska. Harris used his Civil War accomplishments to further his interest in politics and became a Nebraska state senator. He and his wife, Mary, had two children, a son and a daughter. The colonel died tragically after an automobile accident in Omaha. He was a passenger in a vehicle that rolled over. Though trapped for a period of time under the automobile, he was released and seemed in good spirits, save for some scratches and bruises. But unfortunately he also had internal bleeding and soon afterward went into shock. A week later, on October 11, 1910, at the age of 75, he passed away.[15]

By the summer of 1865, William Henry Oettiker was traveling up the Missouri River with the Fiftieth Wisconsin Infantry heading to Fort Rice in Dakota, Indian country. In September, after already two months on the march, not long after the Eleventh Wisconsin regiment had returned home and was disbanded, Henry was deep into Dakota, having passed Fort Randall: "Wednesday, September 30th, 1865: Left Fort Randall this morning at 5 oc and martched 12 miles where we camped at 5 oclock in the afternoon and stayed all night. We have traveled over a desolate plane all day."

William Loudon of Company B (Marc and Beth Storch Collection).

Colonel Charles L. Harris and his wife, Mary (left), at the 1906 reunion of the Eleventh Wisconsin regiment. Major Jesse S. Miller and his wife, Lidda, in 1907 (Wisconsin Veterans Museum).

By the end of the month Henry and his regiment had reached Fort Sully, deep in Sioux Indian country. They had seen tough times with "no wood nor scarsely any water." They had also seen thousands of Indians in what he described as cacophonous events. It would not be until October 10 that his regiment finally arrived at Fort Rice. He spent nearly a year on the frontier, and luckily avoided injury while he endured the harsh winter at the fort. The Fiftieth Wisconsin returned home in June of 1866 (the last Civil War Wisconsin regiment to be mustered out of service) and was disbanded. In 1867 Henry married Eva Libert and remained in Lafayette County, where he farmed. In 1879 he sold his farm and moved to Platteville, where he started a well-drilling and pump-making business, which he and Eva sold in 1899. They had four children — one son and three daughters. Henry passed away on April 3, 1908, at the age of 66.

On May 22, 1908, the living members of the Eleventh Wisconsin Volunteer Regiment gathered once more for a reunion, this time on the very ground they fought on outside of

Vicksburg. Jesse Miller, back in Omaha and unable to make the trip, wrote a stirring letter that was read aloud. He ended it by recalling July 4, 1863, when Vicksburg surrendered:

> Looking north and south from the spot where you now stand, as far as the eye can see, simultaneously appeared a line of small white flags, and instantly there were two lines of animated men at varying distances apart, for the first time in more than two years, calmly facing each other, one clad in grey, not unmixed with clay, the other in soiled and faded blue. I shall never forget the joyous shout that rent the air from the line of blue, [and] the silent dignified demeanor of the greys.... The reward to the both Blue and Grey for the four long years of war is in the fact that the Old Glory is still in the sky, the flag of the greatest, grandest, most powerful and wealthiest nation on the globe today.[16]

APPENDIX A

Roster of the 11th Wisconsin

Abbreviations: Bvt.=Brevet; Cpl.=Corporal; Disch.=Discharged; Enl.=Enlisted; Lt.=Lieutenant; M.O.=Mustered Out; Pris.=Prisoner; Prom.=Promoted; Re-enl.=Re-enlisted; Rej.=Rejected; Res.=Resigned; Sgt.=Sergeant; Trans.=Transferred; USCT=United States Colored Troops; Vet.=Veteran; VRC=Veterans Reserve Corps; Wnd.=Wounded

Field and Staff

OFFICERS

Charles L. Harris Colonel; Madison; Rank from Sept. 2, 1861; Wounded Bayou Cache; Brevet Brig. Gen. U.S. Vols., Mar. 13, 1865; Mustered out Sept. 4, 1865.

Charles A. Wood Lt. Colonel; Madison; Rank from Sept. 2, 1861; Resigned June 7, 1863.

Luther H. Whittlesey Lt. Colonel; Mineral Point; Rank from June 7, 1863; From Capt. Co. E; Brevet Col. U.S. Vols., Mar. 13, 1865; Mustered out Sept. 4, 1865.

Arthur Platt Major; Madison; Rank from Sept. 2, 1861; Resigned July 9, 1863.

Jesse S. Miller Major; Richland Center; Rank from July 8, 1863; From Capt. Co. D; Mustered out June 11, 1865.

1907 Reunion of Eleventh Wisconsin Regiment (Wisconsin Veterans Museum).

Otis Remick Major; Madison; Rank from July 26, 1865; From Capt. Co. B; Mustered out Sept. 4, 1865.

Daniel Lincoln Adjutant; Madison; Rank from Sept. 10, 1861; Resigned July 28, 1863.

Ira W. Hunt Adjutant; Neenah; Rank from July 28, 1863; From 1st Lt., Co. K; Resigned June 14, 1864.

James F. Spencer Adjutant; Madison; Rank from June 30, 1864; From Sgt. Major; Mustered out Sept. 4, 1865.

George M. Sabin Quartermaster; Madison; Rank from Sept. 10, 1861; Resigned Nov. 6, 1861.

Charles George Mayers Quartermaster; Madison; Rank from Nov. 6, 1861; Q.M. 2nd Brig. 1st Div 13th A.C., Sept. 25, 1863; Post Q.M. Terre Bonne, May 31, 1864; Brashear City, Aug. 9, 1864; Staff Q.M. Maj Gen. Canby, Comdg. Army and Div West Miss., Mar. 31, 1865; retained in service by order of War Department, until Sept. 30, 1865; Brevet Capt. and Maj. U.S. Vol., Mar. 13, 1865.

Henry P. Strong Surgeon; Beloit; Rank from Sept. 13, 1861; Resigned July 16, 1863.

Edward Everitt Surgeon; Racine; Rank from July 16, 1863; 1st Asst Surg., Sept. 14, 1861; Mustered out Sept. 4, 1865.

Joseph Green 1st Asst. Surgeon; Hudson; Rank from Aug. 10, 1863; Resigned July 20, 1864.

John T. Wilson 1st Asst. Surgeon; Racine; Rank from Aug. 17, 1864; From Hosp. Steward U.S.A.; Mustered out Sept. 4, 1865.

Calvin C. Barnes 2nd Asst. Surgeon; Waukesha; Rank from Oct. 2, 1861; Resigned Oct. 15, 1862.

Hilton W. Boyce 2nd Asst. Surgeon; Geneva; Rank from Nov. 29, 1862; Resigned June 7, 1863.

James R. Britton Chaplain; Madison; Rank from Oct. 1, 1861; Resigned Apr. 24, 1862.

George W. Wells Chaplain; Dodgeville; Rank from June 20, 1864; Resigned June 9, 1865.

Non-Commissioned Officers

Dudley C. Wyman Sgt. Major; Madison; Rank from Oct. 3, 1861; From Co. B; Veteran; Promoted Capt. Co. G, June 30, 1863.

James F. Spencer Sgt. Major; Madison; Rank from July 1, 1863; From Co. F; Veteran; Promoted Adjt., June 30, 1864.

James S. Robinson Sgt. Major; Eagle; Rank from July 10, 1864; From Co. D; Transferred to Co. D, as 1st Sgt., June 25, 1865.

Sylvester Eastman Sgt. Major; Ft. Winnebago; Rank from July 1, 1865; From Principal Musician; Mustered out Sept. 4, 1865.

Frederick A. Bird Quartermaster Sgt.; Sun Prairie; Rank from Sept. 26, 1861; Promoted 2nd. Lt. Co. B, 20th Wis. Inf., Aug. 11, 1862.

Charles C. Robbins Quartermaster Sgt.; Madison; Rank from Aug. 21, 1862; From Co. F; Veteran; Promoted Adjt., June 30, 1864.

Robert Hastie Quartermaster Sgt.; Madison; Rank from Feb. 13, 1864; From Principal Musician; transferred to Co. F., Feb. 8, 1865.

Charles J. Holt Quartermaster Sgt.; Madison; Rank from Feb. 1, 1865; From Co. I; Mustered out Sept. 4, 1865.

Henry A. Sweet Com. Sgt.; Milwaukee; Rank from Sept. 27, 1861; From. Co. F; transferred to Co. K. Feb. 13, 1864.

George W. Welling Com. Sgt.; Black Earth; Rank from June 30, 1862; From Co. A; transferred to Co. A, Feb. 10, 1864.

Rufus J. Hitchcock Com. Sgt.; Dale; Rank from Mar. 1, 1864; From Co. K; Mustered out Sept. 4, 1865.

Henry W. Turner Hospital Steward; Madison; Rank from Sept. 30, 1861; Promoted Asst. Surgeon 16th Wis. Inf., July 17, 1862.

Jay E. Trussell Hospital Steward; Deansville; Rank from Nov. 23, 1862; From Co. C; Discharged June 21, 1865, disability.

Joel B. Wright Hospital Steward; New Chester; Rank from June 22, 1865; From H; Mustered out Sept. 4, 1865.

Eben J. Leavitt Principal Musician; Palmyra; Rank from Oct. 1, 1861; Mustered out July 29, 1862.

Charles C. Chittenden Principal Musician; Madison; Rank from Oct. 23, 1861; Mustered out Nov. 24, 1862.

Sylvester Eastman Principal Musician; Ft. Winnebago; Rank from June 12, 1863; From Co. F; trans. to Co. H. June 1, 1864; from Co. H, Aug. 1, 1864; promoted to Sgt. Major, July 1, 1865.

Robert Hastie Principal Musician; Madison; Rank from June 12, 1863; From CO. F.; Veteran; Promoted Q.M. Sgt., Feb. 13, 1864.

Horace N. Polley Principal Musician; West Point; Rank from Feb. 13, 1864; From Co. H; Mustered out Sept. 4, 1865.

David T. Lindley Principal Musician; Watertown; Rank from July 1, 1865; From Co. D; Mustered out Sept. 4, 1865.

James C. Brown Band; Oregon; Rank from Oct. 12, 1861; Mustered out July 29, 1862.

Thomas P. Camp Band; Oregon; Rank from Oct. 18, 1861; Mustered out July 29, 1862.

Theodore Colliday Band; Dunn; Rank from Oct. 1, 1861; Mustered out July 29, 1862.

John Colliday Band; Dunn; Rank from Oct. 1, 1861; Mustered out July 29, 1862.

George Colliday Band; Dunn; Rank from Oct. 1, 1861; Died July 6, 1862, disease.

John Daws Band; Stoughton; Rank from Oct. 1, 1861; Mustered out July 29, 1862.

John Dodge Band; Stoughton; Rank from Oct. 1, 1861; Mustered out July 29, 1862.

Charles Dodge Band; Stoughton; Rank from Oct. 1, 1861; Mustered out July 29, 1862.

William Gillatt Band; Black Earth; Rank from Oct. 11, 1861; From Co. A; Mustered out July 29, 1862.

William Graham Band; Beaver Dam; Rank from Oct. 18, 1861; Mustered out July 29, 1862.
Willard Graves Band; Palmyra; Rank from Oct. 1, 1861; Mustered out July 29, 1862.
Hiram Graves Band; Palmyra; Rank from Oct. 1, 1861; Mustered out July 29, 1862.
Walter G. Graves Band; Palmyra; Rank from Oct. 12, 1861; Died June 26, 1862.
John Nichols Band; Madison; Rank from Oct. 1, 1861; Mustered out July 29, 1862.
John Panewell Band; Stoughton; Rank from Oct. 1, 1861; Mustered out Jan. 1, 1862.
Henry D. Patte Band; Palmyra; Rank from Oct. 1, 1861; Mustered out July 29, 1862.
Rufus D. Pritchard Band; Dunn; Rank from Oct. 1, 1861; Mustered out July 29, 1862.
Benjamin H. Rolph Band; Stoughton; Rank from Oct. 20, 1861; Mustered out Jan. 21, 1862.
Henry Shutte Band; Concord; Rank from Oct. 1, 1861; Mustered out July 29, 1862.
Charles H. Warren Band; Stoughton; Rank from Oct. 18, 1861; Mustered out July 29, 1862.
John P. Williams Band; Oregon; Rank from Oct. 17, 1861; Mustered out July 29, 1862.
James Woolen Band; Arena; Rank from Sept. 16, 1861; From Co. G; Mustered out July 29, 1862.
Joseph A. Young Band; Waukesha; Rank from Oct. 14, 1861; Mustered out July 29, 1862.

Co. A — The "Watson Guards"

Officers

Daniel E. Hough Captain; Madison; Rank from Sept. 12, 1861; Enlisted Aug. 24, 1861; Wounded Black River Bridge, Miss., May 17, 1863; Died June 3, 1863, of wounds.
William L Freeman Captain; Mazomanie; Rank from June 8, 1863; 2nd Lt., Sept. 12, 1861; 1st Lt., Sept. 5, 1862; Wounded Black River Bridge, Miss., May 17, 1863; Died June 7, 1864, Mazomanie, Wis., of wounds.
Luther T. Park Captain; Black Earth; Rank from July 2, 1864; Enlisted Sept. 6, 1861; Sgt., 1st Sgt.; 1st Lt., June 8, 1863; Mustered out Sept. 4, 1865.
Philo W. Jones 1st Lt.; Mazomanie; Rank from Sept. 9, 1861; Resigned Aug. 5, 1862.
Angus R. McDonald 1st Lt.; Mazomanie; Rank from July 14, 1864; Enlisted Sept. 2, 1861; Veteran, Sgt., 1st Sgt.; 2nd Lt., Apr. 27, 1864; Wounded Blakely, Ala.; Brevet Capt. U.S. Vols., Mar. 26, 1865; Mustered out May 15, 1865.
John B. Miller 2nd Lt.; Springfield; Rank from Sept. 5, 1862; Enlisted Sept. 10, 1861; Sgt., 1st Sgt.; Resigned Sept. 3, 1863.
T.H. Brainard 2nd Lt.; Black Earth; Rank from Sept. 1, 1864; Enlisted Sept. 2, 1861; Veteran, 1st Sgt.; Mustered out Sept. 4, 1865.

Enlisted Men

Charles H. Arland Cross Plains; Enlisted Sept. 19, 1861; Veteran, Corporal; Mustered out Sept. 4, 1865.
John Austin Arena; Enlisted Sept. 10, 1861; Mustered out Nov. 18, 1864, term expired.
William Baker Mazomanie; Enlisted Sept. 2, 1861; Discharged Feb. 7, 1863, disability.
James E. Bardsley Springfield; Enlisted Sept. 5, 1861; Veteran, Corporal, Sgt.; Mustered out Sept. 4, 1865.
John Barrett Madison; Enlisted Feb. 26, 1861; Died Sept. 9, 1864, Brashear City, La., disease.
Sylvester M. Barton Mazomanie; Enlisted Sept. 12, 1861; Discharged Dec. 3, 1862, disability.
George Belor Springfield; Enlisted Sept. 6, 1861; Died Oct. 3, 1862, Helena, Ark., disease.
Charles Berg Mazomanie; Enlisted Sept. 2, 1861; Veteran; Mustered out Sept. 4, 1865.
Henry Berg Mazomanie; Enlisted Mar. 29, 1864; Mustered out Sept. 1, 1865.
John Berg Berry; Enlisted Oct. 8, 1861; Deserted Feb. 21, 1863.
Christian Berrie Mazomanie; Enlisted Jan. 5, 1864; Wounded Blakely; Mustered out Sept. 4, 1865.
Henry Blake Black Earth; Enlisted Mar. 29, 1864; Mustered out Sept. 4, 1865.
Henry M. Blake Cross Plains; Enlisted Sept. 10, 1861; Veteran; Mustered out Sept. 4, 1865.
Ethan A. Blynn Mazomanie; Enlisted Sept. 6, 1861; Discharged June 27, 1862.
James Boardman Mazomanie; Enlisted Sept. 6, 1861; Died Oct. 12, 1862, St. Louis, Mo.
Ransom Bowman Lagrange; Enlisted Sept. 6, 1861; Killed in action, May 17, 1863, Black River Bridge, Miss.
Peter C. Bradshaw Black Earth; Enlisted Sept. 2, 1861; Veteran; Wounded Vicksburg and Blakely; Discharged Aug. 20, 1865, wounds.
James Brown Horicon; Enlisted Sept. 19, 1861; Transferred to Co. B. Oct. 4, 1861.
Reuben Bunhard York; Enlisted Jan. 13, 1864; Died Sept. 14, 1864, Brashear City, La., disease.
John Burrows Sparta; Enlisted Mar. 29, 1864; Mustered out Sept. 4, 1865.
John Cammack Black Earth; Enlisted Sept. 8, 1861; Veteran; Mustered out Sept. 4, 1865.
Alfred B. Campbell Roxbury; Enlisted Sept. 2, 1861; Veteran; Mustered out Sept. 4, 1865.
Sanders W. Campbell Roxbury; Enlisted Sept. 2, 1861; Died Oct. 25, 1861, Madison, Wis.
Bernard Carpenter Mazomanie; Enlisted Dec. 30, 1863; Died May 17, 1864, Alexandria, La., disease.
John Carpenter Black Earth; Enlisted Sept. 2, 1861; Discharged Aug. 3, 1862, disability.
William Charlesworth Black Earth; Enlisted Sept. 2, 1861; Veteran; Killed Aug. 6, 1865, Mobile, Ala., accident.

Hiram Chase Roxbury; Enlisted Dec. 15, 1863; Discharged Feb. 22, 1865, disability.
Milo Cody Springfield; Enlisted Sept. 10, 1861; Died Jan. 11, 1863, Van Buren, Mo., disease.
Thomas H. Conry Black Earth; Enlisted Sept. 2, 1861; Discharged Mar. 20, 1863, disability; re-enlisted Mar. 29, 1864; Mustered out Sept. 4, 1865.
Joseph B. Crooks Mazomanie; Enlisted Sept. 2, 1861; Veteran, Corporal, Wagoner; Mustered out Sept. 4, 1865.
James Dalaba Black Earth; Enlisted Sept. 2, 1861; Veteran; Mustered out Sept. 4, 1865.
George Davies Mazomanie; Enlisted Sept. 5, 1861; Veteran; Corporal, Sgt.; Mustered out Sept. 4, 1865.
Michael Donahue West Point; Enlisted Oct. 18, 1861; Veteran; Wounded Vicksburg; Mustered out July 27, 1865.
George H. Ellis Mazomanie; Enlisted Sept. 2, 1861; Veteran; Mustered out Sept. 4, 1865.
Thomas G. Ellis Mazomanie; Enlisted Sept. 5, 1861; Corporal; trans. to V.R.C., Nov. 20, 1863; Mustered out Sept. 27, 1864, term expired.
Abram W. Emily Berry; Enlisted Sept. 2, 1861; Veteran; Musician; Mustered out Sept. 4, 1865.
Anthony Emily Berry; Enlisted Sept. 29, 1861; From Co. K; Veteran, Corporal; Mustered out July 24, 1865.
Webster L. Emily Berry; Enlisted Sept. 10, 1861; Prisoner Sabine Cross Roads; Mustered out July 6, 1865, term expired.
William H. Emily Berry; Enlisted Sept. 2, 1861; Veteran, Corporal, Sgt.; Mustered out Sept. 4, 1865.
Henry E. Enderly Mazomanie; Enlisted Sept. 2, 1861; Corporal; Died Apr. 26, 1862, Reeves Station, Mo., disease.
Patrick Enright Mazomanie; Enlisted Oct. 3, 1861; Veteran, Corporal; Mustered out Sept. 4, 1865.
Richard Enright Mazomanie; Enlisted Sept. 19, 1861; Wounded Vicksburg; Died May 31, 1863, Vicksburg, Miss., of wounds.
Dennis Enwright Prairie Du Chien; Mustered out July 29, 1865.
John Enwright Madison; Enlisted Mar. 23, 1864; Mustered out Sept. 4, 1865.
Lewis P. Flagler Springfield; Enlisted Oct. 1, 1861; Died Jan. 25, 1863, Ironton, Mo.
John Ford Mazomanie; Enlisted Sept. 11, 1861; Veteran; Mustered out Sept. 4, 1865.
Warren A. Ford Black Earth; Enlisted Sept. 2, 1861; Died Jan. 23, 1863, New Alton, Mo.
Benjamin F. Fowler Mazomanie; Enlisted Sept. 2, 1861; Veteran, Corporal; Mustered out Sept. 4, 1865.
John G. Fowler Mazomanie; Enlisted Sept. 2, 1861; Veteran; Mustered out Sept. 4, 1865.
Abijah Fox Madison; Enlisted Mar. 30, 1864; Died May 1, 1864, Madison, Wis., disease.
John Fox Cross Plains; Enlisted Sept. 9, 1861; Died Oct. 9, 1862, Cairo, Ill., disease.
John Gartshore Black Earth; Enlisted Sept. 2, 1861; Veteran; Mustered out Sept. 4, 1865.
Robert Gillott Springfield; Enlisted Sept. 6, 1861; Veteran; Discharged May 30, 1865, disability.
William Gillott Springfield; Enlisted Sept. 6, 1861; Transferred to Band, Oct. 11, 1861.
Charles Greening Mazomanie; Enlisted Jan. 4, 1864; Mustered out Aug. 22, 1865.
Robert Grimshaw Madison; Enlisted Jan. 5, 1864; Transferred to V.R.C. June 22, 1864.
Josiah Hadiman Cross Plains; Enlisted Sept. 19, 1861; Died Aug. 25, 1863, Cross Plains, Wis., disease.
Joseph Halter Springfield; Enlisted Sept. 6, 1861; Died Aug. 18, 1862, Oldtown, Ark., disease.
Milton M. Haney Cross Plains; Enlisted Sept. 12, 1861; Veteran, Corporal; Wounded Blakely; Mustered out Sept. 4, 1865.
Jonas E. Hazeltine Black Earth; Enlisted Sept. 12, 1861; Wounded Vicksburg; Died May 28, 1863, Vicksburg, Miss., of wounds.
Nathanel S. Hazeltine Black Earth; Enlisted Sept. 6, 1861; Wounded Vicksburg; Died July 30, 1863, Memphis, Tenn., disease.
James Henderson West Point; Enlisted Sept. 12, 1861; Veteran, Corporal; Mustered out Sept. 4, 1865.
William F. Hicks Madison; Enlisted Mar. 7, 1864; Wounded Blakely; Mustered out Sept. 4, 1865.
Joseph Hiller Springfield; Enlisted Sept. 10, 1861; Veteran, Corporal; Wounded Vicksburg; Mustered out Sept. 4, 1865.
Milo Houghton Prairie Du Sac; Enlisted Sept. 4, 1861; Deserted Oct. 17, 1863.
William Howard Springfield; Enlisted Sept. 12, 1861; Veteran; pris. Port Gibson; Mustered out Sept. 4, 1865.
Robert Isam Black Earth; Enlisted Feb. 25, 1864; Died Oct. 11, 1864, New Orleans, La., disease.
Henry N. Johnson Black Earth; Enlisted Sept. 2, 1861; Died Jan. 21, 1863, Ironton, Mo., disease.
Nelson Johnson Mazomanie; Enlisted Sept. 2, 1861; Veteran; Mustered out Sept. 4, 1865.
John Katenberger Roxbury; Enlisted Oct. 8, 1861; Veteran; Mustered out Sept. 4, 1865.
Peter C. Kellech Mazomanie; Enlisted Sept. 8, 1861; Wounded Black River Bridge; transferred to V.R.C., Aug. 10, 1864; Mustered out Sept. 27, 1864, term expired.
David Kerr Mazomanie; Enlisted Sept. 4, 1861; Died Oct. 27, 1862, Ironton, Mo., disease.
Francis Kerr Mazomanie; Enlisted Sept. 5, 1861; Mustered out Nov. 18, 1864, term expired.
Edgar Lampman Arena; Enlisted Sept. 7, 1864; Veteran, Corporal; Mustered out Sept. 4, 1865.
Andrew Lanagan York; Enlisted Feb. 1, 1864; Died Oct. 5, 1864, Madison, Wis., disease.

Harmon R. Learnard Mazomanie; Enlisted Sept. 2, 1861; Veteran, Musician; Mustered out Sept. 4, 1865.

Henry W. Learnard Mazomanie; Enlisted Sept. 2, 1861; Veteran; Died June 8, 1865, Montgomery, Ala., disease.

Robert Lent Springfield; Enlisted Sept. 6, 1861; Veteran; Mustered out Sept. 4, 1865.

John Lloyd Arena; Enlisted Sept. 9, 1861; Veteran; Mustered out Sept. 4, 1865.

James Logerson Cross Plains; Enlisted Sept. 2, 1861; Died July 30, 1862, Jefferson Barracks, Mo., disease.

William Madison West Point; Enlisted Sept. 12, 1861; Veteran, Corporal, Sgt.; Discharged July 1, 1865, disability.

Julius H. Mason Mazomanie; Enlisted Sept. 6, 1861; Veteran, Sgt.; Mustered out Sept. 4, 1865.

John McKay Oldtown, Ark.; Enlisted Aug. 4, 1862; Veteran; Mustered out June 6, 1865.

Patrick McLeany Blue Mounds; Enlisted Sept. 2, 1861; Veteran; Mustered out Sept. 1, 1865.

Edwin Middicot Reedstown; Enlisted Feb. 27, 1864; Mustered out Sept. 4, 1865.

Elias A. Millard Black Earth; Enlisted Dec. 30, 1863; Died Aug. 14, 1864, Brashear City, La., disease.

Aaron Miller Ridgeway; Enlisted Jan. 25, 1864; Mustered out Sept. 4, 1865.

Franklin Miller Madison; Enlisted Jan. 23, 1864; Mustered out Sept. 4, 1865.

William Miller Mazomanie; Enlisted Jan. 27, 1864; Mustered out Sept. 4, 1865.

John C. Morrill Mazomanie; Enlisted Sept. 6, 1861; Corporal; Discharged June 27, 1862, disability.

George I. Nelson Black Earth; Enlisted Mar. 29, 1864; Mustered out Sept. 4, 1865.

Otto Ostenberg Ridgeway, Otto; Enlisted Jan. 24, 1864; Mustered out Sept. 4, 1865.

Highland H. Park Black Earth; Enlisted Sept. 2, 1861; Discharged Dec. 3, 1862, disability.

Joseph Parker Mazomanie; Sept, 19, 1861; Mustered out Nov. 18, 1864, term expired.

Benjamin Parkin Mazomanie; Enlisted Sept. 8, 1862; Mustered out June 6, 1865.

Francis E. Peabody Black Earth; Enlisted Sept. 2, 1861; Corporal; Discharged Aug. 17, 1863, disability.

Timothy A. Perry Springfield; Enlisted Sept. 6, 1861; Died Oct. 24, 1862, Ironton, Mo.

Nehemiah W. Porter Mazomanie; Enlisted Jan. 21, 1864; Mustered out Sept. 4, 1865.

Stephen V. Porter Mazomanie; Enlisted Sept. 8, 1861; Veteran, Corporal, Sgt.; Mustered out Sept. 4, 1865.

James Pritchard Mazomanie; Enlisted Sept. 6, 1861; Mustered out Nov. 18, 1864, term expired.

John B. Pritchett Roxbury; Enlisted Sept. 2, 1861; Veteran; Died Dec. 17, 1864, New Orleans, La., diesase.

Michael Quinard Springfield; Enlisted Sept. 6, 1861; Veteran, Corporal; Wounded Vicksburg; Mustered out Sept. 4, 1865.

James Ray Madison; Enlisted Mar. 30, 1864; Died Apr. 30, 1864, Madison, Wis., disease.

Frederick Raymer Cedar Creek; Enlisted Nov. 5, 1861; Veteran; Mustered out Sept. 4, 1865.

Charles Reeves Mazomanie; Enlisted Sept. 2, 1861; Wounded Vicksburg; Died June 7, 1863, Memphis, Tenn., of wounds.

John H. Remington Black Earth; Enlisted Sept. 2, 1861; Veteran; Mustered out Sept. 4, 1865.

Bayis C. Rice Cross Plains; Enlisted Oct. 29, 1861; Transferred to 23rd Wis. Inf., Feb. 10, 1864.

Obadiah H. Rice Cross Plains; Enlisted Sept. 9, 1861; Veteran; Mustered out Sept. 4, 1865.

Thaddeus Rice Cross Plains; Enlisted Sept. 9, 1861; Died Jan. 5, 1863, Ironton, Mo., disease.

Lloyd A. Robarts Black Earth; Enlisted Sept. 19, 1861; Discharged July 26, 1862, disability.

Lyman H. Robarts Mazomanie; Enlisted Dec. 30, 1863; Died Sept. 1, 1864, Brashear City, La., disease.

William B. Robarts Black Earth; Enlisted Sept. 4, 1861; Veteran; Mustered out Sept. 4, 1865.

Charles H. Robinson Springfield; Enlisted Sept. 7, 1861; Died Oct. 8, 1863, New Orleans, La., disease.

Hollis Roundy Berry; Enlisted Sept. 5, 1861; Died Oct. 15, 1862, St. Louis, Mo., disease.

John Ryan Mazomanie; Enlisted Sept. 12, 1861; Veteran; Mustered out Sept. 4, 1865.

John Salter Oldtown, Ark.; Enlisted Aug. 21, 1862; Veteran; Mustered out June 6, 1865.

Jacob Shaffer Black Earth; Enlisted Sept. 2, 1861; Wounded Vicksburg; absent sick at Mustered out of Regt.

Thomas B. Shew Mazomanie; Enlisted Jan. 2, 1864; Died May 1, 1864, Alexandria, La., disease.

William Skinner Ridgeway; Enlisted Feb. 2, 1864; Died Dec. 16, 1864, Moscow, Wis., disease.

John Slater Moscow; Enlisted Feb. 11, 1864; Died Sept. 17, 1864, Brashear City, La., disease.

Frederick T. Stevens Mazomanie; Enlisted Sept. 8, 1861; Killed May 1, 1863, Port Gibson, Miss.

John Story West Point; Enlisted Sept. 11, 1861; Veteran; Mustered out Sept. 4, 1865.

Byron Swift Edgerton; Enlisted Sept. 4, 1861; Died June 15, 1862, Batesville, Ark., disease.

James Thompson Cross Plains; Enlisted Sept. 9, 1861; Veteran; Wounded Blakely; Mustered out Sept. 4, 1865.

Albert A. Tinker Black Earth; Enlisted Mar. 29, 1864; Mustered out Sept. 4, 1865.

Frank Trautman Sheboygan; Enlisted Sept. 22, 1862; Veteran; Mustered out June 6, 1865.

Alfred E. Turk Black Earth; Enlisted Sept. 2, 1861; Died Aug. 4, 1863, Vicksburg, Miss., disease.

William B. Turk Black Earth; Enlisted Sept. 2,

1861; Veteran, Corporal; Wounded Blakely; Died Apr. 10, 1865, Blakely, Ala., of wounds.
Washington A. Vaughn Madison; Enlisted Mar. 30, 1864; Wounded Blakely; Mustered out Sept. 4, 1865.
Loren Walker Black Earth; Enlisted Sept. 2, 1861; Veteran, Corporal, Sgt., 1st Sgt.; Wounded Vicksburg; Mustered out Sept. 4, 1865.
Marcus Walt Dover; Enlisted Sept. 2, 1861; Discharged Aug. 22, 1863.
Jacob H. Webster Cross Plains; Enlisted Sept. 9, 1861; Died July 10, 1862, Clarendon, Ark., disease.
George E. Welling Black Earth; Enlisted Oct. 12, 1861; Com. Sgt., June 30, 1862; rej. Co. Feb. 10, 1864; Mustered out Nov. 18, 1864, term expired.
Henry N. Wells Mazomanie; Enlisted Sept. 7, 1861; Died July 8, 1862, August, Ark., disease.
Joel F. Wheeler Mazomanie; Enlisted Sept. 8, 1861; Veteran, Corporal; Killed in action, Apr. 9, 1865, Blakely, Ala.
Edwin Williams Black Earth; Enlisted Sept. 2, 1861; Veteran; Mustered out Sept. 4, 1865.
Robert Williams Black Earth; Enlisted Mar. 29, 1864; Mustered out Sept. 4, 1865.
Ambrosius Winkler Berry; Enlisted Sept. 19, 1861; Veteran; Mustered out Sept. 4, 1865.
Horace A. Woodbury Ridgeway; Enlisted Jan. 15, 1864; Mustered out Sept. 4, 1865.
James H. Woolworth Arena; Enlisted Sept. 7, 1861; Discharged Mar. 19, 1862, disability; re-enlisted, Mar. 10, 1864; Mustered out Sept. 4, 1865.
Leonard Yeager Mazomanie; Enlisted Sept. 2, 1861; Corporal; Discharged Apr. 6, 1862, disability; re-enlisted Dec. 24, 1863; Mustered out Sept. 4, 1865.
John Zirbel Mazomanie; Enlisted Jan. 14, 1864; Musician; Died Aug. 6, 1864, Brashear City, La., disease.

Co. B — The "Mendota Guard"

Officers

James H. Hubbard Captain; Madison; Rank from Sept. 30, 1861; Resigned Feb. 7, 1862.
Eri S. Oakley Captain; Madison; Rank from Feb. 15, 1862; 1st Lt., Sept. 30, 1861; Resigned Jan. 23, 1863.
Otis Remick Captain; Madison; Rank from Jan. 23, 1863; Enlisted Sept. 23, 1861; Veteran, Sgt.; 1st Lt., Feb. 15, 1862; Promoted Major, July 26, 1865.
William Charleton Captain; Verona; Rank from Aug. 23, 1865; Enlisted Nov. 8, 1861; Veteran, 1st Sgt.; 2nd Lt. Jan. 23, 1863; 1st Lt. July 14, 1863; Wounded Blakely; Mustered out Sept. 4, 1865.
Wallace W. Day 1st Lt.; Oregon; Rank from Jan. 23, 1863; Enlisted Sept. 30, 1861; Sgt., 1st Sgt.; 2nd Lt. Dec. 20, 1862; Resigned July 11, 1863.
James Bull 2nd Lt.; Middleton; Rank from Sept. 30, 1861; Resigned Mar. 8, 1862.
Henry D. Smith 2nd Lt.; Middleton; Rank from Mar. 11, 1862; Enlisted Sept. 12, 1861; Sgt.; Died July 12, 1862, Clarendon, Ark., disease.
Marvin Colby 2nd Lt.; Oregon; Rank from July 10, 1862; Enlisted Sept. 23, 1861; Corporal, Sgt., 1st Sgt.; Resigned Nov. 28, 1862.
Henry J. Luneburg 2nd Lt.; Middleton; Rank from Jan. 13, 1865; Enlisted Oct. 19, 1861; Veteran, Corporal, Sgt., 1st Sgt.; Wounded Vicksburg; Mustered out Sept. 4, 1865.

Enlisted Men

James Henry Allen Sun Prairie; Enlisted Sept. 16, 1861; Died Oct. 8, 1863, New Iberia, La., disease.
Charles Andersen Blue Mounds; Enlisted Oct. 28, 1861; See Charles Anderson.
John Anderson Enlisted Oct. 29, 1861; Died Sept. 9, 1862, Oldtown, Ark., disease.
George Andrew Boscobel; Enlisted Dec. 30, 1863; From 33rd Wis. Inf.; Mustered out June 23, 1865.
Benjamin Annis Middleton; Enlisted Sept. 12, 1861; Veteran; Mustered out Sept. 4, 1865.
William Annis Middleton; Enlisted Sept. 12, 1861; Veteran; Mustered out Sept. 4, 1865.
Charles Arpin Carlton; Enlisted Oct. 14, 1864; Drafted; Mustered out Sept. 4, 1865.
John W. Baily Boscobel; Enlisted Nov. 18, 1863; From 33rd Wis. Inf.; Corporal; Mustered out Sept. 4, 1865.
Ira Barnes Middleton; Enlisted Sept. 12, 1861; Veteran, Corporal, Sgt.; Mustered out Sept. 4, 1865.
James Barnes Blue Mounds; Enlisted Sept. 17, 1861; Discharged Jan. 6, 1863.
Samuel Barry Dunn; Enlisted Aug. 29, 1862; Veteran; Mustered out June 6, 1865.
Andrew Baumann Fitchburg; Enlisted Oct. 20, 1864; Killed Apr. 9, 1865, Blakely, Ala.
John Baumgartner Lake; Enlisted Mar. 8, 1865; Mustered out Sept. 4, 1865.
Daniel Beagle Middleton; Enlisted Sept. 16, 1861; Veteran, Corporal; Mustered out Sept. 4, 1865.
Walter Bedford Oregon; Enlisted Sept. 18, 1861; Veteran; Wounded Jackson, Miss.; Mustered out Sept. 4, 1865.
David Beers Middleton; Enlisted Sept. 24, 1861; Veteran, Corporal, Sgt.; Mustered out Sept. 4, 1865.
Frederick Beers Middleton; Enlisted Sept. 16, 1861; Discharged May 21, 1864, disability.
David Bell Wiota; Enlisted Feb. 22, 1865; Mustered out Sept. 4, 1865.
Stephen R. Bentley Sun Prairie; Enlisted Sept. 14, 1861; Discharged Oct. 30, 1862, disability.
Samuel N. Blatchford Black Earth; Enlisted Oct. 11, 1861; Veteran; Mustered out Sept. 4, 1865.

William W. Blatchford Black Earth; Enlisted Mar. 29, 1864; Wounded Blakely; Mustered out June 17, 1865.

George Blighton Sun Prairie; Enlisted Sept. 12, 1861; Deserted Nov. 25, 1862.

Anton Bock Middleton; Enlisted Sept. 20, 1864; Discharged May 22, 1865, disability.

Christopher Bohn Berry; Enlisted Oct. 10, 1864; Mustered out Nov. 18, 1864, term expired.

Richard Bond Windsor; Enlisted Jan. 4, 1864; From 33rd Wis. Inf.; Mustered out Sept. 4, 1865.

Billy Bonner Enterprise, Miss; Enlisted Feb. 24, 1864; From 33rd Wis. Inf.; Colored Cook; Mustered out Sept. 4, 1864.

William Boyce Fennimore; Enlisted Jan. 21, 1864; From 33rd Wis. Inf.; Mustered out Sept. 4, 1865.

Warren Boyle Pulaski; Enlisted Dec. 14, 1863; From 33rd Wis. Inf.; Mustered out Sept. 4, 1865.

Josiah P. Bradbury Sun Prairie; Enlisted Sept. 23, 1861; Corporal; Discharged Apr. 10, 1863, disability.

Frederick Brasse Madison; Enlisted Oct. 22, 1864; Mustered out Sept. 4, 1865.

Daniel Briggs Madison; Enlisted Sept. 30, 1861; Corporal, Sgt.; Discharged Aug. 16, 1864, disability.

George W. Brosshard Fountain Prairie; Enlisted Oct. 29, 1861; Veteran; Died Sept. 25, 1864, New Orleans, La., disease.

James Brown Horicon; Enlisted Sept. 18, 1861; From Co. A; Deserted Oct. 4, 1861.

Christopher Brunswick Middleton, Enlisted Jan. 17, 1865; Mustered out Sept. 4, 1865.

Joseph W. Buck Madison; Enlisted Mar. 31, 1864; Died Sept. 29, 1864, New Orleans, La., disease.

John A. Bull Middleton; Enlisted Sept. 12, 1861; Promoted 1st Lt. Co. E, 23rd Wis. Inf., Aug. 21, 1862.

William R. Campbell Mount Hope; Enlisted Jan. 21, 1864; From 33rd Wis. Inf.; Mustered out Sept. 4, 1865.

John Carty Oregon; Enlisted Sept. 27, 1861; Discharged June 12, 1863, disability.

George Clark Marinette; Enlisted Nov. 18, 1863; From 33rd Wis. Inf.; Mustered out Sept. 4, 1865.

Chester C. Clewitt Middleton; Enlisted Sept. 12, 1861; Discharged Apr. 10, 1863, disability.

Truman W. Cole Boscobel; Enlisted Jan. 20, 1864; From 33rd Wis. Inf.; Mustered out Sept. 4, 1865.

Dennis Collins Madison; Enlisted Sept. 19, 1861; Deserted Mar. 17, 1863.

Daniel Cook Verona; Enlisted Nov. 8, 1861; Corporal; Wounded Vicksburg; Mustered out Nov. 18, 1864, term expired.

Theophilus Cross West Blue Mounds; Enlisted Nov. 5, 1861; Died Aug. 19, 1862, Oldtown, Ark., of wounds.

Manter Daggett Madison; Enlisted Sept. 16, 1861; Died Aug. 25, 1862, Reeves Station, Mo., disease.

Daniel Daley Oregon; Enlisted Oct. 14, 1861; Deserted Nov. 3, 1861.

Michael Daley Madison; Enlisted Oct. 4, 1864; Mustered out Sept. 4, 1865.

Isaac Damon Madison; Enlisted Sept. 14, 1861; Wounded Vicksburg; Mustered out Nov. 18, 1864, term expired.

Ezra Darrow Oregon; Enlisted Sept. 14, 1861; Died Oct. 25, 1862, St. Louis, Mo., disease.

Benjamin Davison Middleton; Enlisted Aug. 28, 1864; Mustered out June 6, 1865.

Alvin L. Day Dunn; Enlisted Aug. 16, 1862; Veteran; Absent sick at Mustered out of Regt.

Phillip M. Day Dunn; Enlisted Aug. 17, 1862; Discharged Feb. 23, 1863, disability.

George Dearborn Madison; Enlisted Sept. 19, 1861; Musician; Discharged Nov. 20, 1862, disability.

John Dengle Madison; Enlisted Sept. 14, 1861; Died Apr. 26, 1863, Perkins' Plantation, La., disease.

Francis Depas Scott; Enlisted Mar. 1, 1865; Drafted; Mustered out Sept. 4, 1865.

Nelson R. Doan Madison; Enlisted Sept. 28, 1861; Transferred to Co. I, Sept. 30, 1864.

George W. Doud Dunn; Enlisted Oct. 5, 1861; Discharged Oct. 2, 1862, disability.

Silas Drake Middleton; Enlisted Mar. 24, 1864; Died Dec. 5, 1864, Brashear City, La., disease.

Charles M. Eaton Madison; Enlisted Sept. 17, 1861; Wounded Vicksburg; Mustered out Nov. 18, 1864, term expired.

Edwin A. Eaton Madison; Enlisted Sept. 16, 1861; Veteran, Cpl.; Mustered out Aug. 15, 1865.

Frank Elier Middleton; Enlisted Sept. 22, 1864; Mustered out June 6, 1865.

Henry F. Emery Middleton; Enlisted Sept. 12, 1861; Discharged Feb. 26, 1863, disability.

Andrew Everson Vermont; Enlisted Oct. 11, 1861; Died Nov. 18, 1862, Ironton, Mo., disease.

Thomas Everson Vermont; Enlisted Oct. 28, 1861; Died Jan. 3, 1863, St. Louis, Mo., disease.

Antonie Fontaine Green Bay; Enlisted Mar. 1, 1865; Drafted; Died July 13, 1865, Montgomery, Ala., disease.

Asa Foster Little Suamico; Enlisted Dec. 29, 1864; Drafted; Mustered out Sept. 4, 1865.

Louis Fralich Middleton; Enlisted Sept. 12, 1861; Discharged Mar. 29, 1863, disability.

Henry Gabert Manitowoc; Enlisted Mar. 17, 1865; Mustered out Sept. 4, 1865.

Henry Gacker Two Rivers; Enlisted Mar. 17, 1865; Mustered out Sept. 4, 1865; Died en route home.

John H. Gilbert Madison; Enlisted Oct. 9, 1861; Died Dec. 9, 1863, New Orleans, La., disease.

Jacob N. Glidden Janesville; Enlisted Oct. 31, 1861; Wounded Vicksburg; Died Nov. 23, 1863, New Orleans, La., disease.

Lysander Glidden Oregon; Enlisted Sept. 25, 1861; Corporal, Sgt.; Wounded Vicksburg; Mustered out Nov. 16, 1864, term expired.

Ambrose A. Grout Middleton; Enlisted Sept. 12, 1861; Sgt., 1st Sgt.; Died Mar. 12, 1862, Sulpher Springs, Mo.

Enos Grout Fall River; Enlisted Oct. 29, 1861; Discharged Apr. 6, 1863, disability.

Patrick Hannan Madison; Enlisted Oct. 29, 1861; Deserted Nov. 20, 1861.

Robert H. Henry Verona; Enlisted Sept. 26, 1861; Veteran, Corporal; Promoted 2nd Lt., Co. H, 42nd Wis. Inf., July 29, 1864.

John Hicks Fountain Prairie; Enlisted Oct. 1, 1861; Discharged Feb. 27, 1863, disability.

Edward Hines Pewaukee; Enlisted Mar. 13, 1865; Mustered out Sept. 4, 1865.

Lucius Hitchcock Boscobel; Enlisted Dec. 7, 1863; From 33rd Wis. Inf.; Mustered out Sept. 4, 1865.

Russel S. Howard Watertown; Enlisted Oct. 28, 1861; Died Nov. 2, 1862, Ironton, Mo., disease.

Edward S. Hunt Verona; Enlisted Oct. 1, 1864; Mustered out Sept. 4, 1865.

Xavier Hunt Lomira; Enlisted Mar. 22, 1865; Mustered out Sept. 2, 1865.

Joseph L.S. Jackson Boscobel; Enlisted Nov. 18, 1863; From 33rd Wis. Inf.; Mustered out Sept. 4, 1865.

Daniel Kelly Dunn; Enlisted Sept. 30, 1861; Discharged July 1, 1862, disability; re-enlisted July 10, 1864; Mustered out Sept. 4, 1865.

Henry E. Kelly Dunn; Enlisted Aug. 25, 1864; Mustered out June 6, 1865.

Michael Kelly Madison; Enlisted Sept. 28, 1864; Mustered out Sept. 4, 1865.

Thomas Kelly Rutland; Enlisted Aug. 27, 1864; Mustered out June 6, 1865.

Robert King Avoca; Enlisted Oct. 30, 1862; From 33rd Wis. Inf.; Mustered out Sept. 4, 1865.

Frederick Kropf Middleton; Enlisted Oct. 21, 1861; Veteran; Mustered out Sept. 4, 1865.

Charles B. Lindsley Rutland; Enlisted Aug. 27, 1864; Died Nov. 1, 1862, Old Mills, Mo., disease.

Francis S. Livermore Fountain Prairie; Enlisted Oct. 1, 1861; Veteran; Mustered out Sept. 4, 1865.

William London Middleton; Enlisted Oct. 31, 1861; Veteran, Corporal; Mustered out Sept. 4, 1865.

Frederick Loudon Middleton; Enlisted Mar. 17, 1862; Killed May 22, 1863, Vicksburg, Miss.

John Maas Greenville; Enlisted Mar. 13, 1865; Mustered out Sept. 4, 1865, Also written Mass.

Martin Maas Greenville; Enlisted Mar. 13, 1865; Mustered out Sept. 4, 1865. Also written Mass.

Thomas Manion Dunn; Enlisted Sept. 26, 1861; Vet, Corporal; Mustered out Sept. 4, 1865.

John N. Martin Boscobel; Enlisted Nov. 18, 1863; From 33rd Wis. Inf.; Mustered out Sept. 4, 1865.

Presley Martin Boscobel; Enlisted Nov. 18, 1863; From 33rd Wis. Inf.; Mustered out Sept. 4, 1865.

Michael Mattimore Madison; Enlisted Oct. 29, 1861; Veteran; Mustered out Sept. 4, 1865.

Richard McConnell Madison; Enlisted Dec. 14, 1864; Mustered out Sept. 4, 1865.

James K. McCord Boscobel; Enlisted Dec. 17, 1863; From 33rd Wis. Inf.; Mustered out Sept. 4, 1865.

James McGowan Dunn; Enlisted Oct. 1, 1861; Veteran; Killed Apr. 9, 1865, Blakely, Ala.

Robert McPherson Ellenboro; Enlisted Jan. 4, 1864; From 33rd Wis. Inf.; Mustered out Sept. 4, 1865.

Conrad Meyer Theresa; Enlisted Mar. 6, 1865; Mustered out Sept. 4, 1865.

Layton Miles Middleton; Enlisted Nov. 9, 1861; Discharged May 31, 1863, disability.

William Miles Middleton; Enlisted Sept. 12, 1861; Veteran, Corporal, Sgt., 1st Sgt.; Mustered out Sept. 4, 1865.

George W. Miller Middleton; Enlisted Aug. 26, 1864; Mustered out June 6, 1865.

Jacob Miller Lomira; Enlisted Mar. 22, 1865; Died June 7, 1865, Montgomery, Ala., disease.

James R. Miller Middleton; Enlisted Aug. 26, 1864; Mustered out June 6, 1865.

Jaques Minsart Scott; Enlisted Mar. 1, 1865; Drafted; Mustered out Sept. 4, 1865.

Samuel D. Moran Boscobel; Enlisted Jan. 19, 1864; From 33rd Wis. Inf.; Mustered out Sept. 4, 1865.

Frederick Muelinweg Milford; Enlisted Sept. 12, 1861; Killed in action, Apr. 9, 1865, Blakely, Ala.

Edwin Nichols Dunn; Enlisted Sept. 30, 1861; Veteran; Wounded Vicksburg; Promoted 2nd Lt. Co. H, 51st Wis. Inf., Feb. 22, 1865.

Benjamin M. Niles Windsor; Enlisted Oct. 4, 1861; Veteran; Absent sick at Mustered out of regt.

Bryant F. Nobie Dunn; Enlisted Dec. 1, 1862; Mustered out Sept. 4, 1865.

Henry J. Norton Middleton; Enlisted Sept. 12, 1861; Veteran, Corporal, Sgt.; Wounded May 22, 1863, Vicksburg; Discharged July 8, 1865, disability.

Warren W. Nye Fitchburg; Enlisted Sept. 28, 1861; Veteran; Discharged Mar. 8, 1865, disability; Died Mar. 9, 1865, New Orleans, La.

Patrick O'Brien Madison; Enlisted Oct. 14, 1861; Veteran; Wounded May 22, 1863. Vicksburg; Died Sept. 6, 1865, New Orleans, La.

Peter J. Peters Prible; Enlisted Dec. 28, 1864; Drafted; Mustered out Sept. 4, 1865.

August Piersdorf Springdale; Enlisted Sept. 21, 1864; Mustered out June 6, 1865.

Henry Plackett Westport; Enlisted Sept. 23, 1861; Died Oct. 20, 1864, New York, disease.

Frank D. Powers Oregon; Enlisted Sept. 27, 1861; Discharged Mar. 8, 1863, disability.

Philander Purrington Boscobel; Enlisted Nov. 4, 1863; From 33rd Wis. Inf.; Mustered out June 28, 1865.

James Quigley Boscobel; Enlisted Dec. 28, 1863; From 33rd Wis. Inf.; Mustered out Sept. 4, 1865.

William Reshaw Middleton; Enlisted Sept. 1, 1864; Mustered out June 6, 1865.

Joseph Rewshaw Middleton; Enlisted Sept. 14, 1861; Veteran; Mustered out Sept. 4, 1865.

George W. Reinehart Sun Prairie; Enlisted Sept. 14, 1861; Died Oct. 7, 1862, Helena, Ark., disease.

Erastus Richardson Middleton; Enlisted Aug. 26, 1864; Mustered out June 6, 1865.

Lyman Richardson Middleton; Enlisted Sept. 24, 1861; Veteran; Mustered out Sept. 4, 1861.

William Richardson Madison; Enlisted Sept. 18, 1861; Corporal; Killed July 11, 1863, Jackson, Miss.

Franklin Rogers Madison; Enlisted Aug. 5, 1862; Died Sept. 1, 1862, Oldtown, Ark., disease.

Lyaman A. Rogers Madison; Enlisted Sept. 14, 1861; Veteran, Corporal; Mustered out Sept. 4, 1865.

George W. Sandford Middleton; Enlisted Aug. 31, 1864; Mustered out June 6, 1865.

James M. Sanford Middleton; Enlisted Sept. 12, 1861; Veteran, Corporal; Wounded Vicksburg; Mustered out Sept. 2, 1865.

James Scanlan Rutland; Enlisted Oct. 24, 1861; Deserted Nov. 3, 1861.

Jacob Schneider Middleton; Enlisted Sept. 20, 1864; Mustered out Sept. 4, 1865.

Mathias Schuester Berry; Enlisted Mar. 6, 1865; Mustered out Sept. 4, 1865.

Alfred P. Searles Rutland; Enlisted Sept. 30, 1861; Discharged July 1, 1862, disability.

Peter Sehr Berry; Enlisted Mar. 23, 1865; Mustered out Sept. 4, 1865.

David Sheldon Watertown; Enlisted Oct. 28, 1861; Died Apr. 20, 1862, Reeves' Station, Mo., disease.

Valentine Simon Fond Du Lac; Enlisted Mar. 7, 1865; Mustered out Sept. 4, 1865.

Theophilis Y. Skinner Black Earth; Enlisted Oct. 29, 1861; Discharged Feb. 27, 1863, disabiltiy.

Byron J. Smith Madison; Enlisted Sept. 19, 1861; Veteran Musician; Mustered out Sept. 4, 1865.

Christian F. Smith Madison; Enlisted Oct. 4, 1861; Wounded Vicksburg; Killed July 11, 1863, Jackson, Miss.

Frank P. Smith Mifflin; Enlisted Jan. 19, 1864; From 33rd Wis. Inf.; Mustered out Sept. 4, 1865.

John W. Smith Vermont; Enlisted Oct. 31, 1861; Veteran, Corporal; Mustered out Sept. 4, 1865.

Levi D. Smith Windsor; Enlisted Jan. 5, 1864; From 33rd Wis. Inf.; Mustered out Sept. 4, 1865.

William E. Smith Middleton; Enlisted Sept. 24, 1861; Died June 27, 1862, Jacksonport, Ark., disease.

Frank Steisman Ridgeway; Enlisted Sept. 23, 1861; Died May 27, 1862, Pocahontas, Ark., disease.

William C. Stilson Kilbourn City; Enlisted Nov. 12, 1862; From 33rd Wis. Inf.; Mustered out Sept. 4, 1865.

Isreal Stowell Madison; Enlisted Oct. 14, 1861; Died July 16, 1863, Vicksburg, Miss., disease.

Charles A. Swan Madison; Enlisted Oct. 4, 1861; Deserted Feb. 19, 1863.

Thomas Taylor Middleton; Enlisted Oct. 22, 1861; Veteran, Corporal; Mustered out Sept. 4, 1865.

William Taylor Madison; Enlisted Sept. 14, 1861; Veteran, Corporal; Wounded Vicksburg; Mustered out Sept. 4, 1865.

William W. Taylor Middleton; Enlisted Jan. 5, 1864; Died Oct. 27, 1864, Brashear City, La., disease.

Patrick Thompson Blue Mounds; Enlisted Sept. 24, 1861; Mustered out Nov. 18, 1864, term expired.

Robert M. Thompson Verona; Enlisted Oct. 10, 1864; Mustered out Sept. 4, 1865.

Gaylord Towsley Rutland; Enlisted Sept. 18, 1861; Corporal; Discharged Mar. 22, 1862, disability.

John M. Utter Madison; Enlisted Oct. 9, 1861; Veteran; Mustered out Sept. 4, 1865.

William H. Utter Madison; Enlisted Sept. 15, 1862; Veteran, Wagoner; Mustered out June 6, 1865.

Andrew D. Van Buren Middleton; Enlisted Aug. 29, 1864; Mustered out June 6, 1865.

Joseph Vannasse Casco; Enlisted Mar. 30, 1865; Died Aug. 7, 1865, Mobile, Ala., disease.

George W. Vosler Middleton; Enlisted Sept. 12, 1861; Deserted Feb. 8, 1863.

Andrew S. Wakefield Fetchburg; Enlisted Oct. 31, 1861; Veteran; Mustered out Sept. 4, 1865.

Edgar Ward Boscobel; Enlisted Dec. 10, 1863; From 33rd Wis. Inf.; Mustered out Sept. 4, 1865.

Andrew J. Warren Cross Plains; Enlisted Sept. 12, 1861; Sgt.; Died Jan. 30, 1862, Merrimac Bridge, Mo.; Mustered out Jan. 30, 1862, disease.

Ezra Warren Cross Plains; Enlisted Sept. 30, 1861; Discharged Jan. 3, 1863, disability.

Edward Watkinson Sun Prairie; Enlisted Sept. 18, 1861; Discharged Dec. 11, 1862, disability.

Christian Weber Milford; Enlisted Sept. 22, 1864; Mustered out June 6, 1865.

John B. Weber Benton; Enlisted Mar. 20, 1865; Mustered out Sept. 4, 1865.

William Weber Milford; Enlisted Sept. 28, 1864; Mustered out Sept. 4, 1865.

Charles J. White Madison; Enlisted Oct. 4, 1861; Veteran, Corporal, Sgt.; Wounded Blakely; Mustered out Aug. 18, 1865.

Erastus B. Whitmore Oregon; Enlisted Sept. 27, 1861; Veteran; Mustered out Sept. 4, 1865.

William Widener Middleton; Enlisted Oct. 22, 1861; Corporal; Discharged Jan. 5, 1863, disability.

William P. Williams Fountain Prairie; Enlisted Oct. 29, 1861; Died Apr. 4, 1862.

Wirt C. Williams Middleton; Enlisted Sept. 22, 1864; Musician; Mustered out June 6, 1865.

Henry Winter Madison; Enlisted Oct. 21, 1861; Discharged July 25, 1862, disability.

Jacob Wolf Sun Prairie; Enlisted Mar. 27, 1865; Mustered out Sept. 4, 1865.

Barry J. Woren Middleton; Enlisted Sept. 12, 1861; Veteran; Mustered out Sept. 4, 1865.

Dudley C. Wyman Madison; Enlisted Sept. 21, 1861; Promoted Sgt. Major, Oct. 3, 1861.

Co. C — The "Waterloo Rifles"

Officers

Charles Perry Captain; Waterloo; Rank from Aug. 8, 1861; Resigned Mar. 8, 1863.

James Lang Captain; Waterloo; Rank from Mar. 18, 1863; Veteran; 1st Lt., Aug. 8, 1861; Mustered out Sept. 4, 1865.

Mart V.B. Hutchinson 1st Lt.; Waterloo; Rank from Mar. 18, 1863; Enlisted Aug. 26, 1861; Sgt., 1st Sgt.; 2nd Lt., July 8, 1862; res. June 12, 1863.

Azel Grover 1st Lt.; Beaver Dam; Rank from June 12, 1863; Enlisted Sept. 6, 1861; Corporal, Sgt.; Resigned Feb. 6, 1864.

John Sewright 1st Lt.; Whitewater; Rank from Apr. 13, 1864; Enlisted Sept. 2, 1861; Veteran, 1st Sgt.; Mustered out Sept. 4, 1863.

Oscar F. Mattice 2nd Lt.; Waterloo; Rank from Aug. 17, 1861; Resigned July 8, 1862.

Hiram E. Smith 2nd Lt.; Waterloo; Rank from Mar. 18, 1863; Enl Sept. 6, 1862; Sgt.; Killed Mar. 22, 1863, Vicksburg, Miss.

Enlisted Men

Philander Aden Cold Spring; Enlisted Aug. 26, 1861; Corporal; Discharged Oct. 30, 1862, disability.

Obediah T. Alexander Cold Spring; Enlisted Aug. 26, 1861; Discharged Aug. 24, 1863, disability.

William Alexander Cold Spring; Enlisted Aug. 26, 1861; Veteran, Corporal; Wounded Blakely; right arm amputated; Mustered out Aug. 22, 1865.

John Anderson Kroghville; Enlisted Aug. 26, 1861; Wounded Black River Bridge; Died July 18, 1864, Brashear City, La., disease.

Florence E. Andrus Albany; Enlisted Jan. 27, 1864; Musician; Mustered out Sept. 4, 1863.

John D. Armes Cottage Grove; Enlisted Sept. 16, 1861; Discharged Oct. 17, 1862, disability.

Azariah Babcock Portland; Enlisted Sept. 2, 1861; Discharged Aug. 13, 1863, disability.

George W. Bashford Hanchetville; Enlisted Sept. 7, 1861; Discharged June 14, 1864.

William Beam Ellington; Enlisted Mar. 20, 1865; Drafted; Died Aug. 22, 1865, Mobile, Ala., disease.

William Beattie Portage; Enlisted Dec. 13, 1864; Drafted; Mustered out Sept. 4, 1865.

Andrew M. Bottleson Kroghville; Enlisted Aug. 26, 1861; Discharged Feb. 9, 1863, disability.

Elijah A. Bowman Edgerton; Enlisted Nov. 6, 1861; Deserted Jan. 1862.

Henry Brink Milford; Enlisted Aug. 26, 1861; Veteran, Corporal; Wounded Vicksburg; Mustered out Sept. 4, 1865.

John Brink Milford; Enlisted Aug. 26, 1861; Sgt.; Wounded Vickburg; Discharged Oct. 3, 1863, disability.

Lindsey S. Brown Waterloo; Enlisted Aug. 26, 1861; Corporal, Sgt.; Discharged June 9, 1863, disability.

Loren E. Bump Koshkonong; Enlisted Sept. 27, 1861; Veteran; Mustered out Sept. 4, 1865.

Jonathan A. Burnett Stoughton; Enlisted Sept. 9, 1861; Died July 8, 1862, Bayou Devieu, disease.

Scott Case Johnsons Creek; Enlisted Aug. 26, 1861; Wounded Vicksburg; Discharged Aug. 19, 1863, disability.

Friend F. Coleman Eolia; Enlisted Sept. 12, 1861; Discharged Aug. 23, 1862, disability.

James B. Connant Jefferson; Enlisted Oct. 29, 1861; Deserted Apr. 10, 1862.

John Connoly Green Bay; Enlisted Aug. 5, 1864; Mustered out Sept. 1, 1865.

John A. Connoly Brookfield; Enlisted Mar. 15, 1865; Mustered out Sept. 1, 1865.

John C. Conroy Lowell, Mass; Enlisted Nov. 5, 1861; Veteran; Mustered out Sept. 4, 1865.

James H. Cook Hanchetville; Enlisted Sept. 16, 1861; Discharged Nov. 18, 1862, by order.

Major Cooley Johnson Creek; Enlisted Sept. 12, 1861; Discharged Feb. 23, 1863, disability.

Adrian Cornish Hortonia; Enlisted Mar. 22, 1865; Drafted; Mustered out Sept. 4, 1865.

Patrick Desmond Waterloo; Died Nov. 29, 1862; Ironton, Mo., disease.

George Dietrich Morrison; Enlisted Mar. 20, 1865; Drafed; Mustered out Sept. 4, 1865.

George Doen Barton; Enlisted Oct. 12, 1864; Drafed; Mustered out Sept. 1, 1865.

August Drager Waterloo; Enlisted Sept. 9, 1861; Transferred to V.R.C., Feb. 10, 1864; Mustered out Oct. 14, 1864.

James Dunbar Shullsburg; Enlisted Jan. 26, 1864; From 33rd Wis. Inf; Mustered out Sept. 4, 1865.

Norman A. Eddy Herman; Enlisted Mar. 3, 1865.; Mustered out Sept. 1, 1865.

William Folendorf Eldorado; Enlisted Sept. 23, 1861; Veteran; Wounded Black River Bridge; Mustered out Sept. 4, 1863.

Solmon S. Frank Lima; Enlisted Mar. 16, 1865.; Mustered out Sept. 4, 1865.

Henry Fryer Whitewater; Enlisted Aug. 26, 1861; Died July 5, 1862, Augusta, Ark., disease.

Ephriam H. Fuller Hancherville; Enlisted Sept. 14, 1861; Discharged Apr. 19, 1863, disability.

James H. Fuller Hebron; Enlisted Aug. 26, 1861; Musician; Discharged Nov. 30, 1863.

Christian Goldschmidt New Denmark; Enlisted Mar. 2, 1865.; Drafted; Mustered out Sept. 1, 1865.

Charles Gould Preble; Enlisted Mar. 2, 1865; Drafted; Mustered out Sept. 4, 1865.

John Graham Bristol; Enlisted Mar. 25, 1864; Mustered out Sept. 4, 1865.

Z.T. Griffin Caledonia; Enlisted Dec. 16, 1864; Mustered out Sept. 4, 1865.

Owen Griffith Waterloo; Enlisted Oct. 29, 1861; Died July 6, 1862, Cache River, Ark., disease.

Daniel Grindle Johnsons Creek; Enlisted Oct. 29, 1861; Veteran; Mustered out Sept. 4, 1865.

Henry W. Hamilton Rockton, Ill; Enlisted Sept. 24, 1861; Transferred to V.R.C., July 15, 1863.

Daniel Hartman Newbury, Pa; Enlisted Sept. 15, 1861; Veteran, Corporal; Mustered out Sept. 3, 1865.

Geroge D. Hascall Waterloo; Enlisted Sept. 12, 1861; Discharged Nov. 18, 1862, disability.

William Hitchcock Lake Mills; Enlisted Aug. 26, 1861; Died Nov. 14, 1862, St. Louis, Mo., disease.

William Hoyt Sun Prairie; Enlisted Apr. 23,1864; Mustered out Sept. 1, 1865.

Frederick Huckbert Eldorado; Enlisted Sept. 23, 1861; Died Nov. 9, 1863, New Orleans, La.

Charles Huff Farmington; Enlisted Dec. 18, 1863; Died June 15, 1864, New Orleans, La., disease.

John Huff Johnsons Creek; Enlisted Aug. 26, 1861; Mustered out Dec. 14, 1864. term expired.

Frank A. Huntley Whitewater; Enlisted Sept. 26, 1861; Musician; Mustered out Dec. 14, 1864, term expired.

Seldon Huntley Whitewater; Enlisted Jan. 4, 1864; Musician; Mustered out July 9, 1865.

Frank H. Hurd Beloit; Enlisted Aug. 8, 1864; Mustered out June 6, 1865.

Lovinus S. Hurd Ironton; Enlisted Oct. 25, 1861; Veteran, Corporal, Sgt.; Mustered out Sept. 4, 1865.

Albert G. Hutchinson Packwaukee; Enlisted Oct. 20, 1862; Veteran; Mustered out Sept. 4, 1865.

Nelson C. Hyer Portland; Enlisted Sept. 12, 1861; Wounded Vicksburg; Died 64, New Orleans, La.

Charles Ingamells Waterloo; Enlisted Sept. 7, 1861; Wounded Vicksburg; Died June 16, 1863, Memphis, Tenn., of wounds.

George R. Ingamells Waterloo; Enlisted Sept. 7, 1861; Veteran, Corporal; Killed Apr. 9, 1865, Blakely, Ala.

Andreas Johnson Madison; Enlisted Nov. 1, 1864; Mustered out Sept. 4, 1865.

Franklin J. Jones Packwaukee; Enlisted Oct. 20, 1862; Veteran, Corporal; Mustered out July 25, 1865.

Gjert Jorgenson Madison; Enlisted Nov. 1, 1864; Mustered out May 22, 1865.

Patrick Judge Waterloo; Enlisted Sept. 7, 1861; Veteran; Mustered out Sept. 4, 1865.

Alfred H. Kelly Springvale, Me.; Enlisted Sept. 16, 1861; Discharged Sept. 1, 1862.

Jesse Kimber Nasewaunee; Enlisted Mar. 30, 1865; Drafted; Mustered out Sept. 4, 1865.

William C. King Hancherville; Enlisted Sept. 16, 1861; Died Nov. 29, 1862. Ironton, Mo., disease.

Gustav Klose Two Rivers; Enlisted Mar. 16, 1865; Drafted; Mustered out Sept. 4, 1865.

Henry P. Knapp Waterloo; Enlisted Sept. 9, 1861; Veteran, 1st Sgt.; Died Aug. 14, 1864, Brashear City, La., disease.

Michael Kolters Perry; Enlisted Mar. 6, 1865; Drafted; Mustered out Sept. 1, 1865.

Nicholas Krause Greenville; Enlisted Mar. 22, 1865; Drafted; Mustered out Sept. 4, 1865.

Bernard J. Krough Kroughville; Enlisted Aug. 26, 1861; Veteran, Corporal; Mustered out Sept. 4, 1865.

Frederick Kuder Aztalan; Enlisted Sept. 18, 1861; Transferred to V.R.C., Feb. 10, 1864.

John Lafferty Madison; Enlisted Oct. 28, 1861; Veteran, Corporal; Mustered out Sept. 4, 1865.

Clark Lang Waterloo; Enlisted Oct. 3, 1862; Veteran; Mustered out July 9, 1865.

Leviras A. Lee Milwaukee; Enlisted Mar. 29, 1865; Mustered out Sept. 4, 1865.

Frederick Lehman Watertown; Enlisted Sept. 17, 1861; Veteran; Mustered out Sept. 4, 1865.

Henry C. Leland Reeseville; Enlisted Sept. 17, 1861; Wounded Port Gibson; Discharged Sept. 29, 1864, disability.

Peter Liefbroer Holland; Enlisted Mar. 13, 1865; Drafted; Mustered out Sept. 4, 1865.

John W. Linderman Beloit; Enlisted Sept. 14, 1861; Discharged Oct. 25, 1861.

John Lusted Lake Mills; Enlisted Aug. 26, 1861; Died Sept. 15, 1861, Brashear City, La., disease.

William Mason Oxford; Enlisted Oct. 28, 1861; Discharged Mar. 31, 1862, disability.

Albert F. Mattice Waterloo; Enlisted Sept. 16, 1861; Veteran, Corporal; Promoted 1st Lt. Co. H, 1st Wis, H. Art., Sept. 7, 1864.

Daniel McCaskel Brookfield; Enlisted Mar. 21, 1865; Mustered out Sept. 4, 1865.

John McNulty Fond Du Lac; Enlisted Feb. 14, 1865; Drafted; Mustered out Sept. 2, 1865.

Alonzo Meracle Whitewater; Enlisted Sept. 16, 1861; Veteran; Mustered out Sept. 4, 1865.

Peter D. Merserman Milwaukee; Enlisted Mar. 30, 1865; Mustered out Sept. 4, 1865.

Lawrence Meyer Eolia; Enlisted Sept. 16, 1861; Veteran; Mustered out Sept. 4, 1865.

William Mullen Shullsburg; Enlisted Jan. 13, 1864; From 33rd Wis. Inf.; Mustered out Sept. 4, 1865.

Austin L. Muzzy Hanchetville; Enlisted Sept. 16, 1861; Veteran, Sgt.; Mustered out Sept. 4, 1865.

William Nelson Packard Waterloo; Enlisted

Aug. 26, 1861; Mustered out Dec. 14, 1864, term expired.

George F. Peckham Milford; Enlisted Sept. 24, 1861; Veteran, Wagoner; Mustered out Sept. 4, 1865.

George Peterson Madison; Enlisted Nov. 1, 1864; Mustered out Sept. 4, 1865.

Lars Peterson Shullsburg; Enlisted Dec. 10, 1863; From 33rd Wis. Inf.; Mustered out Sept. 4, 1865.

Edgar E. Pierce Waterloo; Enlisted Jan. 4, 1864; Veteran Recruit; Mustered out Sept. 4, 1865.

Benjamin F. Pixley Cold Spring; Enlisted Aug. 26, 1861; Veteran, Corporal; Died Dec. 6, 1864, Brashear City, La., disease.

Frederick Polhman Aztalan; Enlisted Sept. 23, 1861; Wounded Vicksburg; trans. to V.R.C., Dec. 15, 1863; Mustered out Sept. 26, 1864, term expired.

Reuben Prame Waterloo; Enlisted Aug. 26, 1861; Discharged Feb. 26, 1863, disability.

Warren E. Ranney York; Enlisted Sept. 6, 1861; Corporal; transferred to Miss. M. Brigade, Jan. 3, 1863.

John G. Rawson York; Enlisted Sept. 7, 1861; Veteran, Corporal; Mustered out Sept. 5, 1865.

John W. Reynolds Johnsons Creek; Enlisted Sept. 21, 1861; Discharged Aug. 11, 1864.

Melegor Rhod Eolia; Enlisted Sept. 9, 1861; Discharged Mar. 20, 1863, disability.

Phillip E. Rhodes Herman; Enlisted Mar. 22, 1865; Mustered out July 9, 1865.

Charles S. Riley Irving; Enlisted Oct. 19, 1864; Mustered out Sept. 4, 1865.

James B. Roach Milford; Enlisted Sept. 7, 1861; Sgt.; 2nd Lt., May 22, 1863, not mustered; Disch.

Nelson Roach Waterloo; Enlisted Aug. 26, 1861; Veteran, Cpl; Died July 22, 1865, Montgomery, Ala., disease.

William R. Roach Waterloo; Enlisted Sept. 7, 1861; Veteran; Mustered out Sept. 4, 1865.

George Robinson Reeseville; Enlisted Oct. 29, 1861; Died Apr. 27, 1862, Ironton, Mo., disease.

John Robinson Brookfield; Enlisted Mar. 10, 1865; Mustered out Sept. 1, 1865.

Samuel Robinson Portland; Enlisted Aug. 26, 1861; Veteran; Corporal; Mustered out Sept. 4, 1865; Killed in R.R. accident en route home.

Moritz Rost Little Suamica; Enlisted Mar. 22, 1865; Drafted; Mustered out Sept. 4, 1865.

John F. Sander Medina; Enlisted Aug. 31, 1864; Mustered out June 6, 1865.

Phillip Sanfried Oconomowoc; Enlisted Sept. 22, 1864; Drafted; Mustered out June 6, 1865.

Charles Semple Bloomfield; Enlisted Mar. 13, 1865; Drafted; Mustered out Sept. 4, 1865.

James Sharp Rochester, NY; Enlisted Sept. 17, 1861; Veteran; Wounded Blakely; Mustered out Sept. 4, 1865.

Taber A. Sherman Eolia; Enlisted Sept. 16, 1861; Wounded Vicksburg; Discharged Oct. 10, 1863, of wounds.

William H. Sickles Waterloo; Enlisted Jan. 4, 1864; Died May 12, 1865, Waterloo, Wis., disease.

Nicholas Simm Nasewaupee; Enlisted Mar. 21, 1865; Drafted; Mustered out Sept. 4, 1865.

William Smith Johnsons Creek; Enlisted Sept. 6, 1861; Died Dec. 29, 1862, St. Louis, Mo.

John H. Stonebraker Shullsburg; Enlisted Jan. 9, 1864; From 33rd Wis. Inf.; Mustered out Sept. 4, 1865.

Patrick H. Swift Edgerton; Enlisted Aug. 26, 1861; Sgt.; Promoted 2nd Lt. Co. E, 33rd Wis. Inf, Aug. 30, 1862.

Edward Terryberry Shullsburg; Enlisted Jan. 5, 1864; From 33rd, Wis. Inf.; Mustered out Sept. 4, 1865.

John Tessin Whitewater; Enlisted Aug. 26, 1861; Transferred to V.R.C. July 1, 1863.

Alpheus M. Thayer Waterloo; Enlisted Sept. 17, 1861; Veteran; Corporal; Wounded Vicksburg; Mustered out Sept. 4, 1865.

Martin V. Thompson Columbus; Enlisted Sept. 6, 1861; Died Jan. 8, 1863, St. Louis, Mo., disease.

Henry Tolliver Hubbard; Enlisted Mar. 29, 1865; Mustered out Sept. 4, 1865.

William H. Tripp Waterloo; Enlisted Dec. 30, 1863; Mustered out Sept. 4, 1865.

Andrew Tropp York; Enlisted Sept. 6, 1861; Discharged Mar. 26, 1863, disability.

Jay E. Trussel Deansville; Enlisted Aug. 12, 1861; Promoted Hospital Steward. Nov. 23, 1863.

Aaron Twining Hanchetville; Enlisted Nov. 1, 1861; Died Aug. 25, 1862, Oldtown, Ark., disease.

Henry H. Twining Waterloo; Enlisted Sept. 11, 1861; Veteran, Corporal, Sgt.; Absent sick at Mustered out of regt.

John Q. Twining Waterloo; Enlisted Aug. 26, 1861; Died Mar. 21, 1862, Pilot Knob, Mo., disease.

Conarad A. Unger Hanchetville; Enlisted Sept. 7, 1861; Veteran, Sgt., 1st Sgt.; Wounded Blakely, Ala.; Mustered out Sept. 4, 1865.

Alphonso Weed Waterloo; Enlisted Aug. 26, 1861; Discharged disability.

Theodore Weed Waterloo; Enlisted Sept. 2, 1861; Veteran, Corporal, Sgt.; Died Nov. 25, 1864, Cairo, Ill., disease.

Philander Wilber Whitewater; Enlisted Sept. 16, 1861; Veteran, Corporal, Sgt.; Died Apr. 11, 1865, Blakely, Ala., of wounds.

Edmond Wilcox Reeseville; Enlisted Sept. 9, 1861; Wounded Port Gibson; Died June 25, 1863, Memphis, Tenn., of wounds.

George Wilcox Reeseville; Enlisted Sept. 2, 1861; Veteran, Corporal; Mustered out Sept. 4, 1865.

Lester C. Wilcox Reeseville; Enlisted Sept. 9, 1861; Transferred to V.R.C., Dec. 15, 1863.

Thomas A. Williams Sun Prairie; Enlisted Sept. 11, 1861; Veteran, Corporal, Sgt.; Mustered out Sept. 4, 1865.

Darwin Wilson Waterloo; Enlisted Sept. 10, 1861; Discharged Oct. 25, 1864., disability.

Joseph R. Winslow Eolia; Enlisted Sept. 19, 1861; Veteran, Corporal; Mustered out Sept. 4, 1865.

Theodore Wise Onalaska; Enlisted Sept. 2, 1861; Died Jan. 6, 1862, Camp Curtis., disease.

William Wittcho Aztalan; Enlisted Sept. 23, 1861; Died Feb. 15, 1863, Jacks Fork, Ark., disease.

Ira A. Wood York; Enlisted Sept. 9,1861; Died June 29, 1862, Battesville, Ark., disease.

Albert Wooden Johnsons Creek; Enlisted Aug. 26,1862; Corporal; Discharged Feb. 23, 1863, disability.

George Wright Farmington; Enlisted Mar. 27, 1864; Died Aug. 2, 1864, Brashear City, La., disease.

William H. Wright Racine; Enlisted Nov. 3, 1862; From 33rd, Wis. Inf.; Mustered out Sept. 4, 1862.

Co. D — "Richland County Plowboys"

Officers

Jesse S. Miller Captain; Richland Center; Rank from Sept. 11, 1861; Promoted Major, July 8, 1863.

Henry Toms Captain; Richland Center; Rank from Sept. 3, 1863; Enlisted Sept. 12, 1861; Veteran, Corporal, Sgt., 1st Sgt.; 1st Lt., Aug. 17, 1863; Mustered out Sept. 4, 1865.

William Hill 1st Lieutenant; Richland Center; Rank from Sept. 11, 1861; Res Feb. 28, 1863.

George W. Dale 1st Lieutenant; Richland Center; Rank from Sept. 3, 1863; Enlisted Sept. 12, 1861; Veteran, Corporal, Sgt., 1st Sgt.; Mustered out Sept. 4, 1865.

William H. Dawson 2nd Lieutenant; Orion; Rank from Sept. 11, 1861; Res Apr. 7, 1862.

Alfred A. Chamberlain 2nd Lieutenant; Richland Center; Rank from Apr. 7, 1862; Enl Sept. 12, 1861; Sgt., 1st Sgt.; 1st Lt.; Revoked; Deserted June 8, 1863.

Richard Caddell 2nd Lieutenant; Marshall; May 6, 1864; Enlisted Sept. 12, 1861; Cpl,; Discharged Feb. 28, 1863, disability; Re-enlisted Nov. 29, 1863; 1st Sgt.; Killed Apr. 9, 1865, Blakely Ala.

James S. Robinson 2nd Lieutenant; Eagle; Rank from June 13, 1865; Enlisted Sept. 12, 1861; Veteran, Corporal, Sgt., 1st Sgt.; Sgt. Maj July 10, 1864; Wounded Black River Bridge: Mustered out Sept. 4, 1865.

Enlisted Men

Philip Acton Richland Center; Enlisted Sept. 12, 1861; Wounded Bayou Cache and Vicksburg; Died June 4, 1863, Memphis Tenn., of wounds.

Perry Adney Eagle; Enlisted Oct. 8, 1861; Mustered out Nov. 18, 1864, term expired.

Ephraim Alderman Port Andrew; Enlisted Sept. 12, 1861; Corporal; Discharged Nov. 18, 1862, disabilty.

George Allbaugh Bloom; Enlisted Sept. 12, 1861; Vet; Corporal; Killed Apr. 9, 1865, Blakely, Ala.

Solomon Allbaugh Bloom; Enlisted Feb. 1, 1864; Mustered out July 10, 1865.

Calvin P. Alling Sylvan; Enlisted Sept. 12, 1861; Musician; Transferred to Co. E, Nov. 4, 1861; Rejoined Co, Mar. 1, 1864 Mustered out Sept. 4, 1865.

William Allpress Richland Center; Enlisted Oct. 18, 1861; Deserted, Feb. 24, 1863.

Reuben Amey Richland Center; Enlisted Mar. 4, 1864; Killed Apr. 9, 1865 at Blakeley, Ala.

David Ayslworth Richland Center; Enlisted Sept. 12, 1861; Vet; Died Aug. 17, 1864, Richland Center, Wis., Disease.

Alvin S. Bailey Marshall; Enlisted Feb. 15, 1864; Mustered out Sept. 4, 1865.

David Barrett Bloom; Enlisted Sept. 12, 1861; Cpl; Wounded Bayou Cache; Discharged May 1, 1863, Disability.

Enos Barrett Marshall; Enlisted Sept. 12, 1861; Transferred to V.R.C., Feb. 10, 1864.

Lewis Barry Dayton; Enlisted Feb. 10, 1864; Mustered out Sept. 4, 1865.

Thomas Barry Dayton; Enlisted Feb. 12, 1864; Mustered out Sept. 4, 1865.

John D. Beighle Sylvan; Enlisted Sept. 12, 1861; Drowned Dec. 15, 1862, Black River, Mo.

Washington Bennett Bloom; Enlisted Feb. 25, 1864; Wounded Blakely, Ala.; Died Apr. 29, 1865, Greenville, La, of wounds.

George Benton Marshall; Enlisted Feb. 8, 1864; Cpl; Mustered out Sept. 4, 1865.

Newel H. Bingham Richland; Enlisted Sept. 12, 1861; Deserted Nov. 19, 1861.

Thomas Bond Marshall; Enlisted Oct. 18, 1861; Died Nov. 16, 1862, St. Louis, Mo, Disease.

Jonathan Bowman Bloom; Enlisted Feb. 4, 1864; Mustered out Sept. 4, 1865.

Joseph Brace Richland Center; Enlisted Sept. 12, 1861; Wounded Cache River, Ark.; Died July 31, 1862, Jefferson Bks, Mo., of wounds.

John Brannan Marshall; Enlisted Sept. 12, 1861; Died July 22, 1863, Jefferson Bks., Mo.; Disease.

David Briggs Sylvan; Enlisted Sept. 12, 1861; Veteran, Corporal; Mustered out Sept. 4, 1865.

Anson Brown Henrietta; Enlisted Feb. 8, 1864; Mustered out Sept. 5, 1865.

Horace G. Bryant Sugar Creek; Enlisted Feb. 8, 1864; Died en route to regt.

Joseph Burke Rockbridge; Enlisted Sept. 12, 1861; Died Dec. 11, 1862, St. Louis, Mo.; Disease.

Cyrus Butler Rockbridge; Enlisted Sept. 12, 1861; Veteran, Cpl,; Wounded Port Gibson; Mustered out Sept. 4, 1865.

Seth Butler Rockbridge; Enlisted Sept. 12, 1861; Corporal; Sgt.; Mustered out Nov. 18, 1864, Term Exp.

Andrew Campbell Bear Creek; Enlisted Feb. 8, 1864; Died July 29, 1864, New Orleans, LA, Disease.
William H. Campbell Dayton; Enlisted Feb. 12, 1864; Died Mar. 17, 1864, Madison, Wis. Disease.
Albert Carlton Richland Center; Enlisted Sept. 12, 1861; 1st Sgt.; Died Jan. 20, 1862, Victoria, Mo., Disease.
Dighton Chesmore Rockbridge; Enlisted Sept. 12, 1861; Veteran, Wagoner; Mustered out Sept. 2, 1865.
Daniel F. Coats Aiken; Enlisted Sept. 12, 1861; Discharged May 1862, Disability.
Francis M. Coats Dayton; Enlisted Dec. 30, 1863; Mustered out July 2, 1865.
William Collins Orion; Enlisted Sept. 12, 1861; Discharged, Feb. 23, 1863, Disability.
Daniel Conkel Dayton; Enlisted Oct. 31, 1861; Deserted Mar. 15, 1863.
Johnson J. Conkel Marshall; Enlisted Sept. 12, 1861; Deserted Apr. 15, 1863.
Judson A. Cook Sylvan; Enlisted Oct. 31, 1861; Veteran, Corporal; Mustered out Sept. 4, 1865.
Israel Cooper Bloom; Enlisted Oct. 25, 1861; Died July 30, 1862, Oldtown, Ark, Disease.
William M. Core Eagle; Enlisted Sept. 12, 1861; Veteran, Corporal, Wagoner; Died Feb. 14, 1865, Brashear City, LA, Disease.
Jackson Creekpaum Jackson; Enlisted Feb. 29, 1864; Died Mar. 31, 1864, Madison, Wis, disease.
John Creekpaum Jackson; Enlisted Feb. 29, 1864; Transferred to V.R.C., Apr. 12, 1865; Mustered out Sept. 19, 1865.
John Dary Rockbridge; Enlisted Feb. 20, 1864; Wounded Fort Blakely, Ala., Mustered out Sept. 4, 1865.
Fieldon Davis Sylvan; Enlisted Mar. 30, 1864; Discharged Oct. 26, 1864, disability.
Lewis D. Davis Sylvan; Enlisted Feb. 9, 1864; Mustered out Sept. 4, 1865.
Philip A. Davis Bloom; Enlisted Dec. 29, 1863; Mustered out Sept. 4, 1865.
Townsend Davis Marshall; Enlisted Feb. 15, 1864; Mustered out Sept. 4, 1865.
William A. Davis Dayton; Enlisted Dec. 30, 1863; Mustered out Sept. 4, 1865.
Joseph DeFord Bloom; Enlisted Dec. 29, 1863; Mustered out Sept. 4, 1865.
Shedrick Dicks Dayton; Enlisted Dec. 30, 1863; Mustered out Sept. 4, 1865.
Clifton L. Dillingham Richland Center; Enlisted Sept. 12, 1861; Musician; Died Oct. 24, 1862, Victoria, Mo., Disease.
John M. Dowdna Marshall; Enlisted Sept. 12, 1861; Deserted Apr. 15, 1863.
Henry C. Evans Dayton; Enlisted Mar. 4, 1864; Mustered out Sept. 4, 1865.
James H. Ewing Marshall; Enlisted Feb. 2, 1864; Cpl; Mustered out July 5, 1865.
William Favorite Bloom; Enlisted Dec. 4, 1863; Absent Sick at Mustered out of Regt.
James Fazel Sylvan; Enlisted Sept. 12, 1861; Mustered out Nov. 18, 1864, term expired.
Charles Fife Dayton; Enlisted Oct. 31, 1861; Died Nov. 8, 1862, disease.
William Fischer Bloom; Enlisted Feb. 22, 1864; Mustered out Sept. 4, 1865.
David Fogo Marshall; Enlisted Sept. 12, 1861; Corporal, Sgt.; Wounded Bayou Cache, Ark.; Transferred to V.R.C. Feb. 2, 1864.
Richard J. Fowler Henrietta; Enlisted Oct. 23, 1861; Discharged May 1862, disability.
James W. Fox Richland; Enlisted Sept. 12, 1861; Veteran, Drummer; Mustered out Sept. 4, 1865.
Philemon P. Fox Richland; Enlisted Sept. 12, 1861; Corporal, Sgt.; Discharged Oct. 14, 1863, disability.
Hiram Freeman Rockbridge; Enlisted Sept. 12, 1861; Sgt., 1st Sgt.; 2nd Lt., Feb. 28, 1863, revoked; Deserted May 10, 1863.
James M. Fruit Richland; Enlisted Jan. 4, 1864; Mustered out Sept. 4, 1865.
William Gillingham Marshall; Enlisted Feb. 8, 1864; Wounded Blakely, Ala, Mustered out June 8, 1865.
John Gray Henrietta; Enlisted Sept. 12, 1861; Discharged July 26, 1862, disability.
Jerome Grimes Dayton; Enlisted Sept. 12, 1861; Deserted Feb. 23, 1863.
Edmund F. Gustin Waupaca; Enlisted Feb. 29, 1864; Mustered out Sept. 4, 1865.
John Gwin Ithaca; Enlisted Sept. 12, 1861; Veteran, Corporal, Sgt.; Wounded Blakely, Ala. Mustered out Sept. 4, 1865.
Charles Hamlin Richland Center; Enlisted Sept. 12, 1861; Discharged Jan. 22, 1863, disability.
Matthew D. Hankins Richland; Enlisted Mar. 28, 1864; Mustered out Sept. 4, 1864.
Simon Harris Henrietta; Enlisted Feb. 29, 1864; Mustered out Sept. 4, 1865.
Peter Hebert Marshall; Enlisted Feb. 12, 1864; Mustered out Sept. 4, 1865.
David J. Heckendorn Eagle; Enlisted Oct. 1, 1861; Mustered out Nov. 18, 1864, term expired.
William Hennan Rockbridge; Enlisted Jan. 4, 1864; Died Sept. 19, 1864, New Orleans, La., disease.
William Hill Brown; Enlisted Oct. 25, 1862; Veteran; Wounded Black River Bridge; Died Sept. 14, 1864 Brashear City, La., disease.
Miles B. Hively Marshall; Enlisted Feb. 20, 1864; Died Mar. 24, 1864, Madison, Wis., disease.
Albert Hoke Willow; Enlisted Sept. 12, 1861; Veteran, Corporal, Sgt.; Mustered out Sept. 4, 1865.
John Hook Dayton; Enlisted Feb. 5, 1864; Died Mar. 8, 1864, Madison, Wis., disease.
Nathan Hoyt Bloom; Enlisted Sept. 12, 1861; Sgt., 1st Sgt.; Killed July 7, 1862, Bayou Cache, Ark.
Joseph M. Huffman Dayton; Enlisted Sept. 12, 1861; Discharged Oct. 14, 1863, disability; Re-enl. Dec. 30, 1863; Corporal, Mustered out Sept. 4, 1865.

Daniel W. Huffman Dayton; Enlisted Sept. 12, 1861; Died May 6, 1862, Ironton, Mo., disease.

James A. Huffman Dayton; Enlisted Sept. 12, 1861; Discharged June 26, 1862, disability; Re-enlisted Dec. 30, 1863; Mustered out Sept. 4, 1865.

Thomas H.C. Hull Marshall; Enlisted Jan. 26, 1864; Wounded Blakely, Ala.; Mustered out Sept. 4, 1865.

William Johnson Rockbridge; Enlisted Jan. 4, 1864; Died Sept. 5, 1864, Brashear City, LA, disease.

John M. Jaquish Ithaca; Enlisted Sept. 12, 1861; Veteran, Corporal, Sgt.; Wounded Vicksburg; Discharged Jan. 31, 1865, disability.

Adam Karnes Dayton; Enlisted Jan. 29, 1864; Died Sept. 27, 1864, Brashear City, LA, disease.

John W. Kennedy Bloom; Enlisted Jan. 4, 1864; Killed Apr. 9, 1865, Blakely, Ala.

Joseph M. Kennedy Bloom; Enlisted Jan. 16, 1864; Died Mar. 1, 1864, Madison, Wis, disease.

Avander Kimball Boscobel; Enlisted Jan. 15, 1864; Mustered out Sept. 4, 1865.

Reuel E. Kimball Marshall; Enlisted Nov. 1, 1861; Mustered out Nov. 18, 1864, term expired.

Andrew J. Kinney Richland Center; Enlisted Sept. 12, 1861; Veteran, Corporal, Sgt., Mustered out Sept. 4, 1865.

Sylvester Kitelinger Boscobel; Enlisted Apr. 12, 1864; Mustered out June 14, 1865.

Samuel Kramer Portage; Enlisted Jan. 25, 1864; Mustered out Sept. 4, 1865.

Levi J. Leach Van Buren, Mo.; Enlisted Jan. 14, 1863; Deserted Jan. 16, 1863.

David T. Lindley Watertown; Enlisted Mar. 29, 1864; Promoted Pric Musician, July 1, 1865.

Sylvester Linger Mustered out June 14, 1865.

Richard B. Lynn Whitewater; Enlisted Feb. 29, 1864; Mustered out Aug. 10, 1865.

Cary D. Lyons Richland Center; Enlisted Sept. 12, 1861; Died Jan. 22, 1862, Victoria, Mo., disease.

Delos Lyons Richland Center; Enlisted Sept. 12, 1861; Discharged May 1862, disability.

John Mahlor Westford; Enlisted Nov. 1, 1861; Veteran, Mustered out Sept. 4, 1865.

Joseph Manley Willow; Enlisted Feb. 28, 1865; Drafted; Mustered out Sept. 4, 1865.

Jacob Mann Richland, Center; Enlisted Sept. 12, 1861; Discharged May 7, 1863, disability.

William Mapes Eagle; Enlisted Sept. 12, 1861; Discharged Feb. 2, 1862, disability.

Joseph Mark Boscobel; Enlisted Jan. 15, 1864; Mustered out Sept. 4, 1865.

Jacob Marsh Dayton; Enlisted Feb. 12, 1864; Mustered out Sept. 4, 1865.

Thomas W. Marsh Dayton; Enlisted Feb. 10, 1864; Died Oct. 15, 1864, Brashear City, LA, disease.

Robert Mason Benton; Enlisted Mar. 14, 1865; Drafted; Mustered out Sept. 4, 1865.

Daniel Matoxin Green Bay; Enlisted Oct. 28, 1862; Veteran; Mustered out Aug. 31, 1865.

Lysander Matthews Sylvan; Enlisted Sept. 12, 1861; Veteran, Musician; Mustered out Sept. 4, 1865.

Cornelius McCarthy Henrietta; Enlisted Sept. 12, 1861; Cpl,. Wounded Cache River, Ark.; Brevet Capt. July 7, 1862, for gallentry in battle; Discharged Sept. 11, 1862, of wounds.

Amaziah McClintick Eagle; Enlisted Sept. 12, 1861; Veteran, Mustered out Sept. 4, 1865.

John McDermot Dayton; Enlisted Mar. 7, 1864; Mustered out Sept. 4, 1865.

George P. Mcgill Orion; Enlisted Sept. 12, 1861; Corporal, Died My 8, 1862 at Pocahontas, Ark, disease.

James S. Mcgill Orion; Enlisted Sept. 12, 1861; Mustered out Nov. 18, 1864, disability.

John McKey Marshall; Enlisted Mar. 30, 1864; Mustered out Sept. 4, 1865.

Charles W. Meyers Bloom; Enlisted Feb. 28, 1865; Drafted; Mustered out Sept. 4, 1865.

George N. Mickel Richland Center; Enlisted Sept. 12, 1861; Corporal; Wounded Bayou Cache, Ark.; Discharged Feb. 23, 1863, of wounds.

John Miles Akan; Enlisted Feb. 28, 1865; Drafted; Mustered out Sept. 4, 1865.

James L. Miller Eagle; Enlisted Feb. 18, 1864; Mustered out Sept. 4, 1865.

William H. Miller Eagle; Enlisted Sept. 12, 1861; Cpl; Discharged Oct. 1, 1862, disability.

William Moon Marshall; Enlisted Mar. 30, 1864; Mustered out Sept. 4, 1865.

Francis M. Morrison Union; Enlisted Oct. 8, 1861; Wagoner; Discharged Mar. 10, 1863, disability.

Isaac B. Newkirk Willow; Enlisted Feb. 28, 1865; Drafted; Mustered out Sept. 4, 1865.

Angus Noble Marshall; Enlisted Nov. 1, 1861; Died Nov. 28, 1862, Ironton, Mo., disease.

George Norman Henrietta; Enlisted Feb. 20, 1864; Mustered out Sept. 4, 1865.

Edwin W. Owens Richland; Enlisted Sept. 12, 1861; Veteran, Wagoner; Mustered out Sept. 4, 1865.

James Pannell Union; Enlisted Oct. 8, 1861; Mustered out Sept. 4, 1865.

William Parson Marshall; Enlisted Oct. 1, 1861; Veteran, Cpl; Mustered out Sept. 4, 1865.

Louis Peters Buck Creek; Enlisted Oct. 28, 1862; From Co. I; Mustered out Sep 4, 1865.

George W. Reinhart Willow; Enlisted Oct. 12, 1861; Drowned Dec. 15, 1862, Black River, Mo.

John C. Riesbeck Westford; Enlisted Sept. 12, 1861; Veteran; Wounded Cache River and Vicksburg; Mustered out Sept. 4, 1865.

Benjamin F. Robinson Eagle; Enlisted Sept. 12, 1861; Died June 23, 1862, Batesville, Ark, disease.

James H. Robinson Eagle; Enlisted Sept. 12, 1861; Sgt.; Wounded Black River Bridge; Mustered out Nov. 1, 1864, term expired.

John M. Robinson Dayton; Enlisted Sept. 12, 1861; Discharged June 1, 1862, disability; re-enl. Feb. 13, 1864; Killed Apr. 9, 1865, Blakely, Ala.

John S. Robinson Dayton; Enlisted Sept. 12, 1861; Discharged Nov. 18, 1862, disability.

Robert T. Robinson Dayton; Enlisted Sept. 12, 1861; Discharged Jan. 20, 1863, disability.

Matthew G. Rogers Madison; Enlisted Feb. 6, 1864; Absent sick at Mustered out of Regt.

John Salisbury Willow; Enlisted Feb. 28, 1865; Drafted; Mustered out Sept. 5, 1865.

Jonas M. Sellers Bloom; Enlisted Jan. 28, 1864; Mustered out Sept. 4, 1865.

Squier Shafer Akan; Enlisted Feb. 28, 1865; Drafted; Mustered out Sept. 4, 1865.

William A. Sharp Eagle; Enlisted Sept. 12, 1861; Died Jan. 21, 1863, Van Buren, Mo., disease.

Daniel W. Shaw Boscobel; Enlisted Apr. 12, 1864; Died Nov. 5, 1864, Brashear City, LA, disease.

Benjamin F. Slater Eagle; Enlisted Sept. 12, 1861; Discharged Jan. 20, 1863, disability.

Daniel Smalley Forest; Enlisted Feb. 18, 1864; Died May 17, 1864, New Orleans, LA., disease.

Robert Smalley Forest; Enlisted Feb. 20, 1864; Died Mar. 17, 1864, Madison, Wis., disease.

Martin V. Smith Eagle; Enlisted Sept. 12, 1861; Died Dec. 1, 1862, Black River, Mo., disease.

Andrew Snyder Bloom; Enlisted Sept. 12, 1861; Wounded Cache River, Ark.; Discharged Sept. 25, 1862, of wounds.

Franklin Snyder Bloom; Enlisted Sept. 12, 1861; Veteran, Cpl; Mustered out Sept. 4, 1865.

James W. Southard Buena Vista; Enlisted Mar. 20, 1864; Mustered out Sept. 4, 1865.

Benjamin Southern Richland Center; Enlisted Sept. 12, 1861; Killed Nov. 28, 1862, R.R. Accident.

Lyman Sparling Dayton; Enlisted Feb. 13, 1864; Wounded Blakely, Ala.; Mustered out June 15, 1865.

Ansel L. Standish Eagle; Enlisted Sept. 12, 1861; Discharged Apr. 15, 1863. disability.

Charles A. Stevens Henrietta; Enlisted Sept. 12, 1861; Discharged Dec. 8, 1862, disability.

William Sullivan Eagle; Enlisted Sept. 12, 1861; Died Oct. 31, 1862 Ironton, Mo., disease.

Benjamin B. Sutton Richland; Enlisted Oct. 12, 1861; Discharged July 26, 1862, disabiltiy.

German Tadder Rockbridge; Enlisted Sept. 12, 1861; Corporal; Discharged Aug. 7, 1862, disability.

Isaac Talbott Richland Center; Enlisted Sept. 12, 1861; Discharged Feb. 1, 1863.

Edwin Tepier Eagle; Enlisted Sept. 12, 1861; Mustered out Nov. 18, 1864, term expired.

Benjamin F. Thompson Eagle; Enlisted Sept. 12, 1861; Veteran, Corporal; Mustered out Sept. 4, 1865.

James W. Thompson Eagle; Enlisted Sept. 12, 1861; Mustered out Nov. 18, 1864, term expired.

Alfred E. Titus Henrietta; Enlisted Sept. 12, 1861; Veteran, Corporal, Sgt.; Died Aug. 5, 1864, Brashear City, LA, disease.

Samuel Traymer

Joshua Van Dusen Union; Enlisted Feb. 1, 1864; Mustered out Sept. 4, 1865.

Alexander G. Waddell Rockbridge; Enlisted Sept. 12, 1861; Deserted Aug. 20, 1862.

Comfort C. Walker Dayton; Enlisted Sept. 12, 1861; Wagoner; Died Nov. 12, 1862, Patterson, Mo., disease.

Revilo D. Walsworth Chilton; Enlisted July 26, 1864; Mustered out Sept. 4, 1865.

Peter Ward Henrietta; Enlisted Nov. 1, 1864; Died Jan. 4, 1863, Van Buren, Mo., Disease.

Warner W. Welton Richland; Enlisted Mar. 29, 1864; Mustered out Sept. 4, 1865.

Edward C. White Richwood; Enlisted Oct. 22, 1861; Died Oct. 3, 1862. Helena, Ark., disease.

George C. White Richwood; Enlisted Oct. 19, 1861; Corporal; Killed July 7, 1862, Cache River, Ark.

Henry Widner Union; Enlisted Oct. 8, 1861; Wagoner; Died Mar. 16, 1863, St. Genevieve, Mo., disease.

Martin Widner Union; Enlisted Feb. 6, 1864; Mustered out July 5, 1865.

Matthias Widner Union; Enlisted Feb. 1, 1864; Died Sept. 29, 1864, Brashear City, LA, disease.

Edwin C. Wildermuth Willow; Enlisted Feb. 28, 1865; Drafted; Mustered out Sept. 4, 1865.

Benjamin Williams Sylvan; Enlisted Sept. 12, 1861; Veteran, Corporal, Sgt.; Mustered out Sept. 4, 1865.

Robert J. Wilson Brittish Hollow; Enlisted Sept. 12, 1861; Veteran, Corporal, Sgt.; Mustered out Sept. 4, 1865.

Samuel Wiltrout Bloom; Enlisted Dec. 30, 1863; Mustered out Sept. 4, 1865.

Henry H. Wood Richland; Enlisted Mar. 29, 1864; Mustered out Sept. 4, 1865.

William J. Wood Dayton; Enlisted Jan. 25, 1864; Mustered out May 25, 1865.

Eli Woodman Dayton; Enlisted Feb. 13, 1864; Mustered out Sept. 4, 1865.

William Yeager Richland; Enlisted Feb. 22, 1864; Mustered out Sept. 4, 1865.

Peter York Westford; Enlisted Nov. 1, 1861; Veteran; Died Apr. 7, 1865, Blakely, Ala. disease.

Casper Zerving Westford; Enlisted Sept. 17, 1861; Discharged Nov. 22, 1862, disability.

Co. E.— The "Farmers Guards"

OFFICERS

Luther H. Whittlesey Captain; Mineral Point; Rank from Sept. 20, 1861; Promoted Lt. Col. June 7, 1863.

Abner Powell Captain; Mineral Point; Rank from July 12, 1863; Veteran; 1st Lt., Sept. 20, 1861; Mustered out Sept. 4, 1865.

Sidney Shepard 1st Lt.; Mineral Point; Rank from July 12, 1863; Veteran; 2nd Lt., Sept. 20, 1861; Mustered out Sept. 4, 1865.

Enlisted Men

Alfred Allen Cadiz; Enlisted Sept. 4, 1861; Died Aug. 21, 1862; Oldtown, Ark., disease.

Calvin P. Alling Sylvan; Enlisted Sept. 12, 1861; From Co. D.; Vet; transferred to Co. D. Mar. 1, 1864.

Gilbert Anderson Moscow; Enlisted Sept. 18, 1861; Veteran; Mustered out Sept. 4, 1865; Died Sept. 3, 1865, Mobile, Ala.

Grant Andrews Enlisted Sept. 23, 1861; Wounded Vicksburg; Died May 25, 1863, of wounds.

Joseph Arthur Mineral Point; Enlisted Sept. 17, 1861; Veteran; Mustered out Sept. 4, 1865.

Hubert Barber Wilton; Enlisted Jan. 4, 1864; From 33rd Wis. Inf.; Mustered out Sept. 4, 1865.

Abraham Barret Lima; Enlisted Oct. 16, 1861; Mustered out Nov. 18, 1864, term expired.

George Beaumont Kendall; Enlisted Sept. 18, 1861; Veteran, Corporal, Sgt.; absent sick at Mustered out of Regt.

Michael Bender Mineral Point; Enlisted Oct. 5, 1861; Died Dec. 7, 1861, Sulpher Springs, Mo., disease.

Phillip Bennett Cottage Inn; Enlisted Sept. 20, 1861; Veteran; Mustered out Sept. 4, 1865.

William H. Bennett Mineral Point; Enlisted Sept. 7, 1861; Mustered out Sept. 28, 1864, term expired.

William Bleibaum Brookfield; Enlisted Mar. 30, 1865; Mustered out Sept. 4, 1865.

James Bottoms Mineral Point; Enlisted Oct. 7, 1861; Discharged Sept. 11, 1862, disability.

Nelson Bovee Mifflin; Enlisted Jan. 4, 1864; Mustered out Sept. 4, 1865.

Charles J. Bracken Willow Springs; Enlisted Sept. 1, 1861; Veteran, Corporal, Sgt.; Wounded Vicksburg; prom 2nd Lt. Co. G 5th Wis. Inf., Sept. 5, 1864.

John Brazzell Mifflin; Enlisted Sept. 23, 1861; Veteran, Corporal; Mustered out Sept. 4, 1865.

John Brennan Mineral Point; Enlisted Sept. 19, 1861; Veteran; Died July 29, 1864, Brashear City, La. disease.

Jonas Bryan Cottage Inn; Enlisted Sept. 2, 1861; Veteran, Corporal, Sgt.; Mustered out Sept. 4, 1865.

Delos Budlong Mineral Point; Enlisted Aug. 31, 1861; Veteran, Corporal; Mustered out July 9, 1865.

Michael Burns Willow Springs; Enlisted Sept. 21, 1861; Mustered out Nov. 18, 1864, term expired.

Barney A. Callahan Willow Springs; Enlisted Sept. 23, 1861; Veteran; Mustered out Sept. 4, 1865.

John D. Carpenter Belmont; Enlisted Sept. 16, 1861; Mustered out Sept. 4, 1865.

Andrew Carr Kendall; Enlisted Sept. 23, 1861; Veteran, Corporal; Mustered out Sept. 4, 1865.

Ezekiel Cnaney Franklin; Enlisted Sept. 4, 1861; Wounded Vicksburg; Died Sept. 11, 1863, Memphis, Tenn., disease.

John Crabb Mineral Point; Enlisted Sept. 3, 1861; Discharged Apr. 9, 1863, disability.

Matthew T. Curry Linden; Enlisted Sept. 17, 1861; Discharged Jan. 20, 1863.

Moses Glasgow Curry Mineral Point; Enlisted Sept. 18, 1861; Discharged Died 25, 1861, disability.

Thomas W. Curry Linden; Enlisted Sept. 16, 1861; Died Dec. 14, 1862, Black River, Mo., disease.

James M. Dain Kendall; Enlisted Sept. 16, 1861; Died Apr. 17, 1863, Nashville, Tenn., disease.

Thomas T. Dain Mifflin; Enlisted Sept. 4, 1861; Died May 5, 1862, Pocahontas, Ark., disease.

Rees T. Davis Mifflin; Enlisted Oct. 27, 1861; Wounded Port Gibson; Died May 11, 1863, of wounds.

William Dixon Waldwick; May 11, 1864; Mustered out Sept. 4, 1865.

John Doyle Kendall; Enlisted Apr. 14, 1864; Mustered out Sept. 4, 1865.

Francis M. Enloe Mifflin; Enlisted Sept. 23, 1861; Discharged Apr. 22, 1863, disability.

George Erbe Caledonia; Enlisted Apr. 11, 1865; Drafted; Mustered out Sept. 4, 1865.

James H. Evans Mineral Point; Enlisted Oct. 4, 1861; Deserted Nov. 24, 1862.

Jeremiah T. Evans Willow Springs; Enlisted Sept. 17, 1861; Discharged Feb. 12, 1862, disability.

William Evans Belmont; Enlisted Sept. 24, 1861; Missing Jan. 14, 1863 on march.

Joseph Fisher Grafton; Enlisted Mar. 14, 1865; Drafted; Mustered out Sept. 4, 1865.

Louis Forthan Freeman; Enlisted Oct. 5, 1864; Mustered out Sept. 4, 1865.

Charles W. French Willow Springs; Enlisted Sept. 24, 1861; Discharged Feb. 7, 1863, disability.

Henry E. Fuller Lake Mills; Enlisted Oct. 18, 1861; Discharged Nov. 18, 1862, disability.

Henry A. Gardiner Cincinnati, Oh; Enlisted Oct. 8, 1861; Discharged Nov. 30, 1863, disability.

Mial D. Gilson Elk Grove; Enlisted Sept. 9, 1861; Died Jan. 27, 1862, Camp Curtis, Mo., disease.

Ephraim J. Gordan Lynn; Enlisted Mar. 8, 1864; Deserted Apr. 22, 1864.

Dexter H. Gray Elk Grove; Enlisted Sept. 18, 1861; Discharged Oct. 4, 1862, disability.

William A. Gugerty Kendall; Enlisted Apr. 14, 1864; Died July 15, 1864, Brashear City, La., disease.

Rufus Halverson Manitowoc; Enlisted Sept. 30, 1864; Drafted; Mustered out June 7, 1865.

Nelson Hanson Freeman; Enlisted Oct. 5, 1864; Mustered out June 30, 1865.

Peter Hanson Enlisted Mar. 14, 1865; Drafted; Mustered out Sept. 4, 1865.

George Hartley Mineral Point; Enlisted Sept. 3, 1861; Veteran; Mustered out Sept. 4, 1865.

John Haskin Platteville; Enlisted Oct. 22, 1863; Mustered out Sept. 4, 1865.

Abram Hendrickson Reedsburg; Enlisted Sept. 16, 1861; Wounded Black River Bridge; Died Aug. 26, 1863, on steamer "Renford," disease.

Stephen Hoskin Platteville; Enlisted Sept. 17, 1861; Veteran, Corporal; Mustered out Sept. 4, 1865.

Moses Hulin Belmont; Enlisted Sept. 20, 1861; Mustered out Nov. 18, 1864, term expired.

John Hunter Fayette; Enlisted Sept. 17, 1861; Transferred to V.R.C., Oct. 1, 1863.

Joseph Johnson Freeman; Enlisted Oct. 5, 1864; Mustered out Sept. 4, 1865.

Thomas J. Jones Mifflin; Enlisted Oct. 27, 1861; Mustered out Nov. 18, 1864, term expired.

William B. Jones Belmont; Enlisted Sept. 9, 1861; Sgt., 1st Sgt.; Died May 24, 1863, of wounds received Vicksburg, Miss.

James Kilpatrick Cottage Inn; Enlisted Sept. 24, 1861; Discharged Feb. 7, 1863, disability.

Edward King Ridgeway; Enlisted Oct. 4, 1861; Veteran; Mustered out Sept. 4, 1865.

George King Sevastopol; Enlisted Apr. 8, 1865; Mustered out Sept. 4, 1865.

Samuel C. Kirkpatrick Washburn; Enlisted Sept. 11, 1861; Veteran, Corporal, Sgt., 1st Sgt.; Wounded Port Gibson; Mustered out Sept. 4, 1865.

Knud K. Knudson Liberty; Enlisted Mar. 11, 1865; Drafted; Mustered out Sept. 4, 1865.

Peter Knudson Moscow; Enlisted Mar. 14, 1865; Drafted; Died July 25, 1865, on board Steamer "Durand."

Carl F. Krueger Enlisted Mar. 10, 1865; Died July 26, 1865, Mobile, Ala., disease.

John Latch Linden; Enlisted Sept. 1, 1861; Discharged June 8, 1863, disability.

Martin Latch Calamine; Enlisted Sept. 4, 1861; Discharged Oct. 29, 1863, disability; re-enlisted Mar. 30, 1864; Mustered out Sept. 4, 1865.

John Lemke Enlisted Sept. 20, 1864; Mustered out June 6, 1865.

Mark D. Libby Cottage Inn; Enlisted Sept. 16, 1861; Veteran; Mustered out Sept. 4, 1865.

John Logue Willow Springs; Enlisted Sept. 5, 1861; Veteran; Died June 16, 1865, Montgomery, Ala., disease.

Alexander Ludlum Mifflin; Enlisted Sept. 12, 1861; Veteran; Mustered out Aug. 16, 1865.

Andrew Marr Kendall; Enlisted Sept. 19, 1861; Mustered out Nov. 18, 1864, term expired.

James Martin Enlisted Sept. 3, 1861; Mustered out Nov. 18, 1864, term expired.

Charles Mason Mineral Point; Enlisted Sept. 9, 1861; Veteran; Mustered out Sept. 4, 1865.

Frederick Matz Berry; Enlisted Mar. 6, 1865; Drafted; Mustered out Sept. 4, 1865.

Harrison McClennahan Belmont; Enlisted Sept. 21, 1861; Veteran, Musician; Mustered out Sept. 4, 1865.

Daniel McIlhatten Mineral Point; Enlisted Oct. 4, 1861; Veteran; Killed Apr. 9, 1865, Blakely, Ala.

Henry T. Melvin Belmont; Enlisted Sept. 12, 1861; Corporal; Discharged Dec. 4, 1862, disability.

Daniel B. Moore Mifflin; Enlisted Sept. 9, 1861; Veteran, Corporal, Sgt.; Wounded Blakely, Brevet 1st Lt., Apr. 9, 1865; Brevet Capt., Apr. 9, 1865; Mustered out Sept. 4, 1865. Winner of the Congressional Medal of Honor for actions at Blakely, Ala.

Adam Mory Porter; Enlisted Oct. 28, 1862; From 33rd Wis. Inf.; Mustered out Sept. 4, 1865.

Benjamin W. Moulton Fayette; Enlisted Sept. 23, 1861; Discharged July 26, 1862. disability.

Dennis W. Murphy Kendall; Enlisted Sept. 23, 1861; Deserted Mar. 10, 1863.

John Myer Sevastopol; Enlisted Apr. 6, 1865; Drafted; Mustered out Sept. 4, 1865.

Edward Newton Fayette; Enlisted Sept. 17, 1861; Veteran, Wagoner; Wounded; Mustered out Sept. 4, 1865.

Issac Newton Fayette; Enlisted Sept. 23, 1861; Wounded Vicksburg; Died May 24, 1863, of wounds.

Christopher Norton Moscow; Enlisted Sept. 28, 1861; Drafted; Mustered out June 7, 1865.

Nelson O'Connor Ridgeway; Enlisted Sept. 24, 1861; Veteran, Corporal; Wounded May 22, 1863, Vicksburg; Discharged Apr. 1, 1865, disability.

William Odgers Mineral Point; Enlisted Sept. 1, 1861; Discharged Apr. 29, 1863, disability.

William H. Oettiker Belmont; Enlisted Sept. 9, 1861; Veteran; promoted 2nd Lt. Co. K, 50th Wis. Inf., Feb. 21, 1865.

John Ohle Springdale; Enlisted Nov. 2, 1861; Discharged Nov. 20, 1862, disability.

Knud Oleson Moscow; Enlisted Mar. 14, 1865; Mustered out Sept. 4, 1865.

Nathan T. Olmstead Cottage Inn; Enlisted Sept. 9, 1861; Corporal, Sgt.; Discharged Nov. 18, 1862, disability.

Peter Paar Berry; Enlisted Mar. 14, 1865; Mustered out Sept. 4, 1865.

Plimpton M. Palmer Bethel Grove; Enlisted Sept. 24, 1861; Veteran; Died Nov. 27, 1864, Wis., disease.

John J. Parry Mifflin; Enlisted Sept. 9, 1861; Discharged Apr. 6, 1863, disability.

Peter Peterson Moscow; Enlisted Mar. 14, 1865; Drafted; Mustered out Sept. 4, 1865.

David Pfisterer Enlisted Mar. 23, 1865; Drafted; Died Aug. 2, 1865, Mobile, Ala., disease.

Jeremiah J. Phelps Mifflin; Enlisted Oct. 8, 1861; Veteran; Mustered out Sept. 4, 1865.

Jonas M. Phelps Madison; Enlisted Jan. 4, 1864; Mustered out Aug. 16, 1865.

Oliver W. Phelps Mineral Point; Enlisted Sept. 2, 1861; Killed June 23, 1863, Vicksburg, Miss.

William H. Phelps Mifflin; Enlisted Sept. 9, 1861; Veteran, Sgt.; Killed Apr. 9, 1865, Blakely, Ala.

Thomas Powell Mineral Point; Enlisted Sept. 9, 1861; Veteran; Died Oct. 23, 1864, Brashear City, La., disease.

Tyler S. Prentice Mineral Point; Enlisted Sept. 11, 1861; Discharged Sept. 26, 1863, disability.

Thomas Priestly Mineral Point; Enlisted Sept. 9, 1861; 1st Sgt.; Promoted 2nd Lt. Co. B, 30th Wis. Inf., Sept. 8, 1862.

Samuel Prisk Mineral Point; Enlisted Aug. 31, 1861; Veteran, Corporal, Sgt.; Mustered out Sept. 4, 1865.

Thomas W. Prisk Mineral Point; Enlisted Sept. 9, 1861; Veteran, 1st Sgt.; Wounded Vicksburg; Died July 3, 1865, Mineral Point, Wis., disease.

John T. Reeves Waldwick; Enlisted Sept. 15, 1861; Discharged July 26, 1862, disability.

Gottfried Reiner Sheboygan Fall; Enlisted Feb. 14, 1865; Drafted; Mustered out Sept. 4, 1865.

Nathan Richardson Mineral Point; Enlisted Oct. 28, 1861; Veteran; Wounded Blakely; Mustered out Sept. 4, 1865.

Patrick Ruddy Westport; Enlisted Oct. 16, 1861; Veteran, Corporal; Mustered out Sept. 4, 1865.

Henry Rule Mineral Point; Enlisted Sept. 2, 1861; Discharged Apr. 27, 1863, disability.

Thomas M. Satterlee Mineral Point; Enlisted Sept. 16, 1861; Died July 2, 1863, of wounds received at Vicksburg, Miss.

Frederik Schorningen Ahnapee; Enlisted Oct. 3, 1864.; Drafted; Mustered out Sept. 4, 1865.

Jas. Simple Scoggin Belmont; Enlisted Sept. 16, 1861; Died Aug. 16, 1862, Oldtown, Ark., disease.

John Scott Mineral Point; Enlisted Oct. 7, 1861; Killed May 22, 1863, Vicksburg, Miss.

Robert Scott Mineral Point; Enlisted Oct. 7, 1861; Wounded Vicksburg; Died June 16, 1863, Memphis, Tenn., of wounds.

Alexander Shannon Port Andrew; Enlisted Oct. 7, 1861; Veteran; Killed Apr. 9, 1865, Blakely, Ala.

Edward Shea Kendall; Enlisted Apr. 15, 1864; Mustered out Sept. 4, 1865.

John Shea Waldwick; Enlisted Aug. 31, 1861; Veteran; Mustered out Sept. 4, 1865.

Murty Shea Waldwick; Enlisted Sept. 7, 1861; Veteran, Corporal; Killed Apr. 9, 1865, Blakely, Ala.

Robert R. Sherrill Bethel Grove; Enlisted Sept. 16, 1861; Veteran, Corporal; Mustered out July 9, 1865.

Edward T. Shirrell Belmont; Enlisted Aug. 12, 1864; Mustered out July 9, 1865.

Thomas Smith Waldwick; Enlisted Sept. 17, 1861; Wounded Grand Gulf, Miss.; Died July 20, 1863, Millikens Bend, La., disease.

John Stevens Mifflin; Enlisted Sept. 24, 1861; Wounded Vicksburg; Died May 23, 1863, of wounds.

John Stoner Mineral Point; Enlisted Sept. 16, 1861; Veteran; Mustered out Sept. 4, 1865.

Parley E. Stoner Mineral Point; Enlisted Sept. 18, 1861; Veteran; Mustered out July 19, 1865.

Niels Svenson Eaton; Enlisted Sept. 30, 1864; Drafted; Mustered out June 7, 1865.

Daniel Thomas Mineral Point; Enlisted Sept. 1, 1861; Died Aug. 27, 1862, Oldtown, Ark., disease.

John Thrasher Mineral Point; Enlisted Oct. 7, 1861; Veteran, Corporal; Mustered out July 19, 1865.

William Trevillion Mineral Point; Enlisted Sept. 3, 1861; Veteran, Sgt.; Mustered out Sept. 4, 1865.

William Trude Washburn; Enlisted Sept. 11, 1861; Discharged Feb. 22, 1863, disease.

William Truman Lima; Enlisted Nov. 1, 1862; From 33rd Wis. Inf.; Mustered out Sept. 4, 1865.

John Van Nostran Albion; Enlisted Feb. 2, 1864; From 33rd Wis. Inf.; Mustered out Sept. 4, 1865.

Edwin Waldbridge Mineral Point; Enlisted Mar. 5, 1864; Died Nov. 21, 1864, Brashear City, La., disease.

James White Mineral Point; Enlisted Sept. 24, 1861; Veteran; Mustered out Sept. 4, 1865.

Ernest Wiesen Mineral Point; Enlisted Aug. 28, 1861; Corporal; Discharged July 26, 1862, disability.

George Wilcox Oakland; Enlisted Mar. 8, 1864; Deserted Apr. 22, 1864.

Co. F.— The "Harvey Zouaves"

OFFICERS

Edward R. Chase Captain; Madison; Rank from Oct. 2, 1861; Enlisted Sept. 27, 1861; resigned Oct. 3, 1862; appt. Capt. V.R.C. July 20, 1863.

Fernando D. Stone Captain; Baraboo; Rank from Oct. 3, 1862; Enlisted Sept. 9, 1861; 1st Lt., Oct. 2, 1861; Resigned July 20, 1863.

Riel E. Jackson Captain; Waukesha; Rank from July 20, 1862; Veteran; 2nd Lt., Oct. 2, 1861; 1st Lt., Oct. 3, 1862; Mustered out Sept. 4, 1865.

William P. Mcconnell 1st Lt.; Madison; Rank from Sept. 3, 1863; Enlisted Sept. 3, 1861;Veteran, Corporal, Sgt., 1st Sgt.; Mustered out Sept. 4, 1865.

Caleb A. Northrop 2nd Lt.; Pheasant Pr'ch; Rank from Oct. 3, 1862; Enlisted Sept. 16, 1861; 1st Sgt.; Died Sept. 3, 1863, Carrolton, La., disease.

LaFayette Locke 2nd Lt.; Baraboo; Rank from Aug. 23, 1865; Enlisted Sept. 9, 1861;Veteran, Corporal, Sgt., 1st Sgt.; Wounded Blakely; Mustered out Sept. 4, 1865.

Enlisted Men

Martin Abbey Cottage Grove; Enlisted Sept. 26, 1861; Veteran, Corporal; Mustered out Sept. 4, 1865.

Peter Alexander Westfield; Enlisted Sept. 10, 1861; Veteran; Wounded Blakely; right arm amp.; Died May 6, 1865, Memphis, Tenn., disease.

Michael Aman Bloomfield; Enlisted Dec. 31, 1864; Drafted; Mustered out Sept. 4, 1865.

Harvey B. Ames Baraboo; Enlisted Sept. 9, 1861; Corporal; Discharged Feb. 28, 1863, disability.

Edward W. Baker Merrimack; Enlisted Sept. 30, 1861; Veteran; Mustered out Sept. 4, 1865.

Charles Baldwin Pulaski; Enlisted Dec. 16, 1863; From 33rd Wis. Inf.; Mustered out Sept. 4, 1865.

Carl Bartles Fountain City; Enlisted Mar. 10, 1865; Mustered out Sept. 4, 1865.

Phoenix Bartlett Turtle; Enlisted Jan. 5, 1864; From 33rd Wis. Inf.; Mustered out Sept. 4, 1865.

Johnson Beavans Clifton; Enlisted Jan. 13, 1864; From 33rd Wis. Inf.; Mustered out Sept. 4, 1865.

Montgomery F. Billings Madison; Enlisted Sept. 14, 1861; Veteran, Corporal, Sgt.; Mustered out Sept. 4, 1865.

John Birns Preble; Enlisted Mar. 2, 1865; Drafted; Mustered out Sept. 4, 1865.

Ernest Black Freedom; Enlisted Sept. 9, 1861; Died Mar. 26, 1864, Lake Providence, La., disease.

William Black Freedom; Enlisted Sept. 20, 1861; Discharged Apr. 20, 1861, disability.

James H. Bradley Center; Enlisted Feb. 9, 1865; From 33rd Wis. Inf.; Mustered out Sept. 4, 1865.

Richard Bradley From 33rd Wis. Inf.

Mark Brennan Mukwaonago; Enlisted Sept. 22, 1861; Died May 4, 1863, of wounds received at Port Gibson, Miss.

Henry Brill Baraboo; Enlisted Sept. 9, 1861; Died Jan. 13, 1862, Sulpher Springs, Mo., disease.

George W. Brown Baraboo; Enlisted Sept. 30, 1861; Veteran, Corporal; Wounded Vicksburg; Mustered out Sept. 4, 1865.

Joseph Brown Milwaukee; Enlisted Dec. 14, 1864; Drafted; Mustered out Sept. 4, 1865.

Horace Bryant Cross Plains; Enlisted Sept. 23, 1861; Mustered out Nov. 18, 1864, term expired; Mustered out Aug. 28, 1865.

Sylvester F. Buck Shopiere; Enlisted Dec. 30, 1863; From 33rd Wis. Inf.; transferred to V.R.C. May 4, 1865.

Phillip Bugese Forest; Enlisted Mar. 22, 1865; Drafted; Mustered out Sept. 4, 1865.

Ferdinand Butler Peba; Enlisted Mar. 27, 1865; Drafted; Died Aug. 9, 1865, Mobile, Ala., disease.

John Butler Verona; Enlisted Oct. 27, 1861; Killed May 27, 1863, Vicksburg, Miss.

Pierce E. Butler Madison; Enlisted Sept. 21, 1861; Veteran; Wounded Blakely; Mustered out Sept. 4, 1865.

Martin D. Carney Theresa; Enlisted Oct. 13, 1864; Mustered out Sept. 4, 1865.

Austin Carver Wilton; Enlisted Sept. 11, 1861; Veteran, Corporal; Mustered out Sept. 4, 1865.

Roswell M. Clark Verona; Enlisted Sept. 12, 1861; Mustered out Nov. 18, 1864, term expired.

James Costelo Fulton; Enlisted Sept. 14, 1861; Killed Aug. 17, 1863, Carrolton, La., accident.

Josiah O. Curtis Madison; Enlisted Oct. 27, 1861; Veteran, Corporal; Mustered out Sept. 4, 1865.

Burke Dahl Sun Prairie; Enlisted Sept. 17, 1861; Died Feb. 28, 1863. St. Louis, Mo.

Charles Daniels Verona; Enlisted Sept. 12, 1861; Mustered out Nov. 18, 1864, term expired.

Henry P. Dankel Verona; Enlisted Oct. 12, 1861; Veteran; Mustered out Sept. 4, 1865.

William M. Davis Cottage Grove; Enlisted Sept. 12, 1861; Corporal, Sgt.; Killed May 22, 1863, Vicksburg, Miss.

William Devine Sun Prairie; Enlisted Sept. 24, 1861; Veteran; Wounded Vicksburg and Blakely; absent sick at Mustered out of Regt.

Julien J. Dinsmore Springfield; Enlisted Sept. 17, 1861; Veteran, Corporal, Sgt.; Mustered out Sept. 4, 1865.

Thomas Dixon Turtle; Enlisted Jan. 4, 1864; From 33rd Wis. Inf.; absent sick at Mustered out of Regt.

Henry Dobbs Enlisted Mar. 5, 1864; From 33rd Wis. Inf.; Colored Cook; Mustered out Sept. 4, 1865.

Patrick Dolan Madison; Enlisted Sept. 27, 1861; Wounded Black River Bridge; Mustered out Nov. 18, 1864, term expired.

Ole Donalson Baraboo; Enlisted Sept. 19, 1861; Died Sept. 11, 1862, Oldtown, Ark., disease.

Michael J. Donnellon Madison; Enlisted Sept. 17, 1861; Mustered out Nov. 18, 1864, term expired.

William Driebach Verona; Enlisted Sept. 12, 1861; Veteran, Corporal; Wounded Blakely; Mustered out July 8, 1865.

George W. Duryea Cottage Grove; Enlisted Sept. 21, 1861; Corporal, Sgt.; Died June 26, 1862, Batesville, Ark., disease.

John Early Greenfield; Enlisted Sept. 12, 1861; Transferred to V.R.C., Feb. 10, 1864.

Sylvester Eastman Ft. Winnebago; Enlisted Sept. 19, 1864; Musician; Promoted Principal Musician, June 12, 1863.

Henry O. Edwards Clinton; Enlisted Sept. 12, 1864; Mustered out June 6, 1865.

Jeremiah F. Elliott Marceilon; Enlisted Sept. 21, 1864; Drafted; Mustered out Sept. 4, 1865.

Andrew Erickson Cato; Enlisted Mar. 11, 1865; Drafted; Mustered out Sept. 4, 1865.

Michael Farley Madison; Enlisted Sept. 23, 1861; Wounded Port Gibson; Discharged Oct. 15, 1863, disability; re-enl. May 19, 1864; Mustered out Sept. 4, 1865.

William P. Fick Verona; Enlisted Sept. 11, 1861; Mustered out Nov. 18, 1864, term expired.

Joseph G. Finnell Cottage Grove; Enlisted Jan. 4, 1864; From 33rd Wis. Inf.; Mustered out June 12, 1865.

Michael Flannagan Oshkosh; Enlisted Sept. 27, 1861; Veteran, Corporal; Died Aug. 23, 1864, Brashear City, La., disease.

Calvin B. Flick Verona; Enlisted Sept. 11, 1861; Transferred to V.R.C., June 13, 1864; Mustered out Sept. 22, 1864, term expired.

Commodore P. Flora Pulaski; Enlisted Nov. 17, 1863; From 33rd Wis. Inf.; Mustered out Sept. 4, 1865.

David Foot Harrison; Enlisted Mar. 20, 1865; Drafted; Mustered out Sept. 4, 1865.

George E. Foyt Lima; Enlisted Dec. 25, 1863; From 33rd Wis. Inf.; Mustered out Sept. 4, 1865.

Clarkson Freeman Sumpter; Enlisted Sept. 28, 1861; Died Sept. 14, 1862, on Hospital Boat.

Charles Gibbons Woodland; Enlisted Mar. 20, 1865; Drafted; Mustered out Sept. 4, 1865.

James A. Gowdy Springfield; Enlisted Sept. 17, 1861; Died July 1, 1862, Jacksonsprot, Ark., disease.

George L. Graves Westfield; Enlisted Oct. 4, 1861; Discharged Aug. 11, 1862, disability.

Peter Griesman Richfield; Enlisted Sept. 12, 1864; Drafted; Mustered out Sept. 4, 1865.

Stephen Griffith Springfield; Enlisted Sept. 26, 1861; Died May 28, 1862, Batesville, Ark., disease.

Franklin Halpin Madison; Enlisted Mar. 23, 1864; Drummer; Discharged Oct. 12, 1864, disability.

Charles B. Haney Sauk City; Enlisted Mar. 31, 1864; Discharged Sept. 17, 1864, disability.

Lyman L. Hannan Rutland; Enlisted Dec. 3, 1863; From 33rd Wis. Inf.; absent sick at Mustered out of Regt.

Dexter G. Harris Cottage Grove; Enlisted Jan. 2, 1864; From 33rd Wis. Inf.; Mustered out Sept. 4, 1865.

Edmond R. Haskins Woodland; Enlisted Mar. 7, 1865; Mustered out Sept. 4, 1865.

Robert Hastie Madison; Enlisted Sept. 17, 1861; Promoted Principal Musician, June 12, 1863; rejd. from Q.M. Sgt., Feb. 8, 1865; Mustered out Sept. 4, 1865.

Luman C. Hawes Verona; Enlisted Sept. 14, 1861; Veteran, Corporal; Mustered out Sept. 4, 1865.

Richard A. Hawley Janesville; Enlisted Feb. 9, 1865; From 33rd Wis. Inf.; Mustered out Aug. 14, 1865.

Franklin Hayden Monroe; Enlisted Jan. 15, 1864; Musician; Mustered out Sept. 4, 1865.

David A. Hesford Sauk Prairie; Enlisted Sept. 15, 1861; Died Nov. 11, 1862, Mound City, Ill., disease.

Wells R. High Black Earth; Enlisted Sept. 3, 1861; Corporal; Discharged June 13, 1864, for Promoted in U.S.C.T.

Andrew Hodget Sauk Prairie; Enlisted Nov. 1, 1861; Died Sept. 21, 1862, Oldtown, Ark., disease.

James E. Hoyt Rutland; Enlisted Dec. 3, 1863; From 33rd Wis. Inf.; Mustered out Sept. 4, 1865.

John Huffy Lake Mills; Enlisted Jan. 19, 1864; From 33rd Wis. Inf.; Mustered out Sept. 4, 1865.

Elijah D. Hunt Verona; Enlisted Sept. 3, 1861; Corporal; Mustered out Nov. 18, 1864. term expired.

Thomas Hunt Verona; Enlisted Sept. 9, 1861; Wounded Port Gibson; Transferred to V.R.C., June 13, 1864.

Rodney Hurlburt Kingston; Enlisted Sept. 15, 1861; Veteran, Corporal, Sgt.; Mustered out Sept. 4, 1865.

Edward S. Inman Madison; Enlisted Sept. 26, 1861; Discharged June 15, 1864, disability.

William R. Inman Madison; Enlisted Sept. 23, 1861; Veteran; Died Mar. 9, 1865, Madison, Wis., disease.

Christian Jachemick Harrison; Enlisted Mar. 9, 1865; Drafted; Deserted Aug. 21, 1865.

William A. Johnson Kingston; Enlisted Oct. 14, 1861; Corporal; absent on detch. service at Mustered out of Regt.

Abed K. Jones Cottage Grove; Enlisted Mar. 21, 1864; From 33rd Wis. Inf.; Mustered out Sept. 4, 1865.

Frank M. Kern Sumpter; Enlisted Sept. 9, 1861; Sgt.; Discharged Aug. 11, 1863, disability.

Reuben F. King Kingston; Enlisted Sept. 15, 1861; Transferred to V.R.C., June 13, 1864; Discharged Oct. 24, 1864. (?).

Robert King Elk Grove; Enlisted Jan. 18, 1864; From 33rd Wis. Inf.; Mustered out Sept. 4, 1865.

Joseph Klein Milwaukee; Enlisted Mar. 23, 1865; Drafted; Mustered out Sept. 4, 1865.

George W. Kniseley Oshkosh; Enlisted Sept. 27, 1861; Wounded Port Gibson; Died Sept. 6, 1863, Milliken's Bend, La., of wounds.

John Konz Harrison; Enlisted Mar. 9, 1865; Mustered out Sept. 4, 1865.

Ernst Krafft West Bend; Enlisted Oct. 11, 1864; Mustered out May 22, 1865.

Martin Krause Rockland; Enlisted Mar. 11, 1865; Drafted; Mustered out Sept. 4, 1865.

Phillip Laux Edwards; Enlisted Mar. 11, 1865; Drafted,; Mustered out Sept. 4, 1865.

Michael Lawler Milwaukee; Enlisted Nov. 24, 1862; Discharged Apr. 21, 1863, disability.

William V. Le Graff Baraboo; Enlisted Sept. 20, 1861; Discharged Aug. 14, 1863, disability.

James Lenox Kingston; Enlisted Sept. 15, 1861; Discharged Feb. 26, 1863, disability.

Edward Lester Dane; Enlisted Sept. 27, 1861; Veteran, Corporal; Mustered out Sept. 4, 1865.

August Liebertraw Berry; Enlisted Mar. 25, 1865; Drafted; Mustered out Sept. 4, 1865.

Jacob Lips Verona; Enlisted Nov. 6, 1861; Died Feb. 10, 1862, Willow Springs, Mo., disease.

Jacob W. Madou Madison; Enlisted Oct. 9, 1861; Veteran; Mustered out Sept. 4, 1865.

Robert Malone Westport; Enlisted Sept. 23, 1861; Veteran; in confinement at Mustered out of Regt.

Lafayette Y. Marsh Berry; Enlisted Mar. 25, 1865; Drafted; Mustered out Sept. 4, 1865.

Charles W. Martin Dane; Enlisted Sept. 9, 1861; Veteran; trans. to Co. I, Mar. 1, 1864.

David C. Martin Newport; Enlisted Sept. 9, 1861; Corporal; Discharged Feb. 28, 1863, disability.

William E. Martin Newport; Enlisted Sept. 12, 1861; Veteran; Mustered out Sept. 4, 1865.

John W. Mass Sun Prairie; Enlisted Sept. 17, 1861; Sgt.; Brevet Capt., May 22, 1863; Mustered out Sept. 28, 1864, term expired.

Jesse Mather Kingston; Enlisted Oct. 14, 1861; Mustered out Nov. 18, 1864, term expired.

Oliver SS Mather Kingston; Enlisted Oct. 14, 1861; Wounded Vicksburg; Died May 27, 1863, Vicksburg, Miss., of wounds.

John M. McCormick Madison; Enlisted Dec. 29, 1863; From 33rd Wis. Inf.; Mustered out Sept. 4, 1865.

James H. McCurdy Oshkosh; Enlisted Sept. 27, 1861; Veteran; Mustered out Sept. 4, 1865.

Alisius Meyer Winfield; Enlisted Sept. 22, 1864; Drafted; Mustered out June 6, 1865.

Augustus Michael Kingston; Enlisted Sept. 19, 1861; Dishonarably discharged Jan. 5, 1865.

John H. Miller Madison; Enlisted Sept. 14, 1861; Discharged Nov. 30, 1861, disability.

George J. Moog Baraboo; Enlisted Sept. 11, 1861; Wounded Vicksburg; Mustered out Nov. 18, 1864, term expired.

John W. Moore Sun Prairie; Enlisted Oct. 11, 1861; Mustered out Nov. 18, 1864, term expired.

William E. Morgan Madison; Enlisted Dec. 29, 1863; From 33rd Wis. Inf.; Mustered out Sept. 4, 1865.

John Nelson Boscobel; Enlisted Mar. 14, 1865; Drafted; Mustered out Aug. 31, 1865.

Carlos L. Newell Cottage Grove; Enlisted Sept. 12, 1861; Died Oct. 4, 1862, St. Louis, Mo., disease.

John Newkirk Shopiere; Enlisted Dec. 30, 1863; From 33rd Wis. Inf.; Mustered out Sept. 4, 1865.

Charles H. Noble Madison; Enlisted Sept. 12, 1861; Veteran; Mustered out Sept. 4, 1865.

Edward Noon Blue Mounds; Enlisted Oct. 8, 1861; Veteran; Mustered out Sept. 4, 1865.

Tobias Nunamaker Pulaski; Enlisted Dec. 14, 1863; From 33rd Wis. Inf.; Mustered out June 24, 1865.

James M. O'Harrow Lamartine; Enlisted Oct. 19, 1864; Wounded Blakely; absent Wounded at Mustered out of Regt.

Knud Olson Liberty; Enlisted Mar. 29, 1865; Drafted; Mustered out Aug. 31, 1865.

Andrew S. Parsons Oregon; Enlisted Jan. 4, 1864; From 33rd Wis. Inf.; Corporal; Mustered out Sept. 4, 1865.

Daniel H. Parsons Middleton; Enlisted Sept. 12, 1861; Corporal; Mustered out Nov. 18, 1864, term expired.

Charles A. Paul Springfield; Enlisted Sept. 26, 1861; Died Sept. 14, 1863, Keokuk, Ia., disease.

David C. Phillips Lima; Enlisted Feb. 25, 1864; From 33rd Wis. Inf; Mustered out Sept. 4, 1865.

Alfred K. Pierce Springfield; Enlisted Sept. 17, 1861; Discharged Apr. 4, 1863, disability.

Calvin Pierce Springfield; Enlisted Oct. 2, 1861; Veteran, Corporal, Sgt.; Mustered out Sept. 4, 1865.

Augustus F. Poole Verona; Enlisted Sept. 12, 1861; Discharged Dec. 24, 1862, disability.

Francis Prafke Milwaukee; Enlisted Sept. 21, 1864; Drafted; Mustered out June 6, 1865.

Thomas Prideaux Platteville; Enlisted Jan. 4, 1864; From 33rd Wis. Inf; Mustered out Sept. 4, 1865.

Christian Ranchet Caledonia; Enlisted Mar. 27, 1863; Drafted; Mustered out Sept. 4, 1865.

Martin Reding Verona; Enlisted Oct. 5, 1861; Corporal; Wounded Vicksburg; re-enl. Mar. 8, 1864; Mustered out Sept. 4, 1865.

Jacob Renner Caledonia; Enlisted Mar. 27, 1865; Drafted; Mustered out Sept. 4, 1865.

John Riley Sun Prairie; Enlisted Sept. 17, 1861; Veteran; Mustered out Sept. 4, 1865.

Andrew Ripple Oshkosh; Enlisted Sept. 27, 1861; Wounded Port Gibson; transferred to V.R.C., July 7, 1864.

Charles C. Robbins Madison; Enlisted Sept. 18, 1861; Sgt.; Promoted Q.M. Sgt., Aug. 21, 1862.

Amariah Robotham Linden Station; Enlisted Sept. 19, 1861; Died May 8, 1862. Pocahontas, Ark., disease.

Benjamin Rogers Enlisted Dec. 3, 1863; From 33rd Wis. Inf.; Colored Cook; Mustered out Sept. 4, 1865.

Evan Rollins Racine; Enlisted Apr. 6, 1865; Drafted; Died July 5, 1865, Montgomery, Ala., disease.

Christian Rosenbaum Fond Du Lac; Enlisted Oct. 11, 1864; Mustered out Sept. 4, 1865.

Antinas A. Rowly Verona; Enlisted Sept. 22, 1861; Discharged Feb. 26, 1863, disability.

Francis M. Sawdy Baraboo; Enlisted Sept. 11, 1861; Discharged Apr. 3, 1862, disability.

Frederick Schultz Pella; Enlisted Mar. 27, 1865; Drafted; Died Aug. 29, 1865, Madison, Wis.

George Seston Berry; Enlisted Feb. 27, 1865; Drafted; Mustered out Sept. 4, 1865.

John A. Sholtz Rutland; Enlisted Dec. 3, 1863; From 33rd Wis. Inf.; Mustered out Sept. 4, 1865.

Edward Smith Lake, Mills; Enlisted Jan. 19, 1864; From 33rd Wis. Inf.; Mustered out July 17, 1865.

Henry C. Smith Platteville; Enlisted Dec. 25,

1863; From 33rd Wis. Inf.; Mustered out Sept. 4, 1865.

Albert M. Snyder   Harrison; Enlisted Mar. 15, 1864; From 33rd Wis. Inf.; Mustered out Sept. 4, 1865.

James F. Spencer   Madison; Enlisted Sept. 3, 1861; Corporal; prom Sgt. Major, July 1, 1863.

William Stackhouse   Freedom; Enlisted Sept. 11, 1861; Wounded Vicksburg; Mustered out Nov. 18, 1864, term expired.

William S. Stearnes   Baraboo; Enlisted Sept. 9, 1861; Corporal, Sgt., Wounded Vicksburg; Died June 15, 1863, Memphis, Tenn., of wounds.

Henry A. Sweet   Milwaukee; Enlisted Sept. 13, 1861; Com. Sgt., Sept. 27, 1861; rej. June 29, 1862; Discharged Mar. 15, 1863, disability.

Lysander Sweetlon   Stoughton; Enlisted Sept. 18, 1861; Discharged Apr. 4, 1863, disability.

Milton N. Talsey   Madison; Enlisted Sept. 22, 1861; Musician; Discharged Apr. 20, 1863, disability.

Alexander I. Taylor   Shopiere; Enlisted Dec. 30, 1863; From 33rd Wis. Inf.; Died Sept. 21, 1865, Madison, Wis., disease.

Charles Thomas   Verona; Enlisted Sept. 12, 1861; Corporal; Died July 10, 1862, Clarendon, Ark., disease.

Lewis Thompson   Sun Prairie; Enlisted Sept. 17, 1864; Discharged Apr. 4, 1863, disability.

Ole Thompson   Moscow; Enlisted Mar. 14, 1865; Drafed; Died Aug. 2, 1865, Mobile, Ala., disease.

James Thorne   Madison; Enlisted Sept. 3, 1861; Discharged Aug. 11, 1862, disability.

James Ward   Marshall; Enlisted Feb. 28, 1865; Drafted; Mustered out Sept. 4, 1865.

Chauncy S. Warren   Sun Prairie; Enlisted Sept. 19, 1861; Corporal; Mustered out Nov. 18, 1864, term expired.

Alfred Welch   Dane; Enlisted Oct. 14, 1861; Veteran; Killed Apr. 9, 1865, Blakely, Ala.

Martin M. Wells   Fond Du Lac; Enlisted Oct. 18, 1864; Mustered out Sept. 4, 1865.

Alonzo L. Whitcomb   Madison; Enlisted Dec. 2, 1863; From 33rd Wis. Inf.; Mustered out May 26, 1865.

Herman Williams   Bloom'g Grove; Enlisted Mar. 28, 1864; Died Oct. 18, 1864, Brashear City, La., disease.

Martin Wilms   Forest; Enlisted Mar. 22, 1865; Drafted; Mustered out Aug. 31, 1865.

George W. Wing   Baraboo; Enlisted Sept. 10, 1861; Discharged Apr. 4, 1863, disability.

William Wright   Springdale; Enlisted Sept. 28, 1861; Veteran; Discharged June 11, 1865, disability.

Co. G — The "Randall Zouaves"

Officers

Wilbur F. Pelton   Captain; Sun Prairie; Rank from Oct. 10, 1861; Resigned May 14, 1862.

Edwin D. Partridge   Captain; Clayton; May 14, 1862; Enlisted Aug. 26, 1861, 1st Lt., Oct. 10, 1861; resigned Mar. 18, 1863.

John A. Peaslee   Captain; Sun Prairie; Rank from Mar. 18, 1863; Enlisted Oct. 21, 1861; Sgt.; 2nd Lt., May 14, 1862, 1st Lt. Jan. 17, 1863; Wounded Vicksburg; Died May 28, 1863, Vicksburg, Miss., of wounds.

Dudley C. Wyman   Captain; Madison; Rank from June 1, 1863; From Sgt. Major; Dismissed Dec. 21, 1864.

William S. McCready   Captain; Black Hawk; Rank from June 13, 1865; Enlisted Sept. 16, 1861; Veteran, Corporal, Sgt., 1st Sgt.; Wounded Bayou Cache; 1st Lt., Mar. 22, 1864; Mustered out Sept. 4, 1865.

Nathan Downs   1st Lt.; Mazomanie; May 14, 1862; Enlisted Sept. 16, 1861; 1st Sgt.; 2nd Lt., Mar. 20, 1862; resigned Jan. 17, 1863.

Andrew R. Wynn   1st Lt.; Blue Mounds; Rank from Mar. 18, 1863; Enlisted Sept. 1, 1861; Sgt., 1st Sgt.; 2nd Lt., Jan. 17, 1863; resigned Oct. 22, 1863.

George Farwell   1st Lt.; Ridgeway; Rank from June 13, 1865; Enlisted Sept. 16, 1861; Veteran, Corporal, Sgt., 1st Sgt.; Wounded Vicksburg; Mustered out Sept. 4, 1865.

Henry Blake   2nd Lt.; Madison; Rank from Oct. 10, 1861; Enlisted Sept. 11, 1861; resigned Mar. 19, 1862.

James Law   2nd Lt.; Mazomanie; Rank from Mar. 18, 1862; Enlisted Sept. 28, 1861; Sgt., 1st Sgt.; Wounded Vicksburg; Died June 5, 1863, on steamer *Champion*, of wounds.

Enlisted Men

John W. Anderson   Arena; Enlisted Sept. 1, 1861; Discharged Dec. 11, 1862, disability.

George W. Appleby   Arena; Enlisted Sept. 12, 1861; Veteran; Mustered out Sept. 4, 1865.

Henry Armstrong   Westport; Enlisted Sept. 20, 1861; Discharged Feb. 7, 1863, disability.

Tyler F. Ayers   Henrietta; Enlisted Feb. 28, 1865; Drafted; Mustered out Aug. 31, 1865.

John Bahm   Burk; Enlisted Oct. 9, 1861; Discharged Mar. 29, 1863, disability.

George H. Baker   Brothertown; Enlisted Sept. 12, 1861; Veteran, Corporal, Sgt.; Wounded Vicksburg; Mustered out Sept. 4, 1865.

Henry A. Baxter   Summit; Enlisted Sept. 7, 1861; Veteran, Corporal, Sgt.; Mustered out Sept. 4, 1865.

Henry Beach   Henrietta; Enlisted Feb. 28, 1865; Drafted; Mustered out Aug. 31, 1865.

Darwin Beaumont   Arena; Enlisted Aug. 27,

1862; Transferred to V.R.C., Jan. 15, 1864; Mustered out July 5, 1865 (?).

William H. Bender Forest; Enlisted Feb. 28, 1865; Drafted; Mustered out Sept. 4, 1865.

Elias Billington Ridgeway; Enlisted Sept. 12, 1861; Veteran, Corporal, Sgt.; Discharged Mar. 20, 1865, disability.

Thomas C. Bishop Arena; Enlisted Sept. 5, 1861; Discharged Nov. 1, 1861, disability.

Walter Blakely Forest; Enlisted Feb. 28, 1864; Drafted; Mustered out Sept. 4, 1865.

Edward Borwell Mazomanie; Enlisted Oct. 25, 1861; Corporal; Wounded Vicksburg; Discharged July 28, 1863, disability.

Kingsley R. Boyd Boscobel; Enlisted Jan. 4, 1864; From 33rd Wis. Inf.; Mustered out Sept. 4, 1865.

John T. Bradley Madison; Enlisted Sept. 6, 1861; Sgt.; Prisoner Sabine Cross Roads; Brevet 1st Lt., May 1, 1863; Mustered out June 6, 1865.

Charles Bywater Arena; Enlisted Aug. 28, 1861; Veteran, Corporal; Wounded Vicksburg; Mustered out Sept. 4, 1865.

John Bywater Arena; Enlisted Sept. 1, 1861; Prisoner Sabine Cross Roads; Mustered out June 15, 1865.

Anson Calkins Arena; Enlisted Oct. 26, 1861; Veteran; Mustered out Sept. 4, 1865.

Jerome Calkins Arena; Enlisted Aug. 27, 1861; Veteran, Corporal, Sgt., 1st Sgt.; Wounded Bayou Chache and Fort Blakely; Died June 27, 1865, Arena, Wis., of wounds.

Stephen Calkins Arena; Enlisted Aug. 27, 1861; Veteran; Wounded Blakely; Mustered out July 29, 1865.

Charles D. Cleaveland Cross Plains; Enlisted Sept. 13, 1861; Died July 11, 1862, Clarendon, Ark., disease.

Henry D. Crow Haney; Enlisted Dec. 21, 1863; From 33rd Wis. Inf.; Mustered out Sept. 4, 1865.

Festus Daily Cottage Grove; Enlisted Oct. 11, 1861; Killed May 22, 1863, Vicksburg, Miss.

Elijah T. Davis Scott; Enlisted Feb. 3, 1865; From 33rd Wis. Inf.; Mustered out Sept. 4, 1865.

Anthony Dever Baraboo; Enlisted Sept. 9, 1861; Discharged Dec. 11, 1862, disability.

Oscar H. Dilley Scott; Enlisted Feb. 3, 1865; From 33rd Wis. Inf.; Mustered out Sept. 4, 1865.

Bamford Dodge Arena; Enlisted Aug. 31, 1861; Veteran, Corporal; Wounded Blakely; Mustered out Sept. 4, 1865.

George M. Dodge Arena; Enlisted Sept. 8, 1861; Discharged Aug. 21, 1862, disability.

Jacob Dodge Arena; Enlisted Aug. 26, 1861; Corporal, Sgt.; trans. to V.R.C. Feb. 2, 1864.

Adolphus Eastman Leicester; Enlisted Sept. 6, 1861; Musician; Discharged Mar. 15, 1864, disability.

Joseph P. Endries Liberty; Enlisted Sept. 30, 1864; Drafted; Mustered out June 6, 1865.

Valentine Ewing Forest; Enlisted Feb. 28, 1865; Drafted; Mustered out Sept. 4, 1865.

John Fisher Clyman; Enlisted Oct. 6, 1864; Drafted; Mustered out Sept. 4, 1865.

Chauncey Fritz Bloom; Enlisted Feb. 28, 1865; Mustered out Sept. 4, 1865.

Michael Gallagher Cottage Grove; Enlisted Sept. 9, 1861; Discharged May 26, 1862, disability.

Samuel Gallagher Madison; Enlisted Sept. 30, 1861; Discharged Nov. 20, 1861, disability.

Silas Garthwait Kilbourn; Enlisted Sept. 6, 1861; From Co. H; Musician; Discharged Jan. 5, 1863, disability.

Thomas Gilbertson Arena; Enlisted Sept. 16, 1861; Died Nov. 6, 1862. St. Louis, Mo., disease.

Edward D. Gilson Sun Prairie; Enlisted Oct. 7, 1861; Died Nov. 17, 1862. Ironton, Mo., disease.

David Goess Cooperstown; Enlisted Mar. 10, 1865; Drafted; Aug. 1, 1862; Mustered out Sept. 4, 1865.

Charles H.B. Green Madison; Enlisted Oct. 2, 1861; Discharged Aug. 1, 1862, disability; re-enlisted Oct. 26, 1863; Discharged Mar. 14, 1865, disability.

John Griffin Forest; Enlisted Feb. 28, 1865; Drafted; Mustered out Sept. 4, 1865.

Romeo E. Hadley Forest; Enlisted Feb. 28, 1865; Drafted; absent sick at Mustered out of Regt.

B.F. Harmon Summit; Enlisted Mar. 2, 1863; Drafted; Mustered out Sept. 4, 1865.

Warren A. Hart Washington; Enlisted Sept. 11, 1861; Mustered out Nov. 18, 1864, term expired.

Warren Hathaway Arena; Enlisted Aug. 20, 1862; Discharged Nov. 11, 1862, disability.

Valentine Hay Empire; Enlisted Mar. 14, 1865; Mustered out Sept. 4, 1865.

William Hayden Sun Prairie; Enlisted Oct. 9, 1861; Corporal; Killed July 7, 1862, Bayou Cache, Ark.

Josiah Hazen Deerfield; Enlisted Sept. 11, 1861; Discharged July 26, 1862, disability.

Franz Herman Kossuth; Enlisted Mar. 10, 1865; Drafted; Mustered out Sept. 4, 1865.

Curtis Z. Hodgen Sugar Creek; Enlisted Feb. 9, 1864; Died Apr. 13, 1864, St. Louis, Mo., disease.

Daniel Holcomb Arena; Enlisted Aug. 31, 1861; Veteran; Mustered out July 29, 1865.

Frederick Hoppe Pierce; Enlisted Mar. 22, 1865; Mustered out Sept. 4, 1865.

Allen Huey Verona; Enlisted Sept. 20, 1861; Mustered out Nov. 18, 1864, term expired.

Charles B. Jacobs Dexter; Enlisted Oct. 22, 1861; Veteran, Corporal; Wounded Bayou Cache, Mustered out Sept. 4, 1865.

Joseph James Portland; Enlisted Mar. 20, 1865; Mustered out Aug. 31, 1865.

Isaac R. Jenks Utica; Enlisted Jan. 5, 1864; From 33rd Wis. Inf.; Mustered out Sept. 4, 1865.

Samuel Jenks Prairie Du Chien; Enlisted Sept. 30, 1861; Mustered out Nov. 18, 1864, term expired.

Gu—ck B. Johnson   Deerfield; Enlisted Sept. 11, 1861; Veteran; Corporal; Mustered out Sept. 4, 1865.

Sylvester W. Jones   Lyden; Enlisted Sept. 3, 1861; Wounded Bayou Cache; Discharged Nov. 24, 1862, of wounds.

George Kalb   Sun Prairie; Enlisted Sept. 13, 1861; Wounded Vicksburg; right arm amputated; Discharged; Died 5, 1863, disability.

Andrew Kanudson   Freeman; Enlisted Dec. 17, 1863; From 33rd Wis. Inf.; Mustered out Sept. 4, 1865.

Joseph Kastna   Cooperstown; Enlisted Sept. 29, 1864; Drafted; Mustered out June 6, 1865.

Christopher Kelling   Milwaukee; Enlisted Mar. 23, 1865; Drafted; absent sick at Mustered out of Regt.

James Kennedy   Henrietta; Enlisted Feb. 28, 1865; Drafted; Mustered out Sept. 4, 1865.

Joseph Klika   Cooperstown; Enlisted Mar. 27, 1865; Mustered out Sept. 4, 1865.

David Kocher   Sun Prairie; Enlisted Sept. 2, 1861; Wounded Vicksburg; Died July 7, 1863, Memphis, Tenn., of wounds.

Joseph Kozel   Carlton; Enlisted Dec. 29, 1864; Drafted; Mustered out Sept. 4, 1865.

Ferdinand Krohn   Ahnapee; Enlisted Mar. 27, 1865; Drafted; Mustered out Sept. 4, 1865.

Jaco Langennechard   Troy; Enlisted Sept. 16, 1861; Killed May 22, 1863, Vicksburg, Miss.

William E. Lockwood   Rutland; Enlisted Sept. 18, 1861; Discharged Mar. 4, 1863, disability.

Major J. Long   Venua; Enlisted Sept. 11, 1861; Discharged Oct. 28, 1861, by Civil Authority.

John A. Loveless   Forest; Enlisted Feb. 28, 1865; Drafted; Mustered out Sept. 4, 1865.

Edward J. Mabbott   Arena; Enlisted Sept. 12, 1861; Transferred to V.R.C. Mar. 15, 1864; Mustered out Oct. 10, 1864, term expired.

Daniel Mageean   Milwaukee; Enlisted Sept. 30, 1861; Veteran, Corporal; Wounded Blakely; Died Apr. 11, 1865, Blakely, Ala., of wounds.

William H. Mallow   Madison; Enlisted Oct. 12, 1861; Died Nov. 21, 1862, St. Louis, Mo., disease.

James Malory   New Castle, PA; Enlisted Oct. 22, 1861; Died Oct. 30, 1862, Ironton, Mo., disease.

John Marquette   Arena; Enlisted Sept. 2, 1861; Wounded Vicksburg; Died June 16, 1863, Memphis, Tenn., of wounds.

William H. Masterman   Arena; Enlisted Sept. 1, 1861; Corporal; Died Feb. 3, 1863, Van Buren, Mo., disease.

Henry M. May   Enlisted Nov. 6, 1861; Wounded Vicksburg; Died June 26, 1863, Hospital Boat of wounds.

Robert McCann   Richland Center; Enlisted Sept. 1, 1861; Veteran; Mustered out Sept. 4, 1865.

Jacob A. Michael   Sun Prairie; Enlisted Nov. 5, 1861; Killed May 22, 1863, Vicksburg, Miss.

Isaac Miles   Forest; Enlisted Feb. 28, 1865; Drafted; Mustered out Sept. 4, 1865.

Eleazer Moore   Sun Prairie; Enlisted Oct. 26, 1861; Wounded Vicksburg; pris. Sabine Cross Roads; Mustered out June 15, 1865, term expired.

Isaac Moore   Sun Prairie; Enlisted Oct. 9, 1861; Discharged Apr. 3, 1862, disability.

Frederick A. Morsback   Sauk City; Enlisted Sept. 21, 1861; Veteran; Mustered out Sept. 4, 1865.

Michael Murphey   Arena; Enlisted Sept. 10, 1861; Veteran; Died Apr. 6, 1864, Arena, Wis., disease.

James Nary   Arena; Enlisted Sept. 12, 1861; Wounded Vicksburg; Mustered out Nov. 18, 1864, term expired.

Leonard H. Parks   Arena; Enlisted Sept. 7, 1861; Veteran, Corporal, Sgt., 1st Sgt.; Wounded Bayou Cache and Vicksburg; Mustered out Sept. 4, 1865.

Samuel Partloe   Arena; Enlisted Sept. 16, 1861; Veteran; Wounded Blakely; Died May 18, 1865, New Orleans, La., of wounds.

Frank Paulu   Kewaunee; Enlisted Dec. 29, 1864; Drafted; Mustered out Sept. 4, 1865.

William H. Percinger   Richwood; Enlisted Feb. 3, 1865; From 33rd Wis. Inf.; Mustered out Sept. 4, 1865.

Isaac Phifer   Forest; Enlisted Feb. 28, 1865; Drafted; Mustered out Aug. 31, 1865.

John Pickett   Rock Elm; Enlisted Mar. 15, 1865; Mustered out Aug. 31, 1865.

William P. Price   Vienna; Enlisted Sept. 4, 1861; Prisoner Pocahontas, Ark.; Discharged Mar. 9, 1864, disability.

Benjamin W. Queen   Marshall; Enlisted Feb. 28, 1865; Drafted; Died Sept. 3, 1865, Mobile, Ala., disease.

John Ramsey   Milwaukee; Enlisted Mar. 7, 1865; Mustered out Sept. 4, 1865.

William Richard   Ahnapee; Enlisted Mar. 28, 1865; Drafted; Died Aug. 9, 1865, Mobile, Ala., disease.

Russell Richmond   Summit; Enlisted Sept. 22, 1864; Drafted; Mustered out June 6, 1865.

Calvin Rood   Sun Prairie; Enlisted Sept. 9, 1861; Died Aug. 22, 1862, Oldtown, Ark., disease.

John Rowe   Cottage Grove; Enlisted Sept. 19, 1861; Transferred to V.R.C., May 16, 1864.

Benedict Ruchti   Sececa; Enlisted Jan. 4, 1864; From 33rd Wis. Inf.; Mustered out Sept. 4, 1865.

Henry Russell   Seneca; Enlisted Jan. 4, 1864; From 33rd Wis. Inf.; Mustered out Sept. 4, 1865.

John Saenger   Milleville; Enlisted Nov. 19, 1863; From 33rd Wis. Inf.; Mustered out Sept. 4, 1865.

Evan Sanders   Brookfield; Enlisted Mar. 28, 1865; Mustered out Sept. 4, 1865.

Henry Sanders   Arena; Enlisted Sept. 8, 1862; Veteran; Mustered out June 6, 1865.

Thomas Saunders   Brookfield; Enlisted Mar. 28, 1865; Mustered out Sept. 4, 1865.

Carl Schneider   Pierce; Enlisted Oct. 3, 1864; Drafted; Mustered out Sept. 4, 1865.

Jacob Schultz   Berry; Enlisted Mar. 25, 1865;

Drafted; Died June 28, 1865, Montgomery, Ala., disease.

Adam Sechrest Two Rivers; Enlisted Mar. 10, 1865; Drafted; Mustered out Sept. 4, 1865.

Jacob Shadal Sun Prairie; Enlisted Oct. 21, 1861; Veteran; Wounded Bayou Cache; Discharged Oct. 20, 1864, disability.

Hugh Sharkey Madison; Enlisted Oct. 26, 1861; Veteran; Deserted Apr. 22, 1864.

Jeremiah Shay Arena; Enlisted Sept. 16, 1861; Died June 15, 1862, Arena, Wis., disease.

Samuel Showers Cross Plains; Enlisted Sept. 13, 1861; Veteran, Corporal; Mustered out Sept. 4, 1865.

Moses J. Smart Forest; Enlisted Feb. 28, 1865; Drafted; Mustered out Sept. 4, 1865.

John J. Smith Ridgeway; Enlisted Sept. 4, 1861; Veteran, Wagoner; Wounded Bayou Lombrau, La.; Mustered out Sept. 4, 1865.

William Smol Cross Plains; Enlisted Sept. 20, 1861; Died Nov. 7, 1863, Paoli, Wis., disease.

Hall Spink Mazomanie; Enlisted Oct. 26, 1861; Veteran, Musician; Mustered out Sept. 4, 1865.

Edward Sprecher Sun Prairie; Enlisted Sept. 4, 1861; Wagoner; Mustered out Nov. 18, 1864, term expired.

Hugh Stewart Mazomanie; Enlisted Oct. 21, 1861; Veteran, Corporal; Mustered out Sept. 4, 1865.

Samuel L.S. Stickle Cottage Grove; Enlisted Sept. 5, 1861; Corporal; Mustered out Nov. 18, 1864, term expired.

Alonzo L. Stroud Washington; Enlisted Sept. 10, 1861; Veteran; Wounded Vicksburg; Mustered out Sept. 4, 1865.

George W. Stroud Washington; Enlisted Sept. 10, 1861; Wounded Vicksburg; Died Aug. 11, 1863, St. Louis, Mo., of wounds.

William Stubbs Ahnapee; Enlisted Mar. 22, 1865; Drafted; Mustered out Sept. 4, 1865.

Thomas Tiernan Arena; Enlisted Sept. 10, 1861; Corporal; Wounded Vicksburg; Died June 26, 1863, Hospital Boat, of wounds.

Robert A. Tollard Cottage Grove; Enlisted Sept. 2, 1861; Killed Dec. 28, 1861, Sulpher Springs, Mo., accident.

James Tweedall Ahnapee; Enlisted Mar. 22, 1865; Drafted; Mustered out Sept. 4, 1865.

Stephen Weeks Bristol; Enlisted Feb. 2, 1865; Drafted; Mustered out Sept. 4, 1865.

John S. Welch Rockbridge; Enlisted Sept. 2, 1861; Veteran, Corporal; Wounded Bayou Cache; Mustered out Sept. 4, 1865.

Charles H. Wells Westport; Enlisted Sept. 11, 1861; Died Nov. 9, 1862, St. Louis, Mo., disease.

Merit Whitmore Fitchburg; Enlisted Sept. 12, 1861; Veteran, Corporal, Sgt.; Mustered out Sept. 4, 1865.

Alexander Wilkin Haney; Enlisted Aug. 21, 1862; From 33rd Wis. Inf.; Mustered out Sept. 4, 1865.

David Wingad Arena; Enlisted Sept. 20, 1861; Wounded Vicksburg; Mustered out Nov. 18, 1864, term expired.

Abraham Wolf Sun Prairie; Enlisted Oct. 26, 1861; Discharged Mar. 15, 1863, disability.

Christopher Wolf Theresa; Enlisted Mar. 22, 1865; Drafted; Died Aug. 6, 1865, Mobile, Ala., disease.

Hiram Wood Marietta; Enlisted Jan. 4, 1864; From 33rd Wis. Inf.; Mustered out Sept. 4, 1865.

Henry H. Woodcock Arena; Enlisted Sept. 12, 1861; Wounded Vicksburg; transferred to V.R.C., Feb. 2, 1864.

James Wooler Arena; Enlisted Sept. 16, 1861; Transferred to band, Oct. 20, 1861.

Mathew Zemmer Hartford; Enlisted Oct. 12, 1864; Drafted; Mustered out Sept. 4, 1865.

John Zeros Milwaukee; Enlisted Sept. 21, 1864; Drafted; Mustered out June 6, 1865.

Co. H — The "Dixon Guard"

Officers

Charles Allen 1st Lt.; Portage; Rank from July 13, 1863; Enlisted Sept. 3, 1861; Sgt.; 2nd Lt., June 18, 1862; Wounded Vicksburg; right foot amp.; resigned Jan. 11, 1864.

Alexander Chrystie Captain; Portage; Rank from Sept. 25, 1861; Wounded Bayou Cache, Ark and Black River Bridge; Prisoner Sept. 26, 1862; resigned Jan. 11, 1864.

William N. Gates 2nd Lt.; Orion; Rank from Sept. 1, 1865; Enlisted Oct. 21, 1861; Veteran, Corporal, Sgt., 1st Sgt.; Wounded Vicksburg; Mustered out Sept. 4, 1865.

Charles A. Johnson 1st Lt.; Portage; Rank from Dec. 10, 1864; Enlisted Oct. 21, 1861; Veteran, Corporal, Sgt., 1st Sgt.; Died July 5, 1865, Montgomery, Ala, of wounds.

John E. Lyon 1st Lt.; Friendship; Rank from July 29, 1865; Enlisted Sept. 9, 1861; Veteran, Corporal, Sgt., 1st Sgt.; Wounded Vicksburg; Mustered out Sept. 4, 1865.

Eli H. Mix 1st Lt.; Roche-a-Cri; Rank from Sept. 25, 1861; Resigned July 12, 1863; appt. 1st Lt. V.R.C. Feb. 6, 1864.

James O'Neil Captain; Caledonia; Rank from Dec. 10, 1864; Enlisted Sept. 3, 1861; Veteran, Corporal, Sgt., 1st Sgt.; 1st Lt., Apr. 27, 1864; Mustered out Sept. 4, 1865.

Issac J. Wright 2nd Lt.; Port Andrew; Rank from Oct. 24, 1861; Resigned. June 18, 1862.

Enlisted Men

Ephraim Ackerman Easton; Enlisted Sept. 5, 1861; Died Sept. 18, 1862, Oldtown, Ark., disease.

Cyrus Alexander Millville; Enlisted Oct. 7, 1861; Discharged Sept. 10, 1862, disability.

Harvey Almy Portage; Enlisted Sept. 26, 1861; Died Jan. 22, 1863, Alton, Mo., disease.

Samuel Almy Fairfield; Enlisted Oct. 25, 1861; Died Dec. 13, 1862, Ironton, Mo., disease.

Johnson Anderson Cambria; Enlisted Sept. 11, 1861; Died (date Unkown), buried Jefferson Barracks, Mo.

James Atkinson Port Andrew; Enlisted Oct. 21, 1861; Discharged Nov. 4, 1861, disability.

Austin A.C. Bacon Milwaukee; Enlisted Sept. 4, 1861; 1st Sgt.; Killed July 7, 1862, Bayou Cache, Ark.

Roswell Bacon Richford; Enlisted Oct. 10, 1864; Wounded Blakely; Died Apr. 12, 1865, Blakely, Ala., of wounds.

John Baker Paris; Enlisted Nov. 9, 1863; From 33rd Wis. Inf.; absent sick at Mustered out of Regt.

Harvey S. Barnes West Point; Enlisted Sept. 3, 1861; Musician; pris. Sept. 26, 1862; Discharged Jan. 28, 1863, disability.

Zachariah Barnes Port Andrew; Enlisted Mar. 17, 1862; Died Oct. 2, 1862, Cairo, Ill., disease.

John Barrett Roche-a-Cri; Enlisted Nov. 12, 1862; Deserted July 29, 1863.

I.N. Bassett Enlisted Dec. 28, 1864; Drafted; Mustered out Sept. 4, 1865.

Arthur A. Basye Clifton; Enlisted Dec. 30, 1863; From 33rd Wis. Inf.; Mustered out Sept. 4, 1865.

James Baty Hixton; Enlisted Oct. 10, 1864; Mustered out Sept. 4, 1865.

Edwin Bauer Sauk; Enlisted Feb. 12, 1864; Mustered out Sept. 4, 1865.

Jacob Bauer Portage; Enlisted Sept. 20, 1864; Mustered out Sept. 4, 1865.

Cyrus Benjamin Preston; Enlisted Oct. 7, 1861; Transferred to Co. I, Nov. 1, 1861.

Benjamin P. Benson Port Andrew; Enlisted Oct. 15, 1861; Corporal; Wounded Bayou Cache; Died July 20, 1862, St. Louis, Mo., of wounds.

Alonzo Bidwell Easton; Enlisted Sept. 20, 1861; Discharged Mar. 14, 1863.

Erasmus Bidwell Easton; Enlisted Oct. 13, 1861; Wounded Bayou Cache; Died Nov. 25, 1862, Patterson, Mo., disease.

William Bike Merrimack; Enlisted Feb. 12, 1864; Mustered out Sept. 4, 1865.

Vernon V. Bishop Millville; Enlisted Oct. 7, 1861; Deserted Mar. 16, 1863.

Carlisle Blakely Forest; Enlisted Mar. 18, 1865; Mustered out May 30, 1865.

Henry C. Blaker Merrimack; Enlisted Sept. 3, 1861; Veteran, Corporal; Wounded Blakely; Mustered out July 22, 1865.

William Blocksage Racine; Enlisted Nov. 4, 1862; From 33rd Wis. Inf; Mustered out Sept. 4, 1865.

Melancthon Bohanan Paris; Enlisted Mar. 2, 1864; From 33rd Wis. Inf.; Died Mar. 29, 1864, Madison, Wis., disease.

Frederick Bowers Merrimack; Enlisted Sept. 3, 1861; Wounded Vicksburg; Mustered out Nov. 18, 1864, term expired.

James P. Bridge Roche-a-Cri; Enlisted Oct. 29, 1862; Died Aug. 21, 1863, Cairo, Ill., disease.

John W. Brisbois Portage; Enlisted Sept. 3, 1861; Corporal; Discharged July 27, 1862, disability.

William H. Brower Green Bay; Enlisted Dec. 28, 1864; Drafted; Mustered out July 29, 1865.

Balthaser Brown Sauk City; Enlisted Sept. 3, 1861; Veteran, Corporal; Mustered out Sept. 4, 1865.

David Brown Douglas; Enlisted Oct. 8, 1864; Mustered out June 21, 1865.

Henry S. Brown Port Andrew; Enlisted Oct. 15, 1861; Mustered out Nov. 18, 1864, term expired.

Charles Bruneohler Portage; Enlisted Sept. 3, 1861; Corporal, Sgt.; Killed May 22, 1863, Vicksburg, Miss.

Joseph M. Burton Trafton; Enlisted Jan. 16, 1864; From 33rd Wis. Inf.; Mustered out Sept. 4, 1865.

Ithamar S. Chaffee Richford; Enlisted Oct. 10, 1864; Mustered out Sept. 4, 1865.

Thomas Chamberlain Lincoln; Enlisted Sept. 16, 1861; Discharged Dec. 10, 1862, disability.

Titus B. Chapman Fairfield; Enlisted Sept. 9, 1861; Died Apr. 5, 1863, Fairfield, Wis., disease.

John M. Church Millville; Enlisted Oct. 7, 1861; Discharged Dec. 15, 1863, disability.

Robert Clark Port Andrew; Enlisted Oct. 21, 1861; Mustered out Nov. 18, 1864, term expired.

John H. Clary Boscobel; Enlisted Feb. 28, 1865; Drafted; Never joined Co.

Amos Colburn Merrimack; Enlisted Sept. 3, 1864; Died Feb. 1, 1862, Cole's Bridge, Mo., disease.

Frank A. Colburn Kilbourn City; Enlisted Oct. 12, 1864; Mustered out Sept. 5, 1865.

Henry Cook Milwaukee; Enlisted Mar. 15, 1865; Drafted; Never joined Co.

Michael Cook Port Andrew; Enlisted Oct. 26, 1861; Transferred to Co. I, Nov. 1, 1861.

John N. Coon Douglas; Enlisted Oct. 8, 1864; Mustered out Sept. 4, 1865.

John M. Core Port Andrew; Enlisted Oct. 26, 1861; Transferred to Co. I, Nov. 1, 1861.

George W. Coville Warren; Enlisted Feb. 27, 1864; From 33rd Wis. Inf.; Mustered out Sept. 4, 1865.

John B. Cowing Roche-a-Cri; Enlisted Sept. 15, 1861; Wounded Vicksburg; Mustered out Nov. 18, 1864, term. expired.

Charles A. Cox Troy; Enlisted Feb. 6, 1864; Mustered out Sept. 4, 1865.

Andrew M. Crane Douglas; Enlisted Sept. 3, 1861; Discharged Aug. 7, 1862, disability.

Robert G. Crubaugh Millville; Enlisted Oct. 1, 1861; Veteran, Corporal; Mustered out Sept. 4, 1865.

Milo E. Davis Merrimack; Enlisted Aug. 28, 1861; Discharged Apr. 8, 1863, disability.

John H. Delap Millville; Enlisted Oct. 14, 1861; Discharged Apr. 8, 1863, disability.

William A. Delap Millville; Enlisted Oct. 14,

1861; Veteran; Died Sept. 13, 1864, Brashear City, La., disease.

Noah Densmore Merrimack; Enlisted Sept. 3, 1861; Discharged Nov. 5, 1861, disability.

John Deven Madison; Enlisted Nov. 4, 1861; Discharged Mar. 8, 1863, disability.

John Dever Merrimack; Enlisted Sept. 3, 1861; Veteran, Corporal; Mustered out Sept. 4, 1865.

Mahlon Dewing White Creek; Enlisted Sept. 20, 1861; Veteran, Corporal; pris. Friars Pt.; Mustered out Sept. 4, 1865.

James S. Dickinson Friendship; Enlisted Sept. 3, 1861; Veteran, Corporal; Wounded Bayou Cache; Mustered out Sept. 4, 1865.

Jeremiah D. Dingman Port Andrew; Enlisted Oct. 21, 1861; Mustered out Nov. 18, 1864, term expired.

Frank O. Douglass Portage; Enlisted Oct. 21, 1861; Discharged Apr. 4, 1863, disability.

Joseph H. Douglass Lowell; Enlisted Mar. 20, 1865; Drafted; Mustered out Aug. 4, 1865.

Patrick Downey Portage; Enlisted Oct. 21, 1861; Discharged Jan. 6, 1864, disability; Died Feb. 17, 1864, Mound City, Ill. .

Barney W. Doyle Milwaukee; Enlisted Sept. 3, 1861; Discharged Jan. 16, 1863, disability.

Stephen D. Duel Portage; Enlisted Oct. 3, 1861; Transferred to Co. I, Nov. 1, 1861.

Sylvester Eastman Ft. Winnebago; Enlisted Sept. 19, 1861; From Principal Musician; Veteran; Promoted Principal Musician, Aug. 1, 1864. .

Deroy Eaton White Creek; Enlisted Sept. 25, 1864; Mustered out Sept. 4, 1865.

Dewitt Eaton White Creek; Enlisted Sept. 25, 1864; Mustered out Sept. 4, 1865.

Thomas R. Edmonds Portage; Enlisted Sept. 22, 1861; Wounded Port Gibson; trans. to V.R.C., Feb. 15, 1864; Mustered out Nov. 18, 1864; term expired.

Lewis B. Edwards Cassville; Enlisted Feb. 6, 1864; From 33rd Wis. Inf.; Mustered out Sept. 4, 1865.

Hilarius Ehr Lewiston; Enlisted Oct. 18, 1864; Mustered out Sept. 4, 1865.

Nicholas Ehr Lewiston; Enlisted Oct. 19, 1864; Mustered out Sept. 4, 1865.

Warren Emerick Douglas; Enlisted Oct. 8, 1864; Mustered out Sept. 4, 1865.

Thompson Emerson Packwaukee; Enlisted Oct. 20, 1864; Wounded Blakely; Mustered out May 27, 1865.

George W. Faith Port Andrew; Enlisted Oct. 19, 1861; Died Sept. 3, 1862, St. Louis, Mo., disease.

Henderson Faith Port Andrew; Enlisted Oct. 26, 1861; Wounded Bayou Cache; Discharged Oct. 27, 1862, disability.

John Faith Port Andrew; Enlisted Oct. 19, 1861; Died Oct. 31, 1862, Acadia, Mo., disease.

Nathan Farnsworth Merrimack; Enlisted Feb. 12, 1864; Wounded Blakely; Mustered out June 5, 1865.

Mahlon Fawcett Platteville; Enlisted Dec. 30, 1863; From 33rd Wis. Inf.; Mustered out Sept. 4, 1865.

William Fay Preston; Enlisted Sept. 3, 1861; Corporal; Wounded Vicksburg; Died May 28, 1863, Vicksburg, Miss., of wounds.

Alexander Ferber Sauk City; Enlisted Sept. 3, 1861; Veteran, Corporal, Sgt.; Wounded Blakely; Mustered out Sept. 4, 1865.

Bartholomew Ferber Sauk City; Enlisted Sept. 2, 1864; Wounded Blakely, Ala.; Mustered out June 19, 1865, by order.

George E. Finton Rio; Enlisted Sept. 3, 1861; Transferred to Co. I, Nov. 1, 1861.

Robert Fisher Milwaukee; Enlisted Mar. 30, 1865; Never joined Co.

Leonard M. Foster Sylvester; Enlisted Sept. 28, 1864; Mustered out Sept. 4, 1865.

Daniel E. Frazier Madison; Enlisted Feb. 27, 1864; From 33rd Wis. Inf.; Mustered out Sept. 4, 1865.

Silas Garthwait White Creek; Enlisted Sept. 5, 1861; Musician; transferred to Co. G, Nov. 12, 1861.

Mark Geodrich Boscobel; Enlisted Dec. 11, 1863; From 33rd Wis. Inf.; Mustered out Sept. 4, 1865.

Charles George Portage; Enlisted Sept. 3, 1861; Discharged Dec. 1, 1862.

Wilibolt Gnudig Portage; Enlisted Sept. 27, 1861; Wounded Vicksburg; Mustered out Nov. 18, 1864. .

George Gray Port Andrew; Enlisted Oct. 19, 1861; Sgt., 1st Sgt.; Discharged Dec. 4, 1862, disability.

Silas W. Green Portage; Enlisted Sept. 13, 1861; Discharged Nov. 18, 1862, disability.

Nathaniel Grim Boscobel; Enlisted Feb. 28, 1865; Drafted; Discharged Aug. 18, 1865, disability.

Charles W. Grimsey Millville; Enlisted Sept. 28, 1861; Corporal, Sgt.; Discharged Oct. 1, 1862, disability.

Fred L. Grow Friendship; Enlisted Sept. 3, 1861; Sgt.; prom 2nd Lt. Co K, 25th Wis. Inf., Aug. 11, 1862.

William B. Hailings Port Andrew; Enlisted Sept. 5, 1861; Wounded Vicksburg; Mustered out Nov. 18, 1864, term expired.

Adam Halbman Merrimack; Enlisted Feb. 3, 1864; Mustered out Sept. 4, 1865.

Otis Hall Newton; Enlisted Oct. 10, 1864; Absent sick at Mustered out of Regt.

Thomas H. Hancock Tomah; Enlisted Mar. 30, 1864; Mustered out Aug. 31, 1865.

James R. Haney Port Andrew; Enlisted Oct. 22, 1861; Discharged Nov. 5, 1861, disability.

John W. Haney Port Andrew; Enlisted Oct. 21, 1861; Wounded Bayou Cache; trans. to V.R.C., Aug. 14, 1863.

William Hanks Paris; Enlisted Feb. 20, 1864; From 33rd Wis. Inf.; Mustered out Aug. 16, 1865.

Joel A. Harris Cottage Grove; Enlisted Sept. 20, 1864; Mustered out June 8, 1865.

Festus U. Hartson Randolph; Enlisted Sept. 13, 1861; Killed May 1, 1863, Port Gibson, Miss.

William Hasson West Point; Enlisted Sept. 3, 1861; Discharged Nov. 1, 1862, disability.

Albert T. Henderson Fennimore; Enlisted Dec. 30, 1862; From 33rd Wis. Inf.; Mustered out June 14, 1865.

Gottleib Hoefs Lewiston; Enlisted Oct. 19, 1864; Mustered out Sept. 4, 1865.

James Hofus Enlisted Oct. 26, 1861; Discharged Nov. 5, 1861, disability.

Frederick Holzinger Merrimack; Enlisted Feb. 25, 1864; Mustered out Sept. 4, 1865.

Charles E. Hollenbeck Lincoln; Enlisted Oct. 20, 1864; Mustered out Sept. 4, 1865.

Robert Hornby Fairfield; Enlisted Sept. 9, 1861; Died Nov. 4, 1862, Mound City, Ill., disease.

James Hughbanks Port Andrew; Enlisted Oct. 19, 1861; Corporal; Wounded Vicksburg; Died May 31, 1863, Vicksburg, Miss., of wounds.

John Hughbanks Port Andrew; Enlisted Oct. 19, 1861; Veteran; Wagoner, Mustered out Sept. 4, 1865.

Thomas Hyland Lowell; Enlisted Mar. 3, 1865; Absent sick at Mustered out of Regt.

James F. Jacobus White Creek; Enlisted Sept. 28, 1861; Corporal; Mustered out Nov. 18, 1864, term expired.

William H. Jacobus White Creek; Enlisted Sept. 20, 1861; Sgt., 1st Sgt.; Wounded Vicksburg; Died May 27, 1863, Vicksburg, Miss., of wounds. .

Benajah Johnson Portage; Enlisted Sept. 11, 1861; Prisoner Sabine Cross Roads. Mustered out Aug. 16, 1865.

John E. Jones Kingston; Enlisted Sept. 13, 1861; Died Aug. 12, 1862, Oldtown, Ark., disease.

Thomas R. Jones Port Andrew; Enlisted Oct. 23, 1861; Discharged Feb. 26, 1863, disability.

John Kehoe Enlisted Oct. 27, 1861; Discharged Nov. 13, 1861, civil authority.

William Kent Portage City; Enlisted Sept. 3, 1861; Wounded Vicksburg; Died June 4, 1863, Memphis, Tenn., of wounds.

Andrew W. Kerr Packwaukee; Enlisted Oct. 31, 1864; Mustered out July 15, 1865.

Joseph S. Kerr Portage; Enlisted Sept. 17, 1861; Wounded Vicksburg; Died Nov. 1, 1863, on cars near Chicago, Ill.

William Kerr Packwaukee; Enlisted Oct. 31, 1864; Mustered out Sept. 4, 1865.

David H. King Salem; Enlisted Dec. 5, 1863; From 33rd Wis. Inf; Mustered out Sept. 4, 1865.

Friedrich Koch Lewiston; Enlisted Oct. 18, 1864; Mustered out Sept. 4, 1865.

Augustus Kufner Harrison; Enlisted Mar. 2, 1865; Drafted; Mustered out July 29, 1865.

Frederick Langdon Randolph; Enlisted Sept. 17, 1861; Died July 2, 1862, Picket's farm, Ark., disease.

John L. Lavine Portage; Enlisted Sept. 3, 1861; Veteran, Corporal, Sgt.; Wounded Bayou Cache; Mustered out Sept 4, 1865.

James Lee Briggsville; Enlisted Sept. 26, 1861; Discharged Mar. 28, 1862, disability.

Joseph Lee Briggsville; Enlisted Oct. 25, 1864; Wounded Blakely; Mustered out June 5, 1865.

August Lockman Howard; Enlisted Dec. 28, 1864; Drafted; Mustered out Sept. 4, 1865.

George E. Logue Port Andrew; Enlisted Oct. 28, 1861; Transferred to Co. I, Nov. 1, 1861.

James E. Lum Melville; Enlisted Oct. 14, 1861; Discharged Oct. 13, 1863, disability.

John Lyon Tafton; Enlisted Jan. 5, 1864; From 33rd Wis. Inf.; Mustered out Sept. 4, 1865.

Orville B. Lyon Friendship; Enlisted Oct. 28, 1861; Wounded Bayou Cache; Discharged Dec. 16, 1862, disability.

Thomas C. Maley Boscobel; Enlisted Nov. 18, 1863; From 33rd Wis. Inf.; Mustered out Sept. 4, 1865.

John Martain Tafton; Enlisted Jan. 6, 1864; From 33rd Wis. Inf.; Mustered out Sept. 4, 1865.

James F. Mason Fordon; Enlisted Sept. 1, 1861; Veteran; Wounded Vicksburg; Mustered out Sept. 4, 1865.

Charles P. Mathews Paris; Enlisted Dec. 16, 1863; From 33rd Wis. Inf.; Mustered out Sept. 4, 1865.

James McDonald Glen Haven; Enlisted Jan. 5, 1864; From 33rd Wis. Inf.; Mustered out Sept. 4, 1865.

William McElroy Ft. Winnebago; Enlisted Sept. 6, 1861; Died Jan. 26, 1863, Van Buren, Mo.

Alonzo C. Miller Port Andrew; Enlisted Oct. 21, 1861; Died Aug. 10, 1862, St. Louis, Mo., disease.

Ansil Miller Fredericksburg, Mo; Enlisted Mar. 21, 1862; Mustered out Mar. 24, 1865, term expired.

Joseph Minis Salem; Enlisted Dec. 5, 1863; From 33rd Wis. Inf.; Mustered out Sept. 4, 1865.

Sebastian Morris Prairie Du Chien; Enlisted Nov. 30, 1863; From 33rd Wis. Inf.; Mustered out Sept. 4, 1865.

Gideon W. Mott Newton; Enlisted Oct. 10, 1864; Mustered out Sept. 4, 1865.

Walter Motter Port Andrew; Enlisted Oct. 8, 1861; Died Nov. 8, 1862, Ironton, Mo., disease.

Allen H. Mumford Millville; Enlisted Oct. 7, 1861; Veteran, Corporal, Sgt.; Mustered out Sept. 2, 1865.

Frank Munn Roche-a-Cri; Enlisted Sept. 25, 1861; Discharged Nov. 19, 1862, disability.

Robert Murray Caledonia; Enlisted Sept. 3, 1861; Wounded Bayou Cache; Discharged Feb. 16, 1863, disability.

Henry Myers Kenosha; Enlisted Mar. 20, 1863; From 33rd Wis. Inf.; Mustered out Sept. 4, 1865.

James P. Myers Oak Grove; Enlisted Sept. 26, 1864; Mustered out June 14, 1865.

George W. Nevel Richland Center; Enlisted Feb. 28, 1865; Drafted; Mustered out Aug. 31, 1865.

William Newkirk Boscobel; Enlisted Feb. 28, 1865; Drafted; Mustered out Aug. 16, 1865.

William P. Newman Poynette; Enlisted Sept. 18, 1861; Died July 7, 1862, Cache River, Ark., disease.

Andrew J. Nutting Richford; Enlisted Oct. 10, 1864; Mustered out July 6, 1865.

Ole Oleson Port Andrew; Enlisted Oct. 26, 1861; Transferred to Co. I, Nov. 1, 1861.

Darius H. Olmstead White Creek; Enlisted Sept. 22, 1861; Died Oct. 9, 1864, Brashear City, La., disease.

Samuel H. Osmond Port Andrew; Enlisted Oct. 28, 1861; Discharged Nov. 5, 1861, disability.

George Parsons Merrimack; Enlisted Sept. 3, 1861; Corporal, Sgt.; Died Dec. 1, 1862, Ironton, Mo., disease.

James W. Perkins New Chester; Enlisted Sept. 6, 1861; Veteran, Corporal, Sgt.; Mustered out Sept. 4, 1865.

Eugene S. Pettis Str'ng's Prairie; Enlisted Oct. 13, 1861; Discharged Sept. 20, 1862, disability.

Rufus C. Phillips Jackson; Enlisted Sept. 6, 1861; Corporal, Sgt.; Died Dec. 10, 1862, Jackson, Wis.

Martin Pickett White Creek; Enlisted Sept. 25, 1864; Mustered out Sept. 4, 1865.

Orion Pickett White Creek; Enlisted Sept. 25, 1864; Mustered out May 29, 1865.

Horace N. Polley West Point; Enlisted Oct. 24, 1861; Veteran; Promoted Principal Musician, Feb. 13, 1864.

Clinton H. Porter Richford; Enlisted Oct. 14, 1861; Wounded Blakely; Mustered out May 27, 1865, G.O. 48.

Hiram Porter Fairfield; Enlisted Sept. 9, 1861; Died Aug. 20, 1862, Oldtown, Ark., disease.

Gerald O. Potter Richford; Enlisted Oct. 10, 1864; Mustered out Sept. 4, 1865.

William H. Powderly Ft. Winnebago; Enlisted Sept. 3, 1861; Wounded Bayou Cache; Died July 10, 1862, Clarendon, Ark., of wounds.

Morse Powell Stark; Enlisted Nov. 15, 1864; Drafted; Mustered out Sept. 4, 1865.

Samuel M. Quaw Friendship; Enlisted Oct. 13, 1861; Mustered out Nov. 18, 1864, term expired.

Thomas Quinn Wyalusing; Enlisted Jan. 23, 1864; From 33rd Wis. Inf.; Mustered out Sept. 4, 1865.

Royal F. Randall Merrimack; Enlisted Oct. 27, 1861; Prisoner Firar's Point, Miss.; Mustered out Nov. 18, 1864, term expired.

Henry H. Ray Platteville; Enlisted Jan. 18, 1865; Mustered out Sept. 4, 1865.

Stephen B. Rice Millville; Enlisted Oct. 14, 1861; Corporal; Wounded Port Gibson; trans. to V.R.C., Sept. 28, 1864; Mustered out Oct. 27, 1864, term expired.

William L. Richards Glen Haven; Enlisted Feb. 29, 1864; From 33rd Wis. Inf.; Mustered out Sept. 4, 1865.

Gurshum Richardson Friendship; Enlisted Sept. 5, 1861; Died July 19, 1862, Cairo, Ill., disease.

Phillip Richardson Friendship; Enlisted Sept. 3, 1861; Died Sept. 27, 1862, Oldtown, Ark., disease.

William Risk White Creek; Enlisted Sept. 5, 1861; Mustered out Nov. 18, 1864, term, expired.

Oliver S. Robinson Port Andrew; Enlisted Oct. 21, 1861; Wounded Vicksburg; Died May 30, 1863, Vicksburg, Miss., of wounds.

Thomas W. St. John Port Andrew; Enlisted Oct. 19, 1861; Discharged Mar. 13, 1862, disability.

Reuben G. Sawyer Richford; Enlisted Oct. 10, 1864; Died Apr. 27, 1865, New York, NY., disease.

John Seavy Douglass; Enlisted Oct. 10, 1864; Discharged May 27, 1865, disability; Died Apr. 10, 1865, Mound City, Ill.

Gottfried Seiler Lewiston; Enlisted Sept. 20, 1864; Mustered out Sept. 4, 1865.

Horace Sheldon White Creek; Enlisted Sept. 25, 1861; Wounded Port Gibson; Died May 31, 1863, Grand Gulf, Miss., of wounds.

Thomas Singleton Portage; Enlisted Sept. 25, 1861; Discharged Nov. 5, 1863, disability.

Samuel Slack Ridgeway; Enlisted Mar. 29, 1864; Mustered out Sept. 4, 1865.

Charles W. Smith Paris; Enlisted Jan. 8, 1864; From 33rd Wis. Inf.; Mustered out Sept. 4, 1865.

George H. Smith Somers; Enlisted Nov. 7, 1863; From 33rd Wis. Inf.; Mustered out Sept. 4, 1865.

James H. Smith West Troy; Enlisted Feb. 6, 1864; Mustered out Sept. 4, 1865.

Isaac B. Snider Glen Haven; Enlisted Jan. 4, 1864; From 33rd Wis. Inf.; Mustered out May 10, 1865.

Orlando T. Sowie Jackson; Enlisted Jan. 10, 1864; Promoted 2nd Lt. Co. D, 51st Wis. Inf., Feb. 22, 1865.

James F. Spalding Richford; Enlisted Oct. 14, 1864; Mustered out Sept. 4, 1865.

Bradshaw Stearns New Chester; Enlisted Sept. 6, 1861; Corporal, Sgt.; Mustered out Nov. 16, 1864, term expired.

Joel Stout Bloom; Enlisted Feb. 28, 1865; Drafted; Died July 11, 1865, Jefferson Barracks, Mo., disease, never joined co.

Andrew Sullivan Milwaukee; Enlisted Oct. 6, 1864; Absent sick at Mustered out of Regt.

John Sullivan Milwaukee; Enlisted Dec. 2, 1864; Never joined Co.

Austin P. Sutton Port Andrew; Enlisted Oct. 21, 1861; Discharged Mar. 13, 1862, disability.

George W. Swires Clifton; Enlisted Dec. 30, 1863; From 33rd Wis. Inf.; Mustered out Sept. 4, 1865.

Joshua Taylor Port Andrew; Enlisted Oct. 26, 1861; Discharged Mar. 22, 1863, disability.

William H. Taylor Port Andrew; Enlisted Oct. 21, 1861; Transferred to V.R.C., Aug. 14, 1863.

Hermon N. Wadsworth Portage; Enlisted Oct. 14, 1864; Mustered out June 19, 1865.

James Wafer Menomonie; Enlisted Mar. 10, 1865; Never joined Co.

Ludwig Wagner Lewiston; Enlisted Oct. 19, 1864; Mustered out Sept. 4, 1865.

Wiley H. Walter Port Andrew; Enlisted Oct. 21, 1861; Veteran; Mustered out May 31, 1865.

Addison Warren Sugar Creek; Enlisted Feb. 16, 1864; Discharged July 1, 1865, disability.

David I. Washburn Millville; Enlisted Oct. 7, 1861; Corporal; Died Nov. 13, 1862, Ironton, Mo., disease.

Francis E. Washburn Kenosha; Enlisted Jan. 5, 1864; From 33rd Wis. Inf.; Mustered out Sept. 4, 1865.

Orison Washburn Millville; Enlisted Oct. 7, 1861; Died Nov. 9, 1862, Ironton, Mo., disease.

Edgar C. Wheelock Madison; Enlisted Jan. 2, 1864; Died Nov. 29, 1864, Brashear City, La., disease.

Rufus Whitcomb Port Andrew; Enlisted Oct. 26, 1861; Deserted Nov. 14, 1862.

Christian White Wingville; Enlisted Dec. 8, 1863; From 33rd Wis. Inf.; Deserted.

John Williams Packwaukee; Enlisted Oct. 31, 1864; Mustered out Sept. 4, 1865.

Mark Williams Enlisted Sept. 18, 1864; Drafted; Never joined Co.

Gottleib Windus Lewiston; Enlisted Oct. 18, 1864; Wounded Blakely; Discharged Aug. 22, 1865, of wounds.

Joel B. Wright New Chester; Enlisted Oct. 22, 1861; Veteran; Promoted Hospital Steward, June 22, 1865.

Abram Yeomans Portage; Enlisted Oct. 19, 1864; Mustered out Sept. 2, 1865.

Co. I — The "Fox River Zouaves"

Officers

Allen J. Whittier Captain; Markesan; Rank from Oct. 8, 1861; Enlisted Sept. 1, 1861; res. Feb. 18, 1864.

Nelson R. Doan Captain; Rutland; Rank from Mar. 22, 1864; Enlisted Oct. 18, 1861; Veteran, 1st Sgt.; 2nd Lt., Mar. 8, 1862; 1st Lt., Nov. 12, 1863; Wounded Bayou Cache; Mustered out Sept. 4, 1865.

Dewitt C. Benham 1st Lt.; Berlin; Rank from Oct. 8, 1861; Enlisted Aug. 11, 1861; res. Mar. 7, 1862.

Jerome Chesebro 1st Lt.; Markesan; Rank from Mar. 8, 1862; 2nd Lt., Oct. 8, 1861; Died May 3, 1863.

Henry C. Welcome 1st Lt.; Markesan; Rank from Mar. 22, 1864; Enlisted Sept. 20, 1861; Veteran, 1st Sgt.; Mustered out Sept. 4, 1865.

Harvey H. Hopkins 2nd Lt.; Princeton; Rank from Sept. 1, 1865; Enlisted Oct. 5, 1861; Veteran, Sgt., 1st Sgt.; Wounded Bayou Cache; Mustered out Sept. 4, 1865.

Enlisted Men

Joseph Angel Unadilla, Mich; Enlisted Oct. 6, 1861; Discharged Jan. 7, 1864, disability.

Henry W. Bailey Aurora; Enlisted Oct. 4, 1861; Died Feb. 23, 1863, Ironton, Mo., disease.

Samuel Barrett Madison; Enlisted Nov. 19, 1861; Discharged Dec. 12, 1862, disability.

James S. Bedient Berlin; Enlisted Sept. 10, 1861; Wounded Bayou Cache; Died Aug. 16, 1862, Oldtown, Ark., disease.

Samuel C. Benjamin Friendship; Enlisted Oct. 29, 1861; Veteran; Wounded Bayou Cache; Mustered out Sept. 4, 1865.

Charles W. Benlen Aurora; Enlisted Sept. 10, 1861; Died Feb. 13, 1862, Sulpher Springs, Mo., disease.

James H. Benlen Aurora; Enlisted Sept. 23, 1861; Mustered out Nov. 18, 1864, term expired.

Chauncy F. Boylan Princeton; Enlisted Nov. 6, 1861; Veteran; Mustered out Sept. 4, 1865.

Hudson L. Boylan Markesan; Enlisted Oct. 5, 1861; Veteran; Mustered out Sept. 4, 1865.

John D. Burns Markesan; Enlisted Aug. 25, 1862; Vet; Mustered out June 5, 1865.

Theodore Button Kenosha; Enlisted Dec. 1, 1863; From 33rd Wis. Inf.; Mustered out Sept. 4, 1865.

Michael Campbell Port Andrew; Enlisted Nov. 16, 1861; Veteran; Mustered out Sept. 4, 1865.

Robert Carr Enlisted Nov. 5, 1861; Deserted Apr. 6, 1862.

Timothy Carr Princeton; Enlisted Sept. 30, 1864; Died Sept. 1, 1865, Mobile, Ala.

Franklin B. Carter Warren; Enlisted Sept. 30, 1861; Transferred to V.R.C., Feb. 10, 1864.

George W. Chesebro Markesan; Enlisted Jan. 21, 1861; Veteran, Corporal; Mustered out Sept. 4, 1865.

Mason Chesebro Markesan; Enlisted Jan. 31, 1865; Mustered out Sept. 4, 1865.

Leroy W. Chipman Warren; Enlisted Sept. 20, 1861; Mustered out Nov. 18, 1864, term expired.

Theodore S. Chipman Warren; Enlisted Sept. 16, 1861; 1st Sgt.; Mustered out Nov. 18, 1864, term expired.

Hiram C. Cobbett Markesan; Enlisted Oct. 4, 1861; Musician; Died Jan. 10, 1862, Sulpher Springs, Mo., disease.

Dewitt Cole Lomira; Enlisted Mar. 22, 1865; Drafted; Mustered out Sept. 4, 1865.

Michael Cook Port Andrew; Enlisted Oct. 31, 1861; Discharged Aug. 16, 1862, disability.

Nelson Cook Mackford; Enlisted Feb. 9, 1865; Mustered out Sept. 4, 1865.

William W. Coon Berlin; Enlisted Sept. 10, 1861; Wounded Bayou Cache; Mustered out Nov. 18, 1864, term expired.

William H. Cope Colebrook; Enlisted Oct. 30, 1861; Mustered out Nov. 18, 1864, term expired.

John M. Core Port Andrew; Enlisted Oct. 30, 1861; Discharged Dec. 25, 1861, disability.

Joseph Cox Woodland; Enlisted Mar. 20, 1865; Drafted; Mustered out Sept. 4, 1865.

Dennis Crawley Sevastopol; Enlisted Mar. 23, 1865; Drafted; Mustered out Sept. 4, 1865.

James M. Crook Berlin; Enlisted Oct. 7, 1861; Veteran; Wounded Mar. 28, 1862, accident; Mustered out Sept. 4, 1865.

Moses E. Crown Markesan; Enlisted Sept. 20, 1861; Veteran, Corporal; Mustered out Sept. 4, 1865.

Merritt H. Day Markesan; Enlisted Sept. 18, 1861; Veteran, Corporal; Wounded Port Gibson; Mustered out Sept. 4, 1865.

George W. Decker Berlin; Enlisted Sept. 16, 1861; Discharged Dec. 28, 1862, disability.

Henry C. Decker Berlin; Enlisted Oct. 4, 1861; Discharged Oct. 26, 1861, disability.

Joseph Dickerson Randolph; Enlisted Sept. 20, 1861; Discharged Dec. 6, 1862, disability.

Thomas C. Dixon Randolph; Enlisted Sept. 20, 1861; Discharged Nov. 6, 1862, disability.

Francis W. Downs Markesan; Enlisted Sept. 18, 1861; Discharged Nov. 6, 1862, disability.

Stephen D. Duel Enlisted Oct. 4, 1861; Veteran; Mustered out Sept. 4, 1865.

Philander Edwards Markesan; Enlisted Jan. 31, 1865; Died July 20, 1865, Montgomery, Ala., disease.

Joshua Eldred Aurora; Enlisted Sept. 10, 1861; Discharged Oct. 31, 1861, disability.

Melvin Estabrook Aurora; Enlisted Sept. 10, 1861; Veteran; Mustered out Sept. 4, 1865.

Peter Everson Aurora; Enlisted Oct. 10, 1861; Wounded Bayou Cache; Discharged Oct. 21, 1862, disability.

Edward G. Finton Enlisted Oct. 4, 1861; Prisoner Sabine Cross Roads; Mustered out Nov. 18, 1864, term expired.

John Fox Centerville; Enlisted Mar. 11, 1865; Drafted; Mustered out Sept. 4, 1865.

Martin V. Francisco Maion; Enlisted Sept. 30, 1861; Veteran; Mustered out Sept. 4, 1865.

Charles H. Frank Princeton; Enlisted Oct. 1, 1861; Discharged Oct. 10, 1862, disability.

William J. Frank Madison; Enlisted Feb. 8, 1865; Mustered out Sept. 4, 1865.

James B. Frisby Marquette; Enlisted Nov. 21, 1862; Mustered out Sept. 4, 1865.

Abraham Good Woodland; Enlisted Mar. 20, 1865; Drafted; Mustered out Aug. 30, 1865.

Joseph Goodchild Mackford; Enlisted Feb. 9, 1865; Mustered out Sept. 4, 1865.

George H. Gordon Ripon; Enlisted Oct. 9, 1861; Veteran; Wounded Bayou Cache; absent sick at Mustered out of Regt.

Alonzo G. Gregory Berlin; Enlisted Sept. 23, 1861; Deserted Nov. 20, 1861.

W.D. Guptill Markesan; Enlisted Sept. 24, 1862; Veteran; Mustered out Sept. 4, 1865.

Benjamin F. Hake Princeton; Enlisted Mar. 31, 1864; Mustered out Sept. 4, 1865.

James A. Hake Princeton; Enlisted Oct. 5, 1861; Veteran, Corporal, Sgt.; Wounded Vicksburg; Mustered out Sept. 4, 1865.

Heman D. Hall Berlin; Enlisted Sept. 10, 1861; Veteran, Corporal; Mustered out Sept. 4, 1865.

Ole Halverson Watertown; Enlisted Sept. 10, 1861; Wounded Vicksburg; Died May 22, 1863, Vicksburg, Miss., of wounds.

George T. Hamer Princeton; Enlisted Oct. 9, 1861; Wounded Bayou Cache; Discharged Oct. 10, 1862, of wounds.

Newton W. Hamer Princeton; Enlisted Oct. 5, 1861; Veteran, Corporal, Sgt.; Mustered out Sept. 4, 1865.

Emerson H. Harrington Berlin; Enlisted Mar. 24, 1863; Veteran; Wounded Vicksburg; Mustered out Sept. 4, 1865.

Gideon H. Harrington Berlin; Enlisted Mar. 12, 1863; Veteran; Mustered out Sept. 4, 1865.

Henry C. Harrington Berlin; Enlisted Sept. 10, 1861; Veteran; Wounded Bayou Cache and Vicksburg; Discharged June 16, 186?; Disability.

Lavender L. Harris Manchester; Enlisted Sept. 24, 1862; Veteran, Corporal; Mustered out Sept. 4, 1865.

Marion W. Helterbrand Missouri; Enlisted Jan. 1, 1862; Deserted Apr. 6, 1862.

George H. Hobbs Berlin; Enlisted Oct. 7, 1861; Deserted.

Henry C. Hobbs Aurora; Enlisted Sept. 10, 1861; Died Nov. 3, 1862, Ironton, Mo., disease.

Charles J. Holt Madison; Enlisted Nov. 6, 1861; Veteran; Promoted Q.M. Sgt., Feb. 1, 1865.

Albert C. Hopkins Princeton; Enlisted Nov. 6, 1861; Veteran; Corporal; Wounded Black River Bridge; Mustered out Sept. 4, 1865.

Lorenzo D. Hoskins Warren; Enlisted Sept. 30, 1861; Died Feb. 28, 1862, Sulpher Springs, Mo., disease.

Egbert J. Hull Platteville; Enlisted Dec. 24, 1863; From 33rd Wis. Inf.; Mustered out Sept. 4, 1865.

Francis E. Jacobs Berlin; Enlisted Sept. 21, 1861; Mustered out Nov. 18, 1864, term expired.

Chester W. Johnson Milwaukee; Enlisted Jan. 21, 1864; Mustered out Sept. 4, 1865.

Joshua C. Johnson Berlin; Enlisted Sept. 20, 1861; Died Sept. 1, 1862, Jeff. Barracks, Mo., disease.

Thos. F. Jones Lima; Enlisted Jan. 5, 1864; From 33rd Wis. Inf.; Mustered out Sept. 4, 1865.

Henry W. Jordan Aurora; Enlisted Sept. 10, 1861; Corporal, Sgt.; Mustered out Nov. 18, 1864, term expired.

John N. Jordan Aurora; Enlisted Sept. 10, 1861; Sgt.; pris. Sabine Cross Roads; Mustered out Nov. 18, 1864, term expired.

Andrew Kendall Cato; Enlisted Mar. 11, 1865; Drafted; Mustered out Sept. 4, 1865.

John A. Kirkpartrick Lima; Enlisted Jan. 14, 1864; From 33rd Wis. Inf.; Mustered out Sept. 4, 1865.

Randolph A. Kruger Princeton; Enlisted Sept. 26, 1864; Mustered out Sept. 4, 1865.

Theodore Larrabee Princeton; Enlisted Nov. 6, 1861; Died Aug. 2, 1862, Jeff Barracks, Mo., disease.

Leander D. Laughlin Brandon; Enlisted Nov. 5, 1861; Died Nov. 6, 1862, St. Louis, Mo., disease.

Charles B. Livermore Enlisted Oct. 9, 1861; Musician.

George E. Logue Port Andrew; Enlisted Oct. 29, 1861; Veteran, Corporal; Mustered out Sept. 4, 1865.

Reason Lyons Enlisted Nov. 5, 1862; From 33rd Wis. Inf.; Mustered out Sept. 4, 1865.

George E. Marshall Dayton; Enlisted Feb. 2, 1865; Absent sick at Mustered out of Regt.

Frank S. Marston Bristol; Enlisted Feb. 20, 1864; From 33rd Wis. Inf.; Mustered out Sept. 4, 1865.

Charles W. Martin Dane; Enlisted Sept. 9, 1861; From Co. F; Mustered out Sept. 1, 1865.

John M. Martin Madison; Enlisted Oct. 15, 1861; Veteran; Mustered out Sept. 4, 1865.

Stephen Marvin Berlin; Enlisted Oct. 21, 1861; Wounded Bayou Cache; Mustered out Mar. 12, 1863.

Franklin McDonald Mackford; Enlisted Mar. 30, 1864; Mustered out Sept. 4, 1865.

Warren E. McIntyre Princeton; Enlisted Sept. 26, 1864; Mustered out Sept. 4, 1865.

Loren W. Medley Markesan; Enlisted Sept. 20, 1861; Corporal; Wounded Bayou Cache; transferred to V.R.C., Apr. 10, 1864.

Samuel Meservey Markesan; Enlisted Sept. 24, 1862; Veteran; Corporal, Sgt.; Mustered out Sept. 4, 1865.

William H. Meservey Markesan; Enlisted Sept. 24, 1862; Died Apr. 20, 1863, Ironton, Mo., disease.

Simon Meyer Madison; Enlisted Feb. 8, 1865; Mustered out Sept. 4, 1865.

James A. Miller St. Marie; Enlisted Nov. 20, 1862; Veteran; Mustered out Sept. 4, 1865.

John H. Mitchell Princeton; Enlisted Nov. 20, 1862; Veteran; Mustered out Sept. 4, 1865.

Henry H. Moore Mackford; Enlisted Feb. 9, 1865; Mustered out Sept. 4, 1865.

Elmer D. Morse Princeton; Enlisted Oct. 30, 1861; Veteran, Corporal; Mustered out Sept. 4, 1865.

Emery S. Morse Princeton; Enlisted Mar. 29, 1864; Mustered out Sept. 4, 1865.

Nicholas Myers Brandon; Enlisted Oct. 5, 1861; Died Feb. 18, 1863, near Pilot Knob, Mo., disease.

Asahel Nash Aurora; Enlisted Sept. 10, 1861; Wounded Bayou Cache and Sabine Cross Roads, La.,: Mustered out Nov. 18, 1864, term expired.

Ole Oleson Port Andrew; Enlisted Oct. 31, 1861; Discharged July 22, 1862, disability.

Chauncey Ostrander Markesan; Enlisted Nov. 5, 1861; Died Aug. 29, 1862, Oldtown, Ark., disease.

James Otter Oneida; Enlisted Oct. 25, 1862; Deserted June 3, 1863.

Fernando Parker Manchester; Enlisted Oct. 23, 1861; Died Dec. 7, 1862, Ironton, Mo., disease.

Samuel H. Parker Markesan; Enlisted Oct. 11, 1861; Wounded Port Gibson; pris. Sabine Cross Roads; Mustered out Nov. 18, 1864, term expired.

Ormand Parmly Markesan; Enlisted Oct. 1, 1861; Wounded Bayou Cache; Discharged Nov. 20, 1862, disability.

Lewis Peters Duck Creek; Enlisted Oct. 28, 1862; Veteran; trans. to Co. D, Feb. 29, 1864.

Nicholaus Phillips Meeme; Enlisted Sept. 30, 1864; Drafted; Mustered out June 6, 1865.

Adelbert D. Pierce Neshkoro; Enlisted Sept. 10, 1861; Veteran, Corporal, Sgt.; Mustered out Sept. 4, 1865.

Edwin G. Pierce Neshkoro; Enlisted Nov. 25, 1862; Veteran; Mustered out Sept. 4, 1865.

Jonathan Pierce St. Marie; Enlisted Feb. 15, 1865; Mustered out May 12, 1865.

Daniel F. Reilly Warren; Enlisted Sept. 21, 1861; Mustered out Nov. 18, 1864, term expired.

Milton H. Rosemire Highland; Enlisted Jan. 16, 1864; From 33rd Wis. Inf; Mustered out Sept. 4, 1865.

Milton B. Rowland Berlin; Enlisted Sept. 10, 1861; Sgt.; Mustered out Nov. 18, 1864, term expired.

David P. Sergent Kingston; Enlisted Oct. 1, 1861; Discharged Feb. 2, 1863, disability.

Marshall Sergent Kingston; Enlisted Oct. 29, 1861; Transferred to V.R.C., June 5, 1864.

Lester Shadduck Manchester; Enlisted Sept. 20, 1861; Wounded Vicksburg; Discharged June 11, 1864, disability.

Amos Shepard Enlisted Nov. 5, 1861; Wounded Bayou Cache, Ark.; Died Feb. 23, 1863, of wounds.

Hollis Stedman Berlin; Enlisted Sept. 10, 1861; Corporal; Wounded Vicksburg; Mustered out Feb. 9, 1864.

Joseph Stephenson Liberty; Enlisted Mar. 11, 1865; Drafted; Mustered out Sept. 4, 1865.

Thomas C. Steptoe Berlin; Enlisted Oct. 10, 1861; Deserted Nov. 10, 1861.

William E. Stetson Enlisted Nov. 18, 1861; Discharged Feb. 27, 1863, disability.

Martin S. Stow Aurora; Sept, 10, 1861; Died Oct. 30, 1862, Arcadia, Mo., disease.

John Urban Mackford; Enlisted Feb. 9, 1865; Mustered out Sept. 4, 1865.

James Van Buren Madison; Enlisted Feb. 8, 1865; Mustered out May 29, 1865.

Isaac M. Walker Berlin; Enlisted Oct. 2, 1861; Killed May 22, 1863, Vicksburg, Miss.
William W. Walker Berlin; Enlisted Oct. 4, 1861; Veteran, Corporal; Mustered out Sept. 4, 1865.
Frederick Wandry Green Lake; Enlisted Aug. 30, 1862; Veteran; Wounded Vicksburg; Mustered out June 6, 1865.
William Warner Berlin; Enlisted Oct. 29, 1861; Mustered out Nov. 18, 1864, term expired.
Datus E. Washburn Manchester; Enlisted Sept. 20, 1861; Died Apr. 24, 1862, Pittman's Ferry, Ark., disease.
Harvey Weller Berlin; Enlisted Sept. 30, 1861; Corporal; Wounded Vicksburg; Died June 17, 1863, Vicksburg, Miss.
Leander Whicher Hortonville; Enlisted Oct. 1, 1861; Corporal; Died Mar. 24, 1862, Pilot, Knob, Mo., disease.
Charles O. Whipple Aurora; Enlisted Sept. 30, 1861; Died Dec. 7, 1862, St. Louis, Mo., disease.
Daniel Whitney Berlin; Enlisted Sept. 10, 1861; Died Sept. 23, 1862, Mound City, Ill., disease.
William H. Willis Bufton; Enlisted Sept. 26, 1861; Died Dec. 7, 1862, St. Louis, Mo., disease.
Orrin M. Woodruff Mackford; Enlisted Feb. 9, 1865; Absent sick at Mustered out of Regt.
Daniel D. Wrought Mackford; Enlisted Feb. 9, 1865; Discharged Aug. 16, 1865.
Herman Zahr Markesan; Enlisted Mar. 30, 1864; Mustered out Sept. 4, 1865.

Co. K — The "Neenah Rifles"

Officers

Calvin J. Wheeler Captain; Neenah; Rank from July 22, 1861; Resigned Nov. 1, 1861.
Hiram J. Lewis Captain; Neenah; Rank from Nov. 2, 1861; Veteran; 1st Lt., July 22, 1861; Mustered out Jan. 3, 1865.
Alvin Abell Captain; Vinland; Rank from June 27, 1865; Enlisted Sept. 30, 1861; Veteran; Sgt., 1st Sgt.; 1st Lt., Feb. 4, 1865; resigned July 25, 1863.
Ira W. Hunt 1st Lt.; Neenah; Rank from Nov. 2, 1861; Enlisted Sept. 17, 1861; 1st Sgt.; Promoted Adjutant, Oct. 1, 1863.
Artemus Adams 1st Lt.; Neenah; Rank from Nov. 12, 1863; Enlisted Sept. 17, 1861; Sgt.; 2nd Lt., Dec. 20, 1862; resigned Nov. 27, 1864.
Clark S. Gilbert 1st Lt.; Clayton; Rank from Jan. 27, 1865; Enlisted Sept. 30, 1861; Veteran, Corporal, Sgt., 1st Sgt.; Mustered out Sept. 4, 1865.
Robert P. House 2nd Lt.; Neenah; Rank from Oct. 14, 1861; Enlisted Sept. 1, 1861; resigned Nov. 27, 1862.

Enlisted Men

John Abraham Nekimi; Enlisted Mar. 10, 1865; Mustered out Sept. 4, 1865.
John Aldridge Clyman; Enlisted Nov. 27, 1862; Mustered out Feb. 5, 1864.
Henry Althen Mishicot; Enlisted Sept. 29, 1864; Drafted; Mustered out June 6, 1865.
John Anderson Winchester; Enlisted Feb. 22, 1864; Died Aug. 7, 1864, Brashear City, La., disease.
George Applebaker Charlestown; Enlisted Mar. 9, 1865; Drafted; Mustered out Sept. 4, 1865.
Ole Bainson Winchester; Enlisted Feb. 22, 1864; Died Oct. 4, 1864, Brashear City, La., disease.
Samuel A. Bartlett Vinland; Enlisted Sept. 27, 1861; Corporal; Died Nov. 17, 1862, Ironton, Mo., disease.
Peter Bartol Two Rivers; Enlisted Mar. 10, 1865; Mustered out Sept. 4, 1865.
Riley Bashford Clayton; Enlisted Feb. 25, 1864; Died June 14, 1864, New Orleans, La., disease.
Henry Bauer Brookfield; Enlisted Mar. 28, 1865; Mustered out Sept. 4, 1865.
Stephen A. Bell Milwaukee; Enlisted Mar. 29, 1864; Mustered out Sept. 4, 1865.
Lieberhart Berke Green Bay; Enlisted Oct. 19, 1861; Died Jan. 17, 1862, Sulpher Springs, Mo., disease.
John Blake Clayton; Enlisted Sept. 28, 1861; Sgt.; Dropped from rolls by order, Oct. 19, 1863.
Harvey Blue Dale; Enlisted Sept. 25, 1861; Discharged Dec. 8, 1862, disablity; re-enlisted Jan. 14, 1863; Discharged Dec. 30, 1864, disability.
John Branch Milwaukee; Enlisted Apr. 14, 1865; Drafted; Mustered out Sept. 4, 1865.
John C. Brandes Clayton; Enlisted Mar. 21, 1864; Died Sept. 12, 1864, Brashear City, La., disease.
James Brien Clayton; Enlisted Feb. 25, 1864; Corporal; Mustered out Sept. 4, 1865.
Reuben Brockway Vinland; Enlisted Sept. 21, 1861; Corporal; Died Aug. 22, 1862, Oldtown, Ark., disease.
Chester F. Brown Neenah; Enlisted Feb. 29, 1864; Mustered out Sept. 4, 1865.
Joseph Brunett Greenville; Enlisted Apr. 14, 1864; Mustered out Sept. 4, 1865.
Jeremiah Burgess Lowell; Enlisted Nov. 27, 1862; Veteran, Corporal; Mustered out Sept. 4, 1865.
Thomas J. Clark Clyde; Enlisted Dec. 22, 1863; From 33rd Wis. Inf.; Mustered out Sept. 4, 1865.
Charles Cohls Portage; Enlisted Sept. 29, 1864; Drafted; Mustered out June 6, 1865.
James Conley Clayton; Enlisted Sept. 17, 1861; Veteran, Corporal; Died Oct. 20, 1864, Brashear City, La., disease.
William Conley Clayton; Enlisted Sept. 28, 1861; Died Sept. 21, 1862, Helena, Ark., disease.
Marcus Cramer Lowell; Enlisted Nov. 27, 1862; Wounded Vicksburg; Died June 5, 1863, Vicksburg, Miss., of wounds.
Asel Crandall Winneconne; Enlisted Sept. 17, 1861; Discharged Dec. 26, 1862, disability.

George E. Crandall Winneconne; Enlisted Sept. 28, 1861; Veteran; Wounded Blakely, Ala.; Discharged Oct. 17, 1865, disability.

Peter Deml Canton; Enlisted Oct. 1, 1864; Drafted; Mustered out Sept. 4, 1865.

Samuel Donaldson Dale; Enlisted Sept. 24, 1861; Discharged Sept. 10, 1862, disability.

Henry Dorow Winchester; Enlisted Sept. 17, 1861; Veteran, Corporal; Mustered out Sept. 4, 1865.

William Doty Vinland; Enlisted Sept. 17, 1861; Mustered out Nov. 18, 1864, term expired.

Samuel Doughty Oshkosh; Enlisted Sept. 19, 1861; Musician; Died Nov. 11, 1862, Ironton, Mo., disease.

John H. Dubois Vinland; Enlisted Sept. 17, 1861; Veteran, Corporal, Sgt.; Mustered out Sept. 4, 1865.

Henry B. Edwards Clayton; Enlisted Sept. 17, 1861; Died Mar. 13, 1863, Ironton, Mo., disease.

Dan Emery Vinland; Enlisted Sept. 19, 1861; Musician; Discharged Oct. 21, 1863, disability.

Anthony Emily Berry; Enlisted Oct. 29, 1861; Veteran; trans. to Co. A, Feb. 29, 1864.

Ole Everson Winchester; Enlisted Feb. 29, 1864; Mustered out Sept. 4, 1865.

Christian Everts Ahnapee; Enlisted Mar. 22, 1865; Drafted; Mustered out Sept. 4, 1865.

James Farr Beaver Dam; Enlisted Dec. 1, 1862; Corporal; Mustered out Sept. 4, 1865.

Henry C. Fields Clayton; Enlisted Mar. 10, 1864; Mustered out Sept. 4, 1865.

Gottfried Fischer Rockland; Enlisted Mar. 11, 1865; Drafted; Mustered out Sept. 4, 1865.

Seth W. Fitch Neenah; Enlisted Sept. 17, 1861; Discharged Feb. 12, 1862, by order.

John B. Flanegin Vinland; Enlisted Nov. 9, 1861; Wounded Vicksburg; Mustered out Nov. 18, 1864, term expired.

Alexander Forsyth Clayton; Enlisted Sept. 17, 1861; Corporal; Prisoner; transferred to V.R.C., Nov. 24, 1863.

Benjamin D. Franklin Clyde; Enlisted Dec. 31, 1863; From 33rd Wis. Inf.; Mustered out Sept. 4, 1865.

William Franklin Boscobel; Enlisted Sept. 17, 1861; Died Oct. 31, 1862, St. Louis, Mo.

Abram Furney Greenville; Enlisted Apr. 7, 1864; Mustered out Sept. 4, 1865.

August Ganger Cooperstown; Enlisted Dec. 29, 1864; Drafted; Mustered out Sept. 4, 1865.

Frederick Gepp Lake; Enlisted Apr. 4, 1865; Drafted; Mustered out Sept. 4, 1865.

Joseph M. Giddings Clayton; Enlisted Sept. 17, 1861; Veteran, Corporal; Mustered out Sept. 4, 1865.

John Giebel Dale; Enlisted Sept. 24, 1861; Veteran; Wounded, Blakely, Ala.; Died Apr. 10, 1865, Blakely, Ala. of wounds.

Joseph Gotfried Neenah; Enlisted Sept. 17, 1861; Mustered out Nov. 18, 1864, term expired.

Henry Gritt Rantoul; Enlisted Mar. 9, 1865; Drafted; Mustered out Sept. 4, 1865.

Svenning Gunderson Winchester; Enlisted Feb. 22, 1864; Mustered out Sept. 4, 1865.

Frederick Guthschow Clayton; Enlisted Sept. 21, 1861; Veteran; Wounded Vicksburg; Mustered out Sept. 4, 1865.

Andrew Hagerson Winchester; Enlisted Feb. 22, 1864; Mustered out Sept. 4, 1865.

Mathias Hagerson Winchester; Enlisted Feb. 22, 1864; Corporal; Mustered out Sept. 4, 1865.

Halver Halverson Winchester; Enlisted Sept. 23, 1861; Wounded Vicksburg; Discharged Nov. 8, 1863, of wounds.

John Hanson Winchester; Enlisted Feb. 22, 1864; Mustered out Sept. 4, 1865.

Ole Hanson Winchester; Enlisted Feb. 22, 1864; Died Sept. 15, 1861, Brashear City, La., disease.

Jerry Harrington Enlisted Nov. 27, 1862; Wounded Vicksburg; Died July 7, 1863, Memphis, Tenn., of wounds.

James Hart Vinland; Enlisted Sept. 21, 1861; Discharged June 15, 1863, by order.

Thomas Hart Greenville; Enlisted Apr. 7, 1864; Mustered out Sept. 4, 1865.

William D. Hatch Milton; Enlisted Jan. 5, 1864; From 33rd Wis. Inf.; Mustered out Sept. 4, 1865.

Francis Hawkins Clayton; Enlisted Oct. 16, 1861; Veteran, Musician; Discharged June 10, 1865, disability.

Andrew Hayden Suamico; Enlisted Oct. 14, 1861; Died Nov. 27, 1862, Ironton, Mo., disease.

John R. Hedemann Neenah; Enlisted Sept. 17, 1861; Dropped from rolls by order, Oct. 19, 1863.

Henry H. Hendricks Wrightstown; Enlisted Sept. 17, 1861; Corporal; Mustered out Nov. 18, 1864, term expired.

Frederick Henke Watertown; Enlisted Dec. 1, 1864; Drafted; Mustered out Sept. 4, 1865.

George Herman Winchester; Enlisted Oct. 20, 1861; Veteran, Corporal; Wounded Vicksburg; Mustered out Sept. 4, 1865.

John Herman Lomira; Enlisted Mar. 7, 1865; Mustered out Sept. 4, 1865.

Albert Hinman Vinland; Enlisted Sept. 17, 1861; Died St. Louis, Mo.

Rufus I. Hitchcock Dale; Enlisted Sept. 24, 1861; Veteran, Corporal, Sgt.; Promoted Com. Sgt., Mar. 1, 1864.

James W. Hughes Shiocton; Enlisted Oct. 16, 1861; Veteran, Corporal, Sgt.; Wounded Vicksburg; Mustered out Sept. 4, 1865.

Albert H. Hunt Neenah; Enlisted Sept. 17, 1861; Discharged Aug. 3, 1862, disability.

Edward Jones Winchester; Enlisted Sept. 19, 1861; Corporal, Sgt.; Wounded Vicksburg; Mustered out Nov. 18, 1864, term expired.

Robert Jones Neenah; Enlisted Sept. 17, 1861; Discharged June 29, 1862, disability.

Horace Katawamba Kendly Shiocton; Enlisted Sept. 27, 1861; Discharged Apr. 17, 1863, disability.

Hans Kittelsen Winchester; Enlisted Sept. 27, 1861; Discharged Dec. 6, 1862, disability.

Gottleib Klampe Caledonia; Enlisted Oct. 7, 1861; Died May 17, 1862, Jacksonport, Ark., disease.

Andrew Kleiber Meeme; Enlisted Dec. 29, 1864; Drafted; Mustered out Sept. 4, 1865.

John Kleiss Greenville; Enlisted Mar. 9, 1865; Drafted; Mustered out Sept. 15, 1865.

Arnold M. Koppel Madison; Enlisted Nov. 14, 1861; Died Jan. 12, 1863, Ironton, Mo.

August Kruger Winchester; Enlisted Oct. 16, 1861; Veteran; Mustered out Sept. 4, 1865.

William Kruger Caledonia; Enlisted Oct. 1, 1861; Wounded Vicksburg; Mustered out Nov. 18, 1864, term expired.

Samuel Lane Oshkosh; Enlisted Sept. 19, 1861; Discharged Nov. 18, 1862, disability.

Frank Laroy Greenville; Enlisted Apr. 14, 1864; Absent sick at Mustered out of Regt.

Daniel Leach Clyde; Enlisted Dec. 30, 1863; From 33rd Wis. Inf.; Mustered out Sept. 4, 1865.

George H. Lindsley Neenah; Enlisted Sept. 17, 1861; Transferred to V.R.C., Sept. 4, 1863.

Benjamin F. Lisk Neenah; Enlisted Sept. 17, 1861; Sgt., 1st Sgt.; Wounded Vicksburg; Promoted Capt., Co. I, 52nd U.S.C.T., Oct. 12, 1863; Discharged July 10, 1864.

Elias W. Lloyd Neenah; Enlisted Sept. 17, 1861; Died July 3, 1863, Vicksburg, Miss., disease.

Henry Lloyd Clayton; Enlisted Feb. 25, 1864; Mustered out Sept. 4, 1865.

James P. Mark Clayton; Enlisted Sept. 28, 1861; Veteran, Corporal; Mustered out Sept. 4, 1865.

Andrew Marshall Neenah; Enlisted Sept. 17, 1861; Discharged Aug. 17, 1862, disability.

Joseph Matoxin Duck Creek; Enlisted Oct. 28, 1862; Veteran; Mustered out Sept. 4, 1865.

Daniel McAllister Vinland; Enlisted Sept. 17, 1861; Discharged June 2, 1863, disability.

John C. R. McCormick Appleton; Enlisted Sept. 17, 1861; Discharged June 19, 1864, by order.

George Meyer Meeme; Enlisted Mar. 11, 1865; Drafted; Mustered out Sept. 30, 1865.

Andrew Michelson Clayton; Enlisted Sept. 28, 1861; Veteran, Corporal, Sgt., 1st Sgt.; Mustered out Sept. 4, 1865.

Jervis Muttart Neenah; Enlisted Oct. 8, 1861; Veteran, Corporal, Sgt.; Mustered out Sept. 4, 1865.

Christian C. Nelson Clayton; Enlisted Sept. 28, 1861; Veteran, Corporal, Sgt.; Wounded Vicksburg; Died Oct. 10, 1864, New Orleans, La., disease.

Amon L. Newgard Clayton; Enlisted Sept. 17, 1861; Corporal; Disch; Apr. 7, 1863, disability.

Arne Olson Clayton; Enlisted Sept. 19, 1861; Discharged Mar. 6, 1863, disability.

William H. Palmer Clayton; Enlisted Oct. 5, 1861; Dich. Jan. 3, 1863, disability.

Samuel Payawaukie Janesville; Enlisted Jan. 30, 1865; Mustered out Sept. 4, 1865.

John C. Perry Neenah; Enlisted Nov. 5, 1861; Corporal; Mustered out Mar. 7, 1865.

Henry Peterson Winchester; Enlisted Feb. 22, 1864; Mustered out Sept. 4, 1865.

Hiram A. Pohlman Clayton; Enlisted Sept. 28, 1861; Veteran, Corporal, died July 15, 1864, Brashear City, La., disease.

Michael Quinn Milwaukee; Enlisted Dec. 11, 1863; From 33rd Wis. Inf.; transferred to V.R.C., Dec. 21, 1864, Mustered out Aug. 24, 1865.

Herman Rader Greenville; Enlisted Mar. 14, 1865; Mustered out Sept. 4, 1865.

Ai Rice Oshkosh; Enlisted Sept. 17, 1861; Veteran; Mustered out Sept. 4, 1865.

Ebenezer Rifenburgh Neenah; Oct, 9, 1861; Discharged July 30, 1862, disability.

Bernard Riley Neenah; Enlisted Oct. 5, 1861; Deserted Nov. 15, 1861.

Charles C. Robbins Madison; Enlisted Sept. 18, 1861; From Q.M. Sgt.; Mustered out Oct. 6, 1864, term expired.

William B. Robiee Clayton; Enlisted Sept. 25, 1861; Corporal, Sgt.; Wounded Vicksburg; Died May 28, 1863, Vicksburg, Miss., of wounds.

Philip Robinson Lowell; Enlisted Nov. 27, 1862; Killed May 22, 1863, Vicksburg, Miss.

Heinrich Roloff Nekimi; Enlisted Mar. 10, 1865; Mustered out Sept. 4, 1865.

William H.H. Rood Lodi; Enlisted Nov. 6, 1861; Veteran; Wounded Blakely; Mustered out Sept. 4, 1865.

James D. Royer Winchester; Enlisted Oct. 20, 1861; Died June 28, 1862, Batesville, Ark., disease.

James D. Secor Clayton; Enlisted Sept. 28, 1861; Died Jan. 1, 1863, Van Buren, Mo., disease.

George Sengenberger Sulpher Springs, Mo; Enlisted Mar. 12, 1862; Mustered out Mar. 24, 1865, term expired.

Robert Small Vinland; Enlisted Sept. 17, 1861; Mustered out Nov. 18, 1864, term expired.

Jesse S. Smith Prairie Du Chien; Enlisted Sept. 17, 1861; Discharged Feb. 8, 1863, disability.

John Smith Neenah; Enlisted Sept. 17, 1861; Discharged Oct. 13, 1862, disability.

Jonathan Smith Duck Creek; Enlisted Oct. 22, 1862; Veteran; Mustered out Sept. 4, 1865.

Jeremiah Spurgeon Neenah; Enlisted Mar. 2, 1864; Mustered out Sept. 4, 1865.

Jonathan Spurgeon Dale; Enlisted Sept. 24, 1861; Wounded Vicksburg; Died May 29, 1863, Vicksburg, Miss., of wounds.

Philip Spurgeon Dale; Enlisted Sept. 24, 1861; Veteran; Mustered out Sept. 4, 1865.

William H. Stevens Lowell; Enlisted Nov. 20, 1862; Veteran; Mustered out Sept. 4, 1865.

Emery Stickles Neenah; Enlisted Mar. 4, 1864; Discharged Nov. 18, 1864, diability.

Wenzil Striki Pulaski; Enlisted Dec. 14, 1863; From 33rd Wis. Inf.; Mustered out Sept. 4, 1865.

Christian O. Thompson Winneconne; Enlisted Sept. 17, 1861; Wagoner; Died Feb. 13, 1863, St. Louis, Mo., disease.

Creighton Thompson Fremont; Enlisted Oct. 7, 1861; Deserted Dec. 5, 1861.

C.S. Thompson Winneconne; Enlisted Mar. 29, 1864; Died Apr. 12, 1864, Camp Randall, Madison, Wis., disease.

Wilber E. Torrence Vinland; Enlisted Sept. 17, 1861; Died Dec. 3, 1862, St. Louis, Mo., disease.

Delancy H. Tyler Clayton; Enlisted Oct. 17, 1861; Veteran; Mustered out Sept. 4, 1865.

Morris Vaughn Dale; Enlisted Sept. 24, 1861; Transferred to V.R.C., Feb. 8, 1864.

William Voss Meeme; Enlisted Mar. 11, 1865; Drafted; Mustered out Sept. 4, 1865.

Reuben Warner Oshkosh; Enlisted Sept. 17, 1861; Died Aug. 27, 1863, Rolla, Mo., disease.

Henry Webster Duck Creek; Enlisted Oct. 22, 1862; Absent sick at Mustered out of Regt.

Frederick Weiding Charlestown; Enlisted Mar. 9, 1865; Drafted; Mustered out Sept. 4, 1865.

Carver D. Wescott Wrightstown; Enlisted Sept. 17, 1861; Died Oct. 17, 1862, St. Louis, Mo.

George Wetmore Shiocton; Enlisted Oct. 23, 1861; Veteran, Corporal; Mustered out Sept. 4, 1865.

James Wetmore Shiocton; Enlisted Sept. 17, 1861; Veteran, Corporal; Mustered out Sept. 4, 1865.

Samuel Wheeler Neenah; Enlisted Sept. 17, 1861; Transferred to V.R.C., May 22, 1864.

Gaius S. Wooledge Vinland; Enlisted Sept. 21, 1861; Died Nov. 16, 1862, Ironton, Mo., disease.

Joseph E. Wright Vinland; Enlisted Sept. 17, 1861; Veteran; Wounded Blakely; Died June 27, 1865, Philadelphia, Pa., of wounds.

Salomon Yeoman Stockbridge; Enlisted Oct. 12, 1861; Transferred to V.R.C., Dec. 20, 1863.

Charles York Mt. Pleasant; Enlisted Mar. 17, 1865; Mustered out Sept. 4, 1865.

Appendix B

*Civilian Occupations of 11th Wisconsin Soldiers**

Company	Farmers	Skilled Workers	Laborers	White Collar/Student	None Listed	Total
A	94	20	5	10	5	134
B	75	16	4	8	4	107
C	37	6	1	2	50	96
D	97	10	0	0	1	108
E	38	9	2	2	44	95
F	67	24	3	12	2	108
G	77	12	0	1	0	90
H	79	28	5	8	1	121
I	64	17	1	8	5	95
J	58	9	14	6	7	94
Total	686	151	35	57	119	1,048[†]
Percentage	66%	15%	3%	5%	11%	100%

Most Civil War regiments (especially those from rural areas) were dominated by farmers and laborers. The 11th Wisconsin was decidedly made up of farmers and members of the farm community. By comparison, the 12th Wisconsin regiment, made up from a similar combination of soldiers from rural and urban districts, had only 52 percent of its initial members from agricultural communities. Company D of the 11th Wisconsin, known as the "Ploughboys," had the highest percentage of farmers—97 percent. As the data stands now, 66 percent of the regiment listed their occupations as "farmer."

If we combined both laborers (who were most likely farm hands) and farmers the percentage of members from the agricultural community jumps to 72 percent for the 11th Wisconsin. Companies C and E reported a high number of unemployed (no occupation listed), which drastically altered the percentage. If we combined those who listed no occupation, farmers, and laborers, we reach 81 percent of the regiment. Both companies C and E were formed in rural areas (see Appendix C) so the odds of them being unemployed skilled workers seems unlikely.

*11th Wisconsin Descriptive Rolls, *Wisconsin State Historical Archives.*
[†]Official records report the regiment's initial strength at 1,029.

If we keep the average of 3.1 soldiers per regiment for the "None Listed" category, and redistribute the remaining 88 soldiers according to the occupation average per company, we come up with probably the best idea of the regiment's true make up: Farmers, 72 percent; Skilled Workers, 16 percent; Laborers, 3 percent; White Collar, 6 percent; None Listed, 3 percent.

Appendix C

Muster Sites for the 11th Wisconsin Regiment

Company	City	County	Muster Date
A	Mazomania	Dane	September 27, 1861
B	Madison	Dane	September 30, 1861
C	Waterloo	Jefferson	September 27, 1861
D	Richland	Richland	September 27, 1861
E	Mineral Point	Iowa	September 27, 1861
F	Madison	Dane	September 27, 1861
G	Madison	Dane	October 10, 1861
H	Portage City	Columbia	October 4, 1861
I	Berlin	Green Lake	October 12, 1861
K	Neenah	Winnebago	October 18, 1861

APPENDIX D

Victory Sermon by 11th Wisconsin Volunteer George Wells*

June 1865, Fort Blakely, Alabama

Service as performed by the Rev. George Wells following the victory at Fort Blakely and the surrender of Robert E. Lee.

Thanks be to God who giveth us the victory.

War is a terrible calamity. Its scenes of strife and carnage, its destruction of life and ruin of domestic peace, its desolation and blighting influences both national, social and personal, all have a tendency to make it truly terrible; especially as it is of constant occurance, for if one nation enjoys the sweets of peace others are submerged in all the evils of war. If the lava of war subsides in part of the globe it bursts forth with renewed power in another. And if there are no external foes to face, internal enemies arise and plunge a nation into all the terrors of that worst of all evils—civil war. Alas that our own beloved country should know, from sad experience, the truth of these remarks.

For over eighty years unparalleled prosperity attended these United States in their triumphed progress toward the zenith of power and greatness. External foes gave them but little trouble, and had they remained true to themselves no power on earth could have severed the tie that bound together thirty-four great states in a mighty confederation. But dissatisfaction from within displayed itself. Internal discentions arose. A faction of fanatics made fanatical by their blind devotion to and superstitious reverence for the institution of slavery threatened to dissolve the union of states and establish a "Southern Confederacy." While threatenings were all the great mass Northern freeman sat at ease regardless of threats they had little idea would be put into execution. But deceived by a supposed cowardice at the North, and anticipating a division in the ranks of the true and loyal, as well as foreign recognition, they startled the world by passing ordinances of secession, attacking the garrison at Fort Sumpter [sic], and trashing the "Stars and Stripes" in the dust.

What was the duty of the government at the crisis? To allow secession would destroy our nationality and rob the world of a mighty commonwealth. Therefore we could not in honor recognize for a moment a doctrine so destructive to the country we hold so dear. What was their duty in this hour of trial? To await further acts of hostility? Had we not patiently endured contumely and result tall forbearance ceased to be a virtue, and when the emblem of our rights and liberties was smitten, was it honorable? Was it right? To wait till the foe had marshalled his hosts for renewed attacks[?] The flag of the free having been insulted as men, patriots, and Christians it was our duty to sustain the honor of the flag; yes and preserve our own honor for the two are intimately connected. At Sumpter [sic] the gauntlet was thrown down, and it was our duty to take it up, to accept the battle and leave the results with the God of battles. This is the condition of things on the surface. Underneath lay a far more glorious idea than avenging an insult offered the "Star Spangled Banner." Principles were involved. There was then to begin a grand struggle between truth and error. Right and wrong were to meet face to face, and the great battle between glorious heavenly liberty, and hell born, hell bound slavery was to be fought. As to the final results who could doubt but freedom would be triumphant? But it has not always appeared so, for in the struggle we have not been uniformly successful. The history of the war, to the commencement of the present year, has been one of lights and shades, of victory and defeat. The year 1861 gave us victories, but defeats counterbalanced their influence. In 1862 we were successful in many hard fought battles, but their good effects were lost through the influence of disaster. Through 1863 the successes of the Union armies were numerous and important, but two severe reverses tarnished their glory, and partially destroyed their happy results. 1864 is memorable for its successes, and will pass in the record of ages as productive of the greatest military achievement of modern times, but still this year was not entirely clear of failures. But though the first four years show alternate victory and defeat, yet this year presents a record of uniform success. Fort Fisher, Wilmington, Charleston, Columbus, Goldsbourgh, Selma, Mountgerney [Montgomery], Macon, Petersburg, Richmond, Spanish Fort and Blakeley, all testify to the success of the Union armies. Finally the surrender of Lee and Johnson, with the probability that all rebels have ground their arms, assure us victory complete is ours, that the hitherto defiant traitor is beneath our feet, and liberty remains untarnished fair as the sun, clear as the moon and more terrible than an army with banners to slavery propagandists.

But we must speak particularly of the victories of Spanish Fort and Blakeley. As to the former, to others belong the glory of its capture, but when we speak of Blakeley the Eleventh are brought to a scene in their history that will never be forgotten. I was not there. Would to God I had been, if not to share the danger, to participate in your feelings of triumph, and to have the mournful pleasure of giving religious rites to those whom no sound can awake to glory again. But no matter, the mighty work was done, and you took a conspicuous part in its accomplishment. And, truly, while memory retains its seat you will have vivid impressions of that impressive scene. You will never forget the command "Fall in Eleventh," given by your gallant and fearless leader — Major Miller — nor the memorable rifle pits where you heard from the same unfaltering voice, the orders

"Forward Skirmishers!" "Forward Eleventh!" Will never forget the long space over which you ran with almost breathless haste, the fearce storm of shot and shell that greeted your approach to the enemy's works, and the three lines of abattis [?] that obstructed your passage. You will never forget the tripwire, the desperate leap upon the parapet, the demand to surrender, and the willingness manifested by the foe to obey when they were in your power. Oh! And you'll never forget the placid countenances of your brave comrades who lay still in death, and the terrible sufferings of those noble boys who claimed your assistance and sympathy when the glorious work was done. Friends, it must have been a sublime scene, but it is shorn in its glory in the fact that there are connected with it wounded limbs, broken hearts, and lifeless bodies. Your victory was complete. The part of the enemy's works approportioned to you for capture yielded to your resistless charge, and many prisoners with much munition of war fell into your hands. The whole line being successful Blakeley succumbed, and the glorious "Stars and Stripes" superceded the odious rag of secession.

The victories of Spanish Fort and Blakeley that resulted in the evacuation of Mobile are certainly among the most brilliant achievements of the war, and General Canby does well to acknowledge deserved gratitude by thanking his victorious army for displaying so much skill and valor. But he desires us to take into consideration the God of all the earths, and render him thanks for giving us the victory. Now our friends at home have held a day of joy and thanksgiving for all our victories; let us therefore while remembering Spanish Fort and Blakeley take into account the universal success of our nation's army, and return devout thanks to almighty God for the great prosperity attending our glorious cause.

Too many people leave the great Author of all events out of the question as many did General Grant in the glorious campaigns of last fall and winter. Because our Lieut. General was "One still man amidst a blatant land" making little noise, and using others to assist in accomplishing his designs, he was left out in the cold and all the applaudits given to others. But subsequent events show these fickle hero worshipers that the immortal Grant was the maker and mover of the wise means that have resulted in such glorious ends. Go with the God whom we adore. Though men in their willfulness ignore his providence in our national affairs, yet his hand controls events, and though silent and unseen, his purposes have been ripening for our good and the nation's welfare.

I would award the mead if praise to President Lincoln for his honest faithfulness, and to the able Generals who have led our armies from conquering to conquer. I give due credit to the brave soldiers who have fought a good fight and recognize the earnest determination of a patriotic and noble people to sustain so great a war, and yet with a glowing soul I endorse the sentiment of our text — Thanks be to God who giveth us the victory.

But why give thanks to God?

1st because he gave us for a President a good man, devoted Christian, wise statesman, and if an honest man is the noblest work of God, Abraham Lincoln was that noble work, and I do not think I disgrace the "Father of his Country" by placing him by his side, one the maker and other the regenerator of his country. "Honest old Abe" was preeminently the man for the times, and he is to be regarded as an unspeakable gift of God.

2nd because he gave us Generals whose military skill and determined bravery have achieved such great victory. We may with propriety consider our cause honored with the services of the greatest military heroes of the present age. 3rd because we raised up strong armies and willing hearts to fight our battles. It makes a magnificent sight so many thousands leaving the pursuits of civil life to take up arms in defense of their country's honor. History records no scene more sublime, and when the recording Angel shall open the book of time it will be seen that many were inspired by a God given spirit of duty as well as by motives of interest and patriotism! 4th because to him we owe thanks for the vast resources so essential to carry on the conflict. An immense amount of treasure has been expanded, and yet we are far from being exhausted, in fact we are just beginning to realizing our greatness in this particular. We can without exhausting our means employ millions more to bring about a successful termination of war.

But how should we manifest our thanks?

To remain content with a mear expression of thanks is unworthy of us, and yet we too frequently remain satisfied with so doing. But God who searched the heart will accept nothing short of heart felt gratitude, and this alone can repay the debt of love we owe. Of what use is it to say "Oh Lord I thank thee" when the life is Godless and the soul full of hatred to the things of God. Gratitude is the memory of the heart and where this feeling is properly exercised towards God it produces remembrance not only of the blessings received, but of what the donar requires of us. God desires fruits of gratitude. A manifestation of our thanks in prayer and holy living.

1st Prayer. To pray is certainly the will of God concerning us, and gratitude will draw the soul into this delightful exercise. Pray therefore that God would still continue and preserve us as a nation. Though the storm of war may cease its ragings, yet there will remain waves of trouble that will require a God to say "peace be still" before we are blist with a perfect calm. The plusical war is fought and know, but the moral conflict continues and God with us can alone give the victory. Pray for those whose hearts are made sad by war's desolation. The land is full of morning for loved ones who "sleep their last sleep," and full of sorrow for lost limbs and shattered health. Pray that God would bestow consolation and give the oil of joy for mourning with the garment of praise for the spirit of heaviness. And whenever the privilege to render assistance and seccur to these noble suffers presents itself show your gratitude by bestowing your favors, and a gracious God will not suffer you to go unrewarded. But in praying do not forget your own need of pardoning mercy, and a regenerated nature. Pray that God would forgive the past, and give you

"A heart in every thought renewed. And full of love devine."

2nd Holy living. To make our prayers effectual we must lead a holy life, for says Psalmist "If I regard inequity [sic] in my heart the Lord will not hear me." If we are grateful to a friend we show it by corresponding acts, and if we are in earnest in thanking for our success we shall show it not by rebelling against his will, but by keeping his commandments walking in his stature and living to love him. As a nation we have passed through a very firey ordeal, and it ought to purify us as gold is purified by fire. God has chastened us, not for our distruction, but to correct and make us a holy people that we may serve him forever. If we will learn the lesson and obey the teachings of our Almighty Friend our future will be great and glorious beyond our most sanguine expectations, but if we will not serve him we may expect destruction, for the nation that will not serve God shall parish. The laws of our country are so constituted that every man wields an influence. You and I my friends have a power, and we can use it to good advantage if we so choose. Then let us show our gratitude and at the same time benefit our country by living a holy life, and exerting a Christian influence around.

Let it be said of the 11th Wisconsin that besides expressions of thanks, they yielded themselves servants to God, and thereby manifested sincere and hearty thanks to God for giving us the victory. Amen.

APPENDIX E

Army of the Tennessee Officers

Maj. General Ulysses S. Grant

Thirteenth Army Corps
Maj. General John A. McClernand

Seventeenth Army Corps
Maj. General J.B. McPherson

Fifteenth Army Corps
Maj. General William T. Sherman

Sixteenth Army Corps*
Maj. General C.C. Washburn

Each division is typically made up of 2–4 brigades, and each brigade is typically made up of 3–5 regiments.

Thirteenth Army Corps

    Ninth Division
    Brig. Gen. Peter J. Osterhaus

    Tenth Division
    Brig. Gen. Andrew J. Smith

    Twelfth Division
    Brig. Gen. Alvin P. Hovey

    Fourteenth Division
    Brig. Gen. Eugene A. Carr

      First Brigade
      Brig. Gen. William P. Benton
         - **33rd Illinois**, Col. Charles E. Lippincott
         - **99th Illinois**, Col. George W.K. Bailey
         - **8th Indiana**, Col. David Shunk
         - **18th Indiana**, Col. Henry D. Washburn
         - **1st United States Siege Guns**, Maj. Maurice Maloney

      Second Brigade
      Brig. Gen. Michael K. Lawler

---

*Arrived in June 1863 as reinforcements

- **21st Iowa,** Lieut. Col. Cornelius W. Dunlap
- **22nd Iowa,** Col. William M. Stone
- **23rd Iowa,** Col. Samuel L. Glasgow
- **11th Wisconsin,** Col. Charles L. Harris

Chapter Notes

Abbreviations: HOTEWVVI — *History of the 11th Wisconsin Veteran Volunteer Infantry.* HOW — State Historical Society of Wisconsin. LOC — Library of Congress. ORA — *The War of the Rebellion: A Compilation of the Official Records of the Union and Confederate Armies.* ORN — *Official Records of the Union and Confederate Navies in the War of the Rebellion.* USAMHI — United States Army Military History Institute. WSHA — Wisconsin State Historical Archives. WVM — Wisconsin Veterans Museum.

Chapter One

1. *Milwaukee Sentinel*, March 5, 1861.
2. Allan Nevins, *War for the Union 1861–1862: The Improvised War* (New York: Konecky & Konecky, 1971), 74–76; for newspaper quotes, 75.
3. Richard N. Current, *The History of Wisconsin*, vol. 2, *The Civil War Era, 1848–1873* (Madison: State Historical Society of Wisconsin, 1976), 294–295: hereafter cited as HOW.
4. Harry Ellsworth Cole, ed., *A Standard History of Sauk County, Wisconsin*, vol. 1 (Chicago: Lewis, 1918), 229.
5. *Beloit Free Press*, April 18, 1861.
6. E.B. Quiner, *The Military History of Wisconsin: A Record of the Civil and Military Patriotism of the State, in the War for the Union* (Chicago: Clarke & Co., 1866), 43–44: hereafter cited as *The Military History of Wisconsin*.
7. HOW, 296–298; for George E. Smith quote, 298.
8. *Janesville Daily Gazette*, July 29, 1861; Kerry A. Trask, *Fire Within: A Civil War Narrative from Wisconsin* (Kent, Ohio: Kent State University Press, 1995), 42–45.
9. *Janesville Daily Gazette*, April 25, 1861; *Fire Within*, 42–45.
10. *Lancaster Herald*, circa 1861, http://www.wisconsinhistory.org.
11. John D. Billings, *Hard Tack and Coffee: Soldier's Life in the Civil War* (Old Saybrook, CT: Konecky & Konecky, 1887), 41.
12. HOW, 296, 299–300, 336–337; Quiner, *The Military History of Wisconsin*, 63; Frank L. Klement, *Wisconsin in the Civil War* (Madison: State Historical Society of Wisconsin, 1997), 11–13.
13. HOW, 76, 334–335; http://www.wisconsinhistory.org/roster/.
14. David J. Eicher, *The Longest Night: A Military History of the Civil War* (New York: Simon & Schuster, 2001), 58–59; Quiner, *The Military History of Wisconsin*, 52–54; Francis Paul Prucha, "Distribution of Regular Army Troops before the Civil War," *Military Affairs* 16, no. 4: 169–173.
15. *Janesville Daily Gazette*, July 5, 1861, 2–3.
16. Ibid.
17. Ibid., July 22, 1861; Eicher, *The Longest Night*, 88–89, 96, 98–99.
18. Ibid., July 23, 1861.
19. Ibid., July 24, 1861.
20. Ibid., July 23, 1861; Klement, *Wisconsin in the Civil War*, 20.
21. Ibid., September 24, 1861.
22. James M. McPherson, *Drawn with the Sword: Reflections on the American Civil War* (New York: Oxford University Press, 1996), 88; James M. McPherson, *For Cause and Comrades: Why Men Fought in the Civil War* (New York: Oxford University Press, 1997), 92–93, 90–103; for Gustave Paul Cluseret quote, 93; John Keegan, *The Mask of Command* (New York: Penguin, 1988), 91; Henry Strong to Mrs. H.P. Strong, May 23, 1862, Henry P. Strong Letters, Wisconsin State Historical Archives, hereafter cited as WSHA.
23. *Janesville Daily Gazette*, July 22, 1861.
24. Ibid., August 18, 1861.
25. Ibid., July, August, 1861.
26. "Patriot War Correspondence," September 2, 1861, WSHA.
27. *Janesville Daily Gazette*, August 21, 1861; Joseph Schafer, *A History of Agriculture in Wisconsin* (Madison: State Historical Society of Wisconsin, 1922), 87–88, 92–93; Regimental Description Rolls 11th Infantry, reel P68-2474, WSHA.
28. *Janesville Daily Gazette*, August 18, 1861.
29. Ibid., September 21, 1861.

Chapter Two

1. Joseph Schafer, *A History of Agriculture in Wisconsin* (Madison: State Historical Society of Wisconsin [HOW]), 3–13, 86.
2. Ibid.; Harold-Guy Smith, "The Populating of Wisconsin," *Geographical Review* 18, no. 3 (July 1928): 406–407.
3. Hosea W. Rood, *History of Wisconsin Veterans' Home: 1886–1926* (Madison: Democrat Printing, 1926), 9.
4. Schafer, *A History of Agriculture in Wisconsin*, 87.
5. All soldier descriptions and backgrounds, unless otherwise noted, are taken from the Regimental Description Rolls 11th Infantry, reel P68-2474, Wisconsin State Historical Archives (WSHA), and the United States Census Reports, 1860, National Archives.

6. *Madison Capital Times*, November 5, 1931.
7. Twining Papers, WSHA.
8. Samuel Kirkpatrick, The Civil War Letters of Samuel C. Kirkpatrick, WSHA, I-III.
9. Calvin P. Alling, "Four Years with the Western Army: In the Civil War of the United States, 1861–1865," WSHA.
10. Robert R. Sherrill Civil War Letters, Wisconsin Veterans Museum, hereafter sited as WVM.
11. Henry P. Strong letter to Mrs. H.P. Strong, December 20, 1861, in which he says, "For all the items of camp news you will have to consult the *Beloit Journal*— or rather my letters in them." These letters he usually signed as "Major." For example, compare "Correspondences of the Journal & Courier" from Correspondence of Wisconsin Volunteers, 1861–65. E.B. Quiner Papers (hereafter cited as Quiner Papers), WSHA, reel 1, vol. 4, 11th Infantry: May 1, 3, 5, 6, 1862, correspondences signed "Major," with Henry P. Strong to Mrs. H.P. Strong, May 2, 3, 5, 6, 1862, Henry P. Strong Letters, WSHA, in particular, descriptions concerning May 5 encounter with three Southern Union girls. In both instances the retelling is verbatim. Reference concerning the doctor's poor health, Mrs. H.P. Strong to W.H. Watson, October 8, 1862. *Wisconsin Adjutant General's Office: Records of Civil War Regiments*, Correspondences, 1861–1865, box 56, folder 2, WSHA. Brown, Rock County, Wisconsin, 793–794; http://www.freepages.history.rootsweb.com/~wirockbios/Bios/bios1483.html.
12. Obituary for Charles L. Harris, *Omaha Morning World-Herald*, October 12, 1910, p. 3.
13. Henry P. Strong to Mrs. H.P. Strong, May 23, 1862. According to Strong, after 21 days the regiment produced around 1,500 letters. This concerns only those active in the field (these records start in November 1862 when it was recorded that 621 men were fit for duty) of probably around 700–750 at this time, which means that on average each man was writing at least 2 letters per month and probably more. So with 2.5 letters per month per man the regiment produced somewhere around 21,000 letters the first 12 months of service (and this would be a very conservative number); in their second year, 17,000; in the third year 13,000 (this was their hardest year of fighting); and 14,000 the fourth year of service.
14. HOW, 336–337; Quiner, *The Military History of Wisconsin*, 559.
15. Ibid., 338–339. The soldier quoted is Chauncey H. Cook of the 25th Wisconsin.
16. Henry H. Twining to Hattie Perkins, September 29, 1861, Twining Papers, WSHA; HOW, 340.
17. Samuel C. Kirkpatrick to parents, September 29, 1861.
18. Quiner, *The Military History of Wisconsin*, 559.
19. *Janesville Daily Gazette*, July 22 1861, p. 3; HOW, 340–342.
20. Jesse Mather to sister, October 17, 1861, Jesse and Oliver Mather Papers, WSHA.
21. Samuel C. Kirkpatrick to parents, October 3, 1861; Henry H. Twining to Hattie Perkins, September 29, 1861.
22. *The Appleton Crescent*, August 3, 1861, pp. 1–2.
23. Ibid.
24. Ibid., October 5, 1861, p. 2.
25. Ibid.
26. Samuel C. Kirkpatrick to parents, October 3, 1861.
27. Ibid.
28. Ibid.
29. *Janesville Daily Gazette*, November 21, 1861, p. 2.
30. *West Bend Editorial*, November 9, 1861, p. 2.
31. Ibid.; *Janesville Daily Gazette*, November 21, 1861, p. 2.
32. Ibid.; Samuel C. Kirkpatrick to father, November 1861.
33. William H. Cope to father, November 1, 1861, William H. Cope Letters, WSHA.
34. James M. McPherson, *Battle Cry of Freedom: The Civil War Era* (New York: Oxford University Press, 1988), 330–331.

Chapter Three

1. E.B. Quiner, *The Military History of Wisconsin* (Chicago: Clarke, 1866), 560; Bruce Catton, *Grant Moves South* (Boston: Little, Brown, 1960), 85–86; William L. Shea and Earl J. Hess, *Pea Ridge: Civil War Campaign in the West* (Chapel Hill: University of North Carolina Press, 1992), 3.
2. Ibid.; Shelby Foote, *The Civil War: A Narrative*, vol. 1 (New York: Vintage Books, 1986), 89–90, 95–96.
3. Ibid.
4. Allan Nevins, *War for the Union, 1861–1862: The Improvised War* (New York: Konecky & Konecky, 1971), 120–129.
5. United States War Department, *The War of the Rebellion: A Compilation of the Official Records of the Union and Confederate Armies* (hereafter cited as ORA) I, vol. 8, 405–407; Nevins, *War for the Union, 1861–1862: War Becomes Revolution*, 2–4.
6. Ibid., 489.
7. Ibid.; Ulysses S. Grant, *Personal Memoirs*, vol. 1 (New York: Charles L. Webster, 1885), 286–288; Catton, *Grant Moves South*, 123–124; Nevins, *War for the Union, 1861–1862: War Becomes Revolution*, 2–4.
8. Ibid., 14–18.
9. Ibid.
10. *Janesville Daily Gazette*, November 22, 1861, p. 1.
11. Samuel C. Kirkpatrick to parents, brothers and sisters, November 26, 1861.
12. *Janesville Daily Gazette*; Henry H. Twining to Hattie Perkins, February 15, 1862; Kirkpatrick to parents, brothers and sisters, November 26, 1861.
13. Charles A. Stevens to brother, December 15, 1861, Civil War Letters of Charles A. Stevens, WSHA; Quiner Papers, reel 1, vol. 4: February 28, 1862, correspondence to the *Journal & Courier*.
14. Ibid.; Regimental Description Rolls 11th Infantry, reel P68–2474, WSHA.
15. Henry H. Twining to Hattie Perkins, December 3, 1861; Samuel C. Kirkpatrick to parents, brothers and sisters, December 11, 1861.
16. Ibid., Samuel C. Kirkpatrick to father, mother, brother, and sisters, December 15, 1861, and January 2, 1862; Robert R. Sherrill to uncle, December 1, 1861, Robert R. Sherrill Civil War Letters, WVM.
17. Samuel C. Kirkpatrick to father, mother, brother and sisters, December 15, 1861.
18. Ibid., Samuel C. Kirkpatrick to parents, January 2, 1862; Robert R. Sherrill to uncle, December 27, 1861; Henry P. Strong to Mrs. H.P. Strong, December 27, 1861; "This is the first fatal accident that has occurred in our regiment...." Quiner Papers, reel 1, vol. 4: December 26, 31 1861, correspondence. Charles E. Estabrook, ed., *Wisconsin Losses in the Civil War* (Madison, WI: Adjutant General's Dept., 1915), 57, lists seven soldiers who died due to accidents. According to the "Register of Deaths" in the regimental history, Robert Tollard was officially listed as being on picket when he was accidentally shot. Also, according to the Register of Deaths, E.W. Campbell

of Company A was the regiment's first death, having expired from typhoid fever on October 25, 1861; James McMyler, *History of the 11th Wisconsin Veteran Volunteer Infantry* (New Orleans, 1865), hereafter cited as *HOTE WVVI*, 40.

19. Quiner Papers, reel 1, vol. 4: February 6, 1862, and February 9, 1862, correspondence by "Will Hazard"; January 25, 1862, correspondence of the *Journal & Courier*.

20. Samuel C. Kirkpatrick to father, mother, brother, and sisters, December 15, 1861; Henry H. Twining to Hattie Perkins, December 25, 1861.

21. William H. Cope to father, November 27, 1861.

22. Henry P. Strong to Mrs. H.P. Strong, May 23, 1862; Quiner Papers, reel 1, vol. 4. A quick glimpse at both the 8th and the 11th regiments' correspondences to local newspapers shows that the debate was friendly and good-natured, but also serious at times. The two regiments were often camped near each other, allowing more time for each to razz the other.

23. Robert R. Sherrill to uncle, December 27, 1861; Henry H. Twining to Hattie Perkins, December 25, 1861.

24. Samuel C. Kirkpatrick to brother, January 3, 1862.

25. Henry P. Strong to the surgeon general, Sanitary Report for Quarter Ending December 31, 1861, Henry P. Strong Papers, WSHA.

26. Ibid.; Robinson, "Re-enlistment Patterns of Civil War Soldiers," *Journal of Interdisciplinary History* (Summer 2001): 27.

27. Ibid., January 11 1862; February 7, 1862; Henry P. Strong Report, January 26, 1862; Quiner Papers, reel 1, vol. 4: H.A. Reid to *Wisconsin State Journal,* January 8, 1862; Henry P. Strong to *Wisconsin State Journal*, January 18, 1862; G.D.H. correspondence, February 3, 1862.

28. Robert R. Sherrill to uncle, December 1, 1861.

29. Charles A. Stevens to brother, February 23, 1862; William H. Cope to father, December 2, 10, 1861.

30. Jesse Mather to sister, January, 1862, McMyler, *HOTEWVVI*, 12.

31. "Patriot War Correspondence," December 31, 1861; Quiner Papers, reel 1, vol. 4: June 10, 1862, correspondence from "Batesville Ark."

32. Samuel C. Kirkpatrick to brother, February 7, 1862; Abraham Barret to James G. Kirkpatrick and family, January 27, 1862.

33. Ibid., February 10, 1862.

34. Robert R. Sherrill to uncle, January 23, 1862.

35. Samuel C. Kirkpatrick to brother, February 10, 1862.

36. Charles A. Stevens to brother, February 23, 1862; Quiner Papers, reel 1, vol. 4: January 17, 1862, "Monterey" correspondence and February 6, 1862, unknown.

37. Henry P. Strong to Mrs. H.P. Strong, February 9, 1862; Quiner Papers, reel 1, vol. 4, February 1862, *Wisconsin State Journal* correspondence.

38. Richard Crawford, *The Civil War Songbook: Complete Original Sheet Music for 37 Songs* (New York: 1977), 100–103.

39. Oliver Mather to sister, December 15 and January 19, 1862.

40. Ibid.

41. Ibid.

42. Mark K. Christ, ed., *Rugged and Sublime: The Civil War in Arkansas* (Fayetteville: University of Arkansas Press, 1994), 21–22; Shea and Hess, *Pea Ridge: Civil War Campaign in the West*, 14–15; for Van Dorn quote, "I must have St Louis—then huzza," see page 22; Foote, *The Civil War* 1: 277–279.

43. James M. McPherson, *Crossroads of Freedom: Antietam* (New York: Oxford University Press, 2002), 15–22; Foote, *The Civil War* 1:211–212.

44. Ibid; for newspaper quotes, McPherson, *Crossroads of Freedom: Antietam*, 19.

45. Robert R. Sherrill to uncle, February 8, 1862.

46. Foote, *The Civil War* 1:280–285; Francis H. Kennedy, *The Civil War Battlefield Guide* (Boston: Houghton Mifflin, 1990), 20–25. See also Shea and Hess, *Pea Ridge: Civil War Campaign in the West,* for a superb breakdown of the battle and the situation leading up to the events.

47. Henry H. Twining to Hattie Perkins, March 11, 1862.

48. Ibid.; Henry P. Strong to Mrs. H.P. Strong, February 16, 1862.

49. *ORA* I, vol. 53:515.

50. Thaddeus Rice to Mary E. Rice, March 9, 1862; Robert R. Sherrill to uncle, February 8, 1862.

51. Benson Bobrick, *Testament: A Soldier's Story of the Civil War* (New York: Simon & Schuster, 2003), 72. They stayed in Pilot Knob for 10 days according to McMyler, *HOTEWVVI*, 12.

52. *ORA* I, vol. 8:636.

53. Ibid., 662.

54. William H. Cope to father, March 18, 1862.

55. Samuel C. Kirkpatrick to family, March 23, 1862; Quiner Papers, reel 1, vol. 4: April 5, 1862, correspondence to *Journal and Courier*; April 9, 1862, correspondence from "Reeves Station, Mo"; James W. Wheaton, ed., *Surgeon on Horseback: The Missouri and Arkansas Journal and Letters of Dr. Charles Brackett of Rochester, Indiana 1861–1863* (Carmel, IN: Guild Press of Indiana, 1998), 88.

56. Oliver Mather to sister, March 3, 22, and 29, 1862.

57. *Janesville Daily Gazette*, May 12, 1862, p. 2; Quiner Papers, reel 1, vol. 4: March 30, 1862, correspondence to the *Independent*; Quiner, *The Military History of Wisconsin*, 560.

58. Ibid.

59. Henry P. Strong to Mrs. H.P. Strong, February 23, 1862.

60. Samuel C. Kirkpatrick to family, June 10, 1862.

61. Ibid., May 18, 1862.

62. Ibid., June 9, 1862.

63. Mark K. Christ, *Rugged and Sublime: The Civil War in Arkansas* (Fayetteville: University of Arkansas Press, 1994), xi–xx.

64. McMyler, *HOTEWVVI*, 12; Samuel C. Kirkpatrick to family, June 9, 1862.

65. Robert R. Sherrill to uncle, May 27, 1862.

Chapter Four

1. Oliver Mather to sister, April 10, 14 and May 12.

2. Charles A. Stevens to brother, April 18, 1862; Charles E. Estabrook, ed., *Wisconsin Losses in the Civil War* (Madison, WI: Adjutant General's Dept., 1915), 51.

3. Henry P. Strong to Mrs. H.P. Strong, May 20, 1862.

4. *ORA* I, vol. 13:87.

5. *Davenport Daily Democrat and News*, April 2, 1862; Christ, ed., *Rugged and Sublime*, 38–39; *ORA* I, vol. 13:385.

6. Robert R. Mackey, *The Uncivil War: Irregular Warfare in the Upper South, 1861–1865* (University of Oklahoma Press, 2004), 29–49.

7. Ibid., 363–364; Christ, *Rugged and Sublime*, 39–43; Mark Grimsley, *The Hard Hand of War: Union Military Policy toward Southern Civilians, 1861–1865* (New York: Cambridge University Press, 1995), 98.

8. Correspondence to *Janesville Daily Gazette*, July 30, 1862; Quiner Papers, reel 1, vol. 4 and reel 2, vol. 5: August 9, 1862, correspondence from St. Louis.

9. Henry P. Strong to Mrs. H.P. Strong, May 10, 1862; Reid Mitchell, *The Vacant Chair: The Northern Soldier Leaves Home* (New York: Oxford University Press, 1993), 97; Quiner Papers, reel 1, vol. 4; April 18, 1862, correspondence from "Reeves Station"; *Daily Missouri Democrat*, July 17, 1862.

10. *Janesville Daily Gazette*, July 30, 1862; Samuel C. Kirkpatrick to family, July 19, 1862.

11. Elmo Ingenthron, *Borderland Rebellion: A History of the Civil War on the Missouri-Arkansas Border* (Missouri: Ozarks Mountaineer, 1980), 174–175; Michael E. Banasik, *Embattled Arkansas: The Prairie Grove Campaign of 1862* (NC: Broadfoot), 5.

12. *ORA* I, vol. 13:365–367; William Shea, "The Confederate Defeat at Cache River," *Arkansas Historical Quarterly* 52 (Summer 1993): 129–131.

13. *ORA* I, 103–104, 116; "The Confederate Defeat at Cache River," 129–131; Thomas Bringhurst and Frank Swigart, *History of the Forty-Sixth Regiment Indiana Volunteer Infantry* (Logansport, IN: Wilson, Humpreys, 1888), 34–35.

14. *ORA* I, 36–37, 368, 373; Ibid., 129–131; Christ, *Rugged and Sublime*, 42; Shea and Hess, *Pea Ridge: Civil War Campaign in the West*, 301.

15. Ibid; Shea, "The Confederate Defeat at Cache River," *Arkansas Historical Quarterly*, 131–132.

16. Jesse Mather to sister, June 11, 1862; Schafer, *A History of Agriculture in Wisconsin*, 87.

17. Ibid.

18. This is a letter Henry wrote to the *Janesville Daily Gazette* July 25, 1862.

19. Henry P. Strong to Mrs. H.P. Strong, May 20, 1862.

20. Quiner Papers, reel 1, vol. 4, May 20, 1862, correspondence by Barrett.

21. Shea, "The Confederate Defeat at Cache River," 130.

22. Henry Twining's correspondence to *Janesville Daily Gazette*, July 25, 1862.

23. *ORA* I, vol. 13:138–139; Shea, "The Confederate Defeat at Cache River," 132.

24. Ibid.; correspondence to *Janesville Daily Gazette*, July 30, 1862.

25. Ibid.; McMyler, *HOTEWVVI*, 12–13.

26. *Regimental Description Rolls 11th Infantry*, reel P68-2474, WSHA.

27. McMyler, *HOTEWVVI*, 13; *ORA* I, vol. 13:143–145; and see also Henry Twining's correspondence to *Janesville Daily Gazette*, July 25, 1862; Shea, "The Confederate Defeat at Cache River," 134–135; Quiner Papers, reel 1, vol. 4, and reel 2, vol. 5: July 23, 1862, correspondence by "Monterey," and July 7, 1862, correspondence by "The Chip"; As noted, surgeon Henry P. Strong was a prolific writer and preformed correspondent duties during the war for various newspapers. See Henry P. Strong Letters, WSHA, July 23, 1862.

28. Ibid.; *ORA* I, vol. 13:143–145.

29. *ORA* I, vol. 13:143–144; Quiner Papers, July 16 and 18 correspondence by C. McCarthy.

30. *ORA* I, vol. 13:147; Quiner Papers: July 16, 1862, McCarthy correspondence, July 28 correspondence by "The Chip," and July 16 correspondence by "Ralph"; Isaac H. Elliott and Virgil G. Way, *History of the Thirty-Third Regiment*, 28; Henry P. Strong, "Missouri Democrat" correspondence, July 21, 1862, and correspondence to "the Republican," July 23, 1862, Henry P. Strong papers, WSHA.

31. Ibid.; Quiner Papers, reel 1, vol. 4, and reel 2, vol. 5: July 23, 1862, correspondence by "Monterey"; B.P. Gallaway, *The Ragged Rebel: A Common Soldier in W.H. Parson's Texas Cavalry* (Austin: University of Texas Press, 1988), 46–47. In his official report Hovey never stated where his information concerning the prisoner(s) came from, but it appears there were several who were captured. Henry Twining corroborated this in his letter, though it is unknown when or where the executed men were taken. *The New York Times* (July 21, 1862) reprinted an article by the *Cincinnati Gazette* (which was picked up from the *St. Louis Democrat* and Fayel, see below) that offered details not included in the official report. The correspondent reported that Harris and his men "fell in with two Texan regiments of cavalry, with a regiment of conscript infantry drawn up on their right ready to receive them." Shea, "The Confederate Defeat at Cache River," *Arkansas Historical Quarterly*, essentially followed the narrative given by Isaac H. Elliott and Virgil G. Way in their *History of the Thirty-Third Regiment* (1902), which was an account of the battle from that regiment's perspective.

Unfortunately, in his official report, Colonel Hovey seems to have downplayed the contributions of others. When Colonel Wood of the First Indiana Cavalry filed his report with Hovey, it was not accepted and Hovey even wrote another report contradicting most of Wood's accounts. Hovey also accused Wood of making a "reckless" cavalry charge. He gave the impression that Wood was out of control, though he and his men played a key role in scattering the Texans from the field. Interestingly enough, this supposed reckless charge could not have been too deadly, as the First Indiana Cavalry lost not a man, and had only 10 wounded. But the most convincing piece of evidence that supports the success of Wood's charge comes from the officers of the 11th Wisconsin who wrote a letter home to the Governor of Wisconsin. In it they reported that the "entire command of Col. Hovey seemed in imminent danger" until the Indiana Cavalry arrived, led by Wood, and charged the enemy, resulting in the scattering of the rebels, and at that point the "work was done." The letter from the 11th Wisconsin to the governor was dated July 10, 1862: *Wisconsin Adjutant General's Office: Records of Civil War Regiments*, Correspondences, 1861–1865, box 56, folder 2.

Colonel Conrad Baker, commanding Fourth Brigade, spoke out on Wood's behalf during a court of inquiry—though ultimately refused. The men of the 11th Wisconsin hotly contested a description of the battle by a correspondent named "Fayel" (reported William Fayel) with the *St. Louis Democrat*. In an August 1862 "Patriot War Correspondence," a member of the Eleventh Wisconsin, who was in the battle, protested Fayel's description of events; he noted, "gives nearly all the credit to the 33rd Illinois." What is known is that Fayel was not even present during the fight. It is unclear whether the *Cincinnati Gazette* correspondent, who is unnamed, was the same man. After a battle, usually, correspondents from each of the regiments involved wrote letters home to newspapers detailing their deeds, which often did not accurately portray the actions of other regiments. The reports in Wisconsin newspapers do not mention much of the exploits of the Thirty-Third Illinois. Accuracy is always a problem when trying to piece together the actions of one regiment or another during a battle, even one as small as this. Wisconsin historian E.B. Quiner's *The Military History of Wisconsin* follows the narrative as described by Eleventh Wisconsin correspondents.

32. Alling, *Four Years with the Western Army: In the*

Civil War of the United States, 1861–1865 (WSHA), 2; Shea, "The Confederate Defeat at Cache River," 135–137; Quiner, *The Military History of Wisconsin*, 562–563.

33. Gallaway, *The Ragged Rebel: A Common Soldier in W.H. Parson's Texas Cavalry*, 46–47.

34. Ibid.; Quiner Papers, reel 1, vol. 4, and reel 2, vol. 5: July 23, 1862, correspondence by "Monterey."

35. Nelson and Squier, "The Confederate Defense of Northeast Arkansas and the Battle of Cotton Plant, Arkansas, July 7, 1862," *Rivers & Roads & Points in Between* 16 (Spring, 1989): 14 (Woodruff County (Ark.) Historical Society publication).

36. McMyler, *HOTEWVVI*, 13, and see also Henry Twining's correspondence to *Janesville Daily Gazette*, July 25, 1862. Alling, "Four Years with the Western Army," 1–3; *ORA* I, vol. 13:143–144. Also see J.C. Metcalf's correspondence to *Janesville Daily Gazette*, on July 30, 1862; Shea, "The Confederate Defeat at Cache River," 135–137; Quiner, *The Military History of Wisconsin*, 562–563; Henry P. Strong Letters, WSHA, July 23, 1862.

37. Gallaway, *The Ragged Rebel*, 46–47; Nelson and Squier, 14; *ORA* I, vol. 13:143–144; Shea, 138–139, 148

38. *ORA* I, vol. 13:143–144. Also see J.C. Metcalf's correspondence to *Janesville Daily Gazette* on July 30, 1862; Shea, "The Confederate Defeat at Cache River," 135–137; Quiner, *The Military History of Wisconsin*, 562–563; Henry P. Strong Letters, WSHA, July 23, 1862.

39. Ibid.; Robert R. Sherrill to uncle, July, 1862.

40. Henry P. Strong Letters, WSHA, July 23, 1862; Henry Twining correspondence to *Janesville Daily Gazette*, July 25, 1862; Alling, "Four Years with the Western Army," 3–4; *ORA* I, vol. 13:143–144; J.C. Metcalf's correspondence to *Janesville Daily Gazette*, July 30, 1862.

41. Ibid.

42. James W. Wheaton, ed., *Surgeon on Horseback: The Missouri and Arkansas Journal and Letters of Dr. Charles Brackett of Rochester, Indiana, 1861–1863* (Carmel, IN: Guild Press of Indiana, 1998), 162.

43. J.C. Metcalf's correspondence to *Janesville Daily Gazette*, July 30, 1862; *ORA* I, vol. 13:143–144; Quiner Papers, reel 1, vol. 4, and reel 2, vol. 5: July 23, 1862, and July 14, 1862, correspondence from "Helena, Arkansas." Henry P. Strong Letters, July 23, 1862. Also see http://www.cr.nps.gov/hps/abpp/battles/ar003.htm for a common description of the events of the battle that are in question.

44. Elliott and Way, *History of the Thirty-Third Regiment*, 28. Shea, 140–141, puts the 16th Texas Cavalry on the field shortly after the first charge, which is correct. He places Hovey there as well and I contend that is incorrect. It was the dismounted cavalry that forced the 11th Wisconsin back steadily as they faced an almost 10 to 1 disadvantage. As they were pushed back the 12th Texas Cavalry then charged, flushing the 11th back in a panic during the second charge, which is when Hovey arrived. Nelson and Squier also agree that it was after the second massive charge when Hovey arrived. "Parsons led a second mounted charge against the remainder of the Union Line. The Confederate cavalry slammed into the Federals. The Union Commander, Colonel Harris, was severely wounded....": Nelson and Squier, 17; Elliott and Way, *History of the Thirty-Third Regiment*, 131.

45. Ibid.

46. Quiner Papers, reel 1, vol. 4, and reel 2, vol. 5: correspondence by "Monterey"; correspondence by C. McCarthy, July 18, 1862; correspondence to "The Republican," Henry P. Strong Letters, July, 1862.

47. Elliott and Way, *History of the Thirty-Third Regiment*, 28, 131; Shea, 140–141.

48. Ibid.; Henry P. Strong Letters, July 23, 1862.

49. Correspondence to "The Republican," Henry P. Strong Letters, July 23, 1862; Elliott and Way, *History of the Thirty-Third Regiment*, 131; *ORA* I, vol. 13:143–145; Shea, "The Confederate Defeat at Cache River," 144–145.

50. Ibid.

51. Henry Twining correspondence to *Janesville Daily Gazette*, July 25, 1862; Alling, "Four Years with the Western Army"; *ORA* I, vol. 13:143–144; J.C. Metcalf's correspondence to *Janesville Daily Gazette*, July 30, 1862; Quiner, *A Military History of Wisconsin*, 561–562.

52. Henry Twining correspondence to *Janesville Daily Gazette*, July 25, 1862; J.C. Metcalf correspondence to *Janesville Daily Gazette*, on July 30, 1862; Robert R. Sherrill to uncle, July, 1862; *ORA* I, vol. 13:143–144; Shea, "The Confederate Defeat at Cache River," 145–146.

53. Ibid.; Nelson and Squier, "The Confederate Defense of Northeast Arkansas and the Battle of Cotton Plant, Arkansas," 17–18.

54. *ORA* I, vol. 13:146–148.

55. Ibid.; correspondence to "The Republican," Henry P. Strong Letters, July 23, 1862; Shea, "The Confederate Defeat at Cache River," 146.

56. Here again Hovey and Colonel Wood filed reports that contradict the other and in effect make the final twenty minutes of this battle as confusing as the first twenty. For more see *ORA* I, vol. 13:141–151.

57. *ORA* I, vol. 13:145.

58. Henry H. Twining to Hattie Perkins, July 28, 1862.

59. *ORA* I, vol. 13:145.

60. Ibid., 144.

61. Ibid.

62. Henry P. Strong to Mrs. H.P. Strong, August 13, 1862.

63. Quiner Papers, reel 1, vol. 4: April 2, 1862, unknown correspondent.

Chapter Five

1. Henry Twining correspondence to *Janesville Daily Gazette*, July 25, 1862; correspondence to the *Wisconsin State Journal*, "The War in Arkansas," August 25, 1862.

2. James H. Hougland, *Civil War Diary of James H. Hougland Company "G" 1st Indiana Cavalry* (Bloomington, IN: Monroe County Historical Society, 1962), 22.

3. *ORA* I, vol. 13:449; McMyler, *HOTEWVVI*, 12–13; Rhonda M. Kohl, "This Godforsaken Town: Death and Disease at Helena, Arkansas," *Civil War History* 1, no.2 (2004).

4. Ibid.; Henry Twining correspondence to *Janesville Daily Gazette*, July 25, 1862; Oliver Mather to sister, July 22, 1862; Quiner Papers, reel 1, vol. 4: July 23, 1862, correspondence by Henry P. Strong ("Monterey"); Quiner, *A Military History of Wisconsin*, 563.

5. Alling, *Four Years with the Western Army*, 3.

6. Henry P. Strong to Mrs. H.P. Strong, May 2, 1862.

7. Jesse Mather to sister; letter not dated, but based on material most likely written in June 1862.

8. Samuel C. Kirkpatrick to family, July 19, 1862; Robert R. Sherrill to uncle, July 7, 1862.

9. Jesse Mather to sister, June 11, August 7 and August 8, 1862.

10. Oliver Mather to sister, July 22, 1862.

11. Samuel C. Kirkpatrick to family, July 19, 1862, September 5, 1862.

12. Ibid.

13. *ORA* I, vol. 15:486; James M. McPherson, *Cross-*

roads of Freedom: Antietam (New York: Oxford University Press, 2002), 62–63; Quiner Papers, reel 2, vol. 5: July 18, 1862, correspondence from "Oldtown Landing."
14. Samuel C. Kirkpatrick to family, August 7, 1862.
15. Ibid., August 7, 1862; Quiner Papers, reel 2, vol. 5: 310–313.
16. Ibid., August 26, 1862.
17. Henry P. Strong to Mrs. H.P. Strong, March 2, 1862.
18. Ibid.
19. Quiner Papers, reel 2, vol. 5:262.
20. Samuel C. Kirkpatrick to family, August 7, 1862, September 7, 1864.
21. Quiner Papers, reel 2, vol. 5:263.
22. Samuel C. Kirkpatrick to family, March 23, 1865; Bruce Catton, *Grant Moves South* (Boston: Little, Brown, 1960), 363.
23. Allan Nevins, *War for the Union, 1862–1863: War Becomes Revolution* (New York: Konecky & Konecky, 1971), 485–505; Phillip Shaw Paludan, *A People's Contest: The Union & Civil War, 1861–1865* (Lawrence: University of Kansas Press, 1996), 105–115.
24. E.B. Quiner, *The Military History of Wisconsin* (Chicago: Clarke, 1866), 563.
25. Oliver Mather to sister, August 4, 1862.
26. Calvin P. Alling, "Four Years with the Western Army," Wisconsin State Historical Archives (WSHA), 3.
27. *ORA* I, 13:751–753; see http://www.arlingtoncemetery.net/cehovey.htm.
28. Jesse Mather to sister, August 7, 1862; "Our Army Correspondence: From the Eleventh Regiment," October 13, 1862, see http://www.wisconsinhistory.org/libraryarchives/collections/digital.asp.
29. Samuel C. Kirkpatrick to family, July 30, 1862.
30. Henry H. Twining to Hattie Perkins, August 27, 1862; Stephen E. Ambrose, *A Wisconsin Boy in Dixie: Civil War Letters of James K. Newton* (Madison: State Historical Society of Wisconsin), 60.
31. Quiner Papers, reel 2, vol. 5: 310–313: September 24, 1862, correspondence written by "The Chip."
32. Henry P. Strong to Mrs. H.P. Strong, August 3, 1862; Catton, *Grant Moves South*, 347–350.
33. Henry H. Twining to Hattie Perkins, August 27, 1862.
34. Oliver S. Robinson to parents, October 1, 1862, Oliver S Robinson Papers, WSHA.
35. Robert R. Sherrill to aunt, November 3, 1862.
36. Ibid., November 29, 1862.
37. Jesse Mather to sister, November 18, 1862.
38. Daily Returns, Eleventh Wisconsin regiment, November 29, 1862: Present, 621; Absent, 210, WSHA.

Chapter Six

1. Calvin P. Alling, "Four Years with the Western Army: In the Civil War of the United States," Wisconsin State Historical Archives (WSHA), 6; Samuel C. Kirkpatrick to family, November 11, 1862.
2. *Janesville Daily Gazette*, December 6, 1861, p. 2; John Keegan, *Fields of Battle: The Wars for North America* (New York: Vintage Books, 1995), 203; Archer Jones, *The Art of War in the Western World* (New York: Oxford University Press, 1987), 416–417.
3. Samuel C. Kirkpatrick to family, January 1, 1863.
4. James M. McPherson, *Battle Cry of Freedom: The Civil War Era* (New York: Oxford University Press, 1988), 557–563; for the Douglass quote, 558; *Douglass' Monthly* (October 1862): 721; James M. McPherson, *Crossroads of Freedom: Antietam* (New York: Oxford University Press, 2002), 140–141.
5. *Janesville Daily Gazette*, January 2, 1863, p. 2.
6. David J. Eicher, *The Longest Night: A Military History of the Civil War* (New York: Simon & Schuster, 2001), 408–409.
7. Ibid., 405; Steven E. Woodworth, *Nothing But Victory: The Army of the Tennessee, 1861–1865* (New York: Knopf, 2005), 295; for quote from Iowa soldier, 295.
8. Samuel C. Kirkpatrick to family, January 11, 1863; "List of deserters from Aug 1862 to March 1863," *Wisconsin Adjutant General's Office: Records of Civil War Regiments*, Correspondence, 1861–1865, box 56, folder 2; Quiner Papers, reel 1, vol. 4: March 10, 1862, correspondence by "The Chip"; Woodworth, *Nothing But Victory*, 294–295; for Ohio soldier quote, 294.
9. Bruce Catton, *Grant Moves South* (Boston: Little, Brown, 1960), 366; Jerry Frey, *Grandpa's Gone: The Adventures of Daniel Buchwalter in the Western Army, 1862–1865* (Shippensburg, PA: Burd Street Press, 1998), 25–32; Samuel C. Kirkpatrick to family, January 11, 1863.
10. *ORA* I, vol. 24, part III, 13.
11. Catton, *Grant Moves South*, 370–371; for Lincoln quote, 371.
12. *ORA* I, vol. 24, part III, 20; Shelby Foote, *The Civil War: A Narrative*, vol. 2 (New York: Vintage Books), 322–327; Catton, *Grant Moves South*, 371–374.
13. Ibid.
14. Ibid.
15. Letter of General Washburn to Congressman Washburn, January 28, 1863, as cited by Catton, *Grant Moves South*, 374; *ORA* I, vol. 17, part II, 573.
16. *ORA* I, vol. 24, part I, 22.
17. Susan T. Puck, *Sacrifice at Vicksburg: Letters from the Front* (Shippensburg, PA: Burd Street Press, 1997), 55; Eicher, *The Longest Night*, 438–440; Catton, *Grant Moves South*, 376–377.
18. Capt. Elihu Enos to his wife, March 12, 1863, quoted from http://www.28thwisconsin.com/letters/12mar1863.html.
19. Letter of General Washburn to Congressman Washburn, April 11, 1863, as cited in Catton, *Grant Moves South*, 387; *ORA* I, vol. 24, part III, 126.
20. Ibid., 388–389; Mark Grimsley, *The Hard Hand of War: Union Military Policy toward Southern Civilians, 1861–1865* (New York: Cambridge University Press, 1995), 142–143.
21. *ORA* I, vol. 24, part III, 157; Catton, *Grant Moves South*, 391–392.
22. Stephen E. Ambrose, *A Wisconsin Boy in Dixie: Civil War Letters of James K. Newton* (Madison: State Historical Society of Wisconsin, 1961), Newton to father and mother, February 5, 1863, 54–55.
23. Puck, *Sacrifice at Vicksburg: Letters from the Front*, Thomas to Mattie, February 27, 1863, 51; *ORA* I, vol. 24, part I, 23.
24. Henry P. Strong to his wife, January 22, 1863. Bell Irvin Wiley, *The Life of Billy Yank: The Common Soldier of the Union* (Baton Rouge: Louisiana State University Press, 1952), 233–236.
25. Samuel C. Kirkpatrick to father, March 7, 1863.
26. Robert R. Sherrill to aunt, March 13, 1863.
27. Ibid.
28. Quiner, *The Military History of Wisconsin*, 564; James McMyler, *History of the 11th Wisconsin Veteran Volunteer Infantry [HOTEWVV]* (New Orleans: 1865), 14; Samuel C. Kirkpatrick to father, March 14, 1863; Daily Returns, Eleventh Wisconsin regiment, March 15th, 1863: Present, 526; Absent, 190, WSHA.

29. Isaac H. Elliott and Virgil G. Way, *History of the Thirty-Third Regiment* (1902), 35. There is some discrepancy; the 33rd Illinois, who were still traveling with the 11th Wisconsin, believed they arrived at Milliken's Bend on the 26th of March.
30. Quiner, *The Military History of Wisconsin*, 564; McMyler, *HOTEWVVI*, 14.
31. William Charleton Letters, Author's Collection; United States Congressional Set, First Session of the Forty-Ninth Congress, 1885–1886, Report 296: Washington: Government Printing Office, 1886.
32. Constantia Charleton to William Charleton, March 25, 1863, William Charleton Letters, Author's Collection.
33. Ibid, April 7, 1863.
34. Mary P. Charleton to William Charleton, April 7, 1863.
35. Oliver Mather to sister, unknown date, 1863.
36. Foote, *The Civil War* 2:325–327; Eicher, *The Longest Night: A Military History of the Civil War*, 457–460.
37. Ibid.; *ORA* I, vol. 24, part III, 201.
38. *ORA* I, vol. 24, part I, 29–30; Foote, *The Civil War* 2:327–328; Catton, *Grant Moves South*, 414–415.
39. Ibid.
40. Foote, 328–329, 331–332; *ORA* I, vol. 24, part III, 211–212.
41. Frey, *Grandpa's Gone: The Adventures of Daniel Buchwalter in the Western Army, 1862–1865*, 35–36.
42. Catton, *Grant Moves South*, 419; Ulysses S. Grant, *Personal Memoirs*, vol. 1 (New York: Charles L. Webster, 1885), 466–468; Harold-Guy Smith, "The Populating of Wisconsin," *Geographical Review* 18, no. 3 (July 1928): 406–407.
43. Alling, "Four Years with the Western Army," 8.
44. Catton, *Grant Moves South*, 421–422.
45. *ORA* I, vol. 24, part I, 23, 25–27, 28.
46. Robert R. Sherrill to aunt, April 15, 1863.
47. Oliver Mather to sister, July 22, 1862.
48. Jesse Mather to sister, March 9, 1863.
49. Samuel C. Kirkpatrick to family, April 3, 1863.
50. Ibid., March 29, 1863.
51. Ibid.
52. *ORA* I, vol. 24, part I, 615.
53. Samuel C. Kirkpatrick to family, April 28, 1863.
54. Alling, "Four Years with the Western Army," 8; McMyler, *HOTEWVVI*, 15; *ORA* I, vol. 24, part I, 142–143, 615; Timothy B. Smith, *Champion Hill: Decisive Battle for Vicksburg* (New York: Savas Beatie, 2004), 40; William L. Shea and Terrence J. Winschel, *Vicksburg Is the Key: The Struggle for the Mississippi River* (Lincoln: University of Nebraska Press, 2003), 108–109.
55. Samuel C. Jones, *Reminiscences of the Twenty-second Iowa Volunteer Infantry* (Iowa City, IA: 1907), 29.
56. *ORA* I, vol. 24, part I, 658–659, 661–662.
57. Ibid., 663, 672.
58. *ORA* I, vol. 24, part I, 628. Quiner, *The Military History of Wisconsin*, 564; letter concerning Colonel Charles L. Harris from New York City dated July 2, 1863. Colonel Harris's health would deteriorate and force a leave of absence (furlough) on June 2, 1863, according to the Official Military Personnel Files, National Archives.
59. *ORA* I, vol. 24, part I, 628; Smith, *Champion Hill: Decisive Battle for Vicksburg*, 40–43.
60. Ibid., 628, 665; John Fiske, *The Mississippi Valley in the Civil War* (New York: Houghton Mifflin, 1900), 229; John A. McClernand, *Official Report of Maj. Gen. J.A. McClernand Detailing the March of the Thirteenth Army Corps from Miliken's Bend to Vicksburg* (Springfield: Baker & Phillips, 1863), 5–6.
61. Ibid., part I, 664, 672–673.
62. Ibid., part I, 628.
63. See http://www.civilwaralbum.com/vicksburg/port_gibson.htm. This site has some nice photos of the landscape for all of the major engagements during the Vicksburg Campaign.
64. *ORA* I, vol. 24, part I, 628–629; Alling, "Four Years with the Western Army," 9.
65. McMyler, *HOTEWVVI*, 15; *ORA* I, vol. 24, part I, 672–673.
66. McMyler, *HOTEWVVI*, 27; Charles E. Estabrook, ed., *Wisconsin Losses in the Civil War* (Madison, WI: Adjutant General's Dept., 1915), 51–52.
67. *ORA* I, vol. 24, part I, 628–629, 672–673; Frey, *Grandpa's Gone: The Adventures of Daniel Buchwalter in the Western Army, 1862–1865*, 39–40.
68. *ORA* I, vol. 24, part I, 629.
69. Ibid., 32–33.
70. Ibid., 625–626; McClernand, *Official Report of Maj. Gen. J. A. McClernand Detailing the March of the Thirteenth Army Corps from Miliken's Bend to Vicksburg*, 5–6.
71. Ibid., 628–630.
72. Frey, *Grandpa's Gone: The Adventures of Daniel Buchwalter in the Western Army, 1862–1865*, 40–41. He offers a fine rendition of the battle at Port Gibson, which I referred to several times, specifically pages 39–46.
73. *ORA* I, vol. 24, part I, 15, 625–626.
74. Ibid., 15, 602, 610, 625–626.
75. Ibid.
76. Ibid., 15, 629.
77. Ibid., 602–603.
78. Ibid., 626.
79. Frey's *Grandpa's Gone: The Adventures of Daniel Buchwalter in the Western Army, 1862–1865*, 44–46; Smith, *Champion Hill: Decisive Battle for Vicksburg*, 53.
80. *ORA* I, vol. 24, part I, 673.
81. Ibid., 603.
82. Ibid., 629.
83. Samuel C. Kirkpatrick to family, May 28, 1863.
84. *ORA* I, vol. 24, part I, 630.
85. Ibid., 582–585, 673.
86. Smith, *Champion Hill: Decisive Battle for Vicksburg*, 2–3; Oliver S. Robinson to parents, April 26, 1863. It is highly unlikely that Pemberton could not have known that Grant's main move was now coming from the south once the fleet got past Vicksburg, according to historian Timothy B. Smith.

Chapter Seven

1. Samuel C. Kirkpatrick to family, May 28, 1863.
2. Richard L. Kiper, *Major General John Alexander McClernand: Politician in Uniform* (Kent, OH: Kent State University Press), 195–197; *ORA* I, vol. 52, part I, 314; Catton, *Grant Moves South*, 324–327.
3. *ORA* I, vol. 24, part I, 260, 128–129, 594–595; Foote, *The Civil War* 2:348–349.
4. *ORA* I, vol. 24, part I, 32–33.
5. *ORA* I, vol. 24, part III, 268–269, 843.
6. *ORA* I, vol. 24, part III, 807, 821, 834–846, 842; Foote, *The Civil War* 2:351, 353, 358–359; Catton, *Grant Moves South*, 428–429, 430–431.
7. Ibid.
8. *ORA* I, vol. 24, part I, 35.
9. Catton, *Grant Moves South*, 432–433; Foote, *The Civil War* 2:358.
10. *ORA* I, vol. 24, part III, 296.

11. *ORA* I, vol. 24, part III, 296–297; Foote, *The Civil War* 2:358–360, 367; Catton, *Grant Moves South*, 435–436.
12. Ibid.; *ORA* I, vol. 24, part I, 270; part III, 876.
13. *ORA* I, part I, 50–51; *Civil War Journal of O.S. Bereman*, May 15, 1863, http://www.garthhagerman.com/fambly/bereman1.php; Catton, *Grant Moves South*, 442; Foote, *The Civil War* 2:370–371.
14. Ibid.
15. Foote, *The Civil War* 2:360–362, 365; Catton, *Grant Moves South*, 439–440.
16. *Wisconsin State Journal*, June 7, 1863. Otis writes concerning their operations throughout the month of May. This document, among others, can be viewed at http://www.wisconsinhistory.org.
17. *ORA* I, vol. 24, Part I, 270, 51; Foote, *The Civil War* 2:441–442.
18. Ibid.; *ORA* I, vol. 24, Part II, 41; Foote, *The Civil War* 2:442–443.
19. *ORA* I, part II, 41.
20. Ibid.
21. Foote, *The Civil War* 2:370–371; Smith, *Champion Hill: Decisive Battle for Vicksburg*, 103–104, 116–117.
22. *ORA* I, vol. 24, part II, 42.
23. Ibid., 49.
24. Ibid., 55.
25. *ORA* I, vol. 24, part III, 313, 316–318; Kiper, *Major General John Alexander McClernand: Politician in Uniform*, 241–247; Smith, *Champion Hill: Decisive Battle for Vicksburg*, 187, 190–191.
26. Carr's brigade was about a mile and a half from the front and would have heard the sounds of cannon fire.
27. *ORA* I, vol. 24, part I, 42, 49, 55.
28. Foote, *The Civil War* 2:373; Catton, *Grant Moves South*, 443–444.
29. Ibid.; *ORA* I, vol. 24, part II, 42.
30. Ibid., part II, 49; Foote, *The Civil War* 2:370–372.
31. *ORA* I, part I, 56.
32. Ibid., 50.
33. *Centralia Sentinel*, June 11, 1863. The soldier was Sergeant Bernard Zick of the 8th Wisconsin Infantry Regiment.
34. Foote, *The Civil War* 2:373–375; Catton, *Grant Moves South*, 443–445.
35. Ibid.; *ORA* I, vol. 24, part I, 616. There was plenty of blame to go around for why McClernand failed to be more aggressive. For more details see Richard L. Kiper's *Major General John Alexander McClernand: Politician in Uniform*, 245–248, for a detailed account.

Chapter Eight

1. Shelby Foote, *The Civil War: A Narrative* (New York: Vintage Books, 1986), 373–375; Bruce Catton, *Grant Moves South* (Boston: Little, Brown, 1960), 443–445; *ORA* I, vol. 24, part I, 616; *Official Military Personnel Files*, National Archives. Colonel Harris' health continued to deteriorate until his request for furlough on June 1, 1863, which was granted.
2. Foote, *The Civil War* 2:376–377; Calvin P. Alling, "Four Years with the Western Army: In the Civil War of the United States, 1861–1865," 9, Wisconsin State Historical Archives; Catton, *Grant Moves South*, 445–447; Warren E. Grabau, *Ninety-Eight Days: A Geographer's View of the Vicksburg Campaign* (Knoxville: University of Tennessee Press, 2000), 328–330.
3. Grant, *Personal Memoirs* 1:522–523.
4. Ibid.; *ORA* I, vol. 24, part I, 151–152; Foote, *The Civil War* 2:376–380.
5. H.J. Lewis Correspondence, May 28, 1863, Lewis and Moulton Family Papers.
6. Ibid., 376–377; Alling, "Four Years with the Western Army," 9; Catton, *Grant Moves South*, 445–447; Grant, *Personal Memoirs* 1:525–526. Lawler's height and size are up for debate. The smallest it has been reported is six feet one inch and over 200 pounds in "Michael Kelly Lawler: Mexican and Civil War Officer," *Journal of the Illinois State Historical Society* (Winter 1955): 387. The men of the 33rd Illinois described Lawler as weighing "something over 300 pounds." See Elliott and Way, *History of the Thirty-Third Regiment*, 35, Grabau, *Ninety-Eight Days: A Geographer's View of the Vicksburg Campaign*, 329 (which is also an invaluable resource for any historian studying this event), Sylvanus Cadwallader, *Three Years with Grant, As Recalled by War Correspondent Sylvanus Cadwallader* (New York: Alfred A. Knopf, 1955), 83–84, and Lawler Papers: 122a; Jane W. Crichton, "Michael Kelly Lawler: A Southern Illinois Mexican War Captain and Civil War General," thesis, 115, 173.
7. Ibid.; Grabau, *Ninety-Eight Days: A Geographer's View of the Vicksburg Campaign*, 328–330.
8. For a good description of Lawler, see Crichton's "Michael Kelly Lawler: A Southern Illinois Mexican War Captain and Civil War General," 115, 173. Grant, in his memoirs, recalled seeing Lawler "in his shirt sleeves leading a charge upon the enemy," vol. 1, p. 526.
9. *ORA* I, vol. 24, part II, 136–137; J.T. Dorris, "Michael Kelly Lawler: Mexican and Civil War Officer," *Journal of the Illinois State Historical Society* (Winter 1955): 391–396.
10. Ibid.
11. James McMyler, *History of the 11th Wisconsin Veteran Volunteer Infantry [HOTEWVVI]* (New Orleans, 1865), 16. The charge was said to have been made by "the point of the bayonet," so Harris would have had to order his men to fasten them before the charge. See *ORA* I, vol. 24, part II, 133–142.
12. Quiner Papers, reel 3, vol. 9: "Special dispatch to Chicago Times," May 17, 1863; "Letter from the 11th Regiment," May 20, 1863; Lawler Papers, 146.
13. Dorris, "Michael Kelly Lawler: Mexican and Civil War Officer," 396; Samuel C. Kirkpatrick to family, July 1, 1863.
14. *ORA* I, vol. 24, part II, 137; Catton, *Grant Moves South*, 446; Cadwallader, *Three Years with Grant, As Recalled by War Correspondent Sylvanus Cadwallader*, 83–84.
15. According to one eyewitness report, Grant replied, "See that charge! I think it is too late to abandon this campaign," and with that he rode away towards the action. See Otto Eisenschiml and Ralph Newman, *Eyewitness: The Civil War as We Lived It* (New York: Grosset & Dunlap, 1947), 443–444; Howard C. Westwood, "The Vicksburg/ Port Hudson Gap—The Pincers Never Pinched," *Military Affairs* 46, no. 3 (Oct. 1982): 113–119; Catton, *Grant Moves South*, 446–447.
16. *ORA* I, vol. 24, part II, 137; for quote attributed to the colonel of 99th Illinois, see Catton, *Grant Moves South*, 446.
17. Ibid.; Foote, *The Civil War* 2:376–377; McMyler, *HOTEWVVI*, 16; Crichton, "Michael Kelly Lawler: A Southern Illinois Mexican War Captain and Civil War General," 115, 173.
18. H.J. Lewis correspondence, May 28, 1863.
19. *ORA* I, vol. 24, part II, 137; Foote, *The Civil War* 2:376–377; McMyler, *HOTEWVVI*, 16; Smith, *Champion*

Hill: Decisive Battle for Vicksburg, 392–393; for quote attributed to Sergeant Foster, *21st Alabama*, 393.

20. Ibid.; McMyler, *HOTEWVVI*, 16; Quiner Papers, reel 3, vol. 9: "Special dispatch to Chicago Times," May 17, 1863; "Letter from the 11th Regiment," May 20, 1863; *Wisconsin Adjutant General's Office: Records of Civil War Regiments*, correspondence, 1861–1865, box 56, folder 2. The flag was sent to Madison care of W.H. Watson on August 7, 1863.

21. Ibid.; *Grant Moves South*, 446–448; for Grant quote, 446; Foote, *The Civil War* 2:376–377; *ORA* I, vol. 24, part II, 137–138.

22. Ibid.; *ORA* I, vol. 24, part III, 888; Timothy B. Smith, *Champion Hill: Decisive Battle for Vicksburg* (New York: Savas Beatie, 2004), 394–395; Steven E. Woodworth, *Nothing but Victory: The Army of the Tennessee, 1861–1865* (New York: Knopf, 2005), 394.

23. As quoted by Richard Wheeler, *Voices of the Civil War* (New York: Meridian, 1990), 337.

24. *ORA* I, vol. 24, part II, 137–139.

25. Ibid.; Edwin Cole Bearss, *The Vicksburg Campaign*, vol. 3 (Dayton: Morningside House, 1985), 799.

26. H.J. Lewis correspondence, May 28, 1863.

27. *Grant Moves South*, 446–449; Foote, *The Civil War* 2:380–381; *ORA* I, vol. 24, part II, 137–140.

28. *ORA* I, vol. 24, part II, 140; R.W. Burt to Editor *Chicago Times*, Sunday May 30, 1863; http://www.my.ohio.voyager.net/~lstevens/burt/.

29. "From the 11th Wisconsin," correspondence of the *State Journal*, May 29, 1863.

30. Jeffrey C. Burden, "Failed Attack at Vicksburg," *America's Civil War* (May 2000); http://www.historynet.com/magazines/american_civil_war/3031186.html; Foote, *The Civil War* 2:382–384; Woodworth, *Nothing but Victory*, 405.

31. Ibid.; *ORA* I, vol. 24, part III, 891–892.

32. Bearss, *The Vicksburg Campaign* 3:738–739; *ORA* I, vol. 24, part II, 169–170.

33. *ORA* I, vol. 24, part III, 139–140; *Grant Moves South*, 450–452.

34. Foote, *The Civil War* 2:383–384.

35. *ORA* I, vol. 24, part II, 244; Bearss, *The Vicksburg Campaign* 3:800–801; Burden, "Failed Attack at Vicksburg," *America's Civil War*. For a more detailed description of the wicked defenses facing Grant's army see Grabau's *Ninety-Eight Days: A Geographer's View of the Vicksburg Campaign*, 367–382.

36. Oliver S. Robinson to family, April 26, 1863; Samuel Kirkpatrick to family, April 3, 1863.

37. Osborn H. Oldroyd, *A Soldier's Story of the Siege of Vicksburg* (Springfield, 1885), 31–32; Isaac H. Elliott and Virgil G. Way, *History of the Thirty-Third Regiment*, 242; Burden, "Failed Attack at Vicksburg," *America's Civil War*, May 2000.

38. H.J. Lewis Correspondence, May 28, 1863

39. James Manley Sanford, *Autobiography of James Manley Sanford*, dictated to his children from his deathbed, WVM.

40. This fantastic story was dictated by James Manley Sanford to his children on his deathbed on November 25, 1910.

41. Foote, *The Civil War* 2:383–384; McMyler, *HOTEWVVI*, 17. According to F. Stansbury Haydon, Grant was unprepared for a siege because he did not have proper mortars. Grant plainly states in his memoirs (295) that he "had no siege guns" but that Admiral Porter "supplied us with a battery of navy-guns." Porter did supply 6 mortar boats, each mounting a 13-inch siege gun, but they were effective only within a limited range near the river. What Haydon reveals is that, as the Federal lines approached Confederate entrenchments, away from the river, "a number of mortars were constructed of wood." These devices were ingeniously created and inflicted severe casualties on the enemy. See F. Stansbury Haydon, "Grant's Wooden Mortars and Some Incidents of the Siege of Vicksburg," *The Journal of the American Military Institute*, and Grabau, *Ninety-Eighty Days: A Geographer's View of the Vicksburg Campaign*, 427.

42. Bearss, *The Vicksburg Campaign* 3:802, 807, 823.

43. Elliott and Way, *History of the Thirty-Third Regiment*, 242.

44. Colonel Harris has been quoted using this phrase — "Forward, my brave lads!" — numerous times.

45. *ORA* I, vol. 24, part II, 140–141, 242–245; Burden, "Failed Attack at Vicksburg"; William H. Bentley, *History of the 77th Illinois Volunteer Infantry* (Peoria: Edward Hine, 1883), 151–152; H.J. Lewis correspondence, May 28, 1863. Richard L. Kiper, *Major General John Alexander McClernand: Politician in Uniform* (Kent, OH: Kent State University Press), 252–253.

46. "Vicksburg — The Fortress City," Vicksburg National Park Service, 8

47. Bearss, *The Vicksburg Campaign* 3:824–825; Burden, "Failed Attack at Vicksburg."

48. Ibid.; *ORA* I, vol. 24, part II, 140; Grabau, *Ninety-Eighty Days: A Geographer's View of the Vicksburg Campaign*, 375–382.

49. *ORA* I, vol. 24, part II, 140–141, 242–245; Bentley, *History of the 77th Illinois Volunteer Infantry*, 151–152.

50. *ORA* I, vol. 24, part II, 242–245. Burden, "Failed Attack at Vicksburg."

51. Bearss, *The Campaign for Vicksburg* 3:823–825; Grabau, *Ninety-Eight Days*, 378–380; Bentley, *History of the 77th Illinois Volunteer Infantry*, 151–152; *ORA* I, vol. 24, part II, 141.

52. *ORA* I, vol. 24, part I, 172; part II, 273; Foote, *The Civil War* 2:385; Catton, *Grant Moves South*, 452, Kiper, *Major General John Alexander McClernand: Politician in Uniform*, 252–253, 260–262.

53. *ORA* I, vol. 24, part II, 140–141, 242–245; Bentley, *History of the 77th Illinois Volunteer Infantry*, 151–152; Kiper, *Major General John Alexander McClernand: Politician in Uniform*, 260.

54. *ORA* I, vol. 24, part II, 141.

55. Ibid.

56. *Janesville Daily Gazette*, June 1, 1863; Jesse Mather to mother, July 6, 1863; H.J. Lewis correspondence, May 28, 1863.

57. *ORA* I, vol. 24, part I, 276–277; Foote, *The Civil War* 2:387.

58. Susan T. Puck, *Sacrifice at Vicksburg: Letters from the Front* (Shippensburg, PA: Burd Street Press, 1997), 64–65; Richard H. Shryock, "A Medical Perspective on the Civil War," *American Quarterly* 52 (Summer 1993): 162.

59. Puck, *Sacrifice at Vicksburg: Letters from the front*, 63.

60. *Chicago Tribune*, May 22, 1863.

61. *Janesville Daily Gazette*, June 1, 1863; *Chicago Tribune*, May 22, 1863.

62. Ibid., May 29, 1863.

63. H.J. Lewis correspondence, May 28, 1863.

64. *ORA* I, vol. 24, part II, 161; Charles E. Estabrooke, ed., *Wisconsin Losses in the Civil War* (Madison, WI: Adjutant General's Dept., 1915), 51–52.

65. Samuel C. Kirkpatrick to family, May 28, 1863.

66. Ibid., June 2, 1863.

67. http://www.geocities.com/Heartland/Plains/5660/

vicksburg.htm, originally published in *The Century Illustrated Monthly Magazine* by the Century Co, vol. 30 (May 1885 to October 1885).
  68. Stephen E. Ambrose, *A Wisconsin Boy in Dixie: Civil War Letters of James K. Newton* (Madison, WI: State Historical Society of Wisconsin, 1961), 71.
  69. Ibid., 72, 75.
  70. Alling, "Four Years with the Western Army," 10; Daily Returns, Eleventh Wisconsin regiment, June 11, 1863: Present, 465; Absent, 159 , WSHA.
  71. Jesse Miller in a letter to the 11th Wisconsin during their reunion at Vicksburg on May 18, 1908, WVM. Alling, "Four Years with the Western Army," 10.
  72. Jesse Miller letter, May 18, 1908.
  73. Ibid.
  74. Samuel C. Kirkpatrick to family, June 16, June 23, July 1, 1863.
  75. Jesse Miller letter, May 18, 1908.
  76. *ORA* I, vol. 24, part III, 974, 980; David J. Eicher, *The Longest Night: A Military History of the Civil War* (New York: Simon & Schuster, 2001), 556–557; Catton, *Grant Moves South*, 465–467.
  77. Kiper, *Major General John Alexander McClernand: Politician in Uniform*, 465–467; Woodworth, *Nothing But Victory*, 419–424; Sherman to Ellen Ewing Sherman, May 25, 1863; Sherman to John Sherman, May 29, 1863; Brooks D. Simpson and Jean V. Berlin, eds., *Sherman's Civil War: Selected Correspondences of William T. Sherman, 1861–1865* (Chapel Hill: University of North Carolina Press, 1999), 472–473.
  78. Woodworth, *Nothing but Victory*, 440–443, 445–447; Shea and Winschel, *Vicksburg Is the Key*, 158–160.
  79. Ibid., 46; Eicher, *The Longest Night: A Military History of the Civil War*, 470.
  80. Eicher, *The Longest Night*, 556–557; Catton, *Grant Moves South*, 469–470.
  81. *ORA* I, vol. 24, part II, 348.
  82. Catton, *Grant Moves South*, 472; Woodworth, *Nothing but Victory*, 452–454.
  83. H.J. Lewis correspondence, July 3, 1863.
  84. Ibid., 473–478.
  85. *ORA* I, vol. 24, part I, 62; Foote, *The Civil War* 2:623–624.
  86. Henry P. Strong to Mrs. Henry P. Strong, July 1, 1863.
  87. Ibid., July 8, 9, 12, 1863.
  88. Ibid.
  89. Ibid.; Lieut. Whittlesey to Henry P. Strong, July 8, 21, 1863.
  90. Ibid., July 7, 1863.
  91. Ibid., July 12, 1863.
  92. Samuel C. Kirkpatrick to family, July 5, 1863.
  93. *ORA* I, vol. 24, part I, 6, 62; Grant, *Personal Memoirs* 1:572.

Chapter Nine

  1. "List of Killed and Wounded during May 1863, Vicksburg Campaign," *Wisconsin Adjutant General's Office: Records of Civil War Regiments*, Correspondences, 1861–1865, box 56, folder 3.
  2. Jesse Mather to mother, July 6, 1863.
  3. Robert R. Sherrill to aunt, June 22, 1863.
  4. William H. Cope to father, July 6, 1863.
  5. Samuel C. Kirkpatrick to family, July 15, 1863; Quiner Papers, reel 2, vol. 4: letter from the regiment dated March 2, 1863.
  6. Jesse Mather to sister, July 6, 1863.
  7. James McMyler, *History of the 11th Wisconsin Veteran Volunteer Infantry* [HOTEWVVI] (New Orleans: 1865), 17; Isaac H. Elliott and Virgil G. Way, *History of the Thirty-Third Regiment*, 47; Field and Staff Muster Roll, *Official Military Personnel Files*, National Archives.
  8. Samuel C. Kirkpatrick to family, September 2, 1863.
  9. William H. Cope to father, August 18, 1863.
  10. Calvin P. Alling, "Four Years with the Western Army: In the Civil War of the United States, 1861–1865," Wisconsin State Historical Archives, 11.
  11. Samuel C. Kirkpatrick to family, August 13, 1863.
  12. Shelby Foote, *The Civil War: A Narrative*, vol. 2 (New York: Vintage Books), 634–635.
  13. Samuel C. Kirkpatrick to family, August 29, 1863; Foote, *The Civil War* 2:619.
  14. Ulysses S. Grant, *Personal Memoirs*, vol. 1 (New York: Charles L. Webster, 1885), 578–583.
  15. Letter to the governor, September 13, 1863: *Wisconsin Adjutant General's Office: Records of Civil War Regiments*, Correspondences, 1861–1865, box 56, folder 3.
  16. Samuel C. Kirkpatrick to family, August 4 and 29 and December 10, 1863.
  17. Ibid., September 2, 1863.
  18. Ibid., September 15, 1863; Foote, *The Civil War* 2:773–774; *New York Herald*, September 12, 1863.
  19. Quiner, *The Military History of Wisconsin*, 569; Elliott and Way, *History of the Thirty-Third Regiment*, 49; McMyler, *HOTEWVVI*, 17–19; Samuel C. Kirkpatrick to family, September 24, 1863.
  20. McMyler, *HOTEWVVI*, 19–20; Elliott and Way, *History of the Thirty-Third Regiment*, 53.
  21. Ibid., 20–21; Quiner, *The Military History of Wisconsin*, 570.
  22. Alling, "Four Years with the Western Army," 14; Samuel C. Kirkpatrick to brother, December 10, 14, 1863.
  23. William H. Cope to father, December 23, 1863.
  24. Jesse Mather to mother, October 13, 1863.
  25. Puck, *Sacrifice at Vicksburg: Letters from the Front*, 49–50.
  26. James M. McPherson, *For Cause & Comrades: Why Men Fought in the Civil War* (New York: Oxford University Press, 1997), 38–39, 85.
  27. Eicher, *The Longest Night*, 580–592, 624–625.
  28. Ibid.; Foote, *The Civil War* 2:785; Samuel C. Kirkpatrick to family, December 16, 1863.
  29. Alling, *Four Years with the Western Army*, 13–14.
  30. Ibid.; Samuel C. Kirkpatrick to family, November 14, December 10, 14, 1863.

Chapter Ten

  1. *Appletons' Journal* 2, issue 62 (August 1881), "Badeau's Military History of Grant," 141; Adam Badeau, in his *Military History of General Grant*, vol. 2, chapter 28, gives a detailed description of a typical night for Grant in 1864, 135–137; http://www.perseus.tufts.edu/hopper/.
  2. *ORA* I, vol. 32, part II, 142–143; Ulysses S. Grant, *Personal Memoirs*, vol. 1 (New York: Charles L. Webster, 1885), 578–579, and vol. 2, 19–21.
  3. Grant, *Personal Memoirs* 1:578–579 and 2:19–20, 100–101; Sean Michael O'Brien, *Mobile, 1865: Last Stand of the Confederacy* (Westport, CT: Praeger, 2001), 13–17.
  4. For more on Grant's strategy see Archer Jones, *Civil War Strategy: The Process of Victory and Defeat*, 82–84; *ORA* I, vol. 32, part III, 245–246. Grant, *Personal*

Memoirs 2:348–350; Bruce Catton, *Grant Takes Command* (Boston: Little, Brown, 1968), 12–16, 93–95, 101–103, 112, 152–153, 302.
  5. Ned Bradford, *Battles and Leaders of the Civil War*, vol. 4 (Appleton: Century-Crofts, 1956), 345–374; Grant, *Personal Memoirs*, 139–140.
  6. Eicher, *The Longest Night*, 643–644, 653–657, 838–839; Foote, *The Civil War* 3:89.
  7. Abstract returns of the Department of the Gulf, Arkansas, Missouri, Kansas, and New Mexico, *ORA* I, vol. 34, part IV, 153–157; vol. 34, part III, 545–554, 555.
  8. *ORA* I, vol. 34, part IV, 75–76; vol. 34, part III, 545–554, 555.
  9. *ORA* I, vol. 32, part II, 214–216.
  10. Ibid.; Catton, *Grant Takes Command*, 152–153, 302–303, 386–387; Foote, *The Civil War*, 738. Originally, before the Red River debacle, this plan involved General Banks leading the assault on Mobile.
  11. *ORA* I, vol. 39, part II, 79; *Official Records of the Union and Confederate Navies in the War of the Rebellion* (hereafter cited as *ORN* I) I, vol. 21:317.
  12. *ORA* I, vol. 39, part II, 79, and vol. 31, part III, 349–350. Grant believed that a move on Mobile would have opened up a launching point for a thrust into northern Alabama and possibly western Georgia. This would have secured Mississippi as well, but most importantly, it would have opened up another front for the Confederacy, already overstretched, to defend.
  13. *ORA* I, vol. 38, part IV, 418, and vol. 34, part IV, 240–241
  14. Ibid.
  15. Ibid., and vol. 39, part II, 106, 118, 121–122; Jack Hurst, *Nathan Bedford Forrest, A Biography* (New York: Vintage Books), 186–196.
  16. *ORA* I, vol. 39, Part II, page 115; 121–122.
  17. *ORA* I, vol. 34, Part IV, 438–439.
  18. *ORN* I, vol. 21, 612, 626.
  19. Ibid.; Charles G. Hearn, *Mobile Bay and the Mobile Campaign: The Last Great Battles of the Civil War* (Jefferson, NC: McFarland, 1993), 133–135; John C. Waugh, *Last Stand at Mobile* (Abilene: McWhiney Foundation Press, 2001), 15–18.
  20. Ezra J. Warner, *Generals in Blue* (Baton Rouge: Louisiana State University Press, 1964), 67–68.
  21. Max L. Heyman, *Prudent Solider: A Biography of Major General E.R.S. Canby, 1817–1873* (Glendale, CA: A.H. Clark Co., 1959), 189–199; Grant, *Personal Memories* 2:525–526.
  22. Jesse Mather to mother, December 10, 1863.
  23. http://www.ghosttowns.com/states/tx/indianola.html; Samuel C. Kirkpatrick to family, January 11, 1864.
  24. Jesse Mather to sister, January 9, 1864.
  25. McMyler, *HOTEWVVI*, 21–22; Quiner Papers, reel 3, vol. 9: "Correspondence of the State Journal," February 1, 1864.
  26. Ibid.; Samuel C. Kirkpatrick to family, February 1, 1864; E.B. Quiner, *The Military History of Wisconsin* (Chicago: Clarke, 1866), 570.
  27. Ibid.
  28. McMyler, *HOTEWVVI*, 23–24; On March 8, 1864, the regiment reported: Present 373; Absent, 5, Daily Returns, WSHA.
  29. Alling, "Four Years with the Western Army," 15–16; Samuel Kirkpatrick, "The Civil War Letters of Samuel Cotter Kirkpatrick," WSHA, ii.
  30. Jesse Mather to sister, September 16, 1864.
  31. *Baraboo Weekly News*, August 28, 1924, p. 2.
  32. *ORN* I, vol. 21:559; *ORA* I, vol. 39, part I, 426.
  33. *ORN* I, vol. 21:562.
  34. Ibid., 566; *ORA* I, vol. 39, part I, 403, 426.
  35. Hearn, *Mobile Bay and the Mobile Campaign*, 127.
  36. *ORN* I, vol. 21:566; Hearn, *Mobile Bay and the Mobile Campaign*, 131–140.
  37. *ORN* I, vol. 21:566; *ORA* I, vol. 39, part II, 700.
  38. *ORN* I, vol. 21:612.
  39. Ibid., 534–535.
  40. Ibid., 533–534.
  41. *ORA* I, vol. 39, part II, 298, 306–307.
  42. *ORA* I, vol. 39, part I, 404; vol. 39, part II, 231; vol. 41, part II, 494; vol. 34, part IV, 153–161. The real threat would come from General Sterling Price in September when he raided Missouri. Canby was then forced to send a significant portion of his reserves to Alabama.

Chapter Eleven

  1. Hiram J. Lewis, April 24, 1864; *Janesville Weekly Gazette*, June 29, 1864.
  2. Shelby Foote, *The Civil War: A Narrative*, vol. 3 (New York: Vintage Books, 1986), 128–129.
  3. James McMyler, *History of the 11th Wisconsin Veteran Volunteer Infantry* [*HOTEWVVI*] (New Orleans: 1865), 24–25.
  4. Robert R. Sherrill to aunt, October 17, 1864.
  5. McMyler, *HOTEWVVI*, 28; Samuel C. Kirkpatrick to family, May 16, 1864.
  6. Calvin P. Alling, "Four Years with the Western Army: In the Civil War of the United States, 1861–1865," Wisconsin State Historical Archives, 15–16.
  7. Ithamar Stow Chaffee diary, November 8, 1864, Library of Congress.
  8. Robert R. Sherrill to aunt, October 17, 1864.
  9. Henry Oettiker diary, January 13, 14 and 15, 1865, Author's Collection.
  10. Alling, "Four Years with the Western Army," 16–17.
  11. Samuel C. Kirkpatrick to family, September 7, 1864.
  12. Ibid., October 29, 1864.
  13. John W. Kennedy to wife, June 11, 1864, in Civil War letters written by Private John W. Kennedy, WSHA.
  14. John W. Kennedy to children, June 4, 1864.
  15. John W. Kennedy to wife, December 6, 1864.
  16. Ibid., December 6, 1864.
  17. Ibid., December 6, 1864, February 11 and February 23, 1865.
  18. Warren W. Nye to William Charleton, October 19, 1864.

Chapter Twelve

  1. The regiment reported: Present 520, Daily Returns, Wisconsin State Historical Archives; Calvin P. Alling, "Four Years with the Western Army: In the Civil War of the United States, 1861–1865," WSHA 18–19.
  2. *ORA* I, vol. 49, part I, 91–92.
  3. Ibid., 1164; Ulysses S. Grant, *Personal Memoirs*, vol. 2 (New York: Charles L. Webster, 1885), 519–520.
  4. Noah Andre Trudeau, *Like Men of War: Black Troops in the Civil War, 1862–1865* (New York: Back Bay Books, 1998), 396–398.
  5. Alling, "Four Years with the Western Army," 19.
  6. *ORA* I, vol. 49, part I, 93.
  7. William Henry Oettiker diary, Friday March 17, 1865; Stephen E. Ambrose, *A Wisconsin Boy in Dixie: Civil War Letters of James K. Newton* (Madison: State Historical Society of Wisconsin, 1961), 143–146.

8. James B. Lockney to family, March 17, 18 and 19, 1865, Civil War Journal of James B. Lockney, WSHA; A.F. Sperry, *History of the 33d Iowa Infantry Volunteer Regiment, 1863–6*, edited by G.J.W. Urwin and Cathy K. Urwin (University Press of Arkansas, 1999, originally printed 1866), 142.
9. Ibid.
10. Ibid.
11. Lockney noted the fires being set by the advanced troops of his corps in his entry on March 20, 1865.
12. James B. Lockney to family, March 20 and 21, 1865; Thomas G. Rodgers, "Last Stand at Fort Blakely," *America's Civil War* (November 1998): 48–55.
13. Samuel C. Kirkpatrick to family, March 23, 1865.
14. Oettiker diary, Friday, March 23, 1865.
15. William Henry Harrison Clayton, *A Damned Iowa Greyhound: The Civil War letters of William Henry Harrison Clayton*, edited by Donald C. Elder III (Iowa City: University of Iowa Press, 1998), 158.
16. http://www.fortunecity.com/westwood/makeover/347/index.htm.
17. Ibid.
18. Sean Michael O'Brien, *Mobile, 1865: Last Stand of the Confederacy* (Westport, CT: Praeger, 2001), 115–117; John K. Folmar, *From That Terrible Field: Civil War Letters of James M. Williams, Twenty-First Alabama Infantry Volunteers* (Tuscaloosa: University of Alabama Press, 1981), 158.
19. Letter from Corporal D.G. Gammack of Co. D., 38th Inf., to his mother in Clarke County. This can be found at http://www.south-alabama-confederate-records.com/cammack%20letter.htm.
20. William P. Chambers, *Blood and Sacrifice: The Civil War Journal of a Confederate Soldier*, edited by Richard A. Baumgartner (Huntington, WV: Blue Acorn Press, 1994), 204–206; O'Brien, *Mobile, 1865: Last Stand of the Confederacy*, 26–28.
21. Ann K. Blomquist and Robert A. Taylor, eds., *This Cruel War: The Civil War Letters of Grant and Malinda Taylor, 1862–1865* (Macon, GA: Mercer University Press, 2000), 322.
22. *Mobile Register*, April 8, 1865, "Letter from Blakely."
23. The Diary of Joseph W. Hillier, entries for March 27, 28, and 29, 1865, WSHA; ORA I, vol. 49, part I, 94.
24. ORA I, vol. 49, part I, 315–316; O'Brien, *Mobile, 1865: Last Stand of the Confederacy*, 45.
25. ORA I, vol. 49, part I, 315–317; Rodgers, "Last Stand at Fort Blakely," 48–55.
26. ORA I, vol. 49, part I, 315–317; part II, 1180.
27. Ambrose, *A Wisconsin Boy in Dixie*, 148–149.
28. James B. Lockney to family, April 5, 1865.
29. Ibid., April 4, 1865.
30. ORA I, vol. 49, part I, 317; part II, 1180. O'Brien, *Mobile, 1865: Last Stand of the Confederacy*, 55; Hearn, *Mobile Bay and the Mobile Campaign*, 174.
31. ORA I, vol. 49, part II, 1215, 1217–1218, 1219; O'Brien, *Mobile, 1865: Last Stand of the Confederacy*, 173–176.
32. ORA I, vol. 49, part I, 315–317; O'Brien, *Mobile, 1865: Last Stand of the Confederacy*, 175–176; Clayton, *A Damned Iowa Greyhound*, 161.
33. ORA I, vol. 49, part I, 267; O'Brien, *Mobile, 1865: Last Stand of the Confederacy*, 176–177.
34. ORA I, vol. 49, part I, 317; O'Brien, *Mobile, 1865: Last Stand of the Confederacy*, 177–178.
35. Ambrose, *A Wisconsin Boy in Dixie*, 151.
36. ORA I, vol. 46, part I, 56; Jay Winik, *April 1865: The Month That Saved America* (New York: Perennial, 2001), 142–145–150, 166–190; Bruce Catton, *The Army of the Potomac: A Stillness at Appomattox* (New York: Doubleday, 1953), 368–371, 380.
37. Ibid.
38. Ibid.
39. O'Brien, *Mobile, 1865: Last Stand of the Confederacy*, 90.
40. ORA I, vol. 49, part I, 289; O'Brien, *Mobile, 1865: Last Stand of the Confederacy*, 186–187; Michael W. Fitzgerald, "Another kind of glory: Black participation and its consequences in the campaign for confederate mobile," *Alabama Review* (October, 2001); http://www.findarticles.com/p/articles/mi_qa3880/is_200110.
41. ORA I, vol. 49, part I, 97, 289, 293.
42. Ibid., 97, 289.
43. Ibid., 97, 291–296.
44. Henry M. Crydenwise to family, April 9, 1865.
45. ORA I, vol. 49, part I, 97, 298.
46. ORA I, vol. 49, part I, 97, 294–298.
47. Ibid., 97, 294, 296, 298.
48. Fitzgerald, "Another kind of glory: Black participation and its consequences in the campaign for confederate mobile"; http://www.findarticles.com/p/articles/mi_qa3880/is_200110; O'Brien, *Mobile, 1865: Last Stand of the Confederacy*, 189.
49. Ibid.
50. ORA I, vol. 49, part II, 1188.
51. Fitzgerald, "Another kind of glory: Black participation and its consequences in the campaign for confederate mobile"; http:// www.findarticles.com/p/articles/mi_qa3880/is_200110.
52. Ibid.; O'Brien, *Mobile, 1865: Last Stand of the Confederacy*, 79–80; Rodgers, "Last Stand at Fort Blakely," 50–52.
53. William Flenner, "What an awful destruction of human life," *Civil War Times* (December 2004): 26–28, 72.
54. Henry Oettiker diary, April 4, 1865, Author's Collection.
55. ORA I, vol. 49, part 1, 260–262; Jesse Miller's order to "Fall in, Eleventh" was recorded by Reverend George Wells in his sermon delivered a few days after the assault. See Appendix D.
56. ORA I, vol. 49, part 1, 255, 266, 261.
57. Elias D. Moore to his mother, April 10, 1865.
58. O'Brien, *Mobile, 1865: Last Stand of the Confederacy*, 193–194.
59. Martin Roof, "The Diary of Martin Roof, Co. 114th Ohio Volunteer Infantry," April 10, 1865; Clayton, *A Damned Iowa Greyhound*, 160–161.
60. Ibid.
61. Elias D. Moore to mother, April 10, 1865; Roof, "The Diary of Martin Roof," April 10, 1865; Clayton, *A Damned Iowa Greyhound*, 160–161.
62. Trudeau, *Like Men of War*, 405; ORA I, vol. 49, part 1, 287, 291, 294–296
63. Ibid.
64. Ibid.; O'Brien, *Mobile, 1865: Last Stand of the Confederacy*, 193.
65. ORA I, vol. 49, part 1, 261, 266.
66. George F. Rowell, *Mazomain Sickle*, April 19, 1879, WVM; O'Brien, *Mobile, 1865: Last Stand of the Confederacy*, 191–192.
67. John Ritland, *John Ritland Memoirs*, eHistory.com, Chapter Seven: February 1865–April 1865, http://ehistory.osu.edu/osu/sources/letters/ritland/07.cfm#Fort%20Blakely.
68. ORA I, vol. 49, part 1, 287; O'Brien, *Mobile, 1865: Last Stand of the Confederacy*, 197, 198–200; Rodgers, "Last Stand at Fort Blakely," 48–55.

69. Walter A. Chapman to parents, April 11, 1865, Walter A. Chapman Papers, Manuscripts and Archives, Yale University Library; O'Brien, *Mobile, 1865: Last Stand of the Confederacy*, 196–197, 198–201; for "Their eyes glittered like serpents" quote, 198; Trudeau, *Like Men of War*, 404–405.

70. Ibid.; O'Brien, *Mobile, 1865: Last Stand of the Confederacy*, 199; B.C. Bryner, *Bugle Echoes: The Story of the Illinois 47th* (1905), 154; Michael W. Fitzgerald, "Another kind of glory: Black participation and its consequences in the campaign for Confederate Mobile."

71. Sperry, *History of the 33d Iowa Infantry Volunteer Regiment 1863–6*, 158–59.

72. "List of Killed and Wounded during the Siege of Mobile," Wisconsin Adjutant General's Office: Records of Civil War Regiments, Correspondences, 1861–1865, box 56, folder 3.

73. Flenner, "What an awful destruction of human life," 72.

Chapter Thirteen

1. Frank L. Klement, *Wisconsin in the Civil War* (Madison: State Historical Society of Wisconsin, 1997), 123.

2. As quoted by the *Janesville Weekly Gazette*, April 13, 1865, p. 4.

3. Quiner, *The Military History of Wisconsin*, 8; William Henry Oettiker diary, Friday April 20, 25, May 1, 1865.

4. Samuel C. Kirkpatrick to family, May 12, 1865.

5. Ibid., July 17, 1865.

6. Calvin P. Alling, "Four Years with the Western Army: In the Civil War of the United States, 1861–1865," Wisconsin State Historical Archives, 20.

7. Ibid.

8. Ibid., 21.

9. In October 1864, regimental historian James J. McMyler estimated the regiment had traveled 8,000 miles and that 3,500 of them were spent on the march. This was before their efforts in the Mobile Campaign and the taking of Fort Blakely in April 1865.

10. I am indebted to the work of Melvin E. Kirkpatrick, who dutifully transcribed all of Samuel's letters and gave them to the Wisconsin Historical Society.

11. Alling, "Four Years with the Western Army," i.

12. *Mazomain Sickle*, April 19, 1879.

13. Information taken from census reports unless otherwise noted.

14. http://www.freepages.history.rootsweb.com/~wirockbios/Bios/bios1483.html.

15. Obituary for Charles L. Harris, *Omaha Morning World-Herald*, October 12, 1910, p. 3.

16. Jesse Miller in a letter to the 11th Wisconsin reunion at Vicksburg, May 18, 1908.

Bibliography

Abbreviations: HOTEWVVI—*History of the 11th Wisconsin Veteran Volunteer Infantry.* HOW—State Historical Society of Wisconsin. LOC—Library of Congress. ORA—*The War of the Rebellion: A Compilation of the Official Records of the Union and Confederate Armies.* ORN—*Official Records of the Union and Confederate Navies in the War of the Rebellion.* USAMHI—United States Army Military History Institute. WSHA—Wisconsin State Historical Archives. WVM—Wisconsin Veterans Museum.

Books and Articles

Ambrose, Stephen E. *A Wisconsin Boy in Dixie: Civil War Letters of James K. Newton.* Madison: State Historical Society of Wisconsin, 1961.

Andrews, Christopher C. *History of the Campaign of Mobile.* New York, 1867.

Appler, Augustus C. *The Guerrillas of the West.* St. Louis: Eureka, 1876.

Arthur, George Clinton. *Bushwhacker.* Rolla, MO: Rolla Printing, 1938.

Banasik, Michael E. *Embattled Arkansas: The Prairie Grove Campaign of 1862.* Wilmington, NC: Broadfoot, 1996.

Bearss, Edwin Cole. *The Vicksburg Campaign.* Dayton, OH: Morningside House, 1985.

Bentley, William H. *History of the 77th Illinois Volunteer Infantry.* Peoria, IL: Edward Hine Printers, 1883.

Billings, John D. *Hard Tack and Coffee: Soldier's Life in the Civil War.* Old Saybrook, CT: Konecky & Konecky, 1887.

Blomquist, Ann K., and Robert A. Taylor, eds. *This Cruel War: The Civil War Letters of Grant and Malinda Taylor, 1862–1865.* Macon, GA: Mercer University Press, 2000.

Boatner, Mark M., III. *The Civil War Dictionary.* New York: David McKay, 1959.

Bobrick, Benson. *Testament: A Soldier's Story of the Civil War.* New York: Simon & Schuster, 2003.

Bradford, Ned. *Battles and Leaders of the Civil War.* Appleton, WI: Century-Crofts, 1956.

Bringhurst, Thomas, and Frank Swigart. *History of the Forty-Sixth Regiment Indiana Volunteer Infantry.* Logansport, IN: Wilson, Humphreys, 1888.

Bryner B.C. *Bugle Echoes: The Story of the Illinois 47th.* 1905.

Burden, Jeffry C. "Failed Attack at Vicksburg." *America's Civil War* (May 2000).

Bush, Bryan S. *The Civil War Battles of the Western Theatre.* Paducah, KY: Turner, 1998.

Cadwallader, Sylvanus. *Three Years with Grant, As Recalled by War Correspondent Sylvanus Cadwallader.* New York: Alfred A. Knopf, 1955.

Catton, Bruce. *The Army of the Potomac: A Stillness at Appomattox.* New York: Doubleday, 1953.

_____. *Grant Moves South.* Boston: Little, Brown, 1960.

_____. *Grant Takes Command.* Boston: Little, Brown, 1968.

Chambers, William P. *Blood and Sacrifice: The Civil War Journal of a Confederate Soldier.* Edited by Richard A. Baumgartner. Huntington, WV: Blue Acorn Press, 1994.

Christ, Mark K., ed. *Rugged and Sublime: The Civil War in Arkansas.* Fayetteville: University of Arkansas Press, 1994.

Clayton, William Henry Harrison. *A Damned Iowa Greyhound: The Civil War Letters of William Henry Harrison Clayton.* Edited by Donald C. Elder III. Iowa City: University of Iowa Press, 1998.

Cole, Harry Ellsworth, ed. *A Standard History of Sauk County, Wisconsin.* Chicago: Lewis, 1918.

Crawford, Richard. *The Civil War Songbook: Complete Original Sheet Music for 37 Songs.* New York: Dover, 1977.

Current, Richard N. *The History of Wisconsin*, vol. 2, *The Civil War Era, 1848–1873.* Madison: State Historical Society of Wisconsin, 1976.

Daniel, Larry J., and Lynn N. Bock. *Island No. 10: Struggle for the Mississippi Valley.* Tuscaloosa: University of Alabama Press, 1996.

Dorris, J.T. "Michael Kelly Lawler: Mexican and Civil War Officer." *Journal of the Illinois State Historical Society* (Winter 1955).

Dyer, Frederick H. *A Compendium of the War of the Rebellion*, vol. 2. Dayton, OH: Morningside, 1979.

Eicher, David J. *The Longest Night: A Military History of the Civil War*. New York: Simon & Schuster, 2001.

Eisenschiml, Otto, and Ralph Newman. *Eyewitness: The Civil War as We Lived It*. New York: Grosset & Dunlap, 1947.

Estabrook, Charles E., ed. *Records and Sketches of Military Organizations*. Madison, WI: Adjutant General's Dept., 1914.

_____, ed. *Wisconsin Losses in the Civil War*. Madison, WI: Adjutant General's Dept., 1915.

Faust, Patricia L. *Historical Times Illustrated Encyclopedia of the Civil War*. New York: HarperCollins, 1986.

Fiske, John. *The Mississippi Valley in the Civil War*. New York: Houghton Mifflin, 1900.

Fitzgerald, Michael W. "Another kind of glory: Black participation and its consequences in the campaign for confederate mobile." *Alabama Review* (October 2001).

Flenner, William. "What an awful destruction of human life." *Civil War Times* (December 2004).

Folmar, John K. *From That Terrible Field: Civil War Letters of James M. Williams, Twenty-First Alabama Infantry Volunteers*. Tuscaloosa: University of Alabama Press, 1981.

Foote, Shelby. *The Civil War: A Narrative*. New York: Vintage Books, 1986.

Frey, Jerry. *Grandpa's Gone: The Adventures of Daniel Buchwalter in the Western Army, 1862–1865*. Shippensburg, PA: Burd Street Press, 1998.

Gallaway, B.P. *The Ragged Rebel: A Common Soldier in W.H. Parson's Texas Cavalry*. Austin: University of Texas Press, 1988.

Grabau, Warren E. *Ninety-Eight Days: A Geographer's View of the Vicksburg Campaign*. Knoxville: University of Tennessee Press, 2000.

Grant, Ulysses S. *Personal Memoirs*. 2 vols. New York: Charles L. Webster, 1885.

Grimsley, Mark. *The Hard Hand of War: Union Military Policy toward Southern Civilians, 1861–1865*. New York: Cambridge University Press, 1995.

Haydon, F. Stansbury. "Grant's Wooden Mortars and Some Incidents of the Siege of Vicksburg." *The Journal of the American Military Institute* (Spring 1940).

Hearn, Charles G. *Mobile Bay and the Mobile Campaign: The Last Great Battles of the Civil War*. Jefferson, NC: McFarland, 1993.

Heyman, Max L. *Prudent Solider: A Biography of Major General E.R.S. Canby, 1817–1873*. Glendale, CA: A.H. Clark, 1959.

Hougland, James H. *Civil War Diary of James H. Hougland, Company "G" 1st Indiana Cavalry*. Transcribed and edited by Oscar F. Curtis. Bloomington, IN: Monroe County Historical Society, 1962.

Hurst, Jack. *Nathan Bedford Forrest, A Biography*. New York: Vintage Books, 1994.

Ingenthron, Elmo. *Borderland Rebellion: A History of the Civil War on the Missouri-Arkansas Border*. Missouri: Ozarks Mountaineer, 1980.

Jones, Archer. *The Art of War in the Western World*. New York: Oxford University Press, 1987.

_____. *Civil War Command & Strategy*. New York: Free Press, 1992.

Jones, Samuel C. *Reminiscences of the Twenty-second Iowa Volunteer Infantry*. Iowa City, 1907.

Keegan, John. *Fields of Battle: The Wars for North America*. New York: Vintage Books, 1995.

_____. *The Mask of Command*. New York: Penguin, 1988.

Kennedy, Frances H. *The Civil War Battlefield Guide*. Boston: Houghton Mifflin, 1990.

Kiper, Richard L. *Major General John Alexander McClernand: Politician in Uniform*. Kent, OH: Kent State University Press.

Klement, Frank L. *Wisconsin in the Civil War*. Madison: State Historical Society of Wisconsin, 1997.

Kohl, Rhonda M. "'This Godforsaken Town': Death and Disease at Helena, Arkansas." *Civil War History* 50, no. 2 (2004).

Linderman, Gerald F. *Embattled Courage: The Experience of Combat in the American Civil War*. New York: Free Press, 1987.

Love, William De Loss. *Wisconsin in the War of the Rebellion*. New York: Sheldon, 1866.

Mackey, Robert R. *The Uncivil War: Irregular Warfare in the Upper South, 1861–1865*. Norman: University of Oklahoma Press, 2004.

McClernand, John A. *Official Report of Maj. Gen. J. A. McClernand Detailing the March of the Thirteenth Army Corps from Miliken's Bend to Vicksburg Including an Account of the Battles of Port Gibson, Champion Hill, Big Black River, and the Assault upon the Defences of Vicksburg*. Springfield: Steam Press of Messrs. Baker & Phillips, 1863.

McMyler, James. *History of the 11th Wisconsin Veteran Volunteer Infantry*. New Orleans, 1865.

McPherson, James M. *Battle Cry of Freedom: The Civil War Era*. New York: Oxford University Press, 1988.

_____. *Crossroads of Freedom: Antietam*. New York: Oxford University Press, 2002.

_____. *Drawn With the Sword: Reflections on the American Civil War*. New York: Oxford University Press, 1996.

_____. *For Cause and Comrades: Why Men Fought in the Civil War*. New York: Oxford University Press, 1997.

Mitchell, Reid. *Civil War Soldiers*. New York: Viking, 1988.

_____. *The Vacant Chair: The Northern Soldier Leaves Home*. New York: Oxford University Press, 1993.

Nelson, Glenn T., and John D. Squier. "The Confederate Defense of Northeast Arkansas and the Battle of Cotton Plant, Arkansas, July 7, 1862." *Rivers & Roads & Points in Between* 16 (Spring 1989).

Nevins, Allan. *War for the Union.* 4 vols. New York: Konecky & Konecky, 1971.

_____. *Vol. I: The Improvised War, 1861–1862.* New York: Konecky & Konecky, 1971.

_____. *Vol. II: War Becomes Revolution.* New York: Konecky & Konecky, 1971.

O'Brien, Sean Michael. *Mobile, 1865: Last Stand of the Confederacy.* Westport, CT: Praeger, 2001.

Oldroyd, Osborn H. *A Soldier's Story of the Siege of Vicksburg.* Springfield, IL: 1885.

Paludan, Phillip Shaw. *A People's Contest: The Union & Civil War, 1861–1865.* Lawrence: University of Kansas Press, 1996.

Prucha, Francis Paul. "Distribution of Regular Army Troops before the Civil War." *Military Affairs* 16, no.4 (Winter 1952).

Puck, Susan T. *Sacrifice at Vicksburg: Letters from the Front.* Shippensburg, PA: Burd Street Press, 1997.

Quiner, E.B. *The Military History of Wisconsin: Civil and Military Patriotism of the State in the War for the Union.* Chicago, IL: Clarke, 1866.

Robinson, John. "Re-enlistment Patterns of Civil War Soldiers." *Journal of Interdisciplinary History* (Summer 2001).

Rodgers, Thomas G. "Last Stand at Fort Blakely." *America's Civil War* (November 1998).

Rood, Hosea W. *History of Wisconsin Veterans' Home: 1886–1926.* Madison, WI: Democrat Printing, 1926.

Schafer, Joseph. *A History of Agriculture in Wisconsin.* Madison: State Historical Society of Wisconsin, 1922.

Shea, William. "The Confederate Defeat at Cache River." *Arkansas Historical Quarterly* 52 (Summer 1993).

Shea, William L., and Terrence J. Winschel. *Vicksburg Is the Key: The Struggle for the Mississippi River.* Lincoln: University of Nebraska Press, 2003.

Shryock, Richard H. "A Medical Perspective on the Civil War." *American Quarterly* 14, no. 2, part 1 (Summer 1962).

Simpson, Brooks D., and Jean V. Berlin, eds. *Sherman's Civil War: Selected Correspondences of William T. Shermanm, 1861–1865.* Chapel Hill: University of North Carolina Press, 1999.

Smith, Harold-Guy. "The Populating of Wisconsin." *Geographical Review* 18, no. 3 (July 1928).

Smith, Timothy B. *Champion Hill: Decisive Battle for Vicksburg.* New York: Savas Beatie, 2004.

Sperry, A.F. *History of the 33d Iowa Infantry Volunteer Regiment, 1863–6.* Edited by Gregory J.W. Urwin and Cathy Kunzinger Urwin. A reprinting by the University Press of Arkansas, 1999, of the 1866 edition.

Stotherd, R.H. *Notes on Torpedoes, Offensive and Defensive.* Washington: Government Printing Office, 1872.

Trask, Kerry A. *Fire Within: A Civil War Narrative from Wisconsin.* Kent, OH: Kent State University Press, 1995.

Trudeau, Noah Andre. *Like Men of War: Black Troops in the Civil War, 1862–1865.* New York: Back Bay Books, 1998.

Warner, Ezra J. *Generals in Blue.* Baton Rouge: Louisiana State University Press, 1964.

Waugh, John C. *Last Stand at Mobile.* Abilene, Texas: McWhiney Foundation Press, 2001.

Way, Virgil Gilman, and Isaac Hughes Elliott. *History of the Thirty-Third Regiment Illinois Veteran Volunteer Infantry in the Civil War, 22nd August, 1861, to 7th December, 1865.* Gibson City, Ill: [Regimental] Association, 1902.

Westwood, Howard C. "The Vicksburg/ Port Hudson Gap — The Pincers Never Pinched." *Military Affairs* 46, no. 3.

Wheaton, James W., ed. *Surgeon on Horseback: The Missouri and Arkansas Journal and Letters of Dr. Charles Brackett of Rochester, Indiana 1861–1863.* Carmel, IN: Guild Press of Indiana, 1998.

Wheeler, Richard. *Voices of the Civil War.* New York: Meridian, 1990.

Wiley, Bell Irvin. *The Life of Billy Yank: The Common Soldier of the Union.* Baton Rouge: Louisiana State University Press, 1952.

Williams, T. Harry. *Military Analysis of the Civil War.* New York: American Military Institute, 1977.

Winik, Jay. *April 1865: The Month That Saved America.* New York: Perennial, 2001.

Woodworth, Steven E. *Nothing But Victory: The Army of the Tennessee, 1861–1865.* New York: Knopf, 2005.

Theses

Chrichton, Jane W. "Michael K. Lawler, A Southern Illinois Mexican War Captain and Civil War General." Master's thesis, Southern Illinois University, 1965.

Keltner, H.L. "The History of the 33rd Illinois Volunteer Infantry Regiment." Master's thesis, Illinois State University, 1968.

Newspapers

The Appleton Crescent
Beloit Free Press
Chicago Tribune
Cincinnati Gazette
Daily Missouri Democrat
Janesville Daily Gazette
Janesville Gazette
Madison Capital Times
Mazomain Sickle
Milwaukee Sentinel

Mobile Register
New York Herald
New York Times
New York Tribune
Richland County Observer
West Bend Editorial
Wisconsin State Journal

Manuscripts

Alling, Calvin P. "Four Years with the Western Army: In the Civil War of the United States, 1861–1865." WSHA.

Bereman, O.S. Civil War Journal of O.S. Bereman. Private Collection.

Bennett, Lucien B. Papers, 1861–1864. WVM.

Bird, Frederick A. Civil War Papers. WSHA.

Burt, Captain Richard W. Civil War Letters from the 76th Ohio Volunteer Infantry. Private Collection.

Caddell, Richard. Papers, 1862–1896. WSHA.

Chaffee, Ithamar Stowe. "Ithamar Stowe Chaffee Journal, Co. H, 11th Regiment of the Wisconsin Volunteers of the Town of Newton, Marquette County, Wisconsin." Transcribed by Orest A. Ranum. LOC.

Chambers, William Pitt. "Blood and Sacrifice: The Civil War Journal of a Confederate Soldier." Edited by Richard A. Baumgartner.

Chapman, Walter A. Walter A. Chapman Papers. Yale University Library.

Charleton, William. William Charleton Letters, 1862–1864. Author's Collection.

———. William Charleton Papers, 1820–1879. WSHA.

Clayton, William H.H. "A Damned Iowa Greyhound: The Civil War Letters of William Henry Harrison Clayton." Edited by Donald C. Elder II. Private Collection.

Cope, William H. Letters. WSHA.

Corscot, Ruby Peck. Papers, 1850–1962. WSHA.

Crydenwise, Henry M. Letters, 1861–1866. Emory University: Woodruff Library Special Collections.

Grover, Aurelia. Aurelia Grover Letters. WSHA.

Harris, Charles L. Official Military Personnel File. National Archives.

Hillier, Joseph W. The Diary of Joseph W. Hillier. WSHA.

Hough, Daniel E. Daniel E. Hough Papers. WSHA.

Kennedy, John W. Civil War Letters. WSHA.

Kirkpatrick, Samuel. "The Civil War Letters of Samuel C. Kirkpatrick." Edited by Melvin E. Kirkpatrick. WSHA.

Lewis, Hiram J.B. Lewis and Moulton Family Papers, 1862–1932. WSHA.

Livermore, Francis S. A pocket diary, 1861–1865/Francis S. Livermore. USAMHI.

Lockney, James B. Civil War Journal of James B. Lockney. WSHA

Mather, Jesse, and Oliver Mather. Jesse and Oliver Mather Papers. WSHA.

Miller, Jesse. Jesse Miller Letter. WVM.

Minis, Joseph. Joseph Minis Letters. WSHA

Newton, James K. Papers, 1849–1879. WSHA.

Newton, Jones. Papers and photographs, 1863. WVM.

Oettiker, William Henry. 1864 to 1865 Civil War Diary. Author's Collection.

Priestley, Thomas. Papers, 1856–1891. WSHA.

Quiner, E.B. Correspondence of Wisconsin Volunteers, 1861–65. E.B. Quiner Papers. WSHA.

Rice, Thaddeus. Thaddeus Rice Letter. WSHA.

Richardson, Lyman. Civil War Diary of Lyman Richardson, 1862–63. Private Collection.

Ritland, John. John Ritland Memoirs. Private Collection. http://www.ehistory.osu.edu.

Robinson, Oliver S. Oliver S. Robinson Papers. WSHA.

Roof, Martin. The Diary of Martin Roof Co. 114th Ohio Volunteer Infantry. Elias D. Moore Collection.

Rowley Family Papers, 1837–1967. WSHA.

Sanford, James Manley. Autobiography of James Manley Sanford. WVM.

Sherrill, Robert R. Robert R. Sherrill Civil War Letters. WVM.

Smith, Byron J. Civil War Letters, 1861–1865. WSHA.

Stevens, Charles A. Civil War Letters of Charles A Stevens. WSHA.

Strong, Henry P. Henry P. Strong Letters, 1861–1864. WSHA.

Thompson, Martin V. Martin Thompson Letter. Leigh Collection. USAMHI.

Truman, William. Diary. Joseph Riggs Collection. USAMHI.

Twining, Henry H. Henry H. Twining Papers. WSHA.

Wells, George. George Wells Letter. WSHA.

Wheeler, Joel F. Joel Wheeler Letter. Leigh Collection. USAMHI.

Wiley, George, and Luther Wiley. George and Luther Wiley Letters. Earl Hess Collection. USAMHI.

Winslow, Joseph R. Diary of Joseph R. Winslow, Co. C, 11 Reg. Wis. Vols. WSHA.

Documents

United States War Department. "Consolidated Morning Reports." Box 3, 11th Infantry, November 16, 1862 – December 31, 1864. WSHA.

United States War Department. *Official records of the Union and Confederate Navies in the War of the Rebellion*. United States War Department, 1906.

United States War Department. *War of the Rebellion: A Compilation of the Official Records of the Union and Confederate Armies.* United States War Department, 1886.

Wisconsin, Adjutant General's Office. Records of Civil War Regiments, 1861–1900. Boxes 52–57. WSHA.

Websites

http://www.ancestry.com
http://www.cdl.library.cornell.edu (Cornell University)
http://www.civilwaralbum.com
http://www.digicoll.library.wisc.edu/WI/ (State of Wisconsin Digital Collections)
http://www.ehistory.osu.edu
http://www.findarticles.com
http://www.memory.loc.gov/ammem/cwphtml/cwphome.html
http://www.museum.dva.state.wi.us/Res_regiments.asp
http://www.my.execpc.com/~cra1/11thMain.html
http://www.perseus.tufts.edu/hopper/ (Perseus Digital Library)
http://www.rootsweb.com/~wirichla/index.htm
http://www.south-alabama-confederate-records.com
http://www.uwosh.edu/archives/civilwar/civilwar.html
http://www.wisconsinhistory.org (Wisconsin Historical Society)
http://www.wisconsinhistory.org/wlhba/

Index

Numbers in *bold italics* indicate pages with illustrations.

Alexander W. Randall 7–9
Alling, Calvin P. 15, 52, 57, 67, 76, 79, 81–82, 112, 120, 122–123, 125, 132, 137–139, 143–144, 155, 162–163
Alton, Illinois 24, 25
Andrews, Christopher C. 146, 152, 155, 159
Appleton, Wisconsin 18
Appomattox Courthouse 142
Aransas Bay, Texas 122, *123*, 124
Arkansas 38, 39–40, *43*, 44–56
Arkansas Historical Quarterly 49
Arkansas river valley 39–40
Army of the Potomac 12, 136
Army of the Southwest 33
Army of the Tennessee 68, 73, 88, 102
Army of the Trans-Mississippi 20
Atwood, J.P. 8

Baldwin, William E. 84
Baltimore Gazette 120
Banks, Nathaniel P. 69, 98, 121–122, 126–127, 136
Baraboo Range, Wisconsin 13
Baraboo Rangers 12
Barnes, Calvin C. 28
Barret, Abraham 31
baseball 144
Batesville, Arkansas 37, 40
Baton Rouge, Louisiana 69
Battle of Antietam 67
Battle of Bayou Cache 46, *47*, 50–56
Battle of Big Black River 96–97, *98*, 99–101
Battle of Bull Run 10
Battle of Champion Hill 90, *91*, 92–95
Battle of Chickamauga 124
Battle of Fort Blakely *151*, 152–160
Battle of Fredericksburg 68
Battle of Gettysburg 136
Battle of New Orleans (1815) 143
Battle of Pea Ridge 34, 41
Battle of Port Gibson 79, *80*, 81–86
Battle of Shiloh 68–69
Battle of Spotsylvania Courthouse 137

Battle of Wilson's Creek 22–23
Bayou De View 48–49
Beaver Dam Rifles 11
Beloit, Wisconsin 8, 15
Beloit Free Press 7
Beloit Journal 15
Bennet, Lyman O. 44
Benton, William 55
Benton, William P. 82–85
Berdan Sharp Shooters 11
Berlin Light Guard 11
Berwick Bay, Louisiana 119
Big Black River 89, 95, 99, 114
Bird's Point, Arkansas 37
Black Hawk War 13
Black River 37, 66
Blue Mounds, Wisconsin 13
Booth, John Wilkes 161
Boston Mountains 33
Bowen, John S. 79
Brackett, Charles 51
Bragg, Braxton 69
Brashear City, Louisiana 119
Britton, James 61
Bruinsburg, Mississippi 78, 81
Buell, Don Carlos 24, 34
bushwhackers 22, 26, 40, 48, 137
Butler, Benjamin F. 59
Butler, James N. 53

Cache River 45, 48
Cairo, Illinois 22, 161
Callahan, Barney 82
Cameron, Simon 9, 12
Camp Curtis 25, 28
Camp Randall 11, 12, 16, 17–18, 20, 162
Camp Washburn 132
canals *75*
Canby, Edward R.S. *127*, 128–130, 143, 145–148, 150, 152, 161
Cape Girardeau 45
Carr, Eugene A. 73, 78–79, 83–86, 91–96, 106, 109, 111, 116, 148, 150
Carr, Robert 68
Carrollton, Louisiana 119, 121–122
Carson, Kit 22
Chaffee, Ithamar Stowe 137–138
Chambers, William Pitt 147
Champion Hill, Mississippi 91

Charleton, William 73–74, 142
Chesebro, Jerome 48–49, 51, 55
Chicago, Illinois 7, 24, 25, 161
Chicago Tribune 7, 110, 117
Chickasaw bayou 68
Clarendon 57
Clarendon Road 48
Clark, Alfred G. 150
Clark, Roswell 100
Clinton, Mississippi 90
Clinton/Vicksburg Road 90
Cluseret, Gustave Paul 10
Colburn, Amos 27
contraband 59, *60*
Cook, Daniel 103
Cope, William H. 20, 28, 30, 36, 119–120, 123, 133
copperheads 119
Corinth, Mississippi 37, 41, 45
Corps D'Afrique 153
Cottage Grove, Arkansas 27
cotton 39, 62–65, 71
Cotton Plant, Arkansas 49
Crocker, Marcellus 94
Crydenwise, Henry M. 153
Curtis, Samuel R. 23, 33, *34*, 35, 37–38, 40–42, 44–46, 55, 57, 72

Dain, James 15, 29, 35, 77, 118
Dana, Charles A. 71, 96
Dane County 13, 14, 15
Dane Co. Zouaves 12, 16
Dauphin Island 144
Davis, Jefferson 8, 88, 100, 102, 133, 150
Decrows Point, Texas 122
Democrats 7, 8, 67
Denneman, C.A. 49
Densmore, Daniel 153
Department of Alabama 161
Department of the Gulf 126
Department of the Missouri 22
Des Arc Road 49, 54–55
Devine, William *164*
District of Southeast Missouri 35
Done, N.R. 50
Douglas, Stephen A. 7
Douglass, Frederick 68
Drake, George B. 135
Drake, William 74

237

Drew, Charles W. 152–154
Driesbach, John 74
Du Bois, Cornelius 105
Dunlap, Caroline 15, 29, 65, 73, 118–119, 132, 138
Dunlap, John 15, 29, 58, 65–66, 73, 118–119

Edwards Station, Mississippi 90, 94
Eighteenth Alabama regiment 150
Eighth Iowa regiment 150
Eighth Wisconsin regiment 12, 19, 28
Eighty-first Illinois regiment 147
Eighty-second U.S. Colored Infantry 152
Eighty-sixth U.S. Colored Infantry 152
Eleventh Wisconsin regiment 10–17, 19–21, 22, 24–28, 34–37, 40, 42, 44, 46, 48–64, 66, 68, 72–74, 76–78, 81–82, 83–85, 87–89, 92, 95–97, 103–107, 109–110, 112, 118, 122, 124–125, 131–132, 135–140, 142–146, 148, 151–152, 155–158, 160, 163, 166–167, **169**
Elliott, Isaac H. 52
Emancipation Proclamation 67
Essex gunboat 37

Farmers Guards 11, 12, 15, 31, 35, 97, 105
farming 10, 13–14, 29, 59
Farragut, David Glasglow **127**, 128–129
Fifteenth Arkansas regiment 81
Fifteenth Army Corps 89
Fifth Illinois cavalry 36
Fiftieth U.S. Colored Infantry 152, 153–154
Fiftieth Wisconsin regiment 155, 161, 166
Fifty-eight Illinois regiment 145, 155
Fifty-first U.S. Colored Infantry 152
Fifty-second Indiana regiment 145, 155
Fifty-sixth Ohio 84
First Indiana battery 84
First Indiana cavalry 48–49, 52, 54–55
First Louisiana Native Guards 144
First Missouri regiment 100
First Wisconsin battery 97
First Wisconsin regiment 9, 11
Fish River 143, 145
Fitch, Graham 44
Flenner, William 155, 160
Florence, Alabama 34
Foote, Andrew 23
Foote, Shelby 34, 102
Forrest, Nathan Bedford 128–129, 136
Forsyth, Arkansas 42
Fort Blakely 142, 145, 147, 152–160
Fort Donelson 24, 34–35, 59
Fort Esperanza 122, **123**

Fort Gaines 133–134, 143–144
Fort Henry 23–24, 34–35, 59
Fort Monroe 59
Fort Morgan 133–134, 143, 145
Fort Pemberton 70
Fort Pillow 60, 136
Fort Powell 133
Fort Randall 166
Fort Rice 166
Fort Sumter 7, 8
Fortress Monroe 59
Forty-eighth Ohio regiment 107, 109
Forty-eighth U.S. Colored Infantry 152
Forty-fifth Illinois regiment 114
Forty-second Ohio regiment 83
Forty-seventh U.S. Colored Infantry 152
Forty-Sixth Indiana regiment 44
Fourteen Mile Creek 89
Fourteenth Wisconsin regiment 64, 72, 110
Fourth Iowa Cavalry 90
Frémont, John Charles 22

Gammack, D.G. 147
Gardner, Frank 88
Garrard, Kenner 148
Geddes, James L. 150
German Turners 11
Gibson, Randall L. 148–150
Gilchrist, Charles A. 153–154
Grand Gulf, Mississippi 70, 74, 78–79, 87
Granger, Gordon 133, 143, 146
Grant, Ulysses S. 22–24, 34–35, 59, 68, 69, 70, **71**, 72–76, 81–90, 92–93, 95–104, 107, 109–111, 113–117, 120–122, 124–126, 128–129, 134, 143, 150–151
Great Western Railroad 119, 137
Green, Martin E. 79, 81, 84–86, 100
Gregg, John 89
Griffith, Erwin C. 46
Griffith, Joseph 107
guerrillas 22, 26, 40, 128
Gulf of Mexico 122–123, 130
gunboats 37, 76, 104
Guntown, Mississippi 129

Haines Bluff, Mississippi 101
Halleck, Henry W. 22–23, 35–36, 57, 77, 98, 116, 126, 128–129, 133–134
Hamilton, Charles S. 8
Hamilton, Chas A. 12
Hard Times, Louisiana 78
Harris, Charles L. **12**, 16, 25, 30–32, 36, 48–55, 72–74, 79, 95, 97, 99, 105–107, 109, 116, 119–120, 131, 143, 155–158, 162, 166, **167**
Harris, Lavander **164**
Hawkins, John P. 152, 157
Helena, Arkansas 57–59
Hillier, Joseph 146
Hill's Plantation 48, 53–54
Hindman, Thomas 41, 44–45

Hobbs, Charles A. 81
Holly Springs 68
Hoskin, Stephen 82
Hough, Daniel E. 100
Hovey, Alvin P. 83–85, 90
Hovey, Charles E. 36, 48, 53–56, 63–65, 91–94
Hudson Battery 81
Huntley, Seldon **164**
Hyde, Mary 8

Indianola, Texas 130–131
Iron Brigade 10
Iron Mountain Railroad 22, 30, 35
Ironton military hospital 73

Jackson, Andrew 143
Jackson, R.E. 81
Jackson, Thomas J. 10
Jackson, Mississippi 79, 88–90, 95, 118–119
Jacksonport, Arkansas 38, 40, 42, 44
James's Ferry, Arkansas 45
Janesville 8, 13
Janesville Daily Gazette 44, 68
Janesville Light Guard 11
Janesville Weekly Gazette 136
Johnston, Albert S. 41
Johnston, Joseph E. 10, 88, 90, 100, 114, **116**, 118, 121, 128
Jones, Thomas J. 82
Jones, William 112

Kavanaugh, William H. 156
Keegan, John 11
Kennedy, John W. 140–142
Kennedy, Mary Ann 140–142
Kingston, Wisconsin 7
Kinsman, William H. 97–99
Kirkpatrick, Samuel C. 14, **15**, 17, 19, 25, 28, 31, 35–38, 40, 44, 58–59, 61–62, 64, 68, 72, 78, 82, 85, 87, 92, 97–98, 103, 105, 109, 111, 117, 119–123, 125, 131–132, 137, 139, 146, 155, 162–163

landmines 152, 156
Latch, Martin 82
Lawler, Michael K. **96**, 97–100, 103–104, 109, 111
Lee, Robert E. 117, 150–151
Lee, Stephen D. 106
Lewis, Hiram J. 96, 99, 103, 105, 110, 115
Liberty Prairie, Wisconsin 13
Liddell, John R. 154
Lincoln, Abraham 7–9, 22, 24, 34, 67–71, 87, 116, 120, 125, 138, 142, 161
Lincoln, David 51
Lincoln, Mary Todd 161
Lippencott, Charles E. 49, 53
Little Rock, Arkansas 41
Lockney, James 145, 149
Lodi Guards 11
Logan, John A. 93–94
Loring, William W. 91
Loudon, William **166**

Louisiana Redan 114
Luneburg, Henry **164**

Madison Guard 8
Madison, Wisconsin 7, 8, 13, 14, 16, 20, 161
Magnolia Church, Mississippi 81–84
Manitowoc Guards 11
Manitowoc, Wisconsin 8
Marquette Sharpshooters 11
Matagorda Bay, Texas **123**, 125
Mather, Jesse 14, 17, 21, 28, 30, 32–33, 45, 58, 66, 77, 81, 85, 97, 105, 109, 110, 118–119, 124, 130–131, **132**, 133
Mather, Oliver 14, 17, 21, 32–33, 37, 40–41, 45, 57–58, 63, 66, 74, 77, 81, 85, 97, 105, 109–110, 118, 131
Maury, Dabney Herndon 133–134, 143, 145, 148
Maxon's Mill 10
Mazomanie, Wisconsin 163
McCarthy, Joseph 52
McClallan, George 138, 142
McClernand, John A. 69, 76, 78–79, 82, **83**, 84–85, 87–89, 92–95, 100–103, 105, 107, 109, 114
McDonald, Angus R. 158, 163
McGinnis, George F. 83, 84–85, 90–92
McMyler, James 81, 100, 132, 137
McPherson, James 87, 91–95, 101–103, 107, 109, 114
McPherson, James M. 11
Meade, George G. 136
Memphis, Tennessee 24, 37, 66, 70, 73, 136
Mendota Fire 12
Mendota Guards 12
Merriam, Henry C. 152
Metcalf, J.C. 55
Military Division of West Mississippi 127, 134
Miller, Dora 111
Miller, Jesse S. 25–26, 30, 48, 51, 55, 61, 74, 105, 112–113, 155–156, 158, 166, **167**, 168
Milliken's Bend, Louisiana 66, 73–74, 76–77
Milwaukee Sentinel 7
Milwaukee, Wisconsin 9, 163
Milwaukee Zouaves 11
Mineral Point, Wisconsin 13, 16, 132
Mississippi River 24, 35, 59, 63–64, 70, 73–74, 79, 102, 119–120, 137
Missouri State Guard 26
Missouri Swamp Fox *see* Thompson, Jeff
Mobile, Alabama 77, 121, 126–129, 133–134, 145–147
Mobile Bay 129, 133–136, **143**, 145–146
Mobile Register 147
Montgomery, Alabama 126
Moore, Daniel B. 158
Mound City gunboat 45

Nance, David Carey 50
Nashville, Tennessee 24, 69
negroes 38, 59–64, 70, 78, 104, 114, 130, 147, 152, 159
New Carthage, Louisiana 74, 76
New Orleans, Louisiana 119–120, 138, 143
New York Commercial Advertiser 7
New York, N.Y. 7, 130
New York Times 7
New York World 120
newsboys 16
newspapers 7, 11, 16, 30, 34, 62, 67–68, 110
Newton, James K. 72, 149–150
Nineteenth Army corps 122
Nineteenth Indiana 10
Ninety-ninth Illinois regiment 81
Ninety-seventh Illinois 106–107
Ninety-third United States Colored regiment 139
Ninth Division 82
Ninth Illinois Cavalry 36, 51
North Star Hides 11
Nye, Warren W. 142

Oettiker, William Henry 14, 35, 82, 85, 138–139, 145–146, 155, 161–162, 166–167
Old Town, Arkansas 63
114th Ohio 69, 146, 156
130th Illinois regiment 107, 109
178th New York 145, 155
Ord, E.O.C. 114
Osterhaus, Peter J. 82, 84, 152

Parson, William H. 50
Parson's Texas Rangers 46, 50–51, 53
Pelton, Wilbur F. 53
Pemberton, John C. 69, 76–77, 85–86, 88–91, 93–96, 100–101, 109, 114–116
Pensacola, Florida 143
Phelps, Oliver 112
Philadelphia Evening Journal 120
Pile, William A. 152
Pilot Knob 66
Pitman's Ferry 37
Platt, Arthur 12
Platteville, Wisconsin 8, 13
Pocahontas, Arkansas 37
Pollard, Alabama 143
Port Gibson, Mississippi 79, 81–85, 88
Porter, David D. 74, 102, 104, 128
Potter, Leander H. 52, 56
Price, Sterling 23, 33, 36

Queen of the West ram 72
Quiner, E.B. 8

Railroad Redoubt 105–109
Randall, Alexander W. 7, 8, 9, 11, 16
Randall Zouaves 12
Rathbone, Henry R. 161
Raymond, Mississippi 89
Red River Campaign 126–127, 136

Reid, H.A. 29
Revolutionary War 15
Rice, Thaddeus 14, 36
Richland County Plowboys 12, 15, 48
Richland Volunteers 11
Richmond Enquirer 34
Richmond, Virginia 77, 88
Robertson, John 29
Robinson, Oliver S. 15, 65, 86, 102
Rock Prairie, Wisconsin 13
Rock River, Wisconsin 13
Rodney Road 81–85
Rolla, Missouri 33, 44
Rosecrans, William 69, 124
Rust, Albert 50

St. Genevieve, Missouri 73
St. Louis, Missouri 22, 24–25, 35, 62, 64, 162
St. Martinsville, Louisiana 122
Sanford, James M. 103–104, 165
Satterlee, Thomas 113
Sauk County, Wisconsin 7, 13, 27
Savannah, Georgia 77
Scofield, Hiram 152–153
Scott, Winfield 136
secesh 44, 146
Second Teche Expedition 122
Second Wisconsin Cavalry 42, 57
Second Wisconsin regiment 10
Selma, Alabama 128
Seventeenth Texas Cavalry 54
Seventeenth Wisconsin regiment 110
Seventh Wisconsin regiment 10, 12
Seventy-seventh Illinois regiment 107
Seventy-sixth Illinois regiment 155
Seventy-sixth U.S. Colored Infantry 152
Seventy-third U.S. Colored Troops 144, 152
Shea, William L. 49
Sheridan, Philip 143
Sherman, William T. 22, 68, 70, **71**, 74, 76, 86, 88–89, 95–97, 101–102, 113–114, 118, 125, 126, 128–129, 134–135
Sherrill, Robert 15, **27**, 28–29, 31, 36, 40, 51, 53, 58, 65–66, 73, 77, 85, 105, 107, 118–119, 138, 140, 155, 165
Sibley, Henry H. 130
Sixteenth Army Corps 145–146
Sixteenth Texas Cavalry 50
Sixth Mississippi regiment 81
Sixty-eighth U.S. Colored Infantry 153
Sixty-second Alabama regiment 154
Sixty-sixth U.S. Colored Infantry 153
Slack, James R. 83, 90, 92–93
slavery (slaves) 38, 40, 59, 61–62, 67–68, 145, 147, 152
Slocum, H.W. 127
Smith, A.J. 128–129, 134, 143, 147
Smith, George E. 8

Smith, John E. 84
Smith, Kirby 128–129
Spanish Fort 145–150
spies 22
Springfield, Missouri 45, 68
Stanton, Edwin 64, 71, 129, 143
Steele, Frederick 35, 38, 55, 126–127, 143–146, 154
Steele's Bayou 70
Stevens, Charles A. 15, 26, 30–31, 41
Stevens, John 111
Stevenson, Carter L. 91
Stockade Redan 102
Stone, William M. 79, 82–85, 93, 96, 106–107
Strong, Henry P. 15, 27, 29, 32, 35, 37, 41, 46, 48, 50–53, *54*, 55, 58, 61, 64–65, 72, 116–117, 165–66
Sturgis, Samuel D. 129
Sulphur Springs, Missouri 22, 25, 36, 46
Sun Prairie, Wisconsin 13
sutlers 16

Taylor, Annie Roberts 14
Taylor, Richard 127
Tennessee River 24, 34, 126
Texas *123*
Texas Rangers *see* Parson's Texas Rangers
Third Iowa Cavalry 46, 48
Third Louisiana Redan 114
Thirteenth Army Corps 16, 73, 76, 116, 120, 143, 145, 146, 152, 155
Thirteenth Illinois Cavalry 36
Thirty-eighth Alabama regiment 147
Thirty-first Alabama regiment 113
Thirty-fourth Indiana regiment 84
Thirty-fourth New Jersey regiment 145, 155
Thirty-second Iowa regiment 158
Thirty-third Illinois regiment 46, 49, 52–54, 64, 103, 105

Thomas, Bryan M. 154
Thomas, George H. 124–125
Thompson, Jeff 26
Tollard, Robert A. 27
total war 42, 71
Tracy, Edward, D. 81
Trans-Mississippi 22, 34, *39*, 45, 68, 127
Turner, Henry W. 28
Twelfth Arkansas regiment 81
Twelfth Texas Cavalry 50–51, 53
Twenty-eight Wisconsin regiment 70, 145
Twenty-first Alabama regiment 147
Twenty-first Arkansas regiment 81
Twenty-first Iowa regiment 73, 79, 96, 106–107, 111
Twenty-fourth Michigan 10
Twenty-second Iowa regiment 73, 79, 96, 106–107, 111
Twenty-third Iowa regiment 73, 79, 96, 106–107, 111
Twenty-third Wisconsin 58, 89
Twining, Aaron *165*
Twining, Harrison *165*
Twining, Henry 14, 18, 25–26, 28, 35, 46–47, 50–52, 55, 57, 64–65, 85, 97, 105, 165

Union soldiers 10; as a band of brothers 124; battle fatigue 73; dealing with "varmits" 58; death in combat 124; death rate compared to World War II 110; desertion 68; disease 27–28; drilling 17–18; foraging 72, 76; hardships 58–59; interaction with Rebel pickets 113; letter writing 16; morale 46; morality and habits 29; pay 20; poetry 33; reaction to emancipation proclamation 67; sickness 27–28; views towards slavery 60–62

U.S. Sanitary Commission 29
U.S. War Department 9

Van Anda, Salue G. 106
Van Dorn, Earl 34–36, 41–42, 45, 68
Veatch, James C. 155
Vicksburg campaign *5*, 70–72, 74–117, 168
Vicksburg, Mississippi 68–71, 74, 76, 81, 85, 87–89, 94, 100–102; siege of 100–116, *108*, 118, 127
Victoria, Arkansas 31
Victorian America 11, 13
Village Creek 43

Waldo, C.D. 20
Washburn, Cadwallader C. 70–72, 129
Washington, George 136
Washington Artillery 148
Waterloo Rifles 12
Waterloo, Wisconsin 15–16, 18
Watson Guards 12
Waukesha Union Guards 11
Way, Virgil H. 52
Welles, Gideon 133
West Bend Editorial 20
West Point 16
Westover, Alonzo 62
White River 44, 46, 48
Whittlesey, Luther H. 29, *30*, 31, 35, 81, 105, 116–117
Williams, James M. 147
Women's Club of Berry, Wisconsin 14
women's clubs 29
Wood, Charles A. 12, 30, 55, 105
Wood, William F. 49, 54

Yahara River 13
Yazoo Pass Expedition 70
Yazoo River 69, 101

www.ingramcontent.com/pod-product-compliance
Ingram Content Group UK Ltd.
Pitfield, Milton Keynes, MK11 3LW, UK
UKHW050534150426
5217IPUK00026B/1926

9 781476 685205